United Kingdom Balance of Payments

The Pink Book

2011 Edition

Editors: Damian Whittard
Melanie Edwards

Contents

List of contributors

Authors and Production Team:

John Bundey
Julie Crowley
Melanie Edwards
Beverley Davies
Beth Derrett
Simon Harrington
Tony James
Phil Lewin
David Matthewson
Richard McCrae
Jamie Pritchard
Marilyn Thomas
Damian Whittard
Sarah Williams
Jo Wilson
Phil Wood

An introduction to the United Kingdom balance of payments

Introduction

The balance of payments is one of the UK's key economic statistical series. It measures the economic transactions between UK residents and the rest of the world. It also draws a series of balances between inward and outward transactions, provides a net flow of transactions between UK residents and the rest of the world and reports how that flow is funded. Economic transactions include:

- exports and imports of goods, such as oil, agricultural products, other raw materials, machinery and transport equipment, computers, white goods and clothing
- exports and imports of services such as international transport, travel, financial and business services
- income flows, such as dividends and interest earned by foreigners on investments in the UK and by UK residents investing abroad
- financial flows, such as direct investment, investment in shares, debt securities, loans and deposits
- transfers, which are offsetting entries to any one-sided transactions listed above, such as foreign aid and funds brought by migrants to the UK

Closely related to the balance of payments is the international investment position series of statistics. The international investment position measures the levels of financial investment with the rest of the world, inward and outward.

International statistical standards

The Office for National Statistics (ONS) follows the international standards relating to balance of payments and international investment position statistics. There are several reasons for this. First, domestic and foreign analysts will be assured that the UK's official balance of payments and international investment position statistics comply with objective, coherent international standards that reflect current, global analytic needs. Second, the UK is a member of the international community and international users need comparable data for analysis between countries. Third, the UK, as a member of the European Union, as well as organisations such as the IMF and OECD, needs to compile its various economic statistics in conformity with standards set by those organisations. Fourth, the UK can compare and reconcile its data with those of other countries. Statistics need to be as comparable as possible in order to carry out this validation.

To facilitate such consistency and to provide guidelines for its members, the IMF issued the *Balance of Payments Manual*. The first edition appeared in 1948 and the fifth edition in 1993. The conceptual framework of the UK balance of payments corresponds to that underlying the fifth edition of the IMF Manual, referred to as *BPM5*. *BPM5* was implemented in the UK's balance of payments accounts and international investment position statistics in September 1998.

A process of reviewing the existing international standards started in the mid 1980s with the specific objective of harmonising, to the maximum extent possible, the statistical concepts, definitions, statistical units, classifications and terminology. Release of the revised standards started in 1993 with *BPM5* and the third edition of the *System of National Accounts (SNA93)*. *BPM5* was prepared by the IMF in close co-operation with national compilers and with the Statistical Office of the European Communities, the OECD, the United Nations and the World Bank. Those five organisations jointly published *SNA93*. In 1995, the EU produced its own version of *SNA93*, the *European System of Accounts (ESA95)*, upon which the UK's national accounts are based and which is consistent with *BPM5*. Both *SNA93* and *BPM5* were amended in 2000 to give more consistent guidance on the treatment of financial derivatives.

The United Nations Statistics Commission and the IMF Board of Directors have recently completed the comprehensive and parallel updating of the National Accounts (SNA2008) and Balance of Payments manuals (BPM6), in order to ensure their consistency and achieve greater harmonisation. The UK will be publishing statistics in accordance with BPM6 in 2014.

Conceptual framework definitions

Balance of payments

Broadly speaking, the UK balance of payments is a statistical statement designed to provide a systematic record of the UK's economic transactions with the rest of the world. It may be described as a system of consolidated accounts in which the accounting entity is the UK economy and the entries refer to economic transactions between residents of the UK and residents of the rest of the world (non-residents).

The balance of payments accounts are concerned not only with payments made but also any economic transactions during a period that give rise to a payment in an earlier or later period, for example, goods may change ownership in one period, though payment may be made in an earlier period (pre-payment) or in a later period (trade credit). They also include transactions for which there may never be a payment, for example, goods shipped under foreign aid or goods shipped between related enterprises. There is also more than one 'balance': the balance of payments is a system of accounts in which many balances can be derived, such as the balance of goods and services, the current account balance, and capital and financial account balance.

Balance of payments statements cover a wide range of economic transactions which include:

(i) goods, services, income and current transfers

(ii) capital transactions, such as capital transfers, and

(iii) financial transactions involving the UK claims on, and liabilities to, non-residents.

Category (i) is shown in the current account, category (ii) in the capital account and category (iii) in the financial account.

International investment position

The UK's international investment position is a closely related set of statistics. It can be viewed as the balance sheet recording the UK's stock (or level) of foreign financial assets and liabilities at a specific point in time. The net international investment position is the difference between the stock of foreign financial assets and foreign liabilities at a particular date.

Viewed more broadly, the international investment position can be shown as a reconciliation statement of the stock of investment at two different points in time by showing financial transactions and other changes (non-transaction changes) such as price changes, exchange rate effects and other adjustments that occurred during the period. Financial transactions that are included in the reconciliation statement are equivalent to the transactions measured in the financial account of the balance of payments. ONS does not currently publish a full reconciliation of the international investment position showing price, exchange rate and other changes.

Classifications such as assets and liabilities, type of investment (direct, portfolio, other investment, financial derivatives and reserve assets), and instrument of investment, are used consistently in both the balance of payments and the international investment position.

Concepts of territory and residence

In compiling the UK balance of payments and international investment position, the UK economy is conceived as comprising the economic entities that have a closer association with the territory of the UK than with any other territory. Each such economic entity is described as a resident of the UK. Any economic entity which is not regarded as a resident of the UK is described as a non-resident. The concept of residency is not based on nationality.

The UK's economic territory is defined to include the territories lying within its political frontiers and territorial seas, and in the international waters over which it has exclusive jurisdiction. It also includes its territorial enclaves abroad holding, for example, embassies, consulates, military bases, scientific stations, information or immigration offices, or aid agencies, whether owned or rented by the UK Government with the formal agreement of the countries where they are located.

The UK offshore islands – Jersey, Guernsey and Isle of Man – are classified as non-resident to the UK. Therefore transactions between UK residents and the islands are in the balance of payments, but transactions between islanders are not counted in the UK balance of payments. The islands are not part of the EU, so statistics relating to them are not required under *ESA95* and they have to be excluded from the UK's economic territory to ensure full UK consistency with *ESA95*. This treatment is also technically consistent with *BPM5* recommendations that states: 'In a maritime country, economic territory includes islands that belong to the country and are subject to the same fiscal and monetary authorities as the mainland; goods and persons move freely to and from the mainland and islands...'. The offshore islands are subject to their own fiscal authorities and have their own tax systems. Furthermore, there are impediments to taking up residency on the Channel Islands.

For balance of payments purposes, residents of an economy are generally deemed to have a centre of economic interest in the economy and to be resident for at least one year. The residents of the UK comprise:

- Resident general government institutions including the Scottish Government, Welsh Government, Northern Ireland Assembly and local government authorities and statutory bodies. The UK territorial enclaves (for example, embassies, consulates, military bases) physically located abroad are included in the UK's economic territory and are therefore residents. Similar entities of other countries physically located within the UK are outside the UK's economic territory and are therefore non-residents

- Resident financial and trading enterprises which include all enterprises engaged in the production of goods and services on a commercial or equivalent basis within the territory of the UK. Enterprises may be incorporated or unincorporated; privately or government owned and/or controlled; and locally or foreign owned and/or controlled. The definition of an enterprise in terms of the territory in which it is located often makes it necessary to divide a single legal entity into a head office operating in one economy and a branch operating in another economy. Resident enterprises include UK branches of foreign companies and exclude foreign branches of UK companies.

- Resident non-profit bodies, those in which individuals and/or enterprises combine, as owners, to produce goods and services within the territory of the UK for purposes other than to provide a financial return for themselves. Examples are churches, charitable organisations and representative business organisations such as chambers of commerce.

- Resident households and individuals that broadly encompass all persons residing in the territory of the UK for one year or more, whose general centre of economic interest is considered to be the UK. The UK's official diplomatic and consular representatives, the UK's armed forces, other UK Government personnel stationed abroad and their dependants, UK students studying abroad, and UK patients being treated abroad are also included even though they may all be abroad for one year or more. They are treated as UK residents since their centre of interest is considered to be the UK. Generally, the centre of economic interest of persons visiting the UK for less than one year is considered to be outside the UK and they are therefore regarded as non-residents, but if they stay for one year or more they are considered to be residents for balance of payments purposes. Irrespective of their length of stay, non-residents also include foreign diplomatic, consular, military and other government personnel and their dependants, foreign students studying in the UK, and foreign patients being treated in the UK. If an individual maintains residences in the UK and another economy, they are considered to be UK residents if they typically spend more time in their UK residence than their foreign residence during the year.

Double-entry system

Rules for the UK double-entry system

Credit entries, changes in all economic resources provided by the UK to non-residents, including:	**Debit entries,** changes in all economic resources received by the UK from non-residents,including:
Exports of goods and services	Imports of goods and services
Income accruing to the UK from non-residents	Income accruing from the UK to non-residents
Transfers that are offsets to debit entries	Transfers that are offsets to credit entries
Financial liabilities of the UK to non-residents	Financial claims of the UK on non-residents

Examples of UK double-entry recording	**Credits**	**Debits**
1. Sales of goods (value 100) to non-residents for foreign exchange (that is, goods provided and bank payment (a bank deposit) received in an account held abroad)		
Goods	100	
Bank deposits, foreign currency assets		100
2. Purchase of goods (value 120) from a non-resident using trade credit (that is, goods received and a claim on a resident (trade credit liability) provided)		
Goods		120
Trade credit liabilities	120	
3. Food aid (value 5) provided to non-residents (that is, goods provided and transfer imputed)		
Goods	5	
Current transfers		5
4. Repayment of a loan (value 25) by a resident company to a non-resident lender (that is, liability to a non-resident reduced and a reduction in bank deposits held abroad)		
Loan repayment	–25	
Bank deposits, foreign currency assets		–25

Conceptually, an economic transaction has two sides: something of economic value is provided and something of equal value is received. The balance of payments reflects this in a double-entry recording system of credits and debits. When an economic value is provided (for example, UK exports a car) a credit entry is made, and when the corresponding economic value is received (for example, a payment for the car) a debit entry is made. For example, when an exporter sells (provides) goods to a non-resident, the exporter may receive cash (a financial asset) or another type of financial asset (for example, a trade credit claim) in return. The export is represented by a credit entry in the current account and the financial asset acquired is represented by an offset debit entry in the financial account. Similar entries are made when an importer buys a car (debit) and pays for it (credit). So a credit entry represents a change in rest of world ownership of any sort of UK asset (real or financial) while a debit entry represents a change in UK ownership of the rest of the world assets.

An understanding of the double-entry recording system is necessary for a complete understanding of balance of payments statistics.

Under the double-entry system, by definition credit entries must equal debit entries. Credit entries are required for exports of goods and services, income receivable, and changes in financial liabilities. Likewise, debit entries are required for imports of goods and services, income payable, and changes in financial assets. Where something of economic value is provided without something of economic value in exchange (that is, without a quid pro quo) the double-entry system requires an offset to be imputed (a transfer entry) of equivalent value. For example, food exported as aid requires a credit entry for the goods provided and a debit transfer as the aid offset.

Sign convention in the UK balance of payments statistics

The sign convention used in presenting the UK balance of payments statistics is to give a positive sign to an increase in either credit or debit entries and a negative sign to a decrease in credit or debit entries. Balances (calculated as credits less debits) or items that are net credits have no sign, while balances that are net debits have a negative sign.

When considering making international comparisons it should be borne in mind that there is no unique or correct sign convention and other countries/institutions use variations. In particular the convention used by the IMF in their publications gives no sign to credit entries and a minus sign to all debit entries (for example, imports and acquisitions of assets).

Errors and omissions

It follows that, in principle, under a double-entry accounting system, the difference between the sum of credit and debit entries must be zero. In practice, some transactions are not measured accurately (that is, errors) and some are not measured at all (that is, omissions). Data sources used to compile the accounts often measure the credit and debit sides from different data sources and may not always do so consistently. There could be many reasons why these sources may not measure the acquisition side of the transaction and the corresponding payments, either in the same accounting period or at the same value. To restore the equality of credit and debit entries, a net errors and omissions item is included in the balance of payments accounts. The item indicates whether credit or debit transactions would be needed to balance the accounts, but does not show where the discrepancy lies. Usually the financial account is considered to be the most likely source.

Valuation

It is important that the balance of payments and international investment position statistics carry values that have economic meaning to enable useful analysis, and to provide meaningful indicators of cross-border economic activity. It is also important for the double-entry accounting system that a uniform valuation is adopted. This means that the credit and debit entries of each transaction – which in practice may be derived from independent sources – should be valued at the same price. In addition, a uniform valuation is essential to sum different types of transactions on a consistent and comparable basis. The use of a uniform valuation principle aids understanding by users. Moreover, statistics for different countries will not be comparable unless both parties to a transaction adopt the same valuation principle. It is also important to use a principle consistent with national accounting principles. For all these reasons, market price is used in UK economic statistics for valuing transactions.

Market price is the amount of money that a willing buyer pays to acquire something from a willing seller, when such an exchange is between independent parties and involves only commercial considerations. In practice, one or more of the conditions needed to establish a market price may be absent and other valuations may be used.

For the most part, the price at which a transaction is recorded in the accounts of the transactors or in the administrative records used as data sources will be the market price or a very close approximation of it. This valuation is known as the transactions price and is the practical valuation basis used in the balance of payments, both because it aids consistent recording of credits and debits and because of its usual proximity to the ideal market valuation. The following paragraph discusses a special case of transactions where market prices may not apply, namely transfer pricing between affiliated enterprises in different countries.

Transfer pricing

Where transactions are between affiliated enterprises in different countries, the prices adopted in their books for recording transactions in goods and services and any associated indebtedness and interest – referred to as transfer prices – may not correspond to prices that would be charged to independent parties. There will be some departure from the market price principle if transfer prices are different from those charged to enterprises outside the group. However there are practical difficulties in identifying and suitably adjusting individual cases. Transfer pricing to avoid tax is illegal in the UK so the distortions in the international accounts caused by transfer pricing are not considered widespread. For both reasons, adjustments to account for transfer pricing are rarely made in practice.

Assets and liabilities

As with all international investment position statistics, foreign financial assets and liabilities should, in principle, be valued at their current market price at the reference date. In practice this is not always possible and valuation guidelines are adopted in order to approximate market valuation, particularly for those financial assets and liabilities that are only rarely transacted. For example, in measuring the value of direct investment in equity capital, much of which is never traded or is traded infrequently, market value is approximated by one of the following methods: a recent transaction price, directors' value, or net asset value. Over time, this is likely to underestimate the true market value of foreign direct investment.

Unit of account and conversion

Transactions and stock positions originally denominated in foreign currencies need to be converted to pounds sterling using market rates of exchange prevailing at the time of the transaction (balance of payments) or at the reference date (international investment position). Transactions should be converted at the mid-point of the buying and selling exchange rates applying at the time of transaction. Stocks should be converted at the mid-point of the buying and selling exchange rates applying at the beginning or end of the period. In practice, the actual rate used varies according to the source of the transaction or stock

Time of recording

Transactions

The time of recording of transactions in balance of payments and international investment position statistics is, in principle, the time of change of ownership (either actual or imputed). Under the double-entry system, both sides of a transaction should be recorded in the same period. This is consistent with the principle of accrual accounting, which requires that transactions be recorded when economic value is created, transformed, exchanged, transferred or extinguished.

Change of ownership is considered to occur when legal ownership of goods changes, when services are rendered and when income accrues. In the case of transfers, those imposed by one party on another, such as taxes and fines, should ideally be recorded at the moment at which the underlying transactions or other flows occur which give rise to the liability to pay. Other transfers should be recorded when the goods or services change ownership.

For financial transactions, the time of change of ownership is taken to be the time when transactions are entered in the books of the transactors. That is taken to be the time when a foreign financial asset or liability is acquired, relinquished by agreement, sold or repaid. The commitment or pledging of an asset does not constitute an economic transaction, and no entry should be shown unless a change of ownership actually occurs in the period covered. Likewise, the entries for loan drawings should be based on actual disbursements and not on commitments or authorisations. Entries for loan repayments should be recorded at the time they are due rather than on the actual payment date.

Both sides of a transaction should be recorded in the same period. In practice the time of recording of transactions in the balance of payments and international investment position statistics will reflect the practices in data sources, and may diverge from the principle of time of change of ownership. For the UK, transactions in goods credits (exported goods) are mainly recorded at the time when goods are shipped as this is assessed to be a generally good practical approximation of the time when ownership changes. Goods debits (imported goods) are recorded when customs records relating to the movement of the goods across the frontier are processed, again in the expectation that this is the best practical approximation to change of ownership that can be generally achieved. For the remainder of the current account, the time of the recording of transactions generally complies with the time of change of ownership. Exceptions occur mainly because the record-keeping practices of some data providers may not be on this basis. Financial account transactions usually are recorded appropriately, that is, when the parties record transactions in their books. However, some transactions may be derived from information supplied by intermediaries that are not party to the transactions and may not be aware of the time of change of ownership. Also, some enterprises may adopt accounting practices that lead to inconsistent time of recording. A simple example is that different enterprises may close off their accounts at different times of day.

Stock

The time of recognising the stock of a foreign financial asset or liability follows naturally from the time of recording of a transaction in that asset or liability. For example, if a transaction is undertaken to acquire a foreign financial asset, there will also be a consequential increase in the stock of foreign financial assets at the end of that period. Of course, if the asset is disposed of before the end of the period, it will not contribute to the stocks statistics to be recorded for the period, but the disposal will have given rise to another transaction to be recorded for the period.

Types of transactions in the balance of payments

An economic transaction occurs when something of economic value is provided by one party to another. Transactions that are considered to have economic value comprise those in goods, services, income and financial assets and liabilities. The transactions recorded in a balance of payments statement stem from dealings between two parties, one being a resident and the other a non-resident. The types of transactions included in the balance of payments are exchanges, one-sided transactions and imputed transactions.

Exchanges

Exchanges are the most important and numerous type of transaction. They include transactions in which one transactor provides something of economic value to another transactor and receives in return something of equal value.

Special cases of imputation/estimation

Migrants' transfers

A special statistical treatment is required when a person migrates, that is when the person's status changes from non-resident to resident (or vice versa). When this change occurs, the property owned by the migrant becomes the property of a resident instead of that of a non-resident (or vice versa). This change of ownership of net worth between economies is included in the balance of payments. For example, any financial assets held abroad by the migrant become claims by the UK on the rest of the world.

Offset entries are made corresponding to the transfer of net worth and, by their nature, these are included as transfers in the capital account. This treatment amounts to envisaging a transfer of property from the person in their capacity as a non-resident to the person in their capacity as a resident (or vice versa). In principle, this transaction embraces all the migrant's property, whether or not it accompanies the migrant.

Reinvested earnings

A number of special cases of imputed transactions feature in balance of payments compilation. One case involves the reinvestment of earnings in resident enterprises by their non-resident direct investors. These *reinvested earnings* are regarded as being paid out as investment income and then reinvested in the enterprises from which they originated. They are therefore recorded both as a component of investment income in the current account and as a component of direct investment in the financial account. It is considered analytically useful to identify these transactions separately in economic statistics because of the substantial contribution they make to the stock of direct investment finance in a country.

Financial services

A further case relates to estimation for the implicit fees associated with financial services. These include spread earnings on foreign exchange, derivatives and securities trading and Financial Intermediation Services Indirectly Measured (FISIM), which is the implicit margin resulting from interest rate differentials between borrowing and lending.

Exceptions to change of ownership

In economic statistics, transactions are considered to occur when the goods and financial assets change ownership between transactors, when services are provided by one transactor to another, or when income is earned by one transactor from another. However, there are certain situations in which no change of ownership legally occurs, but where transactions are nonetheless considered to have occurred for balance of payments purposes. The situations include financial leases, goods imported into or exported from the UK for processing and return, and transactions between a head office in one country and a branch in another.

Financial leases

A financial lease is regarded as a method of obtaining all the rights, risks and rewards of ownership of real resources without holding legal ownership. Although legal ownership remains with the lessor during the term of the lease, all the risks and responsibilities apply to the lessee. In these cases, the basic nature of the transaction is given precedence over its legal form, by imputing a change of ownership of the resource to the lessee. As a result of this imputation, a financial liability is recognised and lease payments are classified as partly loan repayments in the financial account and partly interest in the current account, rather than as services in the current account.

Goods for processing

In economic statistics, the value of goods entering or leaving the UK for processing and returning to the country of origin after processing should be recorded on a gross basis. That is, recording the goods both when they enter (as imports) and when they leave (as exports), even though there is no legal change of ownership of those goods. A good entering the UK to be processed and returned to the country of origin is therefore recorded as an import at the appropriate value and subsequently as an export – recorded by the customs system at the original value plus the added value of the processing. A symmetrical treatment should be applied to UK goods exported for processing and return. The basis for this treatment is that such goods lose their identity during processing by being transformed or incorporated into different goods. On the other hand, for goods undergoing repairs only the value of the repair, not the gross value of the goods, is included in the goods credits or debits.

Branches

In economic statistics, it is usually necessary to split the activities of a legal entity and recognise two units, a head office in one country and a branch in another. Flows of goods, services, income and finance between the branch and its head office are therefore treated as transactions, even though they are legally part of the same unit. For example, goods and services sent from the head office to its branch are to be treated as exports of goods and services by the head office.

There are two cases where such splitting becomes necessary. The first occurs when production of goods and services is undertaken by the personnel, plant and equipment of the legal entity in an economic territory outside the economic territory of the head office, provided certain conditions apply. These conditions include: the intention to operate in the separate economy indefinitely or over a long period (12 months is used as a rule of thumb); keeping a set of accounts of the branch's activity (that is, income statement, balance sheet, transactions with the parent entity); eligibility to pay income tax in the host country; having a substantial physical presence; and receiving funds for the branch's work which are paid into its own bank account.

The second case occurs when a person or legal entity resident in one economy owns land and buildings located in another economy. Ownership of immovable assets is always attributed in balance of payments and international investment position statistics to residents of the economy in which the assets are located. Thus land in the domestic territory, which is in fact owned by a non-resident, is treated as being owned by a notional resident entity, which in turn has a foreign direct investment liability to the real owner. It should also be recalled that the territorial enclaves (for example, embassies, consulates, military bases) are regarded as part of the economic territory of the economy they represent. When these institutions buy and sell the land in these enclaves they are effectively adding to and subtracting from the economic territory of their government. Such transactions in land owned by foreign embassies are recorded in the capital account as the acquisition/disposal of non-produced, non-financial assets.

Other changes in the international investment position

In addition to the financial transactions included in the balance of payments, the international investment position reconciliation statement includes the other changes which contribute to differences between opening and closing positions for a period.

Other changes in position may occur through price changes, exchange rate changes and other adjustments. Price changes are valuation changes that occur because of changes in the market price of a financial instrument, such as a change in the price of a share or debt security, or through revaluing a company's net worth.

Exchange rate changes are due to fluctuations in the value of the pound, in which the accounts are compiled, relative to the currencies in which foreign assets and liabilities are denominated.

Other adjustments can arise from a number of causes such as write-off of bad debts, classification changes, monetisation/demonetisation of gold, and the allocation/cancellation of Special Drawing Rights. A reclassification would occur where a foreign investor's equity investment in an enterprise increased during the reporting period and the increase was sufficient to change the classification of the investor's total equity holding at the end of the period from portfolio investment to direct investment. Monetisation of gold occurs when the Bank of England monetises commodity stocks of gold and adds these to its monetary gold holdings as part of the UK's official reserve assets. Special Drawing Rights in the IMF are also included in the UK's official reserve assets. Allocations and cancellations of these instruments are included as other adjustments.

Gross and net recording

Entries for current and capital account items are generally treated so that credits for each component are recorded separately from debits. Current and capital account transactions, in this context, are described as being recorded gross.

Gross recording contrasts to the recording of transactions in the financial account, which is mainly on a net basis, although for long-term trade credits and loans, gross drawings and repayments are included in the financial account. The net recording of other financial account items means that, for each item, credit transactions are combined with debit transactions to arrive at a single result – either a net credit or net debit – reflecting the net effect of all increases and decreases in holdings of that type of asset or liability during the recording period. There are several types of netting in the financial account, for example, the netting of purchases and sales within an instrument in an asset position, and netting of assets and liabilities as in the case of direct investment.

Standard balance of payments classification

Balance of payments and international investment position statistics need to be arranged in a coherent structure to facilitate their use and adaptation for purposes such as policy formulation, analytical studies, projections, bilateral comparisons, and regional and global aggregations. *BPM5* contains a standard classification and list of standard components of the balance of payments and international investment position. These standards were developed taking into account the views of national compilers and analysts, and the requirement to harmonise concepts and definitions with related international statistical standards and classifications. The classification also reflects the separation of categories that may exhibit different economic behaviour, may be important in a number of countries, are readily collectable, and are needed for harmonising with other bodies of statistics.

The standard balance of payments classification comprises two main groups of accounts – the **current account** and the **capital and financial account**. Transactions classified to the **current account** include goods and services, income and current transfers. Within the capital and financial account, the **capital account** includes capital transfers and the net acquisition or disposal of non-produced, non-financial assets. The **financial account** includes transactions in financial assets and liabilities.

Transactions in current account and capital account items are generally shown on a gross basis (gross debits and credits separately). Transactions in financial account items are mainly recorded on a net basis.

Current account

Table A (opposite) shows the standard classification of the current account. Each of the broad categories is described briefly below, while individual component items are described in detail in subsequent chapters.

Goods and services are divided into separate accounts. **Goods** comprise most movable goods that change ownership between UK residents and non-residents. **Services** comprise services transactions between UK residents and non-residents, together with some transactions in goods where, by international agreement, it is not practical to separate the goods and services components (for example, goods purchased by travellers are classified to services).

Income refers to income earned by UK residents from non-residents and vice versa. Income covers compensation of employees and investment income. **Compensation of employees** comprises wages, salaries and other benefits earned by individuals from economies other than those in which they are residents, as well as earnings from extraterritorial bodies such as foreign embassies, which often employ staff from the economy in which they are located. **Investment income** comprises income earned from the provision of financial capital and is classified by direct, portfolio and other investment income and income earned on the UK's reserve assets.

Transfers represent offsets to the provision of resources between residents and non-residents with no quid pro quo in economic value (for example, the provision of

A Summary of balance of payments in 2010

£ million

	Credits	Debits
1. Current account		
A. Goods and services	436 796	476 480
1. Goods	265 714	364 176
2. Services	171 082	112 304
2.1. Transportation	20 329	18 710
2.2. Travel	20 969	32 360
2.3. Communications	5 340	4 396
2.4. Construction	1 218	1 229
2.5. Insurance	5 265	1 561
2.6. Financial	42 162	10 667
2.7. Computer and information	8 742	3 968
2.8. Royalties and licence fees	8 678	5 281
2.9. Other business	52 162	28 472
2.10. Personal, cultural and recreational	4 012	1 511
2.11. Government	2 205	4 149
B. Income	163 463	140 424
1. Compensation of employees	1 097	1 486
2. Investment income	162 366	138 938
2.1 Direct investment	81 779	32 421
2.2 Portfolio investment	47 391	59 945
2.3 Other investment	32 484	46 572
2.4 Reserve assets	712	
C. Current transfers	14 608	34 689
1. General government	3 775	18 662
2. Other sectors	10 833	16 027
Total current account	**614 867**	**651 593**
2. Capital and financial accounts		
A. Capital account	5 927	2 219
1. Capital transfers	4 728	1 077
2. Acquisition/disposal of non-produced, non-financial assets	1 199	1 142
B. Financial account	339 983	298 466
1. Direct investment	28 936	7 132
Abroad		7 132
1.1. Equity capital		12 123
1.2. Reinvested earnings		22 920
1.3. Other capital[1]		–27 911
In United Kingdom	28 936	
1.1. Equity capital	33 289	
1.2. Reinvested earnings	–14	
1.3. Other capital[2]	–4 339	
2. Portfolio investment	92 943	82 509
Assets		82 509
2.1. Equity securities		6 778
2.2. Debt securities		75 731
Liabilities	92 943	
2.1. Equity securities	2 524	
2.2. Debt securities	90 419	
3. Financial derivatives (net)		–32 490
4. Other investment	218 104	235 245
Assets		235 245
4.1 Trade credits		–78
4.2 Loans		17 267
4.3 Currency and deposits		216 673
4.4 Other assets		1 383
Liabilities	218 104	
4.1. Trade credits	–	
4.2. Loans	154 597	
4.3. Currency and deposits	62 509	
4.4. Other liabilities	998	
5. Reserve assets		6 070
5.1. Monetary gold		–
5.2. Special drawing rights		18
5.3. Reserve position in the IMF		554
5.4. Foreign exchange		5 605
Total capital and financial accounts	**345 910**	**300 685**
Total current, capital and financial accounts	**960 777**	**952 278**
Net errors and omissions	–8 499	

1 Other capital transaction on direct investment abroad represents claims on affiliated enterprises less liabilities to affiliated enterprises.
2 Other capital transactions on direct investment in the United Kingdom represents liabilities to direct investors less claims on direct investors.

food aid). **Current transfers** are distinguished from **capital transfers**, which are included in the capital account. Current transfers represent the offset to the provision of resources that are normally consumed within a short period (less than twelve months) after the transfer is made. In the example of food aid, the food is presumed to be consumed within twelve months of it being received. The classification of current transfers is by general government and other sectors.

Capital account

The capital account comprises both capital transfers and the acquisition and disposal of non-produced, non-financial assets (such as copyrights). The latter includes land purchases and sales associated with embassies and other extraterritorial bodies. Capital transfers entries are required where there is no quid pro quo to offset the transfer of ownership of fixed assets, or the transfer of funds linked to fixed assets (for example, aid to finance capital works), or the forgiveness of debt. It also includes the counterpart to the transfer of net wealth by migrants, referred to as migrants' transfers.

Financial account

The financial account comprises transactions associated with changes of ownership of the UK's foreign financial assets and liabilities. The main classifications used in the financial account are discussed in conjunction with the international investment position classification below.

The **international investment position** measures the UK's stock of external financial assets and liabilities, whereas the **balance of payments financial account** measures transactions in these assets and liabilities. Hence the classifications used in the financial account and international investment position need to be essentially the same.

Major classifications of the financial account and international investment position

Items in the financial account and international investment position statement are classified on a number of bases. The main ones are **type of investment**, **assets and liabilities**, **instrument of investment**, **sector**, and **original contractual maturity of financial instruments**.

A comparison of the international investment position statement and the balance of payments financial account shows one minor difference. In the category of direct investment in the financial account, reinvested earnings are shown separately whereas, in the international investment position statement, where no separate market price valuation of reinvested earnings can exist, the reinvested earnings are grouped into a composite category for equity and reinvested earnings.

Type of investment

The type of investment used in the UK's balance of payments and international investment position consists of five broad categories:

- **Direct investment** capital refers to capital provided to or received from an enterprise, by an investor in another country (that is, an individual, enterprise or group of related individuals or enterprises) who is in a direct investment relationship with that enterprise. A direct investment relationship exists if the investor has an equity interest in an enterprise, resident in another country, of 10 per cent or more of the ordinary shares or voting stock. The direct investment relationship extends to branches, subsidiaries and to other businesses where the enterprise has significant shareholding.

- **Portfolio investment** refers to transactions in equity and debt securities (apart from those included in direct investment and reserve assets). Debt securities comprise bonds and notes and money market instruments. In comparison with direct investment, it indicates investment where the investor is not assumed to have any appreciable say in the operation of the enterprise (for example, less than 10 per cent of the ordinary share or voting stock).
- **Financial derivatives** cover any financial instrument the price of which is based upon the value of an underlying asset (typically another financial asset). Financial derivatives include options (on currencies, interest rates, commodities, indices), traded financial futures, warrants and currency and interest swaps. Under *BPM5*, transactions in derivatives are treated as separate transactions, rather than being included as integral parts of underlying transactions to which they may be linked as hedges. From 2004 onwards, financial derivatives comprise all UK banks' net derivative transactions. Prior to 2004, only estimates for the settlement receipts/payments on UK banks' interest rate swaps and forward rate agreements are included in financial derivatives. In 2010 and 2011, ONS has introduced financial derivative data, on UK banks and securities dealers respectively, into the main aggregates of the IIP. Prior to this, data on financial derivatives was only available in the financial account and as a supplementary table (FD) in the IIP.
- **Other investment** is a category that captures transactions not classified to direct investment, portfolio investment, financial derivatives or reserve assets of the compiling economy. Other investment covers trade credits, loans (including financial leases), currency and deposits, and a residual category for any other assets and liabilities.
- **Reserve assets** refer to those foreign financial assets that are available to, and controlled by, the monetary authorities such as the Bank of England for financing or regulating payments imbalances. Reserve assets comprise: monetary gold, Special Drawing Rights, reserve position in the IMF and foreign exchange held by the Bank.

Assets and liabilities

A financial **asset** is generally in the form of a financial claim on the rest of the world that is either represented by a contractual obligation (such as a loan) or is evidenced by a security (such as a share certificate). Two financial assets – monetary gold and Special Drawing Rights in the IMF – are not claims on the rest of the world. They are, however, included in international investment assets because they are readily available for payment of international obligations. A financial **liability** represents a financial claim of the rest of the world on the UK. Assets and liabilities in the international investment position statement are components of the balance sheet of an economy with the rest of the world. In the financial account the asset and liability classifications in essence reflect, respectively, transactions in claims on non-residents (assets) and in claims by non-residents (liabilities).

In the international investment position, the difference between assets and liabilities is the net international investment position, also referred to as the net liability position/net asset position, depending on the balance.

For **direct investment**, in both the financial account and international investment position, the main classification is by direction of investment, that is, direct investment abroad and direct investment in the UK. Direct investment abroad is derived by netting liabilities of the UK direct investors to their direct investment enterprises against claims on their direct investment enterprises abroad. Similarly, direct investment in the UK is derived after netting claims of the UK direct investment enterprises against their liabilities to those direct investors abroad.

Instrument of investment

Several instruments of investment are also identified. Some of these are only applicable to one type of capital, that is, the instrument **reinvested earnings** is only applicable to direct investment, while **monetary gold** and **Special Drawing Rights** are only used for reserve assets.

The major instruments and grouping of instruments identified in balance of payments and international investment statistics include:

- monetary gold
- Special Drawing Rights
- foreign exchange
- reserve position in IMF
- equity
- reinvested earnings
- debt securities
- financial derivatives
- trade credit
- loans
- currency and deposits
- other assets/liabilities

Similar instruments may be combined into groups or combined with certain types of investment to make statistical presentations less cluttered. For example:

- trade credit, loans, deposits, and other forms of finance including all debt securities, but excluding equity capital and reinvested earnings, between non-financial enterprises in a direct investment relationship, are combined and shown only as **other capital**. Similar aggregation applies to finance between a financial enterprise and a non-financial enterprise and between financial enterprises only in case of permanent debt
- bonds, bills, notes and money market instruments within portfolio investment are shown separately but under a heading of **debt securities**
- a number of financial assets, held as part of the UK's reserves assets (currency and deposits, bills, bonds, notes and money market instruments), are grouped under the category **foreign exchange** within the reserve assets category

Foreign equity and debt

At a broader level, instruments may be combined to show foreign equity and foreign debt. Foreign equity includes equity capital, reinvested earnings and equity securities. Foreign debt is a residual item containing all other instruments. They may be compiled on a gross basis (for example, foreign debt/assets and liabilities) or on a net basis (for example, net foreign debt).

Sectorisation

Transactor units within an economy may be grouped together into institutional sectors. Units within the same institutional sector may be expected to behave similarly in their financial and other dealings and in response to differing economic and political stimuli. The principle of classification by sector, or sectorisation, in the financial account and international investment position is to identify the sector of the domestic creditor for assets and the sector of the domestic debtor for liabilities.

Four sectors are generally distinguished in the standard components of the ONS balance of payments and international investment statistics:

- **monetary financial institutions**
- **central government**
- **public corporations**
- **other**

Within the current and capital accounts, sectorisation is also applied to current and capital transfers, where a split between **general government** and **other** is used.

Original contractual maturity

The fifth edition of the balance of payments manual looks to distinguish between long-term or short-term investment. Investment longer than one year is deemed to be long-term and investment of one year or less is deemed to be short-term.

Other financial classifications

Other classifications in the financial account and international investment position include the domicile of liabilities issued by residents, drawings and repayments for long-term liabilities in the form of both trade credits and loans and the currency of assets and liabilities.

Country classification

The general principles applying to the compilation of a global balance of payments statement for the UK can be applied to the preparation of a statement for the UK's transactions with an individual country or a group of countries.

Reliability of estimates

All the value estimates are calculated as accurately as possible; however they cannot always be regarded as being absolutely precise to the last digit shown. Similarly, the index numbers are not necessarily absolutely precise to the last digit shown. Some figures are provisional and may be revised later; this applies particularly to many of the detailed figures for the latest years. For example, calendar year data for the International Trade in Services Survey and Foreign Direct Investment Survey are not available until after Pink Book publication. Therefore, the latest Trade in Services and Direct Investment data published in the Pink Book are provisional estimates and subject to annual benchmarking after publication.

The latest data when available for the International Trade in Services Survey can be found at:
http://www.ons.gov.uk/ons/search/index.html?newquery=international+trade+in+services+survey
The latest data when available for the Foreign Direct Investment Survey can be found at:
http://www.ons.gov.uk/ons/search/index.html?pageSize=50&newquery=foreign+direct+investment+survey

Revisions since ONS Pink Book 2010

The data in the Pink Book are subject to revisions following the ONS National Accounts Revision Policy. This can be found at: http://www.ons.gov.uk/ons/guide-method/method-quality/specific/economy/revisions/index.html

The current account balance is revised from 1997 onwards.

Trade in goods – The revisions to trade in goods from 1997 onwards reflect revised data from Her Majesty's Revenue and Customs and other data suppliers and revised estimates of trading associated with VAT MTIC fraud. The revisions are consistent with the 2011 Blue Book.

Trade in services – Revisions from 1997 onwards result from a general reassessment of data following the annual supply use balancing process, the incorporation of updated source data from the Bank of England, Chamber of Shipping and Department for Transport. Revisions from 2010 additionally reflect the use of final results from ONS's International Trade in Services Survey for 2010.

Income, financial account and IIP – the data are revised from 1997. Revisions from 2002 reflect a reassessment of coverage adjustments in the estimates for UK non-banks deposits with, and loans from, non-residents. Revised methodology for estimating UK banks net transactions in financial derivatives with non-residents, introduced from 2006 in the previous edition of the Pink Book, has now been extended back into 2004 and 2005; the associated asset and liability levels, previously shown from 2006, are now shown from 2004. Revised data for UK banks' reinvested earnings and transactions in bonds and notes have been incorporated from 2007.

Revisions from 2008 reflect the use of annual inquiry results from the ONS direct investment surveys. Revisions to 2009 additionally reflect the incorporation of the results of ONS annual surveys of securities dealers, mutual funds, insurance companies, and pension funds.

UK securities dealers' net transactions in financial derivatives with non-residents have been introduced into the accounts in 2010, together with the associated asset and liability levels.

Current transfers – Revisions to current transfers are attributable to revised source data for transfers involving the UK government and the use of the latest data for various ONS surveys.

Capital transfers – Revisions to the capital account are attributable to revised source data from the HM Treasury, Department for International Development and the International Trade in Services survey.

Symbols and conventions used in the tables

Rounding

As figures have been rounded to the nearest final digit, there may be slight discrepancies between the sums of the constituent items and the totals as shown.

Symbols

The following symbols are used throughout:

.. = not available

- = nil or less than a million

References

The internationally agreed framework for the presentation of the Balance of Payments and the National Accounts are described in the following publications:

Balance of Payments Manual (5th edition 1993), International Monetary Fund (ISBN 1-55775-339-3).
www.imf.org/external/np/sta/bop/BOPman.pdf

Balance of Payments Textbook (1996), International Monetary Fund (ISBN 1-55775-570-1).
www.imf.org/external/np/sta/bop/BOPtex.pdf

European System of Accounts (ESA 1995), Office for Official Publications of the European Communities (ISBN 92-827-7954-8)
http://epp.eurostat.ec.europa.eu/portal/page/portal/product_details/publication?p_product_code=CA-15-96-001

System of National Accounts (1993), (ISBN 92-1-161352-3).
http://unstats.un.org/unsd/nationalaccount/docs/1993sna.pdf

Part 1

Current account

Summary of balance of payments

Chapter 1

1.1 Summary of balance of payments

Balances (credits less debits)

£ million

	Current account											
	Trade in goods	Trade in services	**Total goods and services**	Compensation of employees	Investment income	**Total income**	**Current transfers**	**Current balance**	*Current balance as % of GDP*[1]	Capital account	Financial account	Net errors & omissions
	LQCT	KTMS	KTMY	KTMP	HMBM	HMBP	KTNF	HBOG	AA6H	FKMJ	HBNT	HHDH
1946	–101	–274	–375	–20	76	56	166	–153	..	–21	181	–7
1947	–358	–197	–555	–19	140	121	123	–311	..	–21	552	–220
1948	–152	–64	–216	–20	223	203	96	83	*0.7*	–17	–58	–8
1949	–137	–43	–180	–20	206	186	29	35	*0.3*	–12	–103	80
1950	–54	–4	–58	–21	378	357	39	338	*2.6*	–10	–447	119
1951	–692	32	–660	–21	322	301	29	–330	*–2.3*	–15	426	–81
1952	–272	123	–149	–22	231	209	169	229	*1.4*	–15	–229	15
1953	–244	123	–121	–25	207	182	143	204	*1.2*	–13	–177	–14
1954	–210	115	–95	–27	227	200	55	160	*0.9*	–13	–174	27
1955	–315	42	–273	–27	149	122	43	–108	*–0.6*	–15	34	89
1956	50	26	76	–30	203	173	2	251	*1.2*	–13	–250	12
1957	–29	121	92	–32	223	191	–5	278	*1.3*	–13	–313	48
1958	34	119	153	–34	261	227	4	384	*1.7*	–10	–411	37
1959	–116	118	2	–37	233	196	–	198	*0.8*	–5	–68	–125
1960	–404	39	–365	–35	201	166	–6	–205	*–0.8*	–6	–7	218
1961	–144	51	–93	–35	223	188	–9	86	*0.3*	–12	23	–97
1962	–104	50	–54	–37	301	264	–14	196	*0.7*	–12	–195	11
1963	–123	4	–119	–38	364	326	–37	170	*0.6*	–16	–30	–124
1964	–551	–34	–585	–33	365	332	–74	–327	*–1.0*	–17	392	–48
1965	–263	–66	–329	–34	405	371	–75	–33	*–0.1*	–18	49	2
1966	–111	44	–67	–39	358	319	–91	161	*0.4*	–19	22	–164
1967	–601	157	–444	–39	354	315	–118	–247	*–0.6*	–25	179	93
1968	–708	341	–367	–48	303	255	–119	–231	*–0.5*	–26	688	–431
1969	–214	392	178	–47	468	421	–109	490	*1.0*	–23	–794	327
1970	–18	455	437	–56	527	471	–89	819	*1.6*	–22	–818	21
1971	205	617	822	–63	454	391	–90	1 123	*2.0*	–23	–1 330	230
1972	–736	722	–14	–52	350	298	–142	142	*0.2*	–35	477	–584
1973	–2 573	907	–1 666	–68	970	902	–336	–1 100	*–1.5*	–39	1 031	108
1974	–5 241	1 292	–3 949	–92	1 010	918	–302	–3 333	*–4.0*	–34	3 185	182
1975	–3 245	1 708	–1 537	–102	257	155	–313	–1 695	*–1.6*	–36	1 569	162
1976	–3 930	2 872	–1 058	–140	760	620	–534	–972	*–0.8*	–12	507	477
1977	–2 271	3 704	1 433	–152	–678	–830	–889	–286	*–0.2*	11	–3 286	3 561
1978	–1 534	4 215	2 681	–140	–300	–440	–1 420	821	*0.5*	–79	–2 655	1 913
1979	–3 326	4 573	1 247	–130	–342	–472	–1 777	–1 002	*–0.5*	–103	864	241
1980	1 329	4 414	5 743	–82	–2 268	–2 350	–1 653	1 740	*0.8*	–4	–2 157	421
1981	3 238	4 776	8 014	–66	–1 883	–1 949	–1 219	4 846	*1.9*	–79	–5 312	545
1982	1 879	4 261	6 140	–95	–2 336	–2 431	–1 476	2 233	*0.8*	6	–1 233	–1 006
1983	–1 618	5 406	3 788	–89	–1 050	–1 139	–1 391	1 258	*0.4*	75	–3 287	1 954
1984	–5 409	6 101	692	–94	–326	–420	–1 566	–1 294	*–0.4*	107	–7 130	8 317
1985	–3 416	8 499	5 083	–120	–2 609	–2 729	–2 924	–570	*–0.2*	185	–1 657	2 042
1986	–9 617	8 182	–1 435	–156	71	–85	–2 094	–3 614	*–0.9*	135	–122	3 601
1987	–11 698	8 604	–3 094	–174	–730	–904	–3 437	–7 435	*–1.7*	333	10 606	–3 504
1988	–21 553	6 388	–15 165	–64	–1 188	–1 252	–3 293	–19 710	*–4.1*	235	16 989	2 486
1989	–24 724	5 866	–18 858	–138	–2 309	–2 447	–4 228	–25 533	*–4.9*	270	13 614	11 649
1990	–18 707	6 643	–12 064	–110	–4 586	–4 696	–4 802	–21 562	*–3.8*	497	22 272	–1 207
1991	–10 223	6 312	–3 911	–63	–5 642	–5 705	–999	–10 615	*–1.8*	290	7 855	2 470
1992	–13 050	6 353	–6 697	–49	–1 037	–1 086	–5 228	–13 011	*–2.1*	421	16 311	–3 721
1993	–13 066	8 174	–4 892	35	–2 547	–2 512	–5 056	–12 460	*–1.9*	309	22 278	–10 127
1994	–11 126	8 161	–2 965	–170	1 521	1 351	–5 187	–6 801	*–1.0*	33	–3 240	10 008
1995	–12 023	11 165	–858	–296	–546	–842	–7 363	–9 063	*–1.2*	533	–1 717	10 247
1996	–13 722	14 312	590	93	–2 460	–2 367	–4 539	–6 316	*–0.8*	1 260	–940	5 996
1997	–12 400	16 788	4 388	83	242	325	–5 525	–812	*–0.1*	958	–7 294	7 148
1998	–21 870	14 998	–6 872	–10	11 809	11 799	–8 172	–3 245	*–0.4*	489	4 480	–1 724
1999	–28 960	15 565	–13 395	201	–1 243	–1 042	–7 322	–21 759	*–2.3*	747	29 505	–8 493
2000	–33 030	15 013	–18 017	150	1 813	1 963	–9 775	–25 829	*–2.6*	1 703	23 133	993
2001	–41 180	17 208	–23 972	66	9 359	9 425	–6 515	–21 062	*–2.1*	1 318	27 194	–7 450
2002	–47 667	19 633	–28 034	67	18 436	18 503	–8 870	–18 401	*–1.7*	932	16 204	1 265
2003	–48 531	22 216	–26 315	59	17 711	17 770	–9 835	–18 380	*–1.6*	1 466	22 561	–5 647
2004	–60 939	28 296	–32 643	–494	18 523	18 029	–10 276	–24 890	*–2.1*	2 064	29 463	–6 637
2005	–68 784	26 080	–42 704	–610	22 496	21 886	–11 849	–32 667	*–2.6*	1 503	35 235	–4 071
2006	–76 569	35 838	–40 731	–958	10 470	9 512	–11 876	–43 095	*–3.2*	975	33 976	8 144
2007	–90 605	47 956	–42 649	–734	22 103	21 369	–13 546	–34 826	*–2.5*	2 566	24 982	7 278
2008	–94 181	55 057	–39 124	–715	33 851	33 136	–13 765	–19 753	*–1.4*	3 241	25 985	–9 473
2009	–82 852	57 215	–25 637	–259	20 656	20 397	–15 076	–20 316	*–1.5*	3 637	24 765	–8 086
2010	–98 462	58 778	–39 684	–389	23 428	23 039	–20 081	–36 726	*–2.5*	3 708	41 517	–8 499

1 Using series YBHA: GDP at current market prices.

1.1R Summary of balance of payments
Revisions since ONS *Pink Book 2010*

£ million

	Current account											
	Trade in goods	Trade in services	**Total goods and services**	Compensation of employees	Investment income	**Total income**	**Current transfers**	**Current balance**	*Current balance as % of GDP[1]*	Capital account	Financial account	Net errors & omissions
	LQCT	KTMS	KTMY	KTMP	HMBM	HMBP	KTNF	HBOG	AA6H	FKMJ	HBNT	HHDH
1946	–	–	–	–	–	–	–	–	..	–	–	–
1947	–	–	–	–	–	–	–	–	..	–	–	–
1948	–	–	–	–	–	–	–	–	–	–	–	–
1949	–	–	–	–	–	–	–	–	–	–	–	–
1950	–	–	–	–	–	–	–	–	–	–	–	–
1951	–	–	–	–	–	–	–	–	–	–	–	–
1952	–	–	–	–	–	–	–	–	–	–	–	–
1953	–	–	–	–	–	–	–	–	–	–	–	–
1954	–	–	–	–	–	–	–	–	–	–	–	–
1955	–	–	–	–	–	–	–	–	–	–	–	–
1956	–	–	–	–	–	–	–	–	–	–	–	–
1957	–	–	–	–	–	–	–	–	–	–	–	–
1958	–	–	–	–	–	–	–	–	–	–	–	–
1959	–	–	–	–	–	–	–	–	–	–	–	–
1960	–	–	–	–	–	–	–	–	–	–	–	–
1961	–	–	–	–	–	–	–	–	–	–	–	–
1962	–	–	–	–	–	–	–	–	–	–	–	–
1963	–	–	–	–	–	–	–	–	–	–	–	–
1964	–	–	–	–	–	–	–	–	–	–	–	–
1965	–	–	–	–	–	–	–	–	–	–	–	–
1966	–	–	–	–	–	–	–	–	–	–	–	–
1967	–	–	–	–	–	–	–	–	–	–	–	–
1968	–	–	–	–	–	–	–	–	–	–	–	–
1969	–	–	–	–	–	–	–	–	–	–	–	–
1970	–	–	–	–	–	–	–	–	–	–	–	–
1971	–	–	–	–	–	–	–	–	–	–	–	–
1972	–	–	–	–	–	–	–	–	–	–	–	–
1973	–	–	–	–	–	–	–	–	–	–	–	–
1974	–	–	–	–	–	–	–	–	–	–	–	–
1975	–	–	–	–	–	–	–	–	–	–	–	–
1976	–	–	–	–	–	–	–	–	–	–	–	–
1977	–	–	–	–	–	–	–	–	–	–	–	–
1978	–	–	–	–	–	–	–	–	–	–	–	–
1979	–	–	–	–	–	–	–	–	–	–	–	–
1980	–	–	–	–	–	–	–	–	–	–	–	–
1981	–	–	–	–	–	–	–	–	–	–	–	–
1982	–	–	–	–	–	–	–	–	–	–	–	–
1983	–	–	–	–	–	–	–	–	–	–	–	–
1984	–	–	–	–	–	–	–	–	–	–	–	–
1985	–	–	–	–	–	–	–	–	–	–	–	–
1986	–	–	–	–	–	–	–	–	–	–	–	–
1987	–	–	–	–	–	–	–	–	–	–	–	–
1988	–	–	–	–	–	–	–	–	–	–	–	–
1989	–	–	–	–	–	–	–	–	–	–	–	–
1990	–	–	–	–	–	–	–	–	–	–	–	–
1991	–	–	–	–	–	–	–	–	–	–	–	–
1992	–	–	–	–	–	–	–	–	–	–	–	–
1993	–	–	–	–	–	–	–	–	–	–	–	–
1994	–	–	–	–	–	–	–	–	–	–	–	–
1995	–	–	–	–	–	–	–	–	–	–	–	–
1996	–	–	–	–	–	–	–	–	–	–	–	–
1997	–58	–13	–71	–	1	1	220	150	–	–	–	–150
1998	–57	–5	–62	–	–4	–4	–	–66	–	–	–	66
1999	91	3	94	–	1	1	–	95	*0.1*	–	–	–95
2000	–54	11	–43	–	1	1	–	–42	–	–	–	42
2001	32	8	40	–	–	–	–	40	–	–	–	–40
2002	38	1	39	–	217	217	–	256	–	–	–8 000	7 744
2003	76	–396	–320	–	247	247	–	–73	–	–	8	65
2004	–39	–118	–157	–	184	184	–	27	–	–	105	–132
2005	–195	338	143	–	31	31	–	174	–	–	6 211	–6 385
2006	–257	1 063	806	–	1 031	1 031	2	1 839	*0.2*	–	–7 998	6 159
2007	–851	1 158	307	–	1 349	1 349	–	1 656	*0.1*	–	192	–1 848
2008	–1 065	–299	–1 364	–	5 101	5 101	286	4 023	*0.2*	–	174	–4 197
2009	–977	7 363	6 386	429	–11 314	–10 885	–311	–4 810	*–0.4*	418	19 168	–14 776

1 Using series YBHA: GDP at current market prices.

1.2 Current account

£ million

		1989	1990	1991	1992	1993	1994	1995	1996	1997	1998	1999
Credits												
Exports of goods and services												
Exports of goods	LQAD	92 611	102 313	103 939	107 863	122 229	135 143	153 577	167 196	171 825	163 964	166 084
Exports of services	KTMQ	31 542	34 270	34 723	37 617	43 605	48 072	53 570	61 851	65 539	69 226	76 530
Total exports of goods and services	KTMW	124 153	136 583	138 662	145 480	165 834	183 215	207 147	229 047	237 364	233 190	242 614
Income												
Compensation of employees	KTMN	476	543	551	551	595	681	887	911	1 007	840	960
Investment income	HMBN	71 536	76 353	73 652	65 168	70 944	72 585	85 490	89 794	93 360	102 548	100 733
Total income	HMBQ	72 012	76 896	74 203	65 719	71 539	73 266	86 377	90 705	94 367	103 388	101 693
Current transfers												
General government	FJUM	1 507	2 050	4 892	2 180	2 826	2 138	1 730	2 828	2 393	1 767	3 542
Other sectors	FJUN	5 244	6 025	7 611	10 397	9 612	9 521	10 891	13 371	10 735	10 682	8 510
Total current transfers	KTND	6 751	8 075	12 503	12 577	12 438	11 659	12 621	16 199	13 128	12 449	12 052
Total	HBOE	**202 916**	**221 554**	**225 368**	**223 776**	**249 811**	**268 140**	**306 145**	**335 951**	**344 859**	**349 027**	**356 359**
Debits												
Imports of goods and services												
Imports of goods	LQBL	117 335	121 020	114 162	120 913	135 295	146 269	165 600	180 918	184 225	185 834	195 044
Imports of services	KTMR	25 676	27 627	28 411	31 264	35 431	39 911	42 405	47 539	48 751	54 228	60 965
Total imports of goods and services	KTMX	143 011	148 647	142 573	152 177	170 726	186 180	208 005	228 457	232 976	240 062	256 009
Income												
Compensation of employees	KTMO	614	653	614	600	560	851	1 183	818	924	850	759
Investment income	HMBO	73 845	80 939	79 294	66 205	73 491	71 064	86 036	92 254	93 118	90 739	101 976
Total income	HMBR	74 459	81 592	79 908	66 805	74 051	71 915	87 219	93 072	94 042	91 589	102 735
Current transfers												
General government	FJUO	2 055	1 995	3 218	3 506	4 156	4 795	4 811	5 081	5 087	6 585	7 271
Other sectors	FJUP	8 924	10 882	10 284	14 299	13 338	12 051	15 173	15 657	13 566	14 036	12 103
Total current transfers	KTNE	10 979	12 877	13 502	17 805	17 494	16 846	19 984	20 738	18 653	20 621	19 374
Total	HBOF	**228 449**	**243 116**	**235 983**	**236 787**	**262 271**	**274 941**	**315 208**	**342 267**	**345 671**	**352 272**	**378 118**
Balances												
Trade in goods and services												
Trade in goods	LQCT	–24 724	–18 707	–10 223	–13 050	–13 066	–11 126	–12 023	–13 722	–12 400	–21 870	–28 960
Trade in services	KTMS	5 866	6 643	6 312	6 353	8 174	8 161	11 165	14 312	16 788	14 998	15 565
Total trade in goods and services	KTMY	–18 858	–12 064	–3 911	–6 697	–4 892	–2 965	–858	590	4 388	–6 872	–13 395
Income												
Compensation of employees	KTMP	–138	–110	–63	–49	35	–170	–296	93	83	–10	201
Investment income	HMBM	–2 309	–4 586	–5 642	–1 037	–2 547	1 521	–546	–2 460	242	11 809	–1 243
Total income	HMBP	–2 447	–4 696	–5 705	–1 086	–2 512	1 351	–842	–2 367	325	11 799	–1 042
Current transfers												
General government	FJUQ	–548	55	1 674	–1 326	–1 330	–2 657	–3 081	–2 253	–2 694	–4 818	–3 729
Other sectors	FJUR	–3 680	–4 857	–2 673	–3 902	–3 726	–2 530	–4 282	–2 286	–2 831	–3 354	–3 593
Total current transfers	KTNF	–4 228	–4 802	–999	–5 228	–5 056	–5 187	–7 363	–4 539	–5 525	–8 172	–7 322
Total (Current balance)	HBOG	**–25 533**	**–21 562**	**–10 615**	**–13 011**	**–12 460**	**–6 801**	**–9 063**	**–6 316**	**–812**	**–3 245**	**–21 759**

1.2 Current account

continued £ million

		2000	2001	2002	2003	2004	2005	2006	2007	2008	2009	2010
Credits												
Exports of goods and services												
Exports of goods	LQAD	187 826	189 002	186 443	188 241	190 786	211 498	243 564	220 347	251 977	228 126	265 714
Exports of services	KTMQ	81 888	87 773	94 011	101 966	112 826	119 569	135 527	153 685	170 887	167 462	171 082
Total exports of goods and services	KTMW	269 714	276 775	280 454	290 207	303 612	331 067	379 091	374 032	422 864	395 588	436 796
Income												
Compensation of employees	KTMN	1 032	1 087	1 121	1 116	931	974	938	984	1 046	1 176	1 097
Investment income	HMBN	131 902	137 447	120 543	122 069	137 380	185 640	237 505	291 614	262 842	169 313	162 366
Total income	HMBQ	132 934	138 534	121 664	123 185	138 311	186 614	238 443	292 598	263 888	170 489	163 463
Current transfers												
General government	FJUM	2 465	4 991	3 663	3 968	4 177	4 294	4 383	4 318	5 652	6 255	3 775
Other sectors	FJUN	8 018	8 926	8 571	8 079	9 590	13 106	13 791	9 559	10 671	10 809	10 833
Total current transfers	KTND	10 483	13 917	12 234	12 047	13 767	17 400	18 174	13 877	16 323	17 064	14 608
Total	HBOE	**413 131**	**429 226**	**414 352**	**425 439**	**455 690**	**535 081**	**635 708**	**680 507**	**703 075**	**583 141**	**614 867**
Debits												
Imports of goods and services												
Imports of goods	LQBL	220 856	230 182	234 110	236 772	251 725	280 282	320 133	310 952	346 158	310 978	364 176
Imports of services	KTMR	66 875	70 565	74 378	79 750	84 530	93 489	99 689	105 729	115 830	110 247	112 304
Total imports of goods and services	KTMX	287 731	300 747	308 488	316 522	336 255	373 771	419 822	416 681	461 988	421 225	476 480
Income												
Compensation of employees	KTMO	882	1 021	1 054	1 057	1 425	1 584	1 896	1 718	1 761	1 435	1 486
Investment income	HMBO	130 089	128 088	102 107	104 358	118 857	163 144	227 035	269 511	228 991	148 657	138 938
Total income	HMBR	130 971	129 109	103 161	105 415	120 282	164 728	228 931	271 229	230 752	150 092	140 424
Current transfers												
General government	FJUO	7 778	7 340	9 085	10 657	12 225	13 637	13 874	14 082	14 714	17 665	18 662
Other sectors	FJUP	12 480	13 092	12 019	11 225	11 818	15 612	16 176	13 341	15 374	14 475	16 027
Total current transfers	KTNE	20 258	20 432	21 104	21 882	24 043	29 249	30 050	27 423	30 088	32 140	34 689
Total	HBOF	**438 960**	**450 288**	**432 753**	**443 819**	**480 580**	**567 748**	**678 803**	**715 333**	**722 828**	**603 457**	**651 593**
Balances												
Trade in goods and services												
Trade in goods	LQCT	–33 030	–41 180	–47 667	–48 531	–60 939	–68 784	–76 569	–90 605	–94 181	–82 852	–98 462
Trade in services	KTMS	15 013	17 208	19 633	22 216	28 296	26 080	35 838	47 956	55 057	57 215	58 778
Total trade in goods and services	KTMY	–18 017	–23 972	–28 034	–26 315	–32 643	–42 704	–40 731	–42 649	–39 124	–25 637	–39 684
Income												
Compensation of employees	KTMP	150	66	67	59	–494	–610	–958	–734	–715	–259	–389
Investment income	HMBM	1 813	9 359	18 436	17 711	18 523	22 496	10 470	22 103	33 851	20 656	23 428
Total income	HMBP	1 963	9 425	18 503	17 770	18 029	21 886	9 512	21 369	33 136	20 397	23 039
Current transfers												
General government	FJUQ	–5 313	–2 349	–5 422	–6 689	–8 048	–9 343	–9 491	–9 764	–9 062	–11 410	–14 887
Other sectors	FJUR	–4 462	–4 166	–3 448	–3 146	–2 228	–2 506	–2 385	–3 782	–4 703	–3 666	–5 194
Total current transfers	KTNF	–9 775	–6 515	–8 870	–9 835	–10 276	–11 849	–11 876	–13 546	–13 765	–15 076	–20 081
Total (Current balance)	HBOG	**–25 829**	**–21 062**	**–18 401**	**–18 380**	**–24 890**	**–32 667**	**–43 095**	**–34 826**	**–19 753**	**–20 316**	**–36 726**

1.3 Summary of international investment position, financial account and investment income

£ billion

		2000	2001	2002	2003	2004	2005	2006	2007	2008	2009	2010
Investment abroad												
International investment position												
Direct investment	HBWD	618.8	616.9	637.2	691.1	678.1	705.9	733.1	899.8	1 068.7	1 033.6	1 078.5
Portfolio investment	HHZZ	906.1	937.4	844.0	935.8	1 092.1	1 360.9	1 531.0	1 689.7	1 664.3	1 875.3	2 076.1
Financial derivatives	JX96	..	..	..	..	709.4	820.1	853.7	1 378.1	4 040.2	2 176.4	2 962.8
Other investment	HLXV	1 379.7	1 521.9	1 545.2	1 813.7	2 118.0	2 714.8	2 916.6	3 744.5	4 180.6	3 517.1	3 794.3
Reserve assets	LTEB	28.8	25.6	25.5	23.8	23.2	24.7	22.9	26.7	36.3	40.1	49.7
Total	HBQA	**2 933.4**	**3 101.9**	**3 051.9**	**3 464.5**	**4 620.8**	**5 626.4**	**6 057.4**	**7 738.8**	**10 990.1**	**8 642.5**	**9 961.4**
Financial account transactions												
Direct investment	-HJYP	155.6	42.8	35.0	40.9	51.5	44.0	45.0	162.6	99.6	28.5	7.1
Portfolio investment	-HHZC	65.6	86.6	1.0	36.3	141.0	151.0	138.8	91.5	–123.2	164.7	82.5
Financial derivatives (net)	-ZPNN	–1.6	–8.4	–1.0	5.4	6.8	–5.8	–20.6	27.0	121.7	–29.1	–32.5
Other investment	-XBMM	241.7	170.7	70.4	260.4	325.2	506.3	395.9	742.4	–613.0	–336.1	235.2
Reserve assets	-LTCV	3.9	–3.1	–0.5	–1.6	0.2	0.7	–0.4	1.2	–1.3	5.8	6.1
Total	-HBNR	**465.2**	**288.5**	**105.0**	**341.4**	**524.7**	**696.1**	**558.7**	**1 024.7**	**–516.2**	**–166.2**	**298.5**
Investment income												
Direct investment	HJYW	45.0	46.7	51.5	55.1	63.3	79.2	83.6	91.4	69.5	69.6	81.8
Portfolio investment	HLYX	33.0	34.9	32.5	32.5	36.7	45.4	55.1	66.1	67.5	54.6	47.4
Other investment	AIOP	52.9	54.9	35.8	33.6	36.7	60.4	98.1	133.5	125.1	44.4	32.5
Reserve assets	HHCB	1.0	1.0	0.8	0.8	0.7	0.7	0.6	0.6	0.8	0.8	0.7
Total	HMBN	**131.9**	**137.4**	**120.5**	**122.1**	**137.4**	**185.6**	**237.5**	**291.6**	**262.8**	**169.3**	**162.4**
Investment in the UK												
International investment position												
Direct investment	HBWI	310.4	363.5	340.6	355.5	383.3	494.2	577.3	613.8	660.4	652.3	692.9
Portfolio investment	HLXW	1 067.6	1 013.2	925.3	1 082.9	1 227.9	1 461.7	1 703.5	1 945.7	1 980.2	2 405.5	2 523.1
Financial derivatives	JX97	..	..	..	..	715.0	831.1	890.5	1 392.2	3 915.3	2 096.8	2 895.0
Other investment	HLYD	1 651.6	1 861.9	1 898.0	2 135.2	2 511.8	3 109.0	3 270.0	4 115.6	4 518.1	3 792.0	4 047.6
Total	HBQB	**3 029.5**	**3 238.5**	**3 163.9**	**3 573.6**	**4 838.1**	**5 896.0**	**6 441.2**	**8 067.3**	**11 073.9**	**8 946.6**	**10 158.6**
Financial account transactions												
Direct investment	HJYU	80.6	37.3	16.8	16.8	31.2	97.8	84.9	100.0	48.4	45.2	28.9
Portfolio investment	HHZF	172.2	40.8	49.7	105.6	97.3	129.0	152.5	217.9	200.6	191.6	92.9
Other investment	XBMN	235.6	237.6	54.6	241.5	425.6	504.5	355.3	731.8	–739.2	–378.2	218.1
Total	HBNS	**488.3**	**315.7**	**121.2**	**364.0**	**554.2**	**731.3**	**592.7**	**1 049.7**	**–490.2**	**–141.5**	**340.0**
Investment income												
Direct investment	HJYX	27.4	21.4	16.0	21.9	27.6	36.2	51.6	45.1	3.1	26.4	32.4
Portfolio investment	HLZC	32.4	36.1	33.3	32.9	38.7	47.6	57.6	66.8	74.5	60.3	59.9
Other investment	HLZN	70.2	70.5	52.8	49.5	52.5	79.4	117.9	157.7	151.4	61.9	46.6
Total	HMBO	**130.1**	**128.1**	**102.1**	**104.4**	**118.9**	**163.1**	**227.0**	**269.5**	**229.0**	**148.7**	**138.9**
Net investment												
International investment position												
Direct investment	HBWQ	308.4	253.5	296.6	335.6	294.7	211.7	155.8	285.9	408.4	381.3	385.6
Portfolio investment	CGNH	–161.5	–75.7	–81.3	–147.0	–135.8	–100.8	–172.4	–255.9	–315.9	–530.2	–447.0
Financial derivatives	JX98	..	..	..	..	–5.6	–11.0	–36.8	–14.1	124.9	79.6	67.8
Other investment	CGNG	–271.9	–339.9	–352.8	–321.5	–393.9	–394.2	–353.4	–371.0	–337.5	–274.9	–253.4
Reserve assets	LTEB	28.8	25.6	25.5	23.8	23.2	24.7	22.9	26.7	36.3	40.1	49.7
Net investment position	HBQC	**–96.2**	**–136.5**	**–112.0**	**–109.2**	**–217.3**	**–269.6**	**–383.8**	**–328.4**	**–83.8**	**–304.1**	**–197.3**
Financial account transactions												
Direct investment	HJYV	–75.0	–5.5	–18.3	–24.1	–20.3	53.8	39.9	–62.7	–51.2	16.7	21.8
Portfolio investment	HHZD	106.6	–45.7	48.7	69.4	–43.7	–21.9	13.7	126.4	323.8	26.9	10.4
Financial derivatives	ZPNN	1.6	8.4	1.0	–5.4	–6.8	5.8	20.6	–27.0	–121.7	29.1	32.5
Other investment	HHYR	–6.1	66.9	–15.7	–18.9	100.4	–1.8	–40.6	–10.6	–126.2	–42.1	–17.1
Reserve assets	LTCV	–3.9	3.1	0.5	1.6	–0.2	–0.7	0.4	–1.2	1.3	–5.8	–6.1
Net transactions	HBNT	**23.1**	**27.2**	**16.2**	**22.6**	**29.5**	**35.2**	**34.0**	**25.0**	**26.0**	**24.8**	**41.5**
Investment income												
Direct investment	HJYE	17.6	25.3	35.5	33.2	35.7	43.0	32.0	46.3	66.4	43.2	49.4
Portfolio investment	HLZX	0.5	–1.2	–0.8	–0.4	–2.0	–2.2	–2.4	–0.7	–7.0	–5.8	–12.6
Other investment	CGNA	–17.3	–15.7	–17.0	–15.9	–15.9	–19.0	–19.7	–24.1	–26.3	–17.6	–14.1
Reserve assets	HHCB	1.0	1.0	0.8	0.8	0.7	0.7	0.6	0.6	0.8	0.8	0.7
Net earnings	HMBM	**1.8**	**9.4**	**18.4**	**17.7**	**18.5**	**22.5**	**10.5**	**22.1**	**33.9**	**20.7**	**23.4**

Chapter 2

Trade in goods

2.1 Trade in goods
Summary table

£ million

		SITC[1]	2000	2001	2002	2003	2004	2005	2006	2007	2008	2009	2010
Exports													
Food, beverages and tobacco	BQMV	0+1	9 908	9 630	9 993	10 879	10 577	10 647	10 945	11 754	13 776	14 572	16 103
Basic materials	ELBK	2+4	2 603	2 571	2 855	3 335	3 770	3 981	4 892	5 517	6 631	5 194	7 346
Oil													
Crude oil	BQNX	333	10 522	10 489	9 804	9 241	9 338	10 948	12 784	12 644	16 648	12 517	15 825
Oil products	BQNY	334+335	5 076	4 347	4 518	5 356	6 881	8 918	10 439	9 811	15 327	12 139	15 473
Total oil	BOKL	33	15 598	14 836	14 322	14 597	16 219	19 866	23 223	22 455	31 975	24 656	31 298
Coal, gas and electricity	BQNF	32+34+35	1 473	1 571	1 679	1 950	1 685	1 702	2 128	1 942	3 551	2 368	3 813
Semi-manufactured goods													
Chemicals	BQOB	5	24 992	27 514	28 365	31 373	32 009	33 388	37 179	38 939	43 956	47 101	50 925
Precious stones and silver	BQOD	667+681.1	4 744	4 709	4 728	5 138	4 909	5 541	5 024	5 539	7 136	4 207	6 509
Other	BQOC	Rest of 6	17 779	17 938	17 056	17 924	19 416	20 701	22 211	23 827	25 341	20 394	22 756
Total semi-manufactured goods	BQMX	5+6	47 515	50 161	50 149	54 435	56 334	59 630	64 414	68 305	76 433	71 702	80 190
Finished manufactured goods													
Motor cars	BQOE	781	9 178	8 046	10 297	11 183	12 108	13 074	12 557	14 267	15 480	11 921	17 245
Other consumer goods[2]	BQOF		14 292	14 420	14 582	14 978	15 791	17 796	18 753	18 483	19 146	18 341	20 611
Intermediate goods[2]	BQOG		41 130	42 089	40 025	37 370	36 672	38 636	42 317	35 523	38 541	37 027	40 602
Capital goods[2]	BQOH		37 181	37 684	34 944	31 500	29 440	38 131	55 689	32 629	35 617	31 338	35 133
Ships and aircraft	BQOI	792+793	7 262	6 980	6 510	7 144	7 302	6 917	7 338	8 311	9 043	8 845	10 586
Total finished manufactured goods	BQMQ	7+8	109 043	109 219	106 358	102 175	101 313	114 554	136 654	109 213	117 827	107 472	124 177
Commodities and transactions not classified according to kind	BOKJ	9	1 686	1 014	1 087	870	888	1 118	1 308	1 161	1 784	2 162	2 787
Total	LQAD		**187 826**	**189 002**	**186 443**	**188 241**	**190 786**	**211 498**	**243 564**	**220 347**	**251 977**	**228 126**	**265 714**
Imports													
Food, beverages and tobacco	BQMW	0+1	17 663	18 492	19 377	21 189	22 151	23 696	25 014	26 713	31 154	32 336	33 463
Basic materials	BQNA	2+4	6 307	6 442	5 958	6 139	6 338	6 770	7 887	9 560	11 014	7 617	10 279
Oil													
Crude oil	BQNM	333	4 825	4 878	4 752	5 705	8 191	11 222	14 272	13 621	20 291	14 238	19 207
Oil products	BQOA	334+335	4 223	4 650	4 461	5 527	7 116	10 828	11 780	13 532	18 158	13 849	16 817
Total oil	BQAQ	33	9 048	9 528	9 213	11 232	15 307	22 050	26 052	27 153	38 449	28 087	36 024
Coal, gas and electricity	BQNG	32+34+35	968	1 270	1 066	1 079	2 240	3 932	4 921	5 160	10 602	7 444	8 875
Semi-manufactured goods													
Chemicals	BQOJ	5	20 633	22 745	23 987	26 139	27 929	29 208	31 727	34 687	38 001	39 044	44 751
Precious stones and silver	BQOL	667+681.1	5 454	5 260	4 247	4 346	4 673	5 238	6 131	5 450	5 887	5 774	6 537
Other	BQOK		23 609	24 778	24 431	25 519	27 529	28 107	31 298	34 346	36 078	30 160	37 051
Total semi-manufactured goods	BQMR	5+6	49 696	52 783	52 665	56 004	60 131	62 553	69 156	74 483	79 966	74 978	88 339
Finished manufactured goods													
Motor cars	BQOM	781	13 403	16 619	17 800	18 374	18 724	18 988	19 179	21 765	19 772	16 484	19 998
Other consumer goods[2]	BQON		28 075	29 953	32 342	33 404	35 129	37 684	40 773	42 019	44 068	43 663	47 449
Intermediate goods[2]	BQOO		48 455	46 081	44 829	40 869	42 137	45 900	53 176	47 212	50 759	44 240	52 601
Capital goods[2]	BQOP		37 944	38 463	39 473	38 240	40 222	49 118	62 637	45 397	47 111	41 515	48 441
Ships and aircraft	BQOQ	792+793	7 405	9 290	9 929	8 646	7 539	7 771	9 269	9 243	10 378	11 619	15 501
Total finished manufactured goods	BQMY	7+8	135 282	140 406	144 373	139 533	143 751	159 461	185 034	165 636	172 088	157 521	183 990
Commodities and transactions not classified according to kind	BQAO	9	1 892	1 261	1 458	1 596	1 807	1 820	2 069	2 247	2 885	2 995	3 206
Total	LQBL		**220 856**	**230 182**	**234 110**	**236 772**	**251 725**	**280 282**	**320 133**	**310 952**	**346 158**	**310 978**	**364 176**

1 Standard International Trade Classification, Revision 4.
2 Derived from the *Classification by Broad Economic Categories defined in terms of SITC,* published by the United Nations.

2.1 Trade in goods
Summary table

continued

£ million

		SITC[1]	2000	2001	2002	2003	2004	2005	2006	2007	2008	2009	2010
Balances													
Food, beverages and tobacco	BQOS	0+1	-7 755	-8 862	-9 384	-10 310	-11 574	-13 049	-14 069	-14 959	-17 378	-17 764	-17 360
Basic materials	BQOR	2+4	-3 704	-3 871	-3 103	-2 804	-2 568	-2 789	-2 995	-4 043	-4 383	-2 423	-2 933
Oil													
Crude oil	BQMG	333	5 697	5 611	5 052	3 536	1 147	-274	-1 488	-977	-3 643	-1 721	-3 382
Oil products	BQMH	334+335	853	-303	57	-171	-235	-1 910	-1 341	-3 721	-2 831	-1 710	-1 344
Total oil	BQNE	33	6 550	5 308	5 109	3 365	912	-2 184	-2 829	-4 698	-6 474	-3 431	-4 726
Coal, gas and electricity	BQNH	32+34+35	505	301	613	871	-555	-2 230	-2 793	-3 218	-7 051	-5 076	-5 062
Semi-manufactured goods													
Chemicals	BQMI	5	4 359	4 769	4 378	5 234	4 080	4 180	5 452	4 252	5 955	8 057	6 174
Precious stones and silver	BQMK	667+681.1	-710	-551	481	792	236	303	-1 107	89	1 249	-1 567	-28
Other	BQMJ	Rest of 6	-5 830	-6 840	-7 375	-7 595	-8 113	-7 406	-9 087	-10 519	-10 737	-9 766	-14 295
Total semi-manufactured goods	BQOT	5+6	-2 181	-2 622	-2 516	-1 569	-3 797	-2 923	-4 742	-6 178	-3 533	-3 276	-8 149
Finished manufactured goods													
Motor cars	BQML	781	-4 225	-8 573	-7 503	-7 191	-6 616	-5 914	-6 622	-7 498	-4 292	-4 563	-2 753
Other consumer goods[2]	BQMM		-13 783	-15 533	-17 760	-18 426	-19 338	-19 888	-22 020	-23 536	-24 922	-25 322	-26 838
Intermediate goods[2]	BQMN		-7 325	-3 992	-4 804	-3 499	-5 465	-7 264	-10 859	-11 689	-12 218	-7 213	-11 999
Capital goods[2]	BQMO		-763	-779	-4 529	-6 740	-10 782	-10 987	-6 948	-12 768	-11 494	-10 177	-13 308
Ships and aircraft	BQMP	792+793	-143	-2 310	-3 419	-1 502	-237	-854	-1 931	-932	-1 335	-2 774	-4 915
Total finished manufactured goods	BQOV	7+8	-26 239	-31 187	-38 015	-37 358	-42 438	-44 907	-48 380	-56 423	-54 261	-50 049	-59 813
Commodities and transactions not classified according to kind	BQOU	9	-206	-247	-371	-726	-919	-702	-761	-1 086	-1 101	-833	-419
Total	LQCT		**-33 030**	**-41 180**	**-47 667**	**-48 531**	**-60 939**	**-68 784**	**-76 569**	**-90 605**	**-94 181**	**-82 852**	**-98 462**

1 Standard International Trade Classification, Revision 4.
2 Derived from the *Classification by Broad Economic Categories defined in terms of SITC*, published by the United Nations.

2.2 Trade in goods: volume indices

2008=100

		SITC[1]	2000	2001	2002	2003	2004	2005	2006	2007	2008	2009	2010
Exports													
Food, beverages and tobacco	BQPP	0+1	86	81	85	89	89	89	90	96	100	100	107
Basic materials	BQPQ	2+4	45	44	48	57	67	68	72	86	100	86	100
Oil													
Crude oil	BOGH	333	168	184	177	154	135	110	106	103	100	94	90
Oil products	BOGO	334+335	66	60	56	65	69	86	89	87	100	104	100
Total oil	BONC	33	110	114	109	104	99	98	98	95	100	99	95
Coal, gas and electricity	BOGP	32+34+35	104	122	126	138	101	85	83	73	100	78	104
Semi-manufactured goods													
Chemicals	BQLB	5	64	71	75	81	83	85	95	98	100	96	103
Precious stones and silver	BQLD	667+681.1	111	111	107	116	114	126	117	100	100	59	102
Other	BQLC	Rest of 6	93	92	90	89	94	93	101	106	100	76	83
Total semi-manufactured goods	BQPR	5+6	77	81	82	86	89	91	98	101	100	86	96
Finished manufactured goods													
Motor cars	BQLE	781	63	55	71	76	84	90	85	97	100	72	102
Other consumer goods[2]	BQLF		74	75	78	82	88	99	106	106	100	88	99
Intermediate goods[2]	BQLG		100	104	102	99	99	106	119	100	100	88	96
Capital goods[2]	BQLH		85	88	86	77	74	99	143	93	100	81	90
Ships and aircraft	BQLI	792+793	83	79	75	87	91	85	90	102	100	91	107
Total finished manufactured goods	BQPS	7+8	85	87	87	85	86	99	119	99	100	84	96
Total	BPBP		**83.6**	**85.4**	**86.2**	**86.3**	**87.4**	**94.9**	**107.3**	**98.1**	**100.0**	**88.0**	**97.1**
Imports													
Food, beverages and tobacco	BQPT	0+1	70	75	78	83	87	91	96	99	100	97	99
Basic materials	BQPU	2+4	81	82	79	81	82	84	88	97	100	72	86
Oil													
Crude oil	BQPV	333	70	78	79	86	106	100	106	96	100	94	95
Oil products	BQPW	334+335	89	107	80	90	101	107	103	121	100	98	88
Total oil	ELAM	33	77	90	79	88	103	103	104	107	100	96	92
Coal, gas and electricity	BQPX	32+34+35	44	43	40	35	48	57	61	73	100	76	99
Semi-manufactured goods													
Chemicals	BQLQ	5	65	71	78	83	90	91	97	103	100	97	108
Precious stones and silver	BQLS	667+681.1	93	88	77	87	103	111	119	105	100	90	85
Other	BQLR	Rest of 6	77	81	84	88	91	89	96	102	100	80	93
Total semi-manufactured goods	BQPY	5+6	72	77	81	85	92	92	98	103	100	89	100
Finished manufactured goods													
Motor cars	BQLT	781	70	89	95	97	100	102	102	115	100	79	97
Other consumer goods[2]	BQLU		61	64	71	73	78	83	95	102	100	91	101
Intermediate goods[2]	BQLV		91	88	90	86	91	99	115	101	100	80	93
Capital goods[2]	BQLW		65	67	73	74	81	104	130	99	100	80	91
Ships and aircraft	BQLX	792+793	81	100	109	95	83	82	98	96	100	102	137
Total finished manufactured goods	BQPZ	7+8	73	76	82	81	86	96	112	102	100	84	98
Total	BQBJ		**72.2**	**76.2**	**80.2**	**81.5**	**86.9**	**93.4**	**104.4**	**101.3**	**100.0**	**87.4**	**97.5**

1 Standard International Trade Classification, Revision 4.
2 Derived from the *Classification by Broad Economic Categories defined in terms of SITC,* published by the United Nations.

2.3 Trade in goods: price indices

2008=100

		SITC[1]	2000	2001	2002	2003	2004	2005	2006	2007	2008	2009	2010
Exports													
Food, beverages and tobacco	BPAI	0+1	80	82	83	87	84	85	88	89	100	103	106
Basic materials	BPAW	2+4	78	81	80	79	77	82	99	95	100	86	113
Oil													
Crude oil	BQAC	333	37	33	32	35	40	58	68	70	100	76	102
Oil products	BQAD	334+335	44	42	47	50	61	64	71	72	100	76	100
Total oil	BQAL	33	40	37	37	40	48	61	70	71	100	76	101
Coal, gas and electricity	BQAF	32+34+35	40	37	39	42	49	61	70	71	100	78	100
Semi-manufactured goods													
Chemicals	BQLJ	5	84	84	82	86	86	87	88	89	100	110	112
Precious stones and silver	BQLL	667+681.1	60	60	62	62	61	62	63	70	100	100	92
Other	BQLK	Rest of 6	72	74	73	77	80	86	86	88	100	104	108
Total semi-manufactured goods	BQAA	5+6	78	78	77	80	81	84	85	87	100	107	109
Finished manufactured goods													
Motor cars	BQPM	781	95	95	96	96	94	95	96	96	100	106	110
Other consumer goods[2]	BQLM		93	94	93	92	90	91	91	91	100	106	107
Intermediate goods[2]	BQLN		107	106	103	100	97	97	95	92	100	110	111
Capital goods[2]	BQLO		110	108	103	104	102	100	97	93	100	105	111
Ships and aircraft	BQLP	792+793	97	98	96	91	89	90	90	90	100	107	110
Total finished manufactured goods	BQAB	7+8	104	104	100	99	96	96	95	93	100	107	110
Total	BQKR		**84.7**	**84.1**	**82.6**	**83.4**	**83.8**	**86.8**	**88.3**	**87.8**	**100.0**	**101.4**	**107.8**
Imports													
Food, beverages and tobacco	ELAN	0+1	76	77	78	80	80	82	84	86	100	108	110
Basic materials	ELAO	2+4	65	65	62	64	65	68	78	86	100	97	113
Oil													
Crude oil	ELAS	333	35	32	30	33	38	55	66	69	100	76	102
Oil products	ELAT	334+335	28	25	32	35	40	55	65	61	100	79	104
Total oil	ELBB	33	31	28	31	34	38	55	66	65	100	78	103
Coal, gas and electricity	ELAU	32+34+35	17	27	24	26	39	59	70	64	100	90	88
Semi-manufactured goods													
Chemicals	BQLY	5	82	82	80	82	81	84	86	88	100	108	112
Precious stones and silver	BQMA	667+681.1	102	105	99	87	79	83	85	85	100	122	134
Other	BQLZ	Rest of 6	80	80	77	77	81	84	90	93	100	106	114
Total semi-manufactured goods	ELAQ	5+6	83	83	80	80	80	84	88	90	100	108	115
Finished manufactured goods													
Motor cars	BQMB	781	98	95	96	98	96	95	94	95	100	100	102
Other consumer goods[2]	BQMC		94	96	94	94	91	93	93	93	100	102	102
Intermediate goods[2]	BQMD		106	104	98	94	91	92	92	92	100	109	112
Capital goods[2]	BQME		126	124	117	110	105	100	98	94	100	108	112
Ships and aircraft	BQMF	792+793	88	90	88	88	88	92	93	93	100	108	109
Total finished manufactured goods	ELAR	7+8	106	106	102	99	96	95	95	93	100	106	108
Total	BQKS		**85.8**	**85.3**	**82.9**	**82.2**	**81.6**	**85.0**	**87.6**	**87.6**	**100.0**	**102.2**	**108.2**

1 Standard International Trade Classification, Revision 4.
2 Derived from the *Classification by Broad Economic Categories defined in terms of SITC,* published by the United Nations.

2.4 Adjustments to trade in goods on a balance of payments basis

£ million

		2000	2001	2002	2003	2004	2005	2006	2007	2008	2009	2010
Exports												
Overseas trade statistics (f.o.b.)	HGAA	189 666	190 805	187 761	189 040	191 018	212 202	245 236	220 539	248 681	225 040	262 149
Coverage adjustments												
Second-hand ships	HBYK	105	137	187	141	251	248	248	248	248	248	248
Repairs to ships and aircraft	EPAQ	12	12	12	12	12	12	12	12	12	12	12
Goods not changing ownership	HCLJ	–2 343	–2 761	–2 788	–2 744	–2 012	–2 753	–2 471	–2 319	–313	–206	–211
Goods procured in ports	KTPB	865	869	881	982	1 129	1 415	1 562	1 579	2 198	1 678	1 897
Industrial gold	DEJO	33	44	66	76	37	7	9	38	66	9	13
Other	BQPO	57	57	55	57	61	60	66	61	61	61	61
Total coverage adjustments	EHHH	–1 271	–1 642	–1 587	–1 476	–522	–1 011	–574	–381	2 272	1 802	2 020
Other adjustments	EPAR	–569	–161	269	677	290	307	–1 098	189	1 024	1 284	1 545
Total	LQAD	**187 826**	**189 002**	**186 443**	**188 241**	**190 786**	**211 498**	**243 564**	**220 347**	**251 977**	**228 126**	**265 714**
Imports												
Overseas trade statistics (c.i.f.)	HGAD	224 413	229 505	228 608	236 938	253 151	272 850	303 272	311 941	341 972	307 555	361 005
Coverage adjustments												
Second-hand ships	HBTY	112	166	113	248	223	224	224	224	224	224	224
Ships delivered abroad	CGER	540	577	586	572	302	499	304	304	304	304	304
Repairs to ships and aircraft	EPBA	11	9	9	30	54	56	56	56	56	56	56
Goods not changing ownership	HBYS	–2 343	–2 761	–2 788	–2 744	–2 012	–2 753	–2 471	–2 319	–313	–206	–211
Goods procured in ports	KTPC	1 035	1 218	1 438	1 865	2 240	3 331	2 358	3 490	5 207	4 584	4 729
Industrial gold	DEJP	164	145	163	236	230	196	253	273	271	329	409
Smuggling - alcohol	QHCP	279	43	25	29	29	28	28	28	24	28	..
Smuggling - tobacco	QHCT	1 072	1 033	1 063	1 140	1 136	1 144	1 144	1 144	1 136	1 136	..
Other	EHHI	21	10	8	8	7	6	8	7	7	7	..
Total coverage adjustments	EHHJ	891	440	617	1 384	2 209	2 731	1 904	3 207	6 916	6 462	6 567
Valuation adjustments												
Freight	BPGF	–5 106	–5 423	–5 450	–5 465	–5 494	–5 534	–5 548	–5 535	–5 529	–5 519	–5 521
Insurance	ENAG	–654	–662	–662	–704	–736	–774	–848	–874	–934	–849	–981
Total	HCLT	–5 760	–6 085	–6 112	–6 169	–6 230	–6 308	–6 396	–6 409	–6 463	–6 368	–6 502
Other adjustments												
Impact of MTIC fraud	BQHF	2 794	7 060	11 495	4 486	2 689	11 060	22 378	2 138	2 272	2 032	2 522
Other adjustments	EPBB	–1 482	–738	–498	133	–94	–51	–1 025	75	1 461	1 297	584
Total other adjustments	CLAK	1 312	6 322	10 997	4 619	2 595	11 009	21 353	2 213	3 733	3 329	3 106
Total	LQBL	**220 856**	**230 182**	**234 110**	**236 772**	**251 725**	**280 282**	**320 133**	**310 952**	**346 158**	**310 978**	**364 176**

Chapter 3

Trade in services

3.1 Trade in services
Summary table

£ million

		2000	2001	2002	2003	2004	2005	2006	2007	2008	2009	2010
Exports												
Transportation	FJOD	12 676	12 770	12 523	13 628	15 997	17 336	17 094	17 836	21 448	19 787	20 329
Travel	FJPF	14 446	13 110	13 595	13 876	15 414	16 871	18 803	19 292	19 598	19 353	20 969
Communications	FJPH	1 864	2 034	2 219	2 479	3 183	3 697	4 153	4 330	4 463	5 111	5 340
Construction	FJPI	220	174	195	245	278	600	790	996	1 246	1 561	1 218
Insurance	FJPJ	2 680	3 667	5 601	5 427	4 964	1 552	3 832	5 088	5 583	5 641	5 265
Financial	FJPK	16 837	19 370	19 935	22 778	25 440	29 111	34 833	46 470	54 931	46 508	42 162
Computer and information	FJPL	2 865	3 253	4 082	5 261	6 432	6 240	7 013	7 026	7 333	8 488	8 742
Royalties and license fees	FJPM	5 389	5 673	5 786	6 174	6 434	7 315	7 899	8 132	7 985	8 829	8 678
Other business	FJPN	22 399	24 842	26 896	28 272	30 518	32 619	36 918	40 525	43 841	47 399	52 162
Personal, cultural and recreational	FJPR	1 305	1 358	1 601	1 892	2 145	2 243	2 136	1 878	2 279	2 601	4 012
Government	FJPU	1 207	1 522	1 578	1 934	2 021	1 985	2 056	2 112	2 180	2 184	2 205
Total	KTMQ	**81 888**	**87 773**	**94 011**	**101 966**	**112 826**	**119 569**	**135 527**	**153 685**	**170 887**	**167 462**	**171 082**
Imports												
Transportation	FJPV	15 972	16 282	16 922	17 416	18 350	19 897	19 105	18 803	19 225	18 029	18 710
Travel	APQA	25 385	26 376	27 697	29 355	30 873	32 781	34 291	35 692	37 256	32 188	32 360
Communications	FJQZ	1 867	1 993	2 040	2 158	2 642	3 201	3 657	3 514	3 855	4 402	4 396
Construction	FJRA	55	107	104	120	142	570	625	805	1 095	1 346	1 229
Insurance	FJRB	721	762	758	778	830	891	979	1 020	1 108	1 007	1 561
Financial	FJRE	3 789	4 263	4 776	5 903	6 628	8 958	10 338	12 168	13 334	10 958	10 667
Computer and information	FJRF	838	1 175	1 367	1 886	1 961	2 314	2 638	2 756	3 490	4 002	3 968
Royalties and license fees	FJRG	4 379	4 494	4 609	4 810	5 007	5 202	5 183	4 403	5 750	5 374	5 281
Other business	FJRH	11 200	12 416	13 411	13 839	14 632	16 359	19 337	22 517	25 733	27 742	28 472
Personal, cultural and recreational	FJRL	779	724	797	855	884	831	856	952	1 094	1 133	1 511
Government	FJRO	1 890	1 973	1 897	2 630	2 581	2 485	2 680	3 099	3 890	4 066	4 149
Total	KTMR	**66 875**	**70 565**	**74 378**	**79 750**	**84 530**	**93 489**	**99 689**	**105 729**	**115 830**	**110 247**	**112 304**
Balances												
Transportation	FJRP	–3 296	–3 512	–4 399	–3 788	–2 353	–2 561	–2 011	–967	2 223	1 758	1 619
Travel	FJSR	–10 939	–13 266	–14 102	–15 479	–15 459	–15 910	–15 488	–16 400	–17 658	–12 835	–11 391
Communications	FJST	–3	41	179	321	541	496	496	816	608	709	944
Construction	FJSU	165	67	91	125	136	30	165	191	151	215	–11
Insurance	FJSV	1 959	2 905	4 843	4 649	4 134	661	2 853	4 068	4 475	4 634	3 704
Financial	FJTA	13 048	15 107	15 159	16 875	18 812	20 153	24 495	34 302	41 597	35 550	31 495
Computer and information	FJTB	2 027	2 078	2 715	3 375	4 471	3 926	4 375	4 270	3 843	4 486	4 774
Royalties and license fees	FJTC	1 010	1 179	1 177	1 364	1 427	2 113	2 716	3 729	2 235	3 455	3 397
Other business	FJTD	11 199	12 426	13 485	14 433	15 886	16 260	17 581	18 008	18 108	19 657	23 690
Personal, cultural and recreational	FJTH	526	634	804	1 037	1 261	1 412	1 280	926	1 185	1 468	2 501
Government	FJUL	–683	–451	–319	–696	–560	–500	–624	–987	–1 710	–1 882	–1 944
Total	KTMS	**15 013**	**17 208**	**19 633**	**22 216**	**28 296**	**26 080**	**35 838**	**47 956**	**55 057**	**57 215**	**58 778**

3.2 Transportation

£ million

		2000	2001	2002	2003	2004	2005	2006	2007	2008	2009	2010
Exports												
Sea transport												
Passenger												
Passenger revenue	FJAL	630	488	569	993	846	608	444	430	469	621	887
Time charter receipts	FJAM	8	–	11	–	36	51	37	73	75	75	96
Total passenger	FJOF	638	488	580	993	882	659	481	503	544	696	983
Freight												
Dry cargo												
Freight on UK exports	HECV	400	406	481	525	444	544	530	552	636	538	644
Freight on cross-trades	HDVI	1 453	1 609	1 844	2 069	3 180	3 874	3 132	2 924	3 262	2 860	2 821
Time charter receipts	FJAO	140	106	118	196	640	912	1 049	1 491	1 939	2 110	2 289
Wet cargo												
Freight on UK exports	HEIX	98	82	96	126	173	174	130	142	219	120	135
Freight on cross-trades	HECX	458	497	420	742	1 305	1 194	1 222	1 395	2 530	1 315	1 446
Time charter receipts	FJAP	104	336	162	247	472	748	603	554	763	580	413
Total Freight	FJOG	2 653	3 036	3 121	3 905	6 214	7 446	6 666	7 058	9 349	7 523	7 748
Disbursements in the UK	FJAR	1 043	1 088	1 009	951	801	802	940	898	869	924	914
Total sea transport	FJOE	4 334	4 612	4 710	5 849	7 897	8 907	8 087	8 459	10 762	9 143	9 645
Air transport												
Passenger revenue	FJOJ	4 690	4 455	4 162	3 856	3 907	4 073	4 266	4 065	4 584	4 094	4 201
Freight on UK exports and cross trades	FJOK	428	365	350	368	394	397	391	493	562	332	449
Other												
Disbursements in the UK	FJAX	1 994	2 167	1 991	2 111	2 302	2 506	2 973	3 310	4 173	5 054	4 930
Other revenue	HBWB	303	258	247	240	267	182	183	225	127	95	123
Total other	FJOL	2 297	2 425	2 238	2 351	2 569	2 688	3 156	3 535	4 300	5 149	5 053
Total air transport	FJOI	7 415	7 245	6 750	6 575	6 870	7 158	7 813	8 093	9 446	9 575	9 703
Other transport												
Rail												
Passenger	FJOS	109	113	90	91	112	133	139	173	206	182	205
Freight	FJOT	20	16	12	15	16	17	17	16	16	11	15
Total rail	FJOR	129	129	102	106	128	150	156	189	222	193	220
Road												
Passenger	FJOW	–	–	–	–	–	–	–	–	–	–	–
Freight	FJOX	750	728	905	1 042	1 046	1 065	982	1 039	962	820	705
Total road	FJOV	750	728	905	1 042	1 046	1 065	982	1 039	962	820	705
Pipeline transport	FJPD	48	56	56	56	56	56	56	56	56	56	56
Total other transport	FJOM	927	913	1 063	1 204	1 230	1 271	1 194	1 284	1 240	1 069	981
Total	FJOD	**12 676**	**12 770**	**12 523**	**13 628**	**15 997**	**17 336**	**17 094**	**17 836**	**21 448**	**19 787**	**20 329**

3.2 Transportation

continued

£ million

		2000	2001	2002	2003	2004	2005	2006	2007	2008	2009	2010
Imports												
Sea transport												
Passenger												
Passenger expenditure	FJBP	413	450	486	476	476	463	533	627	437	299	297
Time charter payments	FJBQ	24	19	19	15	25	15	38	48	50	124	113
Total passenger	FJPX	437	469	505	491	501	478	571	675	487	423	410
Freight												
Dry cargo												
Freight on UK imports	HCJO	2 531	2 552	2 698	3 023	2 693	2 620	2 848	2 816	2 800	2 868	2 756
Time charter payments	FJBS	149	316	236	221	667	562	279	58	135	143	101
Wet cargo												
Freight on UK imports	HCNJ	280	305	330	355	417	434	422	407	360	371	386
Time charter payments	FJBT	172	176	140	184	359	636	655	721	1 257	1 099	915
Freight on UK coastal routes	HFAA	172	202	199	190	177	194	188	187	189	123	99
Total Freight	FJPY	3 304	3 551	3 603	3 973	4 313	4 446	4 392	4 189	4 741	4 604	4 257
Other												
Disbursements - dry cargo	FJBU	1 036	1 231	1 528	1 508	1 917	2 505	1 202	843	1 093	1 012	1 395
Disbursements - wet cargo	FJBW	55	54	81	118	138	183	164	215	267	245	238
Total other	FJPZ	1 091	1 285	1 609	1 626	2 055	2 688	1 366	1 058	1 360	1 257	1 633
Total sea transport	FJPW	4 832	5 305	5 717	6 090	6 869	7 612	6 329	5 922	6 588	6 284	6 300
Air transport												
Passenger expenditure	FJQB	5 192	5 255	5 559	5 949	6 231	6 761	7 021	6 733	6 739	6 139	6 752
Freight	FJQC	740	822	818	768	681	688	666	650	646	695	639
Disbursements abroad	FJCA	3 951	3 468	3 132	2 880	2 692	2 798	2 996	3 172	2 878	2 659	2 639
Total air transport	FJQA	9 883	9 545	9 509	9 597	9 604	10 247	10 683	10 555	10 263	9 493	10 030
Other transport												
Rail												
Passenger	FJQK	167	168	172	151	167	170	187	193	208	187	204
Freight	FJQL	37	43	44	46	47	44	43	51	44	26	35
Total rail	FJQJ	204	211	216	197	214	214	230	244	252	213	239
Road												
Passenger	FJQO	–	–	–	–	–	–	–	–	–	–	–
Freight	FJQP	1 001	1 169	1 428	1 480	1 611	1 772	1 811	2 030	2 070	1 987	2 089
Total road	FJQN	1 001	1 169	1 428	1 480	1 611	1 772	1 811	2 030	2 070	1 987	2 089
Pipeline transport	FJQV	52	52	52	52	52	52	52	52	52	52	52
Total other transport	FJQE	1 257	1 432	1 696	1 729	1 877	2 038	2 093	2 326	2 374	2 252	2 380
Total	FJPV	**15 972**	**16 282**	**16 922**	**17 416**	**18 350**	**19 897**	**19 105**	**18 803**	**19 225**	**18 029**	**18 710**

3.2 Transportation

continued

£ million

		2000	2001	2002	2003	2004	2005	2006	2007	2008	2009	2010
Balances												
Sea transport												
Passenger	FJRR	201	19	75	502	381	181	–90	–172	57	273	573
Freight												
Dry cargo	FJNJ	–687	–747	–491	–454	904	2 148	1 584	2 093	2 902	2 497	2 897
Wet cargo	FJNM	208	434	208	576	1 174	1 046	878	963	1 895	545	693
Other	FJVC	–172	–202	–199	–190	–177	–194	–188	–187	–189	–123	–99
Total Freight	FJRS	–651	–515	–482	–68	1 901	3 000	2 274	2 869	4 608	2 919	3 491
Other												
Dry cargo	FJVF	–1 036	–1 231	–1 528	–1 508	–1 917	–2 505	–1 202	–843	–1 093	–1 012	–1 395
Wet Cargo	FJVG	–55	–54	–81	–118	–138	–183	–164	–215	–267	–245	–238
Other	FJVI	1 043	1 088	1 009	951	801	802	940	898	869	924	914
Total other	FJRT	–48	–197	–600	–675	–1 254	–1 886	–426	–160	–491	–333	–719
Total sea transport	FJRQ	–498	–693	–1 007	–241	1 028	1 295	1 758	2 537	4 174	2 859	3 345
of which												
Ships owned or chartered-in by UK residents	FLMZ	*1 855*	*1 728*	*1 697*	*2 852*	*3 990*	*4 204*	*4 809*	*5 676*	*7 091*	*5 596*	*5 969*
Ships operated by non-residents	FLNF	*–2 353*	*–2 421*	*–2 704*	*–3 093*	*–2 962*	*–2 909*	*–3 051*	*–3 139*	*–2 917*	*–2 737*	*–2 624*
Air transport												
Passenger	FJRV	–502	–800	–1 397	–2 093	–2 324	–2 688	–2 755	–2 668	–2 155	–2 045	–2 551
Freight	FJRW	–312	–457	–468	–400	–287	–291	–275	–157	–84	–363	–190
Other	FJRX	–1 654	–1 043	–894	–529	–123	–110	160	363	1 422	2 490	2 414
Total air transport	FJRU	–2 468	–2 300	–2 759	–3 022	–2 734	–3 089	–2 870	–2 462	–817	82	–327
Other transport												
Rail												
Passenger	FJSE	–58	–55	–82	–60	–55	–37	–48	–20	–2	–5	1
Freight	FJSF	–17	–27	–32	–31	–31	–27	–26	–35	–28	–15	–20
Total rail	FJSD	–75	–82	–114	–91	–86	–64	–74	–55	–30	–20	–19
Road												
Passenger	FJSI	–	–	–	–	–	–	–	–	–	–	–
Freight	FJSJ	–251	–441	–523	–438	–565	–707	–829	–991	–1 108	–1 167	–1 384
Total road	FJSH	–251	–441	–523	–438	–565	–707	–829	–991	–1 108	–1 167	–1 384
Pipeline transport	FJSP	–4	4	4	4	4	4	4	4	4	4	4
Total other transport	FJRY	–330	–519	–633	–525	–647	–767	–899	–1 042	–1 134	–1 183	–1 399
Total	FJRP	**–3 296**	**–3 512**	**–4 399**	**–3 788**	**–2 353**	**–2 561**	**–2 011**	**–967**	**2 223**	**1 758**	**1 619**

3.3 Travel

£ million

		2000	2001	2002	2003	2004	2005	2006	2007	2008	2009	2010
Exports												
Business												
Expenditure by seasonal & border workers	FJCQ	147	163	219	169	203	234	270	263	260	184	268
Other	FJNO	4 084	3 615	3 618	3 478	3 735	4 110	4 749	4 627	4 574	3 744	4 106
Total business travel	FJPG	4 231	3 778	3 837	3 647	3 938	4 344	5 019	4 890	4 834	3 928	4 374
Personal												
Health related	FJCX	66	83	64	144	68	71	78	81	83	69	132
Education related	FJDD	2 484	2 723	2 592	2 881	3 072	3 357	3 694	3 860	3 957	3 802	5 021
Other	FJDG	7 665	6 526	7 102	7 204	8 336	9 099	10 012	10 461	10 724	11 554	11 442
Total personal travel	FJTU	10 215	9 332	9 758	10 229	11 476	12 527	13 784	14 402	14 764	15 425	16 595
Total	FJPF	**14 446**	**13 110**	**13 595**	**13 876**	**15 414**	**16 871**	**18 803**	**19 292**	**19 598**	**19 353**	**20 969**
Imports												
Business												
Expenditure by seasonal & border workers	FJDO	192	215	102	225	159	202	214	222	228	221	123
Other	FJNP	4 811	4 479	4 336	4 135	4 243	4 695	4 962	5 142	5 282	4 408	4 502
Total business travel	FJQY	5 003	4 694	4 438	4 360	4 402	4 897	5 176	5 364	5 510	4 629	4 625
Personal												
Health related	FJDT	19	16	12	33	45	60	63	66	69	81	62
Education related	FJDV	99	108	110	102	117	165	172	179	187	159	223
Other	APPW	20 264	21 558	23 137	24 860	26 309	27 659	28 880	30 083	31 490	27 319	27 450
Total personal travel	APQW	20 382	21 682	23 259	24 995	26 471	27 884	29 115	30 328	31 746	27 559	27 735
Total	APQA	**25 385**	**26 376**	**27 697**	**29 355**	**30 873**	**32 781**	**34 291**	**35 692**	**37 256**	**32 188**	**32 360**
Balances												
Business												
Expenditure by seasonal & border workers	FJCR	–45	–52	117	–56	44	32	56	41	32	–37	145
Other	FJCW	–727	–864	–718	–657	–508	–585	–213	–515	–708	–664	–396
Total business travel	FJSS	–772	–916	–601	–713	–464	–553	–157	–474	–676	–701	–251
Personal												
Health related	FJCY	47	67	52	111	23	11	15	15	14	–12	70
Education related	FJDE	2 385	2 615	2 482	2 779	2 955	3 192	3 522	3 681	3 770	3 643	4 798
Other	FJDH	–12 599	–15 032	–16 035	–17 656	–17 973	–18 560	–18 868	–19 622	–20 766	–15 765	–16 008
Total personal travel	FJTW	–10 167	–12 350	–13 501	–14 766	–14 995	–15 357	–15 331	–15 926	–16 982	–12 134	–11 140
Total	FJSR	**–10 939**	**–13 266**	**–14 102**	**–15 479**	**–15 459**	**–15 910**	**–15 488**	**–16 400**	**–17 658**	**–12 835**	**–11 391**

3.4 Communications services[1]

£ million

		2000	2001	2002	2003	2004	2005	2006	2007	2008	2009	2010
Exports												
Postal and courier services												
Postal services	FJTN	118	97	110	112	124	121	127	119	122	127	120
Courier services	FJTO	29	80	67	111	320	390	374	415	550	826	814
Total postal and courier services	FJED	147	177	177	223	444	511	501	534	672	953	934
Telecommunications services	FJAS	1 717	1 857	2 042	2 256	2 739	3 186	3 652	3 796	3 791	4 158	4 406
Total	FJPH	**1 864**	**2 034**	**2 219**	**2 479**	**3 183**	**3 697**	**4 153**	**4 330**	**4 463**	**5 111**	**5 340**
Imports												
Postal and courier services												
Postal services	FJTP	260	200	200	225	181	166	159	156	190	218	248
Courier services	FJTQ	18	55	58	90	294	310	280	408	452	373	382
Total postal and courier services	FJEI	278	255	258	315	475	476	439	564	642	591	630
Telecommunications services	FJAT	1 589	1 738	1 782	1 843	2 167	2 725	3 218	2 950	3 213	3 811	3 766
Total	FJQZ	**1 867**	**1 993**	**2 040**	**2 158**	**2 642**	**3 201**	**3 657**	**3 514**	**3 855**	**4 402**	**4 396**
Balances												
Postal and courier services												
Postal services	FJTR	–142	–103	–90	–113	–57	–45	–32	–37	–68	–91	–128
Courier services	FJTS	11	25	9	21	26	80	94	7	98	453	432
Total postal and courier services	FJEE	–131	–78	–81	–92	–31	35	62	–30	30	362	304
Telecommunications services	FJAQ	128	119	260	413	572	461	434	846	578	347	640
Total	FJST	**–3**	**41**	**179**	**321**	**541**	**496**	**496**	**816**	**608**	**709**	**944**

1 The latest year's data for trade in services are provisional as these figures are subject to annual benchmarking.

3.5 Insurance services[1]

£ million

		2000	2001	2002	2003	2004	2005	2006	2007	2008	2009	2010
Exports												
Life insurance and pension funds	FJEU	1 417	2 174	797	8	–713	–1 464	–1 264	–502	–275	–653	–832
Freight insurance	FJJL	41	49	80	129	90	72	43	141	133	230	224
Other direct insurance[2]	FJEW	412	–579	2 164	1 935	3 350	729	1 805	3 504	2 002	1 993	2 115
Reinsurance	FJEX	–296	1 011	1 473	2 241	1 023	970	1 691	399	2 037	2 136	2 012
Auxiliary insurance services (insurance brokers)	FJEY	1 106	1 012	1 087	1 114	1 214	1 245	1 557	1 546	1 686	1 935	1 746
Total[3]	FJPJ	**2 680**	**3 667**	**5 601**	**5 427**	**4 964**	**1 552**	**3 832**	**5 088**	**5 583**	**5 641**	**5 265**
Imports												
Life insurance and pension funds	FJRC	–	–	–	–	–	–	–	–	–	–	–
Freight insurance	FJRD	721	762	758	778	830	891	979	1 020	1 108	1 007	1 561
Other direct insurance	FJFC	–	–	–	–	–	–	–	–	–	–	–
Reinsurance	FJFD	–	–	–	–	–	–	–	–	–	–	–
Auxiliary insurance services	FJFE	–	–	–	–	–	–	–	–	–	–	–
Total	FJRB	**721**	**762**	**758**	**778**	**830**	**891**	**979**	**1 020**	**1 108**	**1 007**	**1 561**
Balances												
Life insurance and pension funds	FJSW	1 417	2 174	797	8	–713	–1 464	–1 264	–502	–275	–653	–832
Freight insurance	FJSX	–680	–713	–678	–649	–740	–819	–936	–879	–975	–777	–1 337
Other direct insurance	FJJM	412	–579	2 164	1 935	3 350	729	1 805	3 504	2 002	1 993	2 115
Reinsurance	FJJN	–296	1 011	1 473	2 241	1 023	970	1 691	399	2 037	2 136	2 012
Auxiliary insurance services	FJJO	1 106	1 012	1 087	1 114	1 214	1 245	1 557	1 546	1 686	1 935	1 746
Total	FJSV	**1 959**	**2 905**	**4 843**	**4 649**	**4 134**	**661**	**2 853**	**4 068**	**4 475**	**4 634**	**3 704**

1 The latest year's data for trade in services are provisional as these figures are subject to annual benchmarking.
2 Other direct insurance by UK insurance companies includes facultative reinsurance on marine, aviation and transport business.
3 Exports of insurance services are net of expenditure abroad by UK insurance companies.

3.6 Financial services[1]

£ million

		2000	2001	2002	2003	2004	2005	2006	2007	2008	2009	2010
Exports												
Monetary financial institutions												
Commissions and fees	APUP	3 041	2 986	3 215	2 677	3 458	4 198	5 562	6 676	6 172	6 300	6 779
Spread earnings	APVA	1 809	2 370	2 922	4 536	5 120	6 334	7 606	10 291	12 942	12 617	10 503
FISIM[2] on loans	TGWM	876	1 585	1 692	2 132	2 004	2 118	2 511	3 798	6 771	4 799	4 382
of which £	LOFR	*480*	*869*	*928*	*1 169*	*998*	*899*	*998*	*1 581*	*1 481*	*589*	*404*
FISIM on deposits	TGWP	1 341	2 141	2 333	3 148	2 939	3 170	3 592	5 412	8 881	5 563	4 877
of which £	LOFU	*772*	*1 233*	*1 344*	*1 813*	*1 573*	*1 461*	*1 481*	*2 364*	*2 399*	*970*	*685*
Total monetary financial institutions	ZXTE	7 067	9 082	10 162	12 493	13 521	15 820	19 271	26 177	34 766	29 279	26 541
Fund managers	FNMM	868	853	1 045	1 528	1 925	2 632	3 199	4 856	5 035	3 590	4 423
Securities dealers												
Commissions and fees	CDFI	5 632	5 211	4 290	3 922	4 316	4 628	6 316	8 429	8 362	6 957	4 835
Spread earnings	QZCM	1 033	1 492	1 168	1 316	1 666	1 918	2 544	2 815	1 779	861	483
Total securities dealers	ZXTF	6 665	6 703	5 458	5 238	5 982	6 546	8 860	11 244	10 141	7 818	5 318
Baltic Exchange	APRJ	336	377	357	398	577	777	744	802	999	724	779
Other institutions	ZSHJ	1 901	2 355	2 913	3 121	3 435	3 336	2 759	3 391	3 990	5 097	5 101
Total including FISIM	FJPK	**16 837**	**19 370**	**19 935**	**22 778**	**25 440**	**29 111**	**34 833**	**46 470**	**54 931**	**46 508**	**42 162**
Total FISIM[2]	C6FD	2 217	3 726	4 025	5 280	4 943	5 288	6 103	9 210	15 652	10 362	9 259
Total excluding FISIM	C9NI	**14 620**	**15 644**	**15 910**	**17 498**	**20 497**	**23 823**	**28 730**	**37 260**	**39 279**	**36 146**	**32 903**
Imports												
Monetary financial institutions	APVW	1 003	1 157	1 475	1 701	1 556	1 693	2 002	2 336	3 055	2 339	3 100
Fund managers	FNMS	160	229	219	336	420	527	574	727	874	689	886
Securities dealers[3]	RWMG	1 199	1 296	1 009	795	862	1 244	1 643	985	1 119	716	437
Baltic Exchange	APSZ	39	27	35	18	26	42	38	33	51	10	33
Other institutions	ZXTG	1 388	1 554	2 038	3 053	3 764	5 452	6 081	8 087	8 235	7 204	6 211
of which FISIM on loans	TGZJ	*387*	*373*	*669*	*864*	*1 142*	*1 571*	*1 748*	*1 939*	*1 777*	*1 777*	*1 679*
FISIM on deposits	TGZU	*443*	*576*	*554*	*966*	*1 480*	*2 251*	*2 658*	*3 201*	*3 950*	*2 754*	*2 720*
Total including FISIM	FJRE	**3 789**	**4 263**	**4 776**	**5 903**	**6 628**	**8 958**	**10 338**	**12 168**	**13 334**	**10 958**	**10 667**
Total FISIM[2]	C6F7	830	949	1 223	1 830	2 622	3 822	4 406	5 140	5 727	4 531	4 399
Total excluding FISIM	C9NJ	**2 959**	**3 314**	**3 553**	**4 073**	**4 006**	**5 136**	**5 932**	**7 028**	**7 607**	**6 427**	**6 268**
Balances												
Monetary financial institutions	ZXLV	6 064	7 925	8 687	10 792	11 965	14 127	17 269	23 841	31 711	26 940	23 441
Fund managers	ZXLW	708	624	826	1 192	1 505	2 105	2 625	4 129	4 161	2 901	3 537
Securities dealers	ZXLX	5 466	5 407	4 449	4 443	5 120	5 302	7 217	10 259	9 022	7 102	4 881
Baltic Exchange	ZXLY	297	350	322	380	551	735	706	769	948	714	746
Other institutions	ZXLZ	513	801	875	68	–329	–2 116	–3 322	–4 696	–4 245	–2 107	–1 110
Total including FISIM	FJTA	**13 048**	**15 107**	**15 159**	**16 875**	**18 812**	**20 153**	**24 495**	**34 302**	**41 597**	**35 550**	**31 495**
Total FISIM[2]	IH3K	1 387	2 777	2 802	3 450	2 321	1 466	1 697	4 070	9 925	5 831	4 860
Total excluding FISIM	IH3L	**11 661**	**12 330**	**12 357**	**13 425**	**16 491**	**18 687**	**22 798**	**30 232**	**31 672**	**29 719**	**26 635**

1 The latest year's data for trade in services are provisional as these figures are subject to annual benchmarking.
2 FISIM is an acronym for Financial Intermediation Services Indirectly Measured. It represents the implicit charge for the service provided by monetary financial institutions paid for by the interest differential between borrowing and lending rather than through fees and commissions.
3 For securities dealers, the move to a gross presentation means that imports of non-financial services are moved to the other business services accounts (see table 3.9).

3.7 Computer and information services[1]

£ million

		2000	2001	2002	2003	2004	2005	2006	2007	2008	2009	2010
Exports												
Computer services	FJCN	2 478	2 725	3 328	3 705	4 747	4 662	4 913	4 964	4 938	5 986	6 441
Information services	FJCO	387	528	754	1 556	1 685	1 578	2 100	2 062	2 395	2 502	2 301
Total	FJPL	**2 865**	**3 253**	**4 082**	**5 261**	**6 432**	**6 240**	**7 013**	**7 026**	**7 333**	**8 488**	**8 742**
Imports												
Computer services	FJDL	745	859	1 122	1 478	1 445	1 832	2 260	2 367	2 934	3 363	3 402
Information services	FJDM	93	316	245	408	516	482	378	389	556	639	566
Total	FJRF	**838**	**1 175**	**1 367**	**1 886**	**1 961**	**2 314**	**2 638**	**2 756**	**3 490**	**4 002**	**3 968**
Balances												
Computer Services	FJJP	1 733	1 866	2 206	2 227	3 302	2 830	2 653	2 597	2 004	2 623	3 039
Information services	FJJQ	294	212	509	1 148	1 169	1 096	1 722	1 673	1 839	1 863	1 735
Total	FJTB	**2 027**	**2 078**	**2 715**	**3 375**	**4 471**	**3 926**	**4 375**	**4 270**	**3 843**	**4 486**	**4 774**

1 The latest year's data for trade in services are provisional as these figures are subject to annual benchmarking.

3.8 Royalties and license fees[1,2]

£ million

		2000	2001	2002	2003	2004	2005	2006	2007	2008	2009	2010
Exports												
Film and television	FJFO	934	982	880	911	890	972	1 252	1 295	1 560	..	..
Other royalties and license fees	FFVJ	4 455	4 691	4 906	5 263	5 544	6 343	6 647	6 837	6 425	..	..
Total	FJPM	**5 389**	**5 673**	**5 786**	**6 174**	**6 434**	**7 315**	**7 899**	**8 132**	**7 985**	**8 829**	**8 678**
Imports												
Film and television	FJFQ	1 020	1 176	1 315	1 449	1 533	1 456	1 385	1 193	1 201	..	..
Other royalties and license fees	FFVP	3 359	3 318	3 294	3 361	3 474	3 746	3 798	3 210	4 549	..	..
Total	FJRG	**4 379**	**4 494**	**4 609**	**4 810**	**5 007**	**5 202**	**5 183**	**4 403**	**5 750**	**5 374**	**5 281**
Balances												
Film and television	FFVV	–86	–194	–435	–538	–643	–484	–133	102	359	..	..
Other royalties and license fees	FFWB	1 096	1 373	1 612	1 902	2 070	2 597	2 849	3 627	1 876	..	..
Total	FJTC	**1 010**	**1 179**	**1 177**	**1 364**	**1 427**	**2 113**	**2 716**	**3 729**	**2 235**	**3 455**	**3 397**

1 The latest year's data for trade in services are provisional as these figures are subject to annual benchmarking.
2 The disaggregation of 'royalties and license fees' into 'film and television' and 'other royalties and license fees' is not available after 2008 due to the incorporation of the Film and Television survey into the International Trade in Services survey.

3.9 Other Business services[1]

£ million

		2000	2001	2002	2003	2004	2005	2006	2007	2008	2009	2010
Exports												
Merchanting and other trade related services												
Merchanting	FJFS	626	782	699	573	549	942	327	1 140	1 148	983	3 962
Other trade related services	FJFX	1 759	1 881	1 720	1 899	1 698	1 780	1 850	1 750	1 740	1 495	1 192
Total merchanting and other trade related services	FJPO	2 385	2 663	2 419	2 472	2 247	2 722	2 177	2 890	2 888	2 478	5 154
Operational leasing services	FJPP	299	248	190	239	342	329	508	394	804	803	383
Miscellaneous business, professional and technical services												
Legal, accounting and management consulting												
Law society	FJGE	1 171	1 339	1 465	1 335	1 470	1 615	2 139	2 611	2 897	3 435	3 348
Commercial bar association	FJCP	61	77	85	95	86	116	113	107	76	84	101
Other legal services	FJGD	288	363	481	600	435	553	450	358	498	71	127
Accounting	FJBX	662	642	728	733	892	1 087	1 327	1 343	1 393	1 137	1 086
Business management and management consulting	FJNV	1 083	1 069	2 545	3 127	3 288	3 998	5 328	6 250	7 543	10 205	9 963
of which Recruitment and training	TVLQ	..	..	*406*	*359*	*350*	*342*	*387*	*389*	*520*	*625*	*768*
Advertising and market research	FJGP	1 432	1 622	1 703	2 155	1 965	2 403	2 295	2 373	2 632	2 652	2 899
Research and development	FJDP	2 421	2 933	2 899	3 467	4 467	4 705	4 846	5 203	5 682	5 592	5 758
Architectural, engineering and other technical services												
Architectural	FJGT	76	153	71	106	110	95	178	271	357	297	381
Engineering	FJGU	2 441	3 239	3 049	3 475	3 501	3 291	3 643	3 596	4 343	4 021	4 167
Surveying	FJGV	68	66	62	57	137	226	149	107	166	148	184
Other Technical	FJGW	1 113	1 220	1 931	1 629	1 698	1 616	1 441	1 087	1 323	1 365	1 459
Agricultural, mining and on-site processing services	FJHC	54	41	31	202	234	259	322	401	786	874	938
Other miscellaneous business services	FJHH	7 565	7 686	7 618	6 475	7 504	7 225	8 952	9 605	7 597	7 110	8 992
of which Other business services exported by UK banks	APVQ	*1 414*	*1 277*	*1 490*	*2 118*	*1 892*	*2 134*	*2 156*	*2 250*	*2 442*	*1 937*	*2 149*
Services between affiliated enterprises, n.i.e.	FJHF	1 280	1 481	1 619	2 105	2 142	2 379	3 050	3 929	4 856	7 127	7 222
Total miscellaneous business, professional, and technical services	FJPQ	19 715	21 931	24 287	25 561	27 929	29 568	34 233	37 241	40 149	44 118	46 625
Total	FJPN	**22 399**	**24 842**	**26 896**	**28 272**	**30 518**	**32 619**	**36 918**	**40 525**	**43 841**	**47 399**	**52 162**
Imports												
Merchanting and other trade related services												
Merchanting	FJHN	71	55	148	35	81	80	81	80	80	80	80
Other trade related services	FJHR	965	952	854	752	1 122	608	589	639	664	631	704
Total merchanting and other trade related services	FJRI	1 036	1 007	1 002	787	1 203	688	670	719	744	711	784
Operational leasing services	FJRJ	560	457	450	456	784	687	807	799	945	1 017	855
Miscellaneous business, professional and technical services												
Legal, accounting and management consulting												
Legal	FJHX	490	380	486	453	416	429	534	533	659	816	765
Accounting	FJVJ	213	228	251	300	324	328	358	314	431	424	403
Business management and management consulting	FJNW	456	569	1 428	1 924	2 328	2 601	2 970	3 481	4 443	5 761	6 075
of which Recruitment and training	TVLV	..	..	*268*	*264*	*357*	*121*	*134*	*142*	*184*	*212*	*397*
Advertising and market research	FJID	789	841	860	946	842	1 100	1 398	1 802	1 970	2 017	2 119
Research and development	FJDQ	723	661	644	1 148	1 806	2 021	2 197	2 264	3 726	3 759	4 154
Architectural, engineering and other technical services												
Architectural	FJIF	13	35	25	50	11	4	21	11	21	19	26
Engineering	FJIG	724	1 075	868	1 107	1 325	1 067	1 278	1 525	1 422	1 338	1 040
Surveying	FJIH	55	31	29	24	48	88	40	28	66	53	68
Other Technical	FJII	429	431	463	368	384	556	433	465	433	505	473
Agricultural, mining and on-site processing services	FJIN	71	142	77	53	63	100	122	136	216	193	204
Other miscellaneous business services	FJIP	4 833	5 490	5 688	5 092	3 900	5 252	6 752	8 450	8 045	7 559	7 680
of which Other business sevices imported by UK banks	APWA	*520*	*448*	*619*	*760*	*497*	*591*	*528*	*820*	*994*	*1 123*	*869*
Other business services imported by Security dealers	RWMH	*2 294*	*2 027*	*1 358*	*1 149*	*1 462*	*3 036*	*4 234*	*5 496*	*5 050*	*5 398*	*5 491*
Services between affiliated enterprises, n.i.e.	FJHG	808	1 069	1 140	1 131	1 198	1 438	1 757	1 990	2 612	3 570	3 826
Total miscellaneous business, professional and technical services	FJRK	9 604	10 952	11 959	12 596	12 645	14 984	17 860	20 999	24 044	26 014	26 833
Total	FJRH	**11 200**	**12 416**	**13 411**	**13 839**	**14 632**	**16 359**	**19 337**	**22 517**	**25 733**	**27 742**	**28 472**

1 The latest year's data for trade in services are provisional as these figures are subject to annual benchmarking.

3.9 Other Business services[1]

continued

£ million

		2000	2001	2002	2003	2004	2005	2006	2007	2008	2009	2010
Balances												
Merchanting and other trade related services												
Merchanting	FJFT	555	727	551	538	468	862	246	1 060	1 068	903	3 882
Other trade related services	FJFY	794	929	866	1 147	576	1 172	1 261	1 111	1 076	864	488
Total merchanting and other trade related services	FJTE	1 349	1 656	1 417	1 685	1 044	2 034	1 507	2 171	2 144	1 767	4 370
Operational leasing services	FJTF	−261	−209	−260	−217	−442	−358	−299	−405	−141	−214	−472
Miscellaneous business, professional and technical services												
Legal, accounting and management consulting												
Legal	FJGG	1 030	1 399	1 545	1 577	1 575	1 855	2 168	2 543	2 812	2 774	2 811
Accounting	FJGI	449	414	477	433	568	759	969	1 029	962	713	683
Business management and management consulting	FJGK	627	500	1 117	1 203	960	1 397	2 358	2 769	3 100	4 444	3 888
Advertising and market research	FJGQ	643	781	843	1 209	1 123	1 303	897	571	662	635	780
Research and development	FJGS	1 698	2 272	2 255	2 319	2 661	2 684	2 649	2 939	1 956	1 833	1 604
Architectural, engineering and other technical services	FJGY	2 477	3 106	3 728	3 718	3 678	3 513	3 639	3 032	4 247	3 916	4 584
Agricultural, mining and on-site processing services	FJHD	−17	−101	−46	149	171	159	200	265	570	681	734
Services between affiliated enterprises, n.i.e.	FJHL	472	412	479	974	944	941	1 293	1 939	2 244	3 557	3 396
Other	FJHI	2 732	2 196	1 930	1 383	3 604	1 973	2 200	1 155	−448	−449	1 312
Total miscellaneous business, professional, and technical services	FJTG	10 111	10 979	12 328	12 965	15 284	14 584	16 373	16 242	16 105	18 104	19 792
Total	FJTD	**11 199**	**12 426**	**13 485**	**14 433**	**15 886**	**16 260**	**17 581**	**18 008**	**18 108**	**19 657**	**23 690**

1 The latest year's data for trade in services are provisional as these figures are subject to annual benchmarking.

3.10 Personal, cultural and recreational services[1]

£ million

		2000	2001	2002	2003	2004	2005	2006	2007	2008	2009	2010
Exports												
Audiovisual and related services[2]												
Film and television	FKJO	726	737	856	1 077	1 274	1 357	1 248	989	1 080	..	..
Other	FFWH	252	172	184	204	286	215	200	162	281	..	..
Total audiovisual and related services	FJPS	978	909	1 040	1 281	1 560	1 572	1 448	1 151	1 361	1 447	2 658
Other personal, cultural and recreational services	FJPT	327	449	561	611	585	671	688	727	918	1 154	1 354
Total	FJPR	**1 305**	**1 358**	**1 601**	**1 892**	**2 145**	**2 243**	**2 136**	**1 878**	**2 279**	**2 601**	**4 012**
Imports												
Audiovisual and related services[2]												
Film and television	FKJX	532	512	615	463	587	584	571	755	867	..	..
Other	FFWN	55	46	39	59	89	44	68	70	68	..	..
Total audiovisual and related services	FJRM	587	558	654	522	676	628	639	825	935	873	1 253
Other personal, cultural and recreational services	FJRN	192	166	143	333	208	203	217	127	159	260	258
Total	FJRL	**779**	**724**	**797**	**855**	**884**	**831**	**856**	**952**	**1 094**	**1 133**	**1 511**
Balances												
Audiovisual and related services	FJTI	391	351	386	759	884	944	809	326	426	574	1 405
Other personal, cultural and recreational services	FJTJ	135	283	418	278	377	468	471	600	759	894	1 096
Total	FJTH	**526**	**634**	**804**	**1 037**	**1 261**	**1 412**	**1 280**	**926**	**1 185**	**1 468**	**2 501**

1 The latest year's data for trade in services are provisional as these figures are subject to annual benchmarking.
2 The disaggregation of 'audiovisual and related services' into 'film and television fees' is not available after 2008 due to the incorporation of the Film & Television survey into the International Trade in Services survey.

3.11 Government services

£ million

		2000	2001	2002	2003	2004	2005	2006	2007	2008	2009	2010
Exports												
Expenditure by foreign embassies and consulates in the UK	FJUK	385	389	393	397	401	405	409	413	418	421	425
Military units and agencies												
Expenditure by US forces in UK	FJKB	271	262	262	264	264	264	264	264	264	264	264
Other military receipts by UK government	HCOJ	58	48	67	248	312	286	366	309	177	193	184
Total military units and agencies	FJIX	329	310	329	512	576	550	630	573	441	457	448
Other												
EU institutions	FKIE	226	525	487	494	543	565	586	607	666	663	734
Other receipts	HCQO	267	298	369	531	501	465	431	519	655	643	598
Total other	FJJA	493	823	856	1 025	1 044	1 030	1 017	1 126	1 321	1 306	1 332
Total	FJPU	**1 207**	**1 522**	**1 578**	**1 934**	**2 021**	**1 985**	**2 056**	**2 112**	**2 180**	**2 184**	**2 205**
Imports												
Expenditure abroad by UK embassies and consulates	FJUJ	106	142	215	190	177	167	187	110	82	193	84
Expenditure abroad by UK military units and agencies	FJJD	1 584	1 629	1 494	2 144	1 892	1 817	2 124	2 499	3 106	3 313	3 213
Civil non-EU services	FJJF	200	202	188	296	512	501	369	490	702	560	852
Total	FJRO	**1 890**	**1 973**	**1 897**	**2 630**	**2 581**	**2 485**	**2 680**	**3 099**	**3 890**	**4 066**	**4 149**
Balances												
Embassies and consulates	FJIW	279	247	178	207	224	238	222	303	336	228	341
Military units and agencies	FJIY	−1 255	−1 319	−1 165	−1 632	−1 316	−1 267	−1 494	−1 926	−2 665	−2 856	−2 765
Other	FJJB	293	621	668	729	532	529	648	636	619	746	480
Total	FJUL	**−683**	**−451**	**−319**	**−696**	**−560**	**−500**	**−624**	**−987**	**−1 710**	**−1 882**	**−1 944**

Chapter 4

Income

4.1 Income

Summary table

£ million

		2000	2001	2002	2003	2004	2005	2006	2007	2008	2009	2010
Credits												
Compensation of employees	KTMN	1 032	1 087	1 121	1 116	931	974	938	984	1 046	1 176	1 097
Investment income												
Earnings on direct investment abroad[1]	HJYW	45 042	46 741	51 473	55 093	63 292	79 192	83 573	91 355	69 498	69 587	81 779
Earnings on portfolio investment abroad												
Earnings on equity securities	HCPL	9 872	9 861	10 530	10 385	11 186	13 254	16 988	20 637	20 038	16 382	15 802
Earnings on debt securities	HLYW	23 101	25 021	21 954	22 165	25 522	32 125	38 155	45 495	47 473	38 173	31 589
Total portfolio investment	HLYX	32 973	34 882	32 484	32 550	36 708	45 379	55 143	66 132	67 511	54 555	47 391
Earnings on other investment abroad	AIOP	52 902	54 863	35 766	33 635	36 675	60 410	98 144	133 517	125 056	44 388	32 484
Earnings on reserve assets	HHCB	985	961	820	791	705	659	645	610	777	783	712
Total investment income	HMBN	131 902	137 447	120 543	122 069	137 380	185 640	237 505	291 614	262 842	169 313	162 366
Total	HMBQ	**132 934**	**138 534**	**121 664**	**123 185**	**138 311**	**186 614**	**238 443**	**292 598**	**263 888**	**170 489**	**163 463**
Debits												
Compensation of employees	KTMO	882	1 021	1 054	1 057	1 425	1 584	1 896	1 718	1 761	1 435	1 486
Investment income												
Foreign earnings on direct investment in the UK[1]	HJYX	27 435	21 437	16 016	21 919	27 620	36 154	51 620	45 051	3 097	26 403	32 421
Foreign earnings on portfolio investment in the UK												
Earnings on equity securities	ZMRB	11 354	14 865	15 351	15 011	16 396	18 440	21 698	23 083	26 326	21 959	22 325
Earnings on debt securities	HLZB	21 085	21 239	17 957	17 891	22 308	29 148	35 865	43 718	48 179	38 355	37 620
Total portfolio investment	HLZC	32 439	36 104	33 308	32 902	38 704	47 588	57 563	66 801	74 505	60 314	59 945
Earnings on other investment in the UK	HLZN	70 215	70 547	52 783	49 537	52 533	79 402	117 852	157 659	151 389	61 940	46 572
Total investment income	HMBO	130 089	128 088	102 107	104 358	118 857	163 144	227 035	269 511	228 991	148 657	138 938
Total	HMBR	**130 971**	**129 109**	**103 161**	**105 415**	**120 282**	**164 728**	**228 931**	**271 229**	**230 752**	**150 092**	**140 424**
Balances (Net earnings)												
Compensation of employees	KTMP	150	66	67	59	−494	−610	−958	−734	−715	−259	−389
Investment income												
Direct investment[1]	HJYE	17 607	25 304	35 457	33 174	35 672	43 038	31 953	46 304	66 401	43 184	49 358
Portfolio investment												
Earnings on equity securities	HLZO	−1 482	−5 004	−4 821	−4 626	−5 210	−5 186	−4 710	−2 446	−6 288	−5 577	−6 523
Earnings on debt securities	HLZP	2 016	3 782	3 997	4 274	3 214	2 977	2 290	1 777	−706	−182	−6 031
Total portfolio investment	HLZX	534	−1 222	−824	−352	−1 996	−2 209	−2 420	−669	−6 994	−5 759	−12 554
Other investment	CGNA	−17 313	−15 684	−17 017	−15 902	−15 858	−18 992	−19 708	−24 142	−26 333	−17 552	−14 088
Reserve assets	HHCB	985	961	820	791	705	659	645	610	777	783	712
Total investment income	HMBM	1 813	9 359	18 436	17 711	18 523	22 496	10 470	22 103	33 851	20 656	23 428
Total	HMBP	**1 963**	**9 425**	**18 503**	**17 770**	**18 029**	**21 886**	**9 512**	**21 369**	**33 136**	**20 397**	**23 039**

1 The latest year's data for foreign direct investment are provisional as these figures are subject to annual benchmarking.

4.2 Investment income
Sector analysis

£ million

		2000	2001	2002	2003	2004	2005	2006	2007	2008	2009	2010
Credits												
(Earnings of UK residents on investment abroad)												
Monetary financial institutions	CGND	69 015	71 354	53 482	52 492	56 616	79 997	114 507	151 659	141 033	62 226	40 916
Central government	CGNY	989	965	823	795	707	669	654	620	786	786	712
Public corporations	CGNP	364	438	371	389	900	1 440	712	870	891	277	251
Other sectors	CGNW	61 534	64 690	65 867	68 393	79 157	103 534	121 632	138 465	120 132	106 024	120 487
Total	HMBN	**131 902**	**137 447**	**120 543**	**122 069**	**137 380**	**185 640**	**237 505**	**291 614**	**262 842**	**169 313**	**162 366**
Debits												
(Foreign earnings on investment in UK)												
Monetary financial institutions	CGPN	70 799	70 621	48 336	47 090	51 600	78 212	113 708	143 581	117 344	49 039	48 960
Central government	CGNZ	4 564	4 233	3 868	4 140	4 803	6 028	7 029	9 059	10 532	8 604	13 384
Local authorities	CGOB	7	4	2	–	–	–	–	–	–	–	–
Public corporations	CGOD	–	–	–	–	16	18	18	18	17	16	16
Other sectors	CGSE	54 719	53 230	49 901	53 128	62 438	78 886	106 280	116 853	101 098	90 998	76 578
Total	HMBO	**130 089**	**128 088**	**102 107**	**104 358**	**118 857**	**163 144**	**227 035**	**269 511**	**228 991**	**148 657**	**138 938**
Balances												
(Net earnings)												
Monetary financial institutions	CGSO	–1 784	733	5 146	5 402	5 016	1 785	799	8 078	23 689	13 187	–8 044
Central government	CGOE	–3 575	–3 268	–3 045	–3 345	–4 096	–5 359	–6 375	–8 439	–9 746	–7 818	–12 672
Local authorities	-CGOB	–7	–4	–2	–	–	–	–	–	–	–	–
Public corporations	CGOF	364	438	371	389	884	1 422	694	852	874	261	235
Other sectors	CGTX	6 815	11 460	15 966	15 265	16 719	24 648	15 352	21 612	19 034	15 026	43 909
Total	HMBM	**1 813**	**9 359**	**18 436**	**17 711**	**18 523**	**22 496**	**10 470**	**22 103**	**33 851**	**20 656**	**23 428**

4.3 Earnings on direct investment[1]

£ million

		2000	2001	2002	2003	2004	2005	2006	2007	2008	2009	2010
Credits												
(Earnings of UK residents on direct investment abroad)												
Earnings on equity												
Dividends and distributed branch profits												
Dividends	CNZN	14 679	14 412	15 255	29 482	26 620	29 623	30 673	25 027	30 431	54 124	49 678
Distributed branch profits	HDNG	2 231	2 552	2 381	2 723	3 573	6 264	5 452	3 857	736	276	5 928
Total dividends and distributed branch profits	HMAE	16 910	16 964	17 636	32 205	30 193	35 887	36 125	28 884	31 167	54 400	55 606
Reinvested earnings	-HDNY	25 178	27 220	32 209	21 456	31 076	43 555	47 878	63 738	38 394	13 241	22 920
Earnings on property investment	HHBW	358	433	380	399	439	453	488	528	653	753	845
Total earnings on equity	HMAK	42 446	44 617	50 225	54 060	61 708	79 895	84 491	93 150	70 214	68 394	79 371
Earnings on other capital[2]	HDNQ	2 596	2 124	1 248	1 033	1 584	–703	–918	–1 795	–716	1 193	2 408
Total	HJYW	**45 042**	**46 741**	**51 473**	**55 093**	**63 292**	**79 192**	**83 573**	**91 355**	**69 498**	**69 587**	**81 779**
Debits												
(Foreign earnings on direct investment in the UK)												
Earnings on equity												
Dividends and distributed branch profits												
Dividends	BCEA	9 472	14 418	7 638	8 170	10 461	14 918	15 292	18 274	22 898	27 107	19 824
Distributed branch profits	CYFD	2 713	2 251	–1 079	56	1 995	2 659	6 338	–5 418	–29 149	–13 918	4 019
Total dividends and distributed branch profits	HMAH	12 185	16 669	6 559	8 226	12 456	17 577	21 630	12 856	–6 251	13 189	23 843
Reinvested earnings	CYFV	10 788	–992	3 647	7 429	8 558	10 501	22 195	23 276	1 542	4 148	–14
Earnings on property investment	HESG	1 258	1 398	1 507	1 614	1 663	1 796	1 901	2 228	2 545	2 354	2 594
Total earnings on equity	HMAG	24 231	17 075	11 713	17 269	22 677	29 874	45 726	38 360	–2 164	19 691	26 423
Earnings on other capital[2]	CYFN	3 204	4 362	4 303	4 650	4 943	6 280	5 894	6 691	5 261	6 712	5 998
Total	HJYX	**27 435**	**21 437**	**16 016**	**21 919**	**27 620**	**36 154**	**51 620**	**45 051**	**3 097**	**26 403**	**32 421**
Balances												
(Net earnings)												
Earnings on equity												
Dividends and distributed branch profits												
Dividends	LTMA	5 207	–6	7 617	21 312	16 159	14 705	15 381	6 753	7 533	27 017	29 854
Distributed branch profits	LTMB	–482	301	3 460	2 667	1 578	3 605	–886	9 275	29 885	14 194	1 909
Total dividends and distributed branch profits	HHZA	4 725	295	11 077	23 979	17 737	18 310	14 495	16 028	37 418	41 211	31 763
Reinvested earnings	LTMC	14 390	28 212	28 562	14 027	22 518	33 054	25 683	40 462	36 852	9 093	22 934
Earnings on property investment	LTMD	–900	–965	–1 127	–1 215	–1 224	–1 343	–1 413	–1 700	–1 892	–1 601	–1 749
Total earnings on equity	HHYY	18 215	27 542	38 512	36 791	39 031	50 021	38 765	54 790	72 378	48 703	52 948
Earnings on other capital[2]	HMAM	–608	–2 238	–3 055	–3 617	–3 359	–6 983	–6 812	–8 486	–5 977	–5 519	–3 590
Total	HJYE	**17 607**	**25 304**	**35 457**	**33 174**	**35 672**	**43 038**	**31 953**	**46 304**	**66 401**	**43 184**	**49 358**

1 The latest year's data for foreign direct investment are provisional as these figures are subject to annual benchmarking.
2 Earnings on other capital consists of interest accrued to/from direct investors from/to associated enterprises abroad.

4.4 Earnings on direct investment[1]

Sector analysis

£ million

		2000	2001	2002	2003	2004	2005	2006	2007	2008	2009	2010
Credits												
(Earnings of UK residents on direct investment abroad)												
Monetary financial institutions	HCVU	3 639	4 596	4 464	5 700	5 806	8 036	8 920	8 010	21	60	–4 525
Insurance companies	CNZD	930	790	628	2 326	3 556	4 385	4 338	5 295	–11	2 972	5 710
Other financial intermediaries	HCWW	3 017	2 924	3 232	4 293	5 097	6 883	7 375	8 057	1 816	3 198	8 982
Private non-financial corporations	HCUS	37 335	38 269	42 949	42 499	48 448	59 465	62 405	69 034	66 755	62 821	71 063
Public corporations	HDMG	17	40	54	87	153	153	219	607	529	118	112
Household sector[2]	HHLI	104	122	146	188	232	270	316	352	388	418	437
Total	HJYW	**45 042**	**46 741**	**51 473**	**55 093**	**63 292**	**79 192**	**83 573**	**91 355**	**69 498**	**69 587**	**81 779**
Debits												
(Foreign earnings on direct investment in UK)												
Monetary financial institutions	GPAZ	4 979	4 795	1 008	2 537	2 858	5 722	6 292	–2 031	–28 397	–11 096	3 681
Insurance companies	HDPK	612	–955	179	898	1 844	2 241	3 544	2 421	1 631	435	719
Other financial intermediaries												
Securities dealers	HDQX	1 495	1 272	1 337	449	1 600	1 489	1 224	3 762	–1 594	5 899	2 602
Other	HFBT	780	593	829	1 754	1 083	2 533	4 594	4 408	826	836	3 575
Total other financial intermediaries	HFCY	2 275	1 865	2 166	2 203	2 683	4 022	5 818	8 170	–768	6 735	6 177
Private non-financial corporations	BCEB	19 569	15 732	12 663	16 281	20 235	24 169	35 966	36 491	30 631	30 329	21 844
Total	HJYX	**27 435**	**21 437**	**16 016**	**21 919**	**27 620**	**36 154**	**51 620**	**45 051**	**3 097**	**26 403**	**32 421**
Balances												
(Net earnings)												
Monetary financial institutions	LTME	–1 340	–199	3 456	3 163	2 948	2 314	2 628	10 041	28 418	11 156	–8 206
Insurance companies	LTMF	318	1 745	449	1 428	1 712	2 144	794	2 874	–1 642	2 537	4 991
Other financial intermediaries	LTMG	742	1 059	1 066	2 090	2 414	2 861	1 557	–113	2 584	–3 537	2 805
Private non-financial corporations	LTMH	17 766	22 537	30 286	26 218	28 213	35 296	26 439	32 543	36 124	32 492	49 219
Public corporations	HDMG	17	40	54	87	153	153	219	607	529	118	112
Household sector[2]	HHLI	104	122	146	188	232	270	316	352	388	418	437
Total	HJYE	**17 607**	**25 304**	**35 457**	**33 174**	**35 672**	**43 038**	**31 953**	**46 304**	**66 401**	**43 184**	**49 358**

1 The latest year's data for foreign direct investment are provisional as these figures are subject to annual benchmarking.
2 The household sector includes non-profit institutions serving households.

4.5 Earnings on portfolio investment

£ million

		2000	2001	2002	2003	2004	2005	2006	2007	2008	2009	2010
Credits												
(Earnings of UK residents on portfolio investment abroad)												
Earnings on equity securities (shares) by:												
Monetary financial institutions	HHRX	865	1 261	1 473	2 299	2 676	3 410	4 132	4 478	3 475	3 321	2 770
Central Government	LOEN	–	–	–	–	–	8	7	8	8	4	–
Insurance companies and pension funds												
Insurance companies[1]	CGOM	2 237	2 289	2 455	2 075	2 194	2 430	2 999	3 366	4 450	4 026	3 899
Self-administered pension funds	HPDL	1 861	1 543	1 598	1 456	1 790	2 428	2 827	2 923	3 122	2 423	3 060
Total insurance companies and pension funds	CGOX	4 098	3 832	4 053	3 531	3 984	4 858	5 826	6 289	7 572	6 449	6 959
Other financial intermediaries	CGOY	4 677	4 465	4 690	4 275	4 202	4 501	6 291	9 006	7 863	5 625	5 304
Private non-financial corporations	EGMS	41	124	127	110	126	135	167	190	244	225	205
Household sector[2]	HEOG	191	179	187	170	198	342	565	666	876	758	564
Total earnings on equity securities	HCPL	9 872	9 861	10 530	10 385	11 186	13 254	16 988	20 637	20 038	16 382	15 802
Earnings on debt securities												
Earnings on bonds and notes by:												
Monetary financial institutions	HPCQ	15 830	16 399	15 596	15 312	17 442	21 277	25 347	32 459	32 362	22 708	16 719
Central Government	HF6Q	–	–	–	–	–	–	–	81	4	-5	30
Insurance companies and pension funds												
Insurance companies[1]	CGON	1 121	1 370	1 718	1 998	1 767	2 161	2 395	2 404	3 277	5 048	4 076
Self-administered pension funds	HPDM	517	565	621	703	903	931	1 086	1 731	2 250	2 235	2 324
Total insurance companies and pension funds	CGOZ	1 638	1 935	2 339	2 701	2 670	3 092	3 481	4 135	5 527	7 283	6 400
Other financial intermediaries	CGPA	2 762	3 468	2 071	2 206	2 808	4 799	5 753	5 141	6 583	6 807	6 783
Private non-financial corporations	EGNF	43	108	111	117	210	206	167	120	178	194	152
Household sector[2]	HEOH	286	260	240	255	238	269	278	285	309	292	268
Total earnings on bonds and notes	HCPK	20 559	22 170	20 357	20 591	23 368	29 643	35 026	42 221	44 963	37 279	30 352
Earnings on money market instruments by:												
Monetary financial institutions	HBMX	2 292	2 569	1 233	984	1 451	1 665	1 937	2 001	1 873	732	1 145
Central government	LSPA	–	18	26	19	9	2	–	–	–	–	–
Other financial intermediaries	NHQV	131	118	130	205	249	319	464	563	297	115	70
Private non-financial corporations	HGBX	119	146	208	366	445	496	728	710	340	47	22
Total earnings on money market instruments	HCHG	2 542	2 851	1 597	1 574	2 154	2 482	3 129	3 274	2 510	894	1 237
Total earnings on debt securities	HLYW	23 101	25 021	21 954	22 165	25 522	32 125	38 155	45 495	47 473	38 173	31 589
Total	HLYX	**32 973**	**34 882**	**32 484**	**32 550**	**36 708**	**45 379**	**55 143**	**66 132**	**67 511**	**54 555**	**47 391**

1 Includes pension funds managed by insurance companies
2 The household sector includes non-profit institutions serving households.

4.5 Earnings on portfolio investment

continued

£ million

		2000	2001	2002	2003	2004	2005	2006	2007	2008	2009	2010
Debits												
(Foreign earnings on portfolio investment in the UK)												
Earnings on equity securities (shares) issued by:												
Monetary financial institutions	HBQJ	132	147	119	123	133	151	176	272	371	349	399
Other sectors[1]	HBQK	11 222	14 718	15 232	14 888	16 263	18 289	21 522	22 811	25 955	21 610	21 926
Total foreign earnings on UK equity securities	ZMRB	11 354	14 865	15 351	15 011	16 396	18 440	21 698	23 083	26 326	21 959	22 325
Earnings on debt securities												
Earnings on bonds and notes												
Issues by central government												
UK foreign currency bonds and notes	ZMRA	339	265	128	20	37	38	37	36	18	–	–
Earnings on British government stocks by:												
Foreign central banks (exchange reserves)	HESK	1 309	1 168	1 119	1 053	1 110	1 190	1 309	1 628	1 876	1 761	2 756
Other foreign residents	HCEV	2 899	2 710	2 530	2 990	3 489	4 614	5 478	7 114	8 211	6 723	10 483
Total foreign earnings on British government stocks	HENI	4 208	3 878	3 649	4 043	4 599	5 804	6 787	8 742	10 087	8 484	13 239
Total issues by central government	HBQU	4 547	4 143	3 777	4 063	4 636	5 842	6 824	8 778	10 105	8 484	13 239
Local authorities' bonds	HHGH	–	–	–	–	–	–	–	–	–	–	–
Public corporations' bonds	HESY	–	–	–	–	–	–	–	–	–	–	–
Issues by monetary financial institutions												
Bonds	HGUV	1 977	1 897	1 945	2 102	2 696	3 271	3 882	4 683	5 026	4 135	3 014
European medium term notes and other medium-term paper	HGMM	1 246	1 450	1 505	1 841	2 658	3 517	4 523	5 991	7 096	8 250	8 766
Total issues by monetary financial institutions	HBOT	3 223	3 347	3 450	3 943	5 354	6 788	8 405	10 674	12 122	12 385	11 780
Issues by other sectors[1]	HGUW	6 153	5 909	6 054	6 539	8 393	10 184	12 086	14 582	15 649	12 871	9 388
Total foreign earnings on UK bonds and notes	HLZA	13 923	13 399	13 281	14 545	18 383	22 814	27 315	34 034	37 876	33 740	34 407
Earnings on money market instruments												
Earnings on treasury bills (issued by central government)												
Sterling treasury bills	XAMR	3	13	20	23	120	144	153	281	427	120	145
Euro treasury bills	HHNV	–	–	–	–	–	–	–	–	–	–	–
Total earnings on treasury bills	HHZU	3	13	20	23	120	144	153	281	427	120	145
Earnings on certificates of deposit issued by monetary financial institutions	HCEE	4 945	6 069	3 490	2 364	2 507	3 915	5 304	6 412	7 136	3 418	2 383
Earnings on commercial paper												
Issued by monetary financial institutions	HCEF	964	923	608	612	841	1 443	2 054	2 159	2 086	886	590
Issued by other sectors[1]	HHZT	1 250	835	558	347	457	832	1 039	832	654	191	95
Total earnings on commercial paper	HHBO	2 214	1 758	1 166	959	1 298	2 275	3 093	2 991	2 740	1 077	685
Total foreign earnings on UK Money Market Instruments	HLYZ	7 162	7 840	4 676	3 346	3 925	6 334	8 550	9 684	10 303	4 615	3 213
Total foreign earnings on UK debt securities	HLZB	21 085	21 239	17 957	17 891	22 308	29 148	35 865	43 718	48 179	38 355	37 620
Total	HLZC	**32 439**	**36 104**	**33 308**	**32 902**	**38 704**	**47 588**	**57 563**	**66 801**	**74 505**	**60 314**	**59 945**

1 These series relate to non-governmental sectors other than monetary financial institutions.

4.5 Earnings on portfolio investment

continued

£ million

		2000	2001	2002	2003	2004	2005	2006	2007	2008	2009	2010
Balances (net earnings)												
Earnings on equity securities (shares)	HLZO	–1 482	–5 004	–4 821	–4 626	–5 210	–5 186	–4 710	–2 446	–6 288	–5 577	–6 523
Earnings on debt securities												
Earnings on bonds and notes	HLZQ	6 636	8 771	7 076	6 046	4 985	6 829	7 711	8 187	7 087	3 539	–4 055
Earnings on money market instruments	HLZR	–4 620	–4 989	–3 079	–1 772	–1 771	–3 852	–5 421	–6 410	–7 793	–3 721	–1 976
Total foreign earnings on UK debt securities	HLZP	2 016	3 782	3 997	4 274	3 214	2 977	2 290	1 777	–706	–182	–6 031
Total	HLZX	**534**	**–1 222**	**–824**	**–352**	**–1 996**	**–2 209**	**–2 420**	**–669**	**–6 994**	**–5 759**	**–12 554**

4.6 Earnings on portfolio investment
Sector analysis

£ million

		2000	2001	2002	2003	2004	2005	2006	2007	2008	2009	2010
Credits												
(Earnings of UK residents on portfolio investment abroad)												
Earnings from portfolio investment abroad by UK:												
Monetary financial institutions	AIND	18 987	20 229	18 302	18 595	21 569	26 352	31 416	38 938	37 710	26 761	20 634
Central government	LOEO	–	18	26	19	9	10	7	89	12	–1	30
Insurance companies and pension funds	AINE	5 736	5 767	6 392	6 232	6 654	7 950	9 307	10 424	13 099	13 732	13 359
Other financial intermediaries	AINF	7 570	8 051	6 891	6 686	7 259	9 619	12 508	14 710	14 743	12 547	12 157
Private non-financial corporations	AINI	203	378	446	593	781	837	1 062	1 020	762	466	379
Household sector[1]	AINK	477	439	427	425	436	611	843	951	1 185	1 050	832
Total	HLYX	**32 973**	**34 882**	**32 484**	**32 550**	**36 708**	**45 379**	**55 143**	**66 132**	**67 511**	**54 555**	**47 391**
Debits												
(Foreign earnings on portfolio investment in the UK)												
Foreign earnings from portfolio investment in UK:												
Monetary financial institutions	HBXI	9 264	10 486	7 667	7 042	8 835	12 297	15 939	19 517	21 715	17 038	15 152
Central government	HBXM	4 550	4 156	3 797	4 086	4 756	5 986	6 977	9 059	10 532	8 604	13 384
Local authorities	HHGH	–	–	–	–	–	–	–	–	–	–	–
Public corporations	HESY	–	–	–	–	–	–	–	–	–	–	–
Other sectors	HBXR	18 625	21 462	21 844	21 774	25 113	29 305	34 647	38 225	42 258	34 672	31 409
Total	HLZC	**32 439**	**36 104**	**33 308**	**32 902**	**38 704**	**47 588**	**57 563**	**66 801**	**74 505**	**60 314**	**59 945**
Balances												
(Net earnings)												
Monetary financial institutions	LTMI	9 723	9 743	10 635	11 553	12 734	14 055	15 477	19 421	15 995	9 723	5 482
Central government	ZPOF	–4 550	–4 138	–3 771	–4 067	–4 747	–5 976	–6 970	–8 970	–10 520	–8 605	–13 354
Local authorities	-HHGH	–	–	–	–	–	–	–	–	–	–	–
Public corporations	-HESY	–	–	–	–	–	–	–	–	–	–	–
Other sectors	LTMJ	–4 639	–6 827	–7 688	–7 838	–9 983	–10 288	–10 927	–11 120	–12 469	–6 877	–4 682
Total	HLZX	**534**	**–1 222**	**–824**	**–352**	**–1 996**	**–2 209**	**–2 420**	**–669**	**–6 994**	**–5 759**	**–12 554**

1 The household sector includes non-profit institutions serving households.

4.7 Earnings on other investment

£ million

		2000	2001	2002	2003	2004	2005	2006	2007	2008	2009	2010
Credits												
(Earnings of UK residents on other investment abroad)												
Earnings on trade credit												
Central government	XBGJ	–	–	–	–	–	–	–	–	–	–	–
Other sectors[1]	HGQD	–	–	–	–	–	–	–	–	–	–	–
Total earnings on trade credit	AIOM	–	–	–	–	–	–	–	–	–	–	–
Earnings on loans												
Long-term												
Bank loans under ECGD[2] guarantee	AINM	508	378	235	205	198	235	258	283	268	240	241
Inter-government loans by the UK	XBGI	4	4	3	4	2	2	2	2	1	–1	–
Loans by Commonwealth Development Corporation (public corporations)	HGEN	101	74	74	74	74	74	74	74	74	74	74
Loans by the ECGD[2]	CY95	246	324	243	228	673	1 213	419	189	288	85	65
Loans by specialist leasing companies[1]	HBXC	–	–	–	–	–	–	–	–	–	–	–
Total long-term loans	AIOO	859	780	555	511	947	1 524	753	548	631	398	380
Short-term loans	VTUN	36	36	36	36	36	36	36	36	36	36	36
Total earnings on loans	CGKJ	895	816	591	547	983	1 560	789	584	667	434	416
Earnings on deposits												
By UK monetary financial institutions (banks)												
Sterling deposits	IFD7	7 159	6 380	4 833	5 034	7 162	8 205	10 723	21 948	23 022	6 192	4 023
Foreign currency deposits	IFD8	38 722	39 771	25 648	22 958	21 881	37 169	63 190	82 480	80 012	28 973	20 543
Total deposits by UK banks	IFD9	45 881	46 151	30 481	27 992	29 043	45 374	73 913	104 428	103 034	35 165	24 566
Deposits by securities dealers	HGTD	1 376	2 908	1 733	1 762	1 904	3 338	5 186	6 071	4 884	3 400	2 986
Deposits by other UK residents[1]	CGJK	4 202	4 499	2 636	3 029	4 416	9 805	17 908	22 079	16 159	5 112	4 241
Total earnings on deposits abroad	CGJQ	51 459	53 558	34 850	32 783	35 363	58 517	97 007	132 578	124 077	43 677	31 793
Earnings on other assets												
Trusts and annuities[1]	HHLF	548	489	325	305	329	333	348	355	312	277	275
Foreign currency exchanges[1]	HHKX	–	–	–	–	–	–	–	–	–	–	–
Miscellaneous central government receipts	HPPK	–	–	–	–	–	–	–	–	–	–	–
Total earnings on other assets	CGKM	548	489	325	305	329	333	348	355	312	277	275
Total	AIOP	**52 902**	**54 863**	**35 766**	**33 635**	**36 675**	**60 410**	**98 144**	**133 517**	**125 056**	**44 388**	**32 484**

1 These series relate to non-governmental sectors other than monetary financial institutions.
2 Export Credits Guarantee Department.

4.7 Earnings on other investment

continued £ million

		2000	2001	2002	2003	2004	2005	2006	2007	2008	2009	2010
Debits												
(Foreign earnings on other investment in the UK)												
Earnings on trade credit												
Public corporations	XBGW	–	–	–	–	–	–	–	–	–	–	–
Other sectors[1]	HHLW	–	–	–	–	–	–	–	–	–	–	–
Total earnings on trade credit	CGMA	–	–	–	–	–	–	–	–	–	–	–
Earnings on loans												
Loans to:												
Central government	CGLF	14	77	71	54	47	42	52	–	–	–	–
Local authorities	CGLG	7	4	2	–	–	–	–	–	–	–	–
Public corporations	CGLH	–	–	–	–	16	18	18	18	17	16	16
Securities dealers	CGLI	8 530	10 525	8 522	7 653	7 557	11 413	15 461	18 243	16 576	14 434	12 838
Other[1]	CGMD	4 074	3 477	3 331	3 076	3 905	6 634	9 801	12 528	9 929	3 611	3 006
Total earnings on loans	CGNO	12 625	14 083	11 926	10 783	11 525	18 107	25 332	30 789	26 522	18 061	15 860
Earnings on deposits[2]												
(Monetary financial institutions)												
Sterling deposits	JJT3	10 519	10 562	8 623	8 890	11 625	13 356	16 206	29 429	33 537	9 913	6 769
Foreign currency deposits	JJT4	46 037	44 778	31 038	28 621	28 282	46 837	75 271	96 666	90 489	33 184	23 358
Total earnings on deposits	HMAS	56 556	55 340	39 661	37 511	39 907	60 193	91 477	126 095	124 026	43 097	30 127
Earnings on other liabilities												
(Non-governmental sectors other than monetary financial institutions)												
Imputed income to foreign households from UK insurance companies technical reserves	HBWS	1 034	1 124	1 196	1 243	1 101	1 102	1 043	775	841	782	585
Other liabilities	CGME	–	–	–	–	–	–	–	–	–	–	–
Total earnings on other liabilities	CGMH	1 034	1 124	1 196	1 243	1 101	1 102	1 043	775	841	782	585
Total	HLZN	**70 215**	**70 547**	**52 783**	**49 537**	**52 533**	**79 402**	**117 852**	**157 659**	**151 389**	**61 940**	**46 572**
Balances												
(Net earnings)												
Trade credit	LTMK	–	–	–	–	–	–	–	–	–	–	–
Loans	LTML	–11 730	–13 267	–11 335	–10 236	–10 542	–16 547	–24 543	–30 205	–25 855	–17 627	–15 444
Currency and deposits	LTMM	–5 097	–1 782	–4 811	–4 728	–4 544	–1 676	5 530	6 483	51	580	1 666
Other investment	LTMN	–486	–635	–871	–938	–772	–769	–695	–420	–529	–505	–310
Total	CGNA	**–17 313**	**–15 684**	**–17 017**	**–15 902**	**–15 858**	**–18 992**	**–19 708**	**–24 142**	**–26 333**	**–17 552**	**–14 088**

1 These series relate to non-governmental sectors other than monetary financial institutions.
2 UK banks' payments on non-resident deposits includes payments on loans received and repurchase agreements.

4.8 Earnings on other investment
Sector analysis

£ million

		2000	2001	2002	2003	2004	2005	2006	2007	2008	2009	2010
Credits												
(Earnings of UK residents on other investment abroad)												
Earnings from other investment by UK:												
Monetary financial institutions	CGMM	46 389	46 529	30 716	28 197	29 241	45 609	74 171	104 711	103 302	35 405	24 807
Central government	CGMN	4	4	3	4	2	2	2	2	1	–1	–
Public corporations	ZPOP	347	398	317	302	747	1 287	493	263	362	159	139
Other sectors	CGMR	6 162	7 932	4 730	5 132	6 685	13 512	23 478	28 541	21 391	8 825	7 538
Total	AIOP	**52 902**	**54 863**	**35 766**	**33 635**	**36 675**	**60 410**	**98 144**	**133 517**	**125 056**	**44 388**	**32 484**
Debits												
(Foreign earnings on other investment in the UK)												
Foreign earnings from other investment in UK:												
Monetary financial institutions	HMAS	56 556	55 340	39 661	37 511	39 907	60 193	91 477	126 095	124 026	43 097	30 127
Central government	CGLF	14	77	71	54	47	42	52	–	–	–	–
Local authorities	CGLG	7	4	2	–	–	–	–	–	–	–	–
Public corporations	CGMV	–	–	–	–	16	18	18	18	17	16	16
Other sectors	CGMZ	13 638	15 126	13 049	11 972	12 563	19 149	26 305	31 546	27 346	18 827	16 429
Total	HLZN	**70 215**	**70 547**	**52 783**	**49 537**	**52 533**	**79 402**	**117 852**	**157 659**	**151 389**	**61 940**	**46 572**
Balances												
(Net earnings)												
Monetary financial institutions	LTMO	–10 167	–8 811	–8 945	–9 314	–10 666	–14 584	–17 306	–21 384	–20 724	–7 692	–5 320
Central government	LTMP	–10	–73	–68	–50	–45	–40	–50	2	1	–1	–
Local authorities	-CGLG	–7	–4	–2	–	–	–	–	–	–	–	–
Public corporations	LTMQ	347	398	317	302	731	1 269	475	245	345	143	123
Other sectors	LTMR	–7 476	–7 194	–8 319	–6 840	–5 878	–5 637	–2 827	–3 005	–5 955	–10 002	–8 891
Total	CGNA	**–17 313**	**–15 684**	**–17 017**	**–15 902**	**–15 858**	**–18 992**	**–19 708**	**–24 142**	**–26 333**	**–17 552**	**–14 088**

Current transfers

Chapter 5

5.1 Current transfers

£ million

		2000	2001	2002	2003	2004	2005	2006	2007	2008	2009	2010
Credits												
General government												
Current taxes on income, wealth etc.	FJKI	357	398	527	375	482	546	681	603	616	672	567
Other taxes on production	FJKH	–	–	–	–	–	–	–	–	–	–	–
Other subsidies on production	FJBC	–	–	–	–	–	–	–	–	–	–	–
Social contributions	FJBH	24	25	24	23	22	22	28	31	40	61	29
Social benefits	FJBL	–	–	–	–	–	–	–	–	–	–	–
EU Institutions:												
(a) Abatement	FKKL	2 084	4 560	3 099	3 560	3 592	3 655	3 570	3 523	4 862	5 392	3 046
(b) Other EU receipts	FKIJ	–	8	13	10	81	71	104	161	134	130	133
Miscellaneous receipts	FKIK	–	–	–	–	–	–	–	–	–	–	–
Total general government	FJUM	2 465	4 991	3 663	3 968	4 177	4 294	4 383	4 318	5 652	6 255	3 775
Other sectors												
Current taxes on income, wealth etc.	FJBJ	–	–	–	–	–	–	–	–	–	–	–
Other taxes on production	FJGC	–	–	–	–	–	–	–	–	–	–	–
Other subsidies on production	FJBA	–	–	–	–	–	–	–	–	–	–	–
Social contributions	FJAB	31	34	53	21	14	–8	28	–5	28	111	54
EU Instititions:												
(a) Agricultural Guarantee Fund	EBGL	2 571	2 336	2 381	2 691	3 315	3 408	3 221	2 952	3 051	3 411	3 032
(b) Social Fund[1]	H5U2	659	370	412	427	364	842	1 225	751	504	505	659
(c) ECSC Grant	FJKP	–	1	–	–	2	–	–	–	–	–	–
Net non-life insurance premiums[2]	NQQP	2 086	3 471	3 008	2 208	3 181	6 133	6 530	3 148	4 477	4 148	4 295
Non-life insurance claims[3]	FJFA	18	25	19	19	47	16	39	50	54	77	315
Other receipts of households[4]	FKIL	2 653	2 689	2 698	2 713	2 667	2 715	2 748	2 663	2 557	2 557	2 478
Total other sectors	FJUN	8 018	8 926	8 571	8 079	9 590	13 106	13 791	9 559	10 671	10 809	10 833
Total	KTND	**10 483**	**13 917**	**12 234**	**12 047**	**13 767**	**17 400**	**18 174**	**13 877**	**16 323**	**17 064**	**14 608**
Of which: Receipts from EU institutions	FKIM	5 314	7 275	5 905	6 688	7 354	7 976	8 120	7 387	8 551	9 438	6 870

1 Social fund receipts by local government are included up to 2003. From 2004 they are included in general government other EU receipts.
2 Premiums paid to UK insurance companies.
3 Claims paid to UK residents by foreign insurance companies.
4 Includes estimates for workers' remittances and for non-profit institutions serving households.

5.1 Current transfers

continued £ million

		2000	2001	2002	2003	2004	2005	2006	2007	2008	2009	2010
Debits												
General government												
Current taxes on income, wealth etc.	FJKK	–	–	–	–	–	–	–	–	–	–	–
Other taxes on production	FJKN	–	–	–	–	–	–	–	–	–	–	–
Other subsidies on production	FJCE	–	–	–	–	–	–	–	–	–	–	–
Social contributions	FJCH	–	–	–	–	–	–	–	–	–	–	–
Social security benefits	FJCK	1 218	1 292	1 388	1 452	1 596	1 650	1 721	1 829	1 999	2 099	2 160
Contributions to international organisations												
EU Institutions:												
(a) GNP: 4th Resource	HCSO	4 243	3 859	5 259	6 622	7 565	8 597	8 358	7 996	8 628	10 692	10 718
(b) GNP adjustments	HCSM	136	–1	76	150	–16	135	163	327	–205	–137	101
(c) Inter governmental agreements	HCBW	–	–	–	–	–	–	–	–	–	–	–
(d) Other	FKIN	6	24	10	18	–3	106	8	6	5	–14	–18
Other organisations:												
(a) Military	HDKF	157	195	192	152	160	141	159	139	193	144	200
(b) Multilateral economic assistance	HCHJ	503	434	539	367	622	495	945	1 102	1 002	1 084	1 434
(c) Other	HCKL	454	403	248	201	394	550	615	505	695	573	392
Bilateral aid:												
(a) Non-project grants	FJKT	175	185	206	268	303	306	300	349	381	485	531
(b) Technical cooperation	FJKU	859	904	1 038	1 320	1 474	1 497	1 467	1 699	1 858	2 367	2 597
Military grants	HDJO	27	45	129	107	130	160	138	130	158	372	547
Total general government	FJUO	7 778	7 340	9 085	10 657	12 225	13 637	13 874	14 082	14 714	17 665	18 662
Other sectors												
Current taxes on income, wealth etc.	FJCI	775	523	644	444	535	589	428	549	793	565	638
Other taxes on production	FJLB	–	–	–	–	–	–	–	–	–	–	–
Other subsidies on production	FJCC	–	–	–	–	–	–	–	–	–	–	–
Social contributions	FJBG	–	–	–	–	–	–	–	–	–	–	–
Social benefits	FJCM	31	34	53	21	14	–8	28	–5	28	111	54
EU Institutions:												
(a) Customs duties and agricultural levies	QYRD	2 086	2 069	1 919	1 937	2 145	2 237	2 329	2 412	2 636	2 645	2 933
(b) Sugar levies	GTBA	44	31	25	18	25	24	–	–	–	–	–
(c) VAT based contributions	HCML	4 104	3 624	2 720	2 775	1 764	1 980	2 165	2 293	2 255	1 733	2 172
(d) VAT adjustments	FSVL	100	–49	88	–35	25	19	2	26	15	–140	81
(e) ECSC Production levy	GTBB	–	–	–	–	–	–	–	–	–	–	–
Net non-life insurance premiums[1]	FJDB	18	25	19	19	47	16	39	50	54	77	315
Non-life insurance claims[2]	NQQR	2 086	3 471	3 008	2 208	3 181	6 133	6 530	3 148	4 477	4 148	4 295
Other payments by households[3]	FKIQ	3 236	3 364	3 543	3 838	4 082	4 622	4 655	4 868	5 116	5 336	5 539
Total other sectors	FJUP	12 480	13 092	12 019	11 225	11 818	15 612	16 176	13 341	15 374	14 475	16 027
Total	KTNE	**20 258**	**20 432**	**21 104**	**21 882**	**24 043**	**29 249**	**30 050**	**27 423**	**30 088**	**32 140**	**34 689**
Of which: Payments to EU institutions	FKIR	10 719	9 557	10 097	11 485	11 505	13 098	13 025	13 060	13 334	14 779	15 987

1 Premiums paid by UK residents to foreign insurance companies.
2 Claims paid by UK insurance companies to non-residents.
3 Includes estimates for workers' remittances and for non-profit institutions serving households.

5.1 Current transfers

continued

£ million

		2000	2001	2002	2003	2004	2005	2006	2007	2008	2009	2010
Balances												
General government												
Current taxes on income, wealth etc.	FJKJ	357	398	527	375	482	546	681	603	616	672	567
Other taxes on production	FJIZ	–	–	–	–	–	–	–	–	–	–	–
Other subsidies on production	FJBD	–	–	–	–	–	–	–	–	–	–	–
Social contributions	FJBI	24	25	24	23	22	22	28	31	40	61	29
Social benefits	FJBM	–1 218	–1 292	–1 388	–1 452	–1 596	–1 650	–1 721	–1 829	–1 999	–2 099	–2 160
Other current transfers	FJKW	–4 476	–1 480	–4 585	–5 635	–6 956	–8 261	–8 479	–8 569	–7 719	–10 044	–13 323
Total general government	FJUQ	–5 313	–2 349	–5 422	–6 689	–8 048	–9 343	–9 491	–9 764	–9 062	–11 410	–14 887
Other sectors												
Current taxes on income, wealth etc.	FJHU	–775	–523	–644	–444	–535	–589	–428	–549	–793	–565	–638
Other taxes on production	FJHT	–	–	–	–	–	–	–	–	–	–	–
Other subsidies on production	FJHV	–	–	–	–	–	–	–	–	–	–	–
Social contributions	FJHJ	31	34	53	21	14	–8	28	–5	28	111	54
Social benefits	FJJG	628	336	359	406	350	850	1 197	756	476	394	605
Other current transfers[1]	FJLT	–4 346	–4 013	–3 216	–3 129	–2 057	–2 759	–3 182	–3 984	–4 414	–3 606	–5 215
Total other sectors	FJUR	–4 462	–4 166	–3 448	–3 146	–2 228	–2 506	–2 385	–3 782	–4 703	–3 666	–5 194
Total	KTNF	**–9 775**	**–6 515**	**–8 870**	**–9 835**	**–10 276**	**–11 849**	**–11 876**	**–13 546**	**–13 765**	**–15 076**	**–20 081**
Of which: EU institutions	FKIS	–5 405	–2 282	–4 192	–4 797	–4 151	–5 122	–4 905	–5 673	–4 783	–5 341	–9 117

1 Includes an estimate for workers' remittances.

Part 2

Capital account, financial account and international investment position

Capital account

Chapter 6

6.1 Capital account

£ million

		2000	2001	2002	2003	2004	2005	2006	2007	2008	2009	2010
Credits												
Capital transfers												
General government												
Debt forgiveness	FJUU	–	–	–	–	–	–	–	–	–	–	–
Other capital transfers	FJLY	–	–	–	–	–	–	–	–	–	–	–
Total general government	FJMD	–	–	–	–	–	–	–	–	–	–	–
Other sectors												
Migrants' transfers	FJMG	1 371	2 267	1 864	1 951	2 298	2 491	2 725	2 953	3 200	3 467	3 688
Debt forgiveness	FJNC	–	–	–	–	–	–	–	–	–	–	–
Other capital transfers												
EU Institutions:												
Regional development fund	FKIT	989	543	296	622	1 062	1 402	618	707	972	640	609
Agricultural fund for regional development[1]	FJXL	82	26	–	2	49	80	50	150	417	215	431
Other capital transfers	EBGO	–	322	–	–	–	–	–	–	–	–	–
Total EU institutions	FKIV	1 071	891	296	624	1 111	1 482	668	857	1 389	855	1 040
Total other sectors	FJMU	2 442	3 158	2 160	2 575	3 409	3 973	3 393	3 810	4 589	4 322	4 728
Total capital transfers	FJMX	2 442	3 158	2 160	2 575	3 409	3 973	3 393	3 810	4 589	4 322	4 728
Sales of non-produced, non-financial assets	FJUX	165	177	172	218	193	337	631	783	1 074	1 515	1 199
Total	FKMH	**2 607**	**3 335**	**2 332**	**2 793**	**3 602**	**4 310**	**4 024**	**4 593**	**5 663**	**5 837**	**5 927**
Debits												
Capital transfers												
General government												
Debt forgiveness	FJUV	22	18	15	16	13	16	13	11	73	49	101
Other capital transfers (project grants)	FJMB	225	237	263	345	389	396	388	449	491	264	239
Total general government	FJME	247	255	278	361	402	412	401	460	564	313	340
Other sectors												
Migrants' transfers	FJMH	461	1 300	582	547	515	551	669	697	744	745	737
Debt forgiveness												
Monetary financial institutions[2]	FJNF	–	–	–	–	–	–	–	–	–	–	–
Public corporations[3]	HMLY	55	188	236	130	109	1 249	1 356	76	–	–	–
Total debt forgiveness	IZZZ	55	188	236	130	109	1 249	1 356	76	–	–	–
Other capital transfers	FJMS	–	–	–	–	–	–	–	–	–	–	–
Total other sectors	FJMV	516	1 488	818	677	624	1 800	2 025	773	744	745	737
Total capital transfers	FJMY	763	1 743	1 096	1 038	1 026	2 212	2 426	1 233	1 308	1 058	1 077
Purchases of non-produced, non-financial assets	FJUY	141	274	304	289	512	595	623	794	1 114	1 142	1 142
Total	FKMI	**904**	**2 017**	**1 400**	**1 327**	**1 538**	**2 807**	**3 049**	**2 027**	**2 422**	**2 200**	**2 219**
Balances												
Capital transfers												
General government												
Debt forgiveness	FJUW	–22	–18	–15	–16	–13	–16	–13	–11	–73	–49	–101
Other capital transfers	FJMC	–225	–237	–263	–345	–389	–396	–388	–449	–491	–264	–239
Total general government	FJMF	–247	–255	–278	–361	–402	–412	–401	–460	–564	–313	–340
Other sectors												
Migrants' transfers	FJMI	910	967	1 282	1 404	1 783	1 940	2 056	2 256	2 456	2 722	2 951
Debt forgiveness	FJNG	–55	–188	–236	–130	–109	–1 249	–1 356	–76	–	–	–
Other capital transfers	FJMT	1 071	891	296	624	1 111	1 482	668	857	1 389	855	1 040
Total other sectors	FJMW	1 926	1 670	1 342	1 898	2 785	2 173	1 368	3 037	3 845	3 577	3 991
Total capital transfers	FJMZ	1 679	1 415	1 064	1 537	2 383	1 761	967	2 577	3 281	3 264	3 651
Non-produced, non-financial assets	NHSG	24	–97	–132	–71	–319	–258	8	–11	–40	373	57
Total	FKMJ	**1 703**	**1 318**	**932**	**1 466**	**2 064**	**1 503**	**975**	**2 566**	**3 241**	**3 637**	**3 708**

1 Up to 2006 this series includes the European Agricultural Guidance Fund.
2 This series also appears in the Financial Account (see Table 7.7).
3 This series also appears in the Financial Account (see Table 7.7) as series HMLW.

Chapter 7

Financial account

7.1 Financial account
Summary table

£ million

		2000	2001	2002	2003	2004	2005	2006	2007	2008	2009	2010
UK investment abroad												
(UK assets = net debits)												
Direct investment abroad[1]												
Equity capital	-HJYM	147 679	16 890	26 155	20 639	19 896	15 612	26 819	60 143	37 703	7 968	12 123
Reinvested earnings	-HDNY	25 178	27 220	32 209	21 456	31 076	43 555	47 878	63 738	38 394	13 241	22 920
Other capital transactions	-HMAB	−17 275	−1 283	−23 323	−1 206	538	−15 162	−29 699	38 758	23 532	7 280	−27 911
Total direct investment abroad	-HJYP	155 582	42 827	35 041	40 889	51 510	44 005	44 998	162 639	99 629	28 489	7 132
Portfolio investment abroad												
Equity securities	-HBVI	20 521	44 464	−3 189	19 684	56 647	61 323	19 597	28 262	−60 117	9 739	6 778
Debt securities	-XBMW	45 042	42 089	4 199	16 584	84 367	89 632	119 241	63 249	−63 058	154 948	75 731
Total portfolio investment abroad	-HHZC	65 563	86 553	1 010	36 268	141 014	150 955	138 838	91 511	−123 175	164 687	82 509
Financial derivatives (net)[2]	-ZPNN	−1 553	−8 417	−1 001	5 401	6 770	−5 767	−20 601	26 990	121 684	−29 104	−32 490
Other investment abroad	-XBMM	241 666	170 663	70 375	260 401	325 220	506 260	395 901	742 391	−612 970	−336 060	235 245
Reserve assets	-LTCV	3 915	−3 085	−459	−1 559	196	656	−426	1 191	−1 338	5 763	6 070
Total	-HBNR	**465 173**	**288 541**	**104 966**	**341 400**	**524 710**	**696 109**	**558 710**	**1 024 722**	**−516 170**	**−166 225**	**298 466**
Investment in the UK												
(UK liabilities = net credits)												
Direct investment in the UK[1]												
Equity capital	HJYR	59 811	20 954	11 809	4 464	23 716	82 949	55 393	82 500	53 397	36 341	33 289
Reinvested earnings	CYFV	10 788	−992	3 647	7 429	8 558	10 501	22 195	23 276	1 542	4 148	−14
Other capital transactions	HMAD	9 967	17 386	1 326	4 883	−1 066	4 395	7 301	−5 802	−6 512	4 677	−4 339
Total direct investment in the UK	HJYU	80 566	37 348	16 782	16 776	31 208	97 845	84 889	99 974	48 427	45 166	28 936
Portfolio investment in the UK												
Equity securities	XBLW	121 302	15 730	1 903	20 088	1 957	6 379	−10 564	16 810	37 946	53 181	2 524
Debt securities	XBLX	50 875	25 099	47 836	85 560	95 387	122 670	163 082	201 102	162 637	138 396	90 419
Total portfolio investment in the UK	HHZF	172 177	40 829	49 739	105 648	97 344	129 049	152 518	217 912	200 583	191 577	92 943
Other investment in the UK	XBMN	235 563	237 558	54 649	241 537	425 621	504 450	355 279	731 818	−739 195	−378 203	218 104
Total	HBNS	**488 306**	**315 735**	**121 170**	**363 961**	**554 173**	**731 344**	**592 686**	**1 049 704**	**−490 185**	**−141 460**	**339 983**
Net transactions												
(net credits *less* net debits)												
Direct investment[1]												
Equity capital	HBWN	−87 868	4 064	−14 346	−16 175	3 820	67 337	28 574	22 357	15 694	28 373	21 166
Reinvested earnings	HBWT	−14 390	−28 212	−28 562	−14 027	−22 518	−33 054	−25 683	−40 462	−36 852	−9 093	−22 934
Other capital transactions	HBWU	27 242	18 669	24 649	6 089	−1 604	19 557	37 000	−44 560	−30 044	−2 603	23 572
Total net direct investment	HJYV	−75 016	−5 479	−18 259	−24 113	−20 302	53 840	39 891	−62 665	−51 202	16 677	21 804
Portfolio investment												
Equity securities	HBWV	100 781	−28 734	5 092	404	−54 690	−54 944	−30 161	−11 452	98 063	43 442	−4 254
Debt securities	HBWX	5 833	−16 990	43 637	68 976	11 020	33 038	43 841	137 853	225 695	−16 552	14 688
Total net portfolio investment	HHZD	106 614	−45 724	48 729	69 380	−43 670	−21 906	13 680	126 401	323 758	26 890	10 434
Financial derivatives[2]	ZPNN	1 553	8 417	1 001	−5 401	−6 770	5 767	20 601	−26 990	−121 684	29 104	32 490
Other investment	HHYR	−6 103	66 895	−15 726	−18 864	100 401	−1 810	−40 622	−10 573	−126 225	−42 143	−17 141
Reserve assets	LTCV	−3 915	3 085	459	1 559	−196	−656	426	−1 191	1 338	−5 763	−6 070
Total	HBNT	**23 133**	**27 194**	**16 204**	**22 561**	**29 463**	**35 235**	**33 976**	**24 982**	**25 985**	**24 765**	**41 517**

1 The latest year's data for foreign direct investment are provisional as these figures are subject to annual benchmarking.
2 Data from 1992 cover the transactions of UK banks with non-residents. From 2010, the transactions of UK securities dealers with non-residents are also included.

7.2 Financial account
Sector analysis

£ million

		2000	2001	2002	2003	2004	2005	2006	2007	2008	2009	2010
UK investment abroad												
(UK assets = net debits)												
By:												
Monetary financial institutions	-HFAQ	229 306	125 392	58 774	179 727	326 078	397 952	416 833	701 178	–382 484	–276 601	95 540
Central government	-HFAN	4 228	–2 568	463	–2 217	1 103	1 588	630	4 698	1 948	10 092	7 932
Public corporations	-HFAO	582	62	–164	–571	–370	–1 671	–4 694	–79	–628	–42	86
Other sectors	-HFAP	231 057	165 655	45 893	164 461	197 899	298 240	145 941	318 925	–135 006	100 326	194 908
Total	-HBNR	**465 173**	**288 541**	**104 966**	**341 400**	**524 710**	**696 109**	**558 710**	**1 024 722**	**–516 170**	**–166 225**	**298 466**
Investment in the UK												
(UK liabilities = net credits)												
In:												
Monetary financial institutions	CGUL	242 746	148 717	114 954	204 512	340 046	321 335	426 637	772 121	–466 832	–203 025	19 517
Central government	HFAR	–243	–97	–4 538	13 657	13 526	29 688	26 220	30 749	41 110	24 415	87 440
Local authorities	HFAS	–188	22	26	204	651	134	232	–42	446	520	175
Public corporations	HFAT	–	–	–	–	283	–7	–12	–6	–9	–4	–
Other sectors	GGCJ	245 991	167 093	10 728	145 588	199 667	380 194	139 609	246 882	–64 900	36 634	232 851
Total	HBNS	**488 306**	**315 735**	**121 170**	**363 961**	**554 173**	**731 344**	**592 686**	**1 049 704**	**–490 185**	**–141 460**	**339 983**
Net transactions												
(net credits *less* net debits)												
In assets and liabilities of:												
Monetary financial institutions	GGCK	13 440	23 325	56 180	24 785	13 968	–76 617	9 804	70 943	–84 348	73 576	–76 023
Central government	HFAV	–4 471	2 471	–5 001	15 874	12 423	28 100	25 590	26 051	39 162	14 323	79 508
Local authorities	HFAS	–188	22	26	204	651	134	232	–42	446	520	175
Public corporations	HFAW	–582	–62	164	571	653	1 664	4 682	73	619	38	–86
Other sectors	GGCL	14 934	1 438	–35 165	–18 873	1 768	81 954	–6 332	–72 043	70 106	–63 692	37 943
Total	HBNT	**23 133**	**27 194**	**16 204**	**22 561**	**29 463**	**35 235**	**33 976**	**24 982**	**25 985**	**24 765**	**41 517**

7.3 Direct investment[1]

£ million

		2000	2001	2002	2003	2004	2005	2006	2007	2008	2009	2010
Direct investment abroad												
(UK assets = net debits)												
Equity capital												
Claims on affiliated enterprises												
(net acquisition of ordinary shares)												
Purchases of ordinary shares	-HDOA	181 488	40 221	35 374	26 128	27 114	24 939	46 960	69 008	40 985	30 541	25 514
Sales of ordinary shares	-HDOC	–34 693	–25 073	–10 440	–8 479	–9 105	–10 691	–21 702	–10 976	–6 868	–25 788	–15 554
Total claims on affiliated enterprises	-HJYL	146 795	15 148	24 934	17 649	18 009	14 248	25 258	58 032	34 117	4 753	9 960
Net acquisition of property	-HHVG	884	1 742	1 221	2 990	1 887	1 364	1 561	2 111	3 586	3 215	2 163
Total equity capital	-HJYM	147 679	16 890	26 155	20 639	19 896	15 612	26 819	60 143	37 703	7 968	12 123
Reinvested earnings	-HDNY	25 178	27 220	32 209	21 456	31 076	43 555	47 878	63 738	38 394	13 241	22 920
Other capital transactions												
Claims on affiliated enterprises												
Debt securities issued by affiliated enterprises												
Purchases of debt securities	-HDOD	952	2 263	513	1 598	1 902	2 260	2 060	3 653	4 665	7 379	1 852
Sales of debt securities	-HDOE	–496	–304	–1 080	–2 312	–608	–1 054	–2 795	–1 708	–2 239	–3 101	–1 584
Other claims on affiliated enterprises												
Change in inter-company accounts	-HDOF	15 110	5 072	17 140	10 178	18 531	17 765	–229	37 171	79 811	–33 135	–1 736
Change in branch indebtedness	-HDOI	–3 360	5 153	–610	1 783	–472	–4 108	585	3 889	8 370	2 141	–8 995
Total claims on affiliated enterprises	-HJYN	12 206	12 184	15 963	11 247	19 353	14 863	–379	43 005	90 607	–26 716	–10 463
Liabilities to affiliated enterprises												
Change in inter-company accounts	-HDOG	28 278	12 880	38 774	10 568	20 950	29 075	26 371	3 718	65 959	–33 558	18 830
Change in branch indebtedness	-HDOJ	1 203	587	512	1 885	–2 135	950	2 949	529	1 116	–438	–1 382
Total liabilities to affiliated enterprises	-HJYO	29 481	13 467	39 286	12 453	18 815	30 025	29 320	4 247	67 075	–33 996	17 448
Total other capital transactions	-HMAB	–17 275	–1 283	–23 323	–1 206	538	–15 162	–29 699	38 758	23 532	7 280	–27 911
Total	-HJYP	**155 582**	**42 827**	**35 041**	**40 889**	**51 510**	**44 005**	**44 998**	**162 639**	**99 629**	**28 489**	**7 132**
Direct investment in the UK												
(UK liabilities = net credits)												
Equity capital												
Liabilities to direct investors												
Quoted ordinary shares												
Purchases of quoted ordinary shares	CYFY	16 253	3 502	5 951	1 739	19 181	64 495	44 436	20 721	24 876	8 368	24 371
Sales of quoted ordinary shares	CYFZ	–2 038	–1 185	–775	–1 200	–	–540	–177	–664	–133	–513	–694
Unquoted ordinary shares												
Purchases of unquoted ordinary shares	CYGA	48 154	20 381	11 068	4 238	6 411	21 681	16 160	64 370	31 202	32 682	11 369
Sales of unquoted ordinary shares	CYGB	–4 187	–2 535	–5 183	–708	–2 499	–3 284	–5 493	–4 285	–4 041	–4 728	–2 289
Total liabilities to direct investors	HJYQ	58 182	20 163	11 061	4 069	23 093	82 352	54 926	80 142	51 904	35 809	32 757
Net acquisition of property	CGLO	1 629	791	748	395	623	597	467	2 358	1 493	532	532
Total equity capital	HJYR	59 811	20 954	11 809	4 464	23 716	82 949	55 393	82 500	53 397	36 341	33 289
Reinvested earnings	CYFV	10 788	–992	3 647	7 429	8 558	10 501	22 195	23 276	1 542	4 148	–14
Other capital transactions												
Liabilities to direct investors												
Debt securities issued by affiliated enterprises												
Purchases of debt securities	CYGC	710	1 318	598	1 844	3 464	2 294	5 135	8 115	5 691	3 619	692
Sales of debt securities	CYGD	–183	–571	–377	–484	–1 153	–269	–745	–2 999	–1 518	–2 530	–1 057
Other liabilities to direct investors												
Change in inter-company accounts	CYGH	11 338	17 420	10 756	–1 264	–931	14 032	5 351	5 862	21 350	–13 593	–445
Change in branch indebtedness	CYGL	869	285	403	1 738	470	351	2 666	–1 413	–1 677	3 940	349
Total liabilities to direct investors	HJYT	12 734	18 452	11 380	1 834	1 850	16 408	12 407	9 565	23 846	–8 564	–461
Claims on direct investors												
Change in inter-company accounts	CYGF	2 495	561	9 990	–2 112	2 723	10 850	5 619	15 779	29 878	–12 794	3 408
Change in branch indebtedness	CYGK	272	505	64	–937	193	1 163	–513	–412	480	–447	470
Total claims on direct investors	HJYS	2 767	1 066	10 054	–3 049	2 916	12 013	5 106	15 367	30 358	–13 241	3 878
Total other capital transactions	HMAD	9 967	17 386	1 326	4 883	–1 066	4 395	7 301	–5 802	–6 512	4 677	–4 339
Total	HJYU	**80 566**	**37 348**	**16 782**	**16 776**	**31 208**	**97 845**	**84 889**	**99 974**	**48 427**	**45 166**	**28 936**

1 The latest year's data for foreign direct investment are provisional as these figures are subject to annual benchmarking.

7.3 Direct investment[1]

continued

£ million

		2000	2001	2002	2003	2004	2005	2006	2007	2008	2009	2010
Net transactions (net credits less net debits)												
Equity capital												
Net acquisition of ordinary shares	LTMS	–88 613	5 015	–13 873	–13 580	5 084	68 104	29 668	22 110	17 787	31 056	22 797
Net acquisition of property	LTMT	745	–951	–473	–2 595	–1 264	–767	–1 094	247	–2 093	–2 683	–1 631
Total equity capital	HBWN	–87 868	4 064	–14 346	–16 175	3 820	67 337	28 574	22 357	15 694	28 373	21 166
Reinvested earnings	HBWT	–14 390	–28 212	–28 562	–14 027	–22 518	–33 054	–25 683	–40 462	–36 852	–9 093	–22 934
Other capital transactions	HBWU	27 242	18 669	24 649	6 089	–1 604	19 557	37 000	–44 560	–30 044	–2 603	23 572
Total	HJYV	**–75 016**	**–5 479**	**–18 259**	**–24 113**	**–20 302**	**53 840**	**39 891**	**–62 665**	**–51 202**	**16 677**	**21 804**

1 The latest year's data for foreign direct investment are provisional as these figures are subject to annual benchmarking.

7.4 Direct investment[1]

Sector analysis

£ million

		2000	2001	2002	2003	2004	2005	2006	2007	2008	2009	2010
Direct investment abroad (UK assets = net debits)												
By:												
Monetary financial institutions	-HCWJ	3 378	4 283	2 825	1 942	16 231	9 533	11 337	10 218	8 275	13 791	–844
Insurance companies	-CNZE	2 166	–256	1 388	3 038	4 357	1 454	8 587	6 902	363	–15	2 165
Other financial intermediaries	-HCXL	9 716	4 468	4 071	13 858	–1 374	2 389	2 122	27 118	–988	–1 927	–183
Private non-financial corporations	-HCVH	139 101	32 575	25 859	18 598	31 048	28 885	23 162	116 232	90 135	14 253	3 599
Public corporations	-HDND	574	201	258	–185	–85	155	–2 003	204	–312	107	115
Household sector[2]	-AAQN	647	1 556	640	3 638	1 333	1 589	1 793	1 965	2 156	2 280	2 280
Total	-HJYP	**155 582**	**42 827**	**35 041**	**40 889**	**51 510**	**44 005**	**44 998**	**162 639**	**99 629**	**28 489**	**7 132**
Direct investment in the UK (UK liabilities = net credits)												
In:												
Monetary financial institutions	GPBQ	4 133	3 387	1 757	2 683	11 715	4 539	4 243	8 291	5 516	4 270	2 460
Insurance companies	HDQI	2 492	1 304	312	876	1 959	–247	3 312	1 716	–1 417	239	–75
Other financial intermediaries												
Securities dealers	HDRU	1 919	938	706	212	1 735	2 956	1 404	14 349	6 141	16 777	787
Other	HFCL	5 792	8 098	3 298	5 395	–5 220	–7 285	4 328	16 673	–3 202	–427	–13
Total other financial intermediaries	HFDR	7 711	9 036	4 004	5 607	–3 485	–4 329	5 732	31 022	2 939	16 350	774
Private non-financial corporations	BCEC	66 230	23 621	10 709	7 610	21 019	97 882	71 602	58 945	41 389	24 307	25 777
Total	HJYU	**80 566**	**37 348**	**16 782**	**16 776**	**31 208**	**97 845**	**84 889**	**99 974**	**48 427**	**45 166**	**28 936**
Net transaction (net credits less net debits)												
In assets and liabilities of:												
Monetary financial institutions	LTMU	755	–896	–1 068	741	–4 516	–4 994	–7 094	–1 927	–2 759	–9 521	3 304
Insurance companies	LTMV	326	1 560	–1 076	–2 162	–2 398	–1 701	–5 275	–5 186	–1 780	254	–2 240
Other financial intermediaries	LTMW	–2 005	4 568	–67	–8 251	–2 111	–6 718	3 610	3 904	3 927	18 277	957
Private non-financial corporations	LTMX	–72 871	–8 954	–15 150	–10 988	–10 029	68 997	48 440	–57 287	–48 746	10 054	22 178
Public corporations	HDND	–574	–201	–258	185	85	–155	2 003	–204	312	–107	–115
Household sector[2]	AAQN	–647	–1 556	–640	–3 638	–1 333	–1 589	–1 793	–1 965	–2 156	–2 280	–2 280
Total	HJYV	**–75 016**	**–5 479**	**–18 259**	**–24 113**	**–20 302**	**53 840**	**39 891**	**–62 665**	**–51 202**	**16 677**	**21 804**

1 The latest year's data for foreign direct investment are provisional as these figures are subject to annual benchmarking.
2 The household sector includes non-profit institutions serving households.

7.5 Portfolio investment

£ million

		2000	2001	2002	2003	2004	2005	2006	2007	2008	2009	2010
Portfolio investment abroad												
(UK assets = net debits)												
Transactions in equity securities (shares) by:												
Monetary financial Institutions	-VTWC	7 195	–1 287	–11 767	18 824	31 597	36 515	21 524	11 413	–67 384	3 114	10 171
Central Government	LOEQ	–	–	–	–	–	43	12	–8	16	24	24
Insurance companies and pension funds												
Insurance companies[1]	-HBHM	–4 297	6 520	2 959	–3 354	6 116	19 601	1 727	12 117	1 586	2 405	261
Self-administered pension funds	-HBHO	–12 798	11 720	15 256	4 394	6 491	8 036	–417	–7 675	–10 247	1 134	–2 834
Total insurance companies and pension funds	-HBRD	–17 095	18 240	18 215	1 040	12 607	27 637	1 310	4 442	–8 661	3 539	–2 573
Other financial intermediaries												
Securities dealers	-HGLG	13 673	24 128	–12 050	–796	9 734	–17 842	–6 505	14 821	17 974	–6 536	–5 418
Unit and Investment Trusts	-HBHQ	9 968	3 913	3 329	2 121	1 174	7 305	2 892	506	26	12 833	6 368
Other	-HBRC	–1 446	–1 077	–856	–1 563	–1 621	–1 668	–1 800	–2 898	–1 863	–1 792	–1 892
Total other financial intermediaries	-HBRE	22 195	26 964	–9 577	–238	9 287	–12 205	–5 413	12 429	16 137	4 505	–942
Private non-financial corporations	-XBNL	9 047	444	–52	17	–380	23	1 381	–1 319	151	101	283
Household sector[2]	HALH	–821	103	–8	41	3 536	9 310	783	1 305	–376	–1 544	–185
Total transactions in equity securities	-HBVI	20 521	44 464	–3 189	19 684	56 647	61 323	19 597	28 262	–60 117	9 739	6 778
Transactions in debt securities												
Transactions in bonds and notes by:												
Monetary financial institutions	-HPCP	36 471	38 458	3 436	–12 713	57 901	62 737	102 238	42 249	–161 193	–10 423	–23 689
Central Government	HQ5P	–	–	–	–	–	–	–	50	–50	165	–36
Insurance companies and pension funds												
Insurance companies[1]	-HBHN	5 363	8 200	8 535	1 618	1 522	3 280	12 777	12 699	13 886	13 161	834
Self-administered pension funds	-HBHP	5 875	1 267	–3 604	1 732	3 980	3 779	11 310	24 433	6 891	5 687	12 192
Total insurance companies and pension funds	-HBRF	11 238	9 467	4 931	3 350	5 502	7 059	24 087	37 132	20 777	18 848	13 026
Other financial intermediaries												
Securities dealers	CGFO	–1 935	–19 589	–1 114	9 912	21 829	13 355	–24 941	–19 292	91 484	121 692	75 466
Unit and investment trusts	-HBHR	664	1 478	720	2 445	1 531	1 430	6 093	4 918	5 655	9 591	9 231
Other	-HBRG	–36	–57	–72	–76	–101	–119	–146	–209	–246	–301	–269
Total other financial intermediaries	-HBRH	–1 307	–18 168	–466	12 281	23 259	14 666	–18 994	–14 583	96 893	130 982	84 428
Private non-financial corporations	-XBNM	1 179	566	300	1 292	197	–727	–1 621	673	2 428	–1 086	3 172
Household sector[2]	HBRI	256	88	88	88	88	88	88	88	88	88	88
Total transactions in bonds and notes	-HEPK	47 837	30 411	8 289	4 298	86 947	83 823	105 798	65 609	–41 057	138 574	76 989
Transactions in Money Market Instruments by:												
Central government	-RUUR	–	458	467	–925	–1	–	–	2 390	–139	2 641	590
Monetary financial institutions	JXG6	345	7 374	–3 982	7 432	–4 461	2 039	5 321	8 534	–14 888	10 690	–831
Insurance companies and pension funds	-HBVK	–106	–159	333	70	602	1 419	–556	154	697	–301	–74
Other financial intermediaries	JXG5	–4 144	2 093	–2 018	1 911	665	1 273	3 920	–3 618	–2 616	1 729	–2 879
Private non-financial corporations	-HBRL	1 110	1 912	1 110	3 798	615	1 078	4 758	–9 820	–5 055	1 615	1 936
Total transactions in Money Market Instruments	-HHZM	–2 795	11 678	–4 090	12 286	–2 580	5 809	13 443	–2 360	–22 001	16 374	–1 258
Total transactions in debt securities	-XBMW	45 042	42 089	4 199	16 584	84 367	89 632	119 241	63 249	–63 058	154 948	75 731
Total	-HHZC	**65 563**	**86 553**	**1 010**	**36 268**	**141 014**	**150 955**	**138 838**	**91 511**	**–123 175**	**164 687**	**82 509**

1 Includes pension funds managed by insurance companies.
2 The household sector includes non-profit institutions serving households.

7.5 Portfolio investment

continued

£ million

		2000	2001	2002	2003	2004	2005	2006	2007	2008	2009	2010
Portfolio investment in the UK												
(UK liabilities = net credits)												
Transactions in equity securities (shares) issued by:												
Monetary financial institutions	HBQG	–3 510	54	–1 276	714	–264	48	651	3 671	1 587	2 229	1 856
Other sectors[1]	HBQH	124 812	15 676	3 179	19 374	2 221	6 331	–11 215	13 139	36 359	50 952	668
Total transactions in equity securities	XBLW	121 302	15 730	1 903	20 088	1 957	6 379	–10 564	16 810	37 946	53 181	2 524
Transactions in debt securities												
Transactions in bonds and notes												
Issues by central government												
UK foreign currency bonds and notes	HEZP	988	–3 342	–2 811	886	38	–32	–138	95	–1 484	–	–
Other central government bonds	HHJM	–	–	–	–	–	–	–	–	–	–	–
Transactions in British government stocks (gilts) by:												
Foreign central banks (exchange reserves)	AING	1 049	1 157	–1 245	–748	–2 339	384	4 212	3 085	4 744	4 618	10 613
Other foreign residents	VTWG	–2 337	1 511	420	11 059	14 908	30 309	20 849	24 057	25 275	18 911	67 877
Total transactions in British government stocks	HEPC	–1 288	2 668	–825	10 311	12 569	30 693	25 061	27 142	30 019	23 529	78 490
Total issues by central government	HBRX	–300	–674	–3 636	11 197	12 607	30 661	24 923	27 237	28 535	23 529	78 490
Local authorities' bonds	HBQT	–	–	–	–	–	–	–	–	–	–	–
Public corporations' bonds	HCEW	–	–	–	–	–	–	–	–	–	–	–
Issues by monetary financial institutions												
Bonds	HBRY	1 886	511	4 884	15 129	13 214	18 828	17 072	28 371	42 763	1 638	15 201
European medium term notes and other medium-term paper	HBRV	2 705	4 055	1 775	13 871	18 747	22 738	26 035	36 499	–22 942	26 967	4 293
Total monetary financial institutions	HMBD	4 591	4 566	6 659	29 000	31 961	41 566	43 107	64 870	19 821	28 605	19 494
Issues by other sectors[1]	HBRT	5 871	1 587	15 210	47 198	40 774	58 619	53 148	88 327	133 130	5 100	47 324
Total transactions in bonds and notes	XBLY	10 162	5 479	18 233	87 395	85 342	130 846	121 178	180 434	181 486	57 234	145 308
Transactions in Money Market Instruments												
Transactions in treasury bills (issued by central government)												
Sterling treasury bills	AARB	–251	304	–180	2 150	1 974	–1 023	747	3 547	12 653	587	8 330
Euro treasury bills	HHNW	–	–	–	–	–	–	–	–	–	–	–
Total treasury bills	HHZO	–251	304	–180	2 150	1 974	–1 023	747	3 547	12 653	587	8 330
Transactions in certificates of deposit issued by UK monetary financial institutions	HBQX	34 954	19 861	4 344	–2 954	–857	–1 512	36 012	17 991	–31 138	72 857	–46 027
Transactions in commercial paper												
Issued by UK monetary financial Institutions	HBRU	3 310	–782	14 620	3 292	8 835	–3 012	8 643	–3 792	–3 501	13 136	–20 476
Issued by other sectors[1]	HHZN	2 700	237	10 819	–4 323	93	–2 629	–3 498	2 922	3 137	–5 418	3 284
Total transactions in commercial paper	HBQW	6 010	–545	25 439	–1 031	8 928	–5 641	5 145	–870	–364	7 718	–17 192
Total transactions in Money Market Instruments	HHZE	40 713	19 620	29 603	–1 835	10 045	–8 176	41 904	20 668	–18 849	81 162	–54 889
Total transactions in debt securities	XBLX	50 875	25 099	47 836	85 560	95 387	122 670	163 082	201 102	162 637	138 396	90 419
Total	HHZF	**172 177**	**40 829**	**49 739**	**105 648**	**97 344**	**129 049**	**152 518**	**217 912**	**200 583**	**191 577**	**92 943**

1 These series relate to non-governmental sectors other than monetary financial institutions.

7.5 Portfolio investment

continued

£ million

		2000	2001	2002	2003	2004	2005	2006	2007	2008	2009	2010
Net transactions (net credits less net debits)												
Equity securities (shares)	HBWV	100 781	–28 734	5 092	404	–54 690	–54 944	–30 161	–11 452	98 063	43 442	–4 254
Debt securities												
Bonds and notes	LTMY	–37 675	–24 932	9 944	83 097	–1 605	47 023	15 380	114 825	222 543	–81 340	68 319
Money Market Instruments	LTMZ	43 508	7 942	33 693	–14 121	12 625	–13 985	28 461	23 028	3 152	64 788	–53 631
Total debt securities	HBWX	5 833	–16 990	43 637	68 976	11 020	33 038	43 841	137 853	225 695	–16 552	14 688
Total	HHZD	**106 614**	**–45 724**	**48 729**	**69 380**	**–43 670**	**–21 906**	**13 680**	**126 401**	**323 758**	**26 890**	**10 434**

7.6 Portfolio investment

Sector analysis

£ million

		2000	2001	2002	2003	2004	2005	2006	2007	2008	2009	2010
Portfolio investment abroad (UK assets = net debits)												
Investment by:												
Monetary financial institutions	-HBRJ	44 011	44 545	–12 313	13 543	85 037	101 291	129 083	62 196	–243 465	3 381	–14 349
Central government	LOFB	–	458	467	–925	–1	43	12	2 432	–173	2 830	578
Insurance companies and pension funds	-HBRO	–5 963	27 548	23 479	4 460	18 711	36 115	24 841	41 728	12 813	22 086	10 379
Other financial intermediaries	-HBRP	16 744	10 889	–12 061	13 954	33 211	3 734	–20 487	–5 772	110 414	137 216	80 607
Private non-financial corporations	-HBRQ	11 336	2 922	1 358	5 107	432	374	4 518	–10 466	–2 476	630	5 391
Household sector[1]	-HBRR	–565	191	80	129	3 624	9 398	871	1 393	–288	–1 456	–97
Total	-HHZC	**65 563**	**86 553**	**1 010**	**36 268**	**141 014**	**150 955**	**138 838**	**91 511**	**–123 175**	**164 687**	**82 509**
Portfolio investment in the UK (UK liabilities = net credits)												
Investment in securities issued by:												
Monetary financial institutions	CGPH	39 345	23 699	24 347	30 052	39 675	37 090	88 413	82 740	–13 231	116 827	–45 153
Central government	HBSO	–551	–370	–3 816	13 347	14 581	29 638	25 670	30 784	41 188	24 116	86 820
Local authorities	HBQT	–	–	–	–	–	–	–	–	–	–	–
Public corporations	HCEW	–	–	–	–	–	–	–	–	–	–	–
Other sectors	CGPL	133 383	17 500	29 208	62 249	43 088	62 321	38 435	104 388	172 626	50 634	51 276
Total	HHZF	**172 177**	**40 829**	**49 739**	**105 648**	**97 344**	**129 049**	**152 518**	**217 912**	**200 583**	**191 577**	**92 943**
Net transactions (net credits less net debits)												
In assets and liabilities of:												
Monetary financial institutions	LTNA	–4 666	–20 846	36 660	16 509	–45 362	–64 201	–40 670	20 544	230 234	113 446	–30 804
Central government	ZPOG	–551	–828	–4 283	14 272	14 582	29 595	25 658	28 352	41 361	21 286	86 242
Local authorities	HBQT	–	–	–	–	–	–	–	–	–	–	–
Public corporations	HCEW	–	–	–	–	–	–	–	–	–	–	–
Other sectors	LTNB	111 831	–24 050	16 352	38 599	–12 890	12 700	28 692	77 505	52 163	–107 842	–45 004
Total	HHZD	**106 614**	**–45 724**	**48 729**	**69 380**	**–43 670**	**–21 906**	**13 680**	**126 401**	**323 758**	**26 890**	**10 434**

1 The household sector includes non-profit institutions serving households.

7.7 Other investment

£ million

		2000	2001	2002	2003	2004	2005	2006	2007	2008	2009	2010
Other investment abroad												
(UK assets = net debits)												
Trade credit												
Long-term												
Central government	-XBMC	–	–	–	–	–	–	–	–	–	–	–
Other sectors[1]	-HCQK	–	–	–	–	–	–	–	–	–	–	–
Total long-term trade credit	-HBRZ	–	–	–	–	–	–	–	–	–	–	–
Short-term												
Other sectors[1]	-XBMF	-42	-315	292	573	-336	-1 395	1 361	120	40	-28	-78
Total trade credit	-XBMB	-42	-315	292	573	-336	-1 395	1 361	120	40	-28	-78
Loans												
Long-term												
Bank loans under ECGD[2] guarantee	-HGBS	-1 476	187	-1 017	113	231	224	-467	-157	54	191	306
Inter-government loans by the UK	-HEUC	-27	-20	-19	-19	-15	-18	-13	-12	-75	-49	-99
Loans by Commonwealth Development Corporation (public corporations)	-HETB	2	–	–	–	–	–	–	–	–	–	–
Loans by the ECGD[2]	CY93	61	49	-186	-259	-176	-577	-1 335	-207	-316	-149	-29
Loans by specialist leasing companies[1]	-HGKU	–	–	–	–	–	–	–	–	–	–	–
Total long-term loans	-HBSG	-1 440	216	-1 222	-165	40	-371	-1 815	-376	-337	-7	178
Short-term loans												
By monetary financial institutions												
Sterling loans	JXH5	1 896	4 797	4 739	462	6 891	20 217	22 119	26 217	5 997	-18 572	1 756
Foreign currency loans	JXH6	53 028	43 294	12 778	70 529	105 145	114 591	97 717	200 310	-128 655	-98 828	15 333
Total monetary financial institutions	ZPOL	54 924	48 091	17 517	70 991	112 036	134 808	119 836	226 527	-122 658	-117 400	17 089
By other sectors	-XBLN	–	–	–	–	–	-3	–	5	2	-9	–
Total short-term loans	VTUL	54 924	48 091	17 517	70 991	112 036	134 805	119 836	226 532	-122 656	-117 409	17 089
Total loans	-XBMG	53 484	48 307	16 295	70 826	112 076	134 434	118 021	226 156	-122 993	-117 416	17 267
Currency and deposits												
Transactions in foreign notes and coin												
Monetary financial institutions	TAAG	-44	1	21	10	-2	-10	58	26	111	-37	-161
Other sectors[1]	-HETF	28	-4	33	20	46	24	66	8	-192	-27	21
Total foreign notes and coin	HEOV	-16	-3	54	30	44	14	124	34	-81	-64	-140
Deposits abroad by UK residents												
Deposits by monetary financial institutions												
Sterling deposits	JXH7	20 090	7 437	-8 012	18 218	-2 646	32 256	47 167	112 101	-24 470	-71 950	-15 874
Foreign currency deposits	JXH8	109 976	29 265	60 754	69 509	108 421	125 617	130 420	263 277	-122 015	-75 473	138 944
Total deposits by monetary financial institutions	HCES	130 066	36 702	52 742	87 727	105 775	157 873	177 587	375 378	-146 485	-147 423	123 070

1 These series relate to non-governmental sectors other than monetary financial institutions.
2 Export Credits Guarantee Department.

7.7 Other investment

continued £ million

		2000	2001	2002	2003	2004	2005	2006	2007	2008	2009	2010
Other investment abroad - *continued*												
Currency and deposits - *continued*												
Deposits abroad by UK residents - *continued*												
Deposits by securities dealers	-HGTF	47 567	58 756	-13 153	53 172	36 186	167 581	48 951	35 468	-338 084	1 725	46 028
Deposits by other UK residents[1]	-HBSI	10 322	27 325	13 907	47 914	70 661	48 095	50 156	104 224	-8 901	-74 402	47 715
Total deposits abroad by UK residents	-HBXV	187 955	122 783	53 496	188 813	212 622	373 549	276 694	515 070	-493 470	-220 100	216 813
Total currency and deposits	-HBVN	187 939	122 780	53 550	188 843	212 666	373 563	276 818	515 104	-493 551	-220 164	216 673
Other assets												
Central government subscriptions to international organisations												
International Development Association	-HEUB	237	200	319	108	185	378	468	460	770	807	1 188
Regional development banks	-HEUD	50	53	69	75	61	42	98	82	176	172	61
European Investment Bank (EIB)	-HEUE	–	–	–	–	–	–	–	–	–	–	–
Other subscriptions	-HEUF	3	3	21	51	37	52	214	159	-13	104	-8
Total central government subscriptions	-HGLR	290	256	409	234	283	472	780	701	933	1 083	1 241
Short-term central government assets	-LOEL	50	-177	65	52	640	435	277	386	2 601	465	142
Total central government other assets	-LOES	340	79	474	286	923	907	1 057	1 087	3 534	1 548	1 383
Debt forgiveness (monetary financial institutions)[2]	-FJNF	–	–	–	–	–	–	–	–	–	–	–
Other sectors (excluding monetary financial institutions)												
Long-term assets	-HHZH	–	–	–	–	–	–	–	–	–	–	–
Short-term assets												
Public corporations assets abroad	-HBSR	–	–	–	–	–	–	–	–	–	–	–
Public corporations debt forgiveness	HMLW	-55	-188	-236	-127	-109	-1 249	-1 356	-76	–	–	–
Other[1]	-HBSK	–	–	–	–	–	–	–	–	–	–	–
Total short-term assets of other sectors	-HHZI	-55	-188	-236	-127	-109	-1 249	-1 356	-76	–	–	–
Total other sectors	-XBLP	-55	-188	-236	-127	-109	-1 249	-1 356	-76	–	–	–
Total other assets	-XBMK	285	-109	238	159	814	-342	-299	1 011	3 534	1 548	1 383
Total	-XBMM	**241 666**	**170 663**	**70 375**	**260 401**	**325 220**	**506 260**	**395 901**	**742 391**	**-612 970**	**-336 060**	**235 245**

1 This series relates to non-governmental sectors other than monetary financial institutions.
2 This series also appears in the capital account (see Table 6.1).

7.7 Other investment

continued

£ million

		2000	2001	2002	2003	2004	2005	2006	2007	2008	2009	2010
Other investment in the UK (UK liabilities = net credits)												
Trade credit												
Long-term[1]	CGJF	–	–	–	–	–	–	–	–	–	–	–
Short-term[1]	XBLQ	–	–	–	–	–	–	–	–	–	–	–
Total trade credit	XBMO	–	–	–	–	–	–	–	–	–	–	–
Loans												
Long-term												
Drawings by:												
Central government	HBSP	–	–	–	–	–	–	–	–	–	–	–
Local authorities	HBSQ	–	–	–	–	–	–	–	–	–	–	–
Public corporations	HHYT	–	–	–	–	–	–	–	–	–	–	–
Other[1]	HIBY	–	–	–	–	–	–	–	–	–	–	–
Total long-term drawings	HBST	–	–	–	–	–	–	–	–	–	–	–
Repayments from:												
Central government	HBSW	–114	–45	–48	–45	–46	–65	7	–3	32	5	–495
Local authorities	HBSX	–188	22	26	204	651	134	232	–42	446	520	175
Public corporations	HHYU	–	–	–	–	283	–7	–12	–6	–9	–4	–
Other[1]	HIBZ	–	–	–	–	–	–	–	–	–	–	–
Total long-term repayments	HBSY	–302	–23	–22	159	888	62	227	–51	469	521	–320
Total long-term loans	HBSZ	–302	–23	–22	159	888	62	227	–51	469	521	–320
Short-term loans to:												
Central government	HBTA	–	–	–	–	–	–	–	–	–	–	–
Local authorities	HBTB	–	–	–	–	–	–	–	–	–	–	–
Public corporations	HIAW	–	–	–	–	–	–	–	–	–	–	–
Securities dealers	HBTD	56 910	77 290	–34 313	31 054	81 239	223 816	–34 085	70 716	–274 515	616	91 579
Other[1]	HBSS	–21 697	38 480	429	39 625	54 549	–1 861	50 204	–15 627	–2 006	–55 187	63 338
Total short-term loans	HBTC	35 213	115 770	–33 884	70 679	135 788	221 955	16 119	55 089	–276 521	–54 571	154 917
Total loans	XBMP	34 911	115 747	–33 906	70 838	136 676	222 017	16 346	55 038	–276 052	–54 050	154 597
Currency and deposits												
Sterling notes and coin												
Notes (issued by Bank of England)	HLYV	67	–51	78	74	102	58	66	41	–22	–150	57
Coins (issued by Royal Mint)	HMAT	8	–6	8	7	11	6	7	4	–3	–17	6
Total notes and coin	AASD	75	–57	86	81	113	64	73	45	–25	–167	63
Deposits from abroad with UK residents												
Deposits with monetary financial institutions												
Sterling deposits	JXH9	33 033	16 820	11 300	23 327	27 080	47 249	57 501	209 574	–42 770	–58 767	–27 882
Foreign currency deposits	JXI2	166 168	104 862	77 472	148 376	261 474	232 399	276 414	471 475	–416 325	–265 205	90 035
Total deposits with monetary financial institutions	HDKE	199 201	121 682	88 772	171 703	288 554	279 648	333 915	681 049	–459 095	–323 972	62 153
Deposit liabilities of UK central government	HEUN	528	–178	–24	232	–877	–57	474	–299	–282	201	293
Total deposits from abroad with UK residents	HBXY	199 729	121 504	88 748	171 935	287 677	279 591	334 389	680 750	–459 377	–323 771	62 446
Total currency and deposits	HMAO	199 804	121 447	88 834	172 016	287 790	279 655	334 462	680 795	–459 402	–323 938	62 509

1 These series relate to non-governmental sectors other than monetary financial institutions.

7.7 Other investment

continued

£ million

		2000	2001	2002	2003	2004	2005	2006	2007	2008	2009	2010
Other investment in the UK - *continued*												
Other liabilities												
Long-term												
Net equity of foreign households in life assurance reserves and pension funds	QZEP	–4	–5	–1	–4	–11	–55	–9	–37	–2	–41	–10
Prepayments of insurance premiums and reserves against outstanding claims	NQMC	942	–157	335	–1 371	1 324	2 675	4 423	–4 223	–3 914	–282	194
Total long-term liabilities	VTUG	938	–162	334	–1 375	1 313	2 620	4 414	–4 260	–3 916	–323	184
Short-term	HJYF	–90	526	–613	58	–158	158	57	245	175	108	814
Total other liabilities	XBMX	848	364	–279	–1 317	1 155	2 778	4 471	–4 015	–3 741	–215	998
Total	XBMN	**235 563**	**237 558**	**54 649**	**241 537**	**425 621**	**504 450**	**355 279**	**731 818**	**–739 195**	**–378 203**	**218 104**
Net transactions (net credits less net debits)												
Trade credit	LTNC	42	315	–292	–573	336	1 395	–1 361	–120	–40	28	78
Loans	LTND	–18 573	67 440	–50 201	12	24 600	87 583	–101 675	–171 118	–153 059	63 366	137 330
Deposits	LTNE	11 865	–1 333	35 284	–16 827	75 124	–93 908	57 644	165 691	34 149	–103 774	–154 164
Other	LTNF	563	473	–517	–1 476	341	3 120	4 770	–5 026	–7 275	–1 763	–385
Total	HHYR	**–6 103**	**66 895**	**–15 726**	**–18 864**	**100 401**	**–1 810**	**–40 622**	**–10 573**	**–126 225**	**–42 143**	**–17 141**

7.8 Other investment

Sector analysis

£ million

		2000	2001	2002	2003	2004	2005	2006	2007	2008	2009	2010
Other investment abroad												
(UK assets = net debits)												
Investment by:												
Monetary financial institutions	HCET	183 470	84 981	69 263	158 841	218 040	292 895	297 014	601 774	–268 978	–264 669	140 304
Central government	-HBSM	313	59	455	267	908	889	1 044	1 075	3 459	1 499	1 284
Public corporations	-HBSV	8	–139	–422	–386	–285	–1 826	–2 691	–283	–316	–149	–29
Other sectors	-HBSN	57 875	85 762	1 079	101 679	106 557	214 302	100 534	139 825	–347 135	–72 741	93 686
Total	-XBMM	**241 666**	**170 663**	**70 375**	**260 401**	**325 220**	**506 260**	**395 901**	**742 391**	**–612 970**	**–336 060**	**235 245**
Other investment in the UK												
(UK liabilities = net credits)												
Investment in:												
Monetary financial institutions	HBWG	199 268	121 631	88 850	171 777	288 656	279 706	333 981	681 090	–459 17	–324 122	62 210
Central government	HBWH	308	273	–722	310	–1 055	50	550	–35	–78	299	620
Local authorities	HBWJ	–188	22	26	204	651	134	232	–42	446	520	175
Public corporations	HBWL	–	–	–	–	283	–7	–12	–6	–9	–4	–
Other sectors	HBWM	36 175	115 632	–33 505	69 246	137 086	224 567	20 528	50 811	–280 437	–54 896	155 099
Total	XBMN	**235 563**	**237 558**	**54 649**	**241 537**	**425 621**	**504 450**	**355 279**	**731 818**	**–739 195**	**–378 203**	**218 104**
Net transactions												
(net credits less net debits)												
In assets and liabilities of:												
Monetary financial institutions	LTNI	15 798	36 650	19 587	12 936	70 616	–13 189	36 967	79 316	–190 139	–59 453	–78 094
Central government	LTNJ	–5	214	–1 177	43	–1 963	–839	–494	–1 110	–3 537	–1 200	–664
Local authorities	HBWJ	–188	22	26	204	651	134	232	–42	446	520	175
Public corporations	LTNK	–8	139	422	386	568	1 819	2 679	277	307	145	29
Other sectors	LTNL	–21 700	29 870	–34 584	–32 433	30 529	10 265	–80 006	–89 014	66 698	17 845	61 413
Total	HHYR	**–6 103**	**66 895**	**–15 726**	**–18 864**	**100 401**	**–1 810**	**–40 622**	**–10 573**	**–126 225**	**–42 143**	**–17 141**

7.9 Reserve assets
Central government sector
Net debits

£ million

		2000	2001	2002	2003	2004	2005	2006	2007	2008	2009	2010
Monetary gold	-HBOX	–883	–786	–266	–	–2	–	–4	–	–	–	–
Special Drawing Rights	-HBOY	–73	–22	26	–2	–35	–8	51	–50	–24	–132	18
Reserve position in the Fund	-HBOZ	–478	633	469	–251	–558	–1 911	–225	–188	802	613	554
Foreign Exchange												
Currency and deposits												
With central banks	-HBPC	–368	6	95	–79	33	28	–43	28	43	–33	–180
With other banks	-HBPD	6	–900	–863	–586	–882	367	–403	–419	–41	–95	49
Total currency and deposits	-HBPB	–363	–892	–767	–664	–849	395	–447	–390	2	–127	–131
Securities												
Bonds and notes	-HBPG	5 418	–1 838	2 280	–390	1 551	370	–854	2 105	–1 035	7 669	5 860
Money market instruments	-HBPH	244	–185	–2 043	–62	107	1 465	1 363	–265	–890	–2 170	–124
Total securities	-HBPE	5 662	–2 023	237	–452	1 658	1 835	509	1 840	–1 925	5 499	5 736
Total foreign exchange	-HBPA	5 299	–2 915	–530	–1 116	809	2 230	62	1 450	–1 923	5 372	5 605
Other claims	-HBPI	50	5	–158	–190	–18	345	–310	–21	–193	–90	–107
Total	-LTCV	**3 915**	**–3 085**	**–459**	**–1 559**	**196**	**656**	**–426**	**1 191**	**–1 338**	**5 763**	**6 070**

International investment position

Chapter 8

8.1 International investment position
Summary table
Balance sheets valued at end of year

£ billion

		2000	2001	2002	2003	2004	2005	2006	2007	2008	2009	2010
UK Assets												
Direct investment abroad[1]												
Equity capital and reinvested earnings	CGMO	586.3	582.2	619.3	670.7	667.2	726.8	762.4	865.7	1 022.1	971.0	1 042.9
Other capital assets	HBUW	32.5	34.8	17.9	20.5	10.9	–20.9	–29.3	34.1	46.7	62.6	35.7
Total direct investment abroad	HBWD	618.8	616.9	637.2	691.1	678.1	705.9	733.1	899.8	1 068.7	1 033.6	1 078.5
Portfolio investment abroad												
Equity securities	HEPX	429.3	404.6	305.9	372.0	455.3	617.2	693.4	748.9	565.2	666.4	743.8
Debt securities	HHZX	476.8	532.8	538.1	563.9	636.8	743.8	837.7	940.8	1 099.1	1 208.9	1 332.3
Total portfolio investment abroad	HHZZ	906.1	937.4	844.0	935.8	1 092.1	1 360.9	1 531.0	1 689.7	1 664.3	1 875.3	2 076.1
Financial derivatives[2]	JX96	..	..	..	..	709.4	820.1	853.7	1 378.1	4 040.2	2 176.4	2 962.8
Other investment abroad	HLXV	1 379.7	1 521.9	1 545.2	1 813.7	2 118.0	2 714.8	2 916.6	3 744.5	4 180.6	3 517.1	3 794.3
Reserve assets	LTEB	28.8	25.6	25.5	23.8	23.2	24.7	22.9	26.7	36.3	40.1	49.7
Total	HBQA	**2 933.4**	**3 101.9**	**3 051.9**	**3 464.5**	**4 620.8**	**5 626.4**	**6 057.4**	**7 738.8**	**10 990.1**	**8 642.5**	**9 961.4**
UK Liabilities												
Direct investment in the UK[1]												
Equity capital and reinvested earnings	HBUY	240.6	259.7	229.2	245.7	267.9	368.7	433.1	495.8	545.7	524.7	570.7
Other capital liabilities	HBVC	69.8	103.7	111.4	109.9	115.5	125.5	144.2	118.0	114.7	127.6	122.3
Total direct investment in the UK	HBWI	310.4	363.5	340.6	355.5	383.3	494.2	577.3	613.8	660.4	652.3	692.9
Portfolio investment in the UK												
Equity securities	HLXX	673.7	584.1	442.7	527.1	574.7	659.3	780.8	835.8	605.5	853.6	944.6
Debt securities	HLXY	393.8	429.1	482.6	555.8	653.2	802.4	922.6	1 109.8	1 374.7	1 551.9	1 578.5
Total portfolio investment in the UK	HLXW	1 067.6	1 013.2	925.3	1 082.9	1 227.9	1 461.7	1 703.5	1 945.7	1 980.2	2 405.5	2 523.1
Financial derivatives[2]	JX97	..	..	..	..	715.0	831.1	890.5	1 392.2	3 915.3	2 096.8	2 895.0
Other investment in the UK	HLYD	1 651.6	1 861.9	1 898.0	2 135.2	2 511.8	3 109.0	3 270.0	4 115.6	4 518.1	3 792.0	4 047.6
Total	HBQB	**3 029.5**	**3 238.5**	**3 163.9**	**3 573.6**	**4 838.1**	**5 896.0**	**6 441.2**	**8 067.3**	**11 073.9**	**8 946.6**	**10 158.6**
Net International Investment Position												
Direct investment[1]												
Equity capital and reinvested earnings	HBSH	345.7	322.4	390.1	425.0	399.3	358.1	329.3	369.8	476.4	446.4	472.2
Other capital	CGKF	–37.3	–69.0	–93.5	–89.4	–104.6	–146.4	–173.5	–83.9	–68.0	–65.0	–86.6
Total net direct investment	HBWQ	308.4	253.5	296.6	335.6	294.7	211.7	155.8	285.9	408.4	381.3	385.6
Portfolio investment												
Equity securities	CGNE	–244.4	–179.4	–136.8	–155.1	–119.4	–42.1	–87.5	–86.9	–40.3	–187.2	–200.8
Debt securities	CGNF	82.9	103.7	55.5	8.1	–16.4	–58.6	–84.9	–169.0	–275.6	–343.0	–246.2
Total net portfolio investment	CGNH	–161.5	–75.7	–81.3	–147.0	–135.8	–100.8	–172.4	–255.9	–315.9	–530.2	–447.0
Financial derivatives[2]	JX98	..	..	..	..	–5.6	–11.0	–36.8	–14.1	124.9	79.6	67.8
Other investment	CGNG	–271.9	–339.9	–352.8	–321.5	–393.9	–394.2	–353.4	–371.0	–337.5	–274.9	–253.4
Reserve assets	LTEB	28.8	25.6	25.5	23.8	23.2	24.7	22.9	26.7	36.3	40.1	49.7
Total	HBQC	**–96.2**	**–136.5**	**–112.0**	**–109.2**	**–217.3**	**–269.6**	**–383.8**	**–328.4**	**–83.8**	**–304.1**	**–197.3**
Allocations of Special Drawing Rights to the UK by the IMF	HEVP	1.7	1.7	1.6	1.6	1.5	1.6	1.5	1.5	2.0	1.9	1.9

1 The latest year's data for foreign direct investment are provisional as these figures are subject to annual benchmarking.
2 Data from 2004 cover the assets and liabilities of UK banks. From 2010, the assets and liabilities of UK securities dealers are also included.

8.2 International investment position Sector analysis

Balance sheets valued at end of year

£ billion

		2000	2001	2002	2003	2004	2005	2006	2007	2008	2009	2010
UK Assets												
Monetary financial institutions	CGNJ	1 421.8	1 535.0	1 572.6	1 737.9	2 700.6	3 248.3	3 530.4	4 838.5	7 991.8	5 556.7	5 786.4
Central government	CGNK	37.7	35.2	36.4	34.2	33.4	35.9	35.2	42.5	55.4	63.6	75.1
Public corporations	CGNL	4.6	3.8	4.2	4.2	4.7	3.4	1.7	1.7	1.6	1.2	1.2
Other sectors	CGNM	1 469.3	1 528.0	1 438.6	1 688.1	1 882.1	2 338.8	2 490.1	2 856.0	2 941.4	3 021.1	4 098.6
Total	HBQA	**2 933.4**	**3 101.9**	**3 051.9**	**3 464.5**	**4 620.8**	**5 626.4**	**6 057.4**	**7 738.8**	**10 990.1**	**8 642.5**	**9 961.4**
UK Liabilities												
Monetary financial institutions	HBYJ	1 486.6	1 623.8	1 707.1	1 893.3	2 895.0	3 413.5	3 707.5	5 082.9	8 137.0	5 802.6	5 931.4
Central government	CGOG	65.6	63.3	59.2	70.9	89.3	115.2	141.2	169.6	226.7	246.1	340.6
Local authorities	CGOH	0.8	0.8	0.9	1.1	1.7	1.9	2.1	2.1	2.5	3.0	3.2
Public corporations	CGOI	–	–	–	–	0.5	0.4	0.4	0.4	0.4	0.4	0.4
Other sectors	HCON	1 476.6	1 550.5	1 396.7	1 608.3	1 851.6	2 365.0	2 590.0	2 812.3	2 707.3	2 894.4	3 883.0
Total	HBQB	**3 029.5**	**3 238.5**	**3 163.9**	**3 573.6**	**4 838.1**	**5 896.0**	**6 441.2**	**8 067.3**	**11 073.9**	**8 946.6**	**10 158.6**
Net International Investment Position												
Monetary financial institutions	HDIJ	–64.8	–88.8	–134.5	–155.4	–194.4	–165.1	–177.0	–244.4	–145.3	–246.0	–145.0
Central government	CGOK	–27.9	–28.2	–22.8	–36.7	–55.9	–79.3	–106.0	–127.0	–171.3	–182.5	–265.5
Local authorities	-CGOH	–0.8	–0.8	–0.9	–1.1	–1.7	–1.9	–2.1	–2.1	–2.5	–3.0	–3.2
Public corporations	CGOL	4.6	3.8	4.2	4.2	4.2	2.9	1.3	1.3	1.2	0.8	0.8
Other sectors	HDKB	–7.3	–22.5	41.9	79.8	30.5	–26.3	–100.0	43.7	234.1	126.6	215.6
Total	HBQC	**–96.2**	**–136.5**	**–112.0**	**–109.2**	**–217.3**	**–269.6**	**–383.8**	**–328.4**	**–83.8**	**–304.1**	**–197.3**

8.3 Direct investment[1]

Balance sheets valued at end of year

£ billion

		2000	2001	2002	2003	2004	2005	2006	2007	2008	2009	2010
Direct investment abroad												
(UK assets)												
Equity capital and reinvested earnings												
Ordinary share capital and reinvested earnings	CVWF	570.6	565.7	600.4	646.1	636.6	689.5	718.9	816.8	966.8	909.6	976.5
Holdings of property	HCHP	15.7	16.5	18.9	24.6	30.6	37.3	43.5	48.9	55.3	61.4	66.4
Total equity capital and reinvested earnings	CGMO	586.3	582.2	619.3	670.7	667.2	726.8	762.4	865.7	1 022.1	971.0	1 042.9
Other capital												
Claims on affiliated enterprises												
Debt securities issued by affiliated enterprises	CVWG	28.1	31.0	31.8	31.9	15.4	18.0	17.8	17.8	21.6	30.8	32.0
Other claims on affiliated enterprises												
Inter-company balance	CVOK	80.7	88.8	103.1	105.2	131.7	137.4	132.3	176.2	251.6	262.3	260.6
Branch indebtedness balance	CVOP	7.9	12.4	11.4	11.1	12.8	8.2	14.8	18.2	27.2	29.7	20.7
Total claims on affiliated enterprises	CGLS	116.8	132.2	146.3	148.2	159.9	163.6	165.0	212.3	300.4	322.8	313.3
Liabilities to affiliated enterprises												
Inter-company balance	-CVOL	–79.1	–93.2	–124.6	–122.4	–144.9	–179.5	–190.2	–173.6	–248.0	–255.1	–273.9
Branch indebtedness balance	-CVOQ	–5.2	–4.2	–3.9	–5.3	–4.1	–5.0	–4.0	–4.6	–5.7	–5.0	–3.7
Total liabilities to affiliated enterprises	-HHDJ	–84.3	–97.4	–128.4	–127.7	–149.0	–184.5	–194.2	–178.2	–253.8	–260.2	–277.6
Total other capital assets	HBUW	32.5	34.8	17.9	20.5	10.9	–20.9	–29.3	34.1	46.7	62.6	35.7
Total	HBWD	**618.8**	**616.9**	**637.2**	**691.1**	**678.1**	**705.9**	**733.1**	**899.8**	**1 068.7**	**1 033.6**	**1 078.5**
Direct investment in the UK												
(UK liabilities)												
Equity capital and reinvested earnings												
Share capital and reinvested earnings												
Quoted share capital and reinvested earnings[2]	CVVB	–	–	20.7	25.8	35.6	73.6	38.9	32.9	30.8	14.5	37.9
Unquoted share capital and reinvested earnings	CVVC	227.1	245.6	192.6	204.0	214.5	276.8	374.0	438.1	490.9	485.6	506.2
Total share capital and reinvested earnings	HBUX	227.1	245.6	213.3	229.8	250.1	350.4	412.9	471.0	521.7	500.1	544.1
Holdings of UK property	HCQM	13.5	14.1	15.9	15.9	17.8	18.4	20.2	24.8	24.0	24.5	26.5
Total equity capital and reinvested earnings	HBUY	240.6	259.7	229.2	245.7	267.9	368.7	433.1	495.8	545.7	524.7	570.7
Other capital												
Liabilities to direct investors												
Debt securities issued by affiliated enterprises	CVVD	11.0	17.5	17.3	16.0	20.4	28.3	38.6	33.1	40.2	43.6	42.3
Other liabilities to direct investors												
Inter-company balance	CVVJ	103.8	133.1	147.0	142.2	147.6	165.7	166.6	150.4	160.1	144.2	143.7
Branch indebtedness balance	CVVM	8.5	9.4	8.7	10.7	8.5	8.5	16.0	9.9	11.7	17.5	17.9
Total liabilities to direct investors	HBVB	123.2	160.0	173.0	168.9	176.5	202.5	221.2	193.5	212.0	205.4	203.9
Claims on direct investors												
Inter-company balance	-CVVI	–51.3	–53.4	–60.5	–55.6	–58.6	–72.7	–73.0	–74.8	–94.8	–77.0	–80.4
Branch indebtedness balance	-CVVL	–2.1	–2.9	–1.1	–3.5	–2.4	–4.3	–3.9	–0.7	–2.5	–0.8	–1.2
Total claims on direct investors	-HBVA	–53.4	–56.3	–61.6	–59.0	–61.0	–77.0	–76.9	–75.5	–97.3	–77.7	–81.6
Total other capital liabilities	HBVC	69.8	103.7	111.4	109.9	115.5	125.5	144.2	118.0	114.7	127.6	122.3
Total	HBWI	**310.4**	**363.5**	**340.6**	**355.5**	**383.3**	**494.2**	**577.3**	**613.8**	**660.4**	**652.3**	**692.9**
Net international investment position												
(UK assets less UK liabilities)												
Equity capital												
Ordinary share capital and reinvested earnings	LTNM	343.5	320.0	387.1	416.3	386.5	339.1	306.0	345.8	445.1	409.5	432.3
Holdings of property	LTNN	2.2	2.4	3.0	8.7	12.8	18.9	23.3	24.1	31.3	36.9	39.9
Total equity capital and reinvested earnings	HBSH	345.7	322.4	390.1	425.0	399.3	358.1	329.3	369.8	476.4	446.4	472.2
Total other capital	CGKF	–37.3	–69.0	–93.5	–89.4	–104.6	–146.4	–173.5	–83.9	–68.0	–65.0	–86.6
Total	HBWQ	**308.4**	**253.5**	**296.6**	**335.6**	**294.7**	**211.7**	**155.8**	**285.9**	**408.4**	**381.3**	**385.6**

1 The latest year's data for foreign direct investment are provisional as these figures are subject to annual benchmarking.
2 Prior to 2002 holdings of quoted share capital were included in series CVVC

8.4 Direct investment[1] Sector analysis

Balance sheets valued at end of year

£ billion

		2000	2001	2002	2003	2004	2005	2006	2007	2008	2009	2010
Direct investment abroad (UK assets)												
By:												
Monetary financial institutions	CVKH	18.1	25.5	27.7	27.6	39.1	47.5	51.7	56.6	66.0	85.2	84.4
Insurance companies	DPYH	24.3	22.8	22.0	24.9	27.1	27.7	38.8	47.1	56.1	59.9	65.9
Other financial intermediaries	CVWH	34.9	37.8	42.0	44.2	32.0	32.2	35.8	68.5	72.9	75.4	82.9
Private non-financial corporations	CVLX	527.9	515.8	527.5	569.9	549.4	561.9	564.5	679.8	821.0	755.5	782.6
Public corporations	CVOF	1.7	0.8	1.5	1.4	1.7	0.8	0.3	0.4	0.2	–	0.1
Household sector[2]	AQHH	12.0	14.3	16.5	23.2	28.7	35.7	41.9	47.3	52.5	57.6	62.7
Total	HBWD	**618.8**	**616.9**	**637.2**	**691.1**	**678.1**	**705.9**	**733.1**	**899.8**	**1 068.7**	**1 033.6**	**1 078.5**
Direct investment in the UK (UK liabilities)												
In:												
Monetary financial institutions	CVJW	26.0	27.2	28.1	30.1	34.2	38.6	41.9	45.0	53.7	57.4	59.9
Insurance companies	CVSM	11.7	13.0	14.1	19.4	18.8	17.5	25.0	21.6	24.1	17.4	18.1
Other financial intermediaries												
Securities dealers	CVTC	9.5	11.0	11.9	12.4	14.3	18.3	15.9	23.0	28.5	42.6	46.1
Other	CVTS	15.8	27.3	29.1	30.3	31.9	26.3	46.4	57.6	36.0	39.5	40.2
Total other financial intermediaries	CVUI	25.2	38.3	41.0	42.7	46.2	44.6	62.4	80.6	64.4	82.1	86.3
Private non-financial corporations	CVKW	247.4	284.9	257.3	263.3	284.1	393.6	448.0	466.8	518.2	495.4	528.7
Total	HBWI	**310.4**	**363.5**	**340.6**	**355.5**	**383.3**	**494.2**	**577.3**	**613.8**	**660.4**	**652.3**	**692.9**
Net international investment position (UK assets less UK liabilities)												
Monetary financial institutions	LTNO	–8.0	–1.7	–0.5	–2.5	4.9	8.9	9.9	11.6	12.3	27.8	24.5
Insurance companies	LTNP	12.6	9.8	7.9	5.4	8.3	10.2	13.7	25.6	32.1	42.5	47.7
Other financial intermediares	LTNQ	9.7	–0.5	1.0	1.4	–14.2	–12.4	–26.5	–12.1	8.4	–6.6	–3.4
Private non-financial corporations	LTNR	280.4	230.8	270.2	306.6	265.2	168.3	116.5	213.1	302.8	260.0	253.9
Public corporations	CVOF	1.7	0.8	1.5	1.4	1.7	0.8	0.3	0.4	0.2	–	0.1
Household sector[2]	AQHH	12.0	14.3	16.5	23.2	28.7	35.7	41.9	47.3	52.5	57.6	62.7
Total	HBWQ	**308.4**	**253.5**	**296.6**	**335.6**	**294.7**	**211.7**	**155.8**	**285.9**	**408.4**	**381.3**	**385.6**

1 The latest year's data for foreign direct investment are provisional as these figures are subject to annual benchmarking.
2 The household sector includes non-profit institutions serving households.

8.5 Portfolio investment
Balance sheets valued at end of year

£ billion

		2000	2001	2002	2003	2004	2005	2006	2007	2008	2009	2010
Portfolio investment abroad (UK assets)												
Investment in equity securities (shares) by:												
Monetary financial institutions	VTWF	19.7	14.3	2.7	20.8	53.0	86.2	109.2	127.0	41.7	49.7	63.5
Central Government	LOER	–	–	–	–	–	0.2	0.2	0.2	0.2	0.2	0.2
Insurance companies and pension funds												
Insurance companies[1]	CGPB	100.7	106.2	82.1	79.1	91.4	132.0	150.2	178.6	149.9	169.0	188.1
Self-administered pension funds	ZPOR	135.5	127.9	104.4	125.7	140.3	192.1	202.0	178.6	136.5	164.6	181.4
Total insurance companies and pension funds	CGPV	236.2	234.1	186.5	204.9	231.7	324.0	352.1	357.2	286.4	333.5	369.6
Other financial intermediaries												
Securities dealers	HCEA	49.3	46.8	22.9	32.4	46.3	33.9	31.3	50.2	60.7	62.9	63.3
Unit and Investment Trusts	CGSN	99.1	88.0	77.3	94.1	100.0	131.0	151.6	162.9	134.6	177.2	205.7
Other	CGTV	–	–	–	–	–	–	–	1.0	1.0	1.0	1.0
Total other financial intermediaries	HDIG	148.4	134.8	100.2	126.5	146.2	164.9	182.9	214.1	196.3	241.2	270.1
Private non-financial corporations	XBNN	10.0	8.9	6.5	7.8	7.9	9.3	11.6	11.3	9.1	10.3	11.3
Household sector[2]	HFLX	15.0	12.5	10.0	12.0	16.5	32.6	37.3	39.1	31.5	31.5	29.1
Total investment in equity securities	HEPX	429.3	404.6	305.9	372.0	455.3	617.2	693.4	748.9	565.2	666.4	743.8
Investment in debt securities												
Investment in bonds and notes by:												
Monetary financial institutions	HPCO	288.7	319.6	332.3	323.1	355.0	409.1	474.5	549.5	561.5	492.8	469.3
Central Government	HQ50	–	–	–	–	–	–	–	0.1	–	0.2	0.1
Insurance companies and pension funds												
Insurance companies[1]	CGTU	39.8	55.9	62.9	64.5	77.0	80.5	103.6	114.7	141.4	165.6	170.9
Self-administered pension funds	JIRX	44.2	49.9	45.7	53.9	64.6	87.0	107.9	141.7	143.2	164.2	209.0
Total insurance companies and pension funds	HBUM	84.0	105.8	108.6	118.3	141.7	167.6	211.4	256.4	284.6	329.8	379.9
Other financial intermediaries												
Securities dealers	HCDZ	45.2	34.9	31.1	38.7	57.3	73.8	40.6	17.9	133.5	239.7	320.2
Unit and investment trusts	HBXZ	6.8	8.4	7.7	10.7	13.4	20.6	29.8	34.1	37.2	50.3	60.8
Other	HCNA	–	–	–	–	–	–	–	–	–	–	–
Total other financial intermediaries	HCOR	52.1	43.3	38.8	49.4	70.7	94.4	70.4	52.0	170.7	290.0	381.0
Private non-financial corporations	XBNK	1.6	2.0	2.2	3.5	3.7	3.0	1.3	2.0	4.7	3.4	6.5
Household sector[2]	HCJC	7.5	7.6	7.8	7.7	7.7	7.7	7.5	7.6	8.5	8.2	8.3
Total investment in bonds and notes	HEPW	433.8	478.3	489.6	502.0	578.8	681.7	765.2	867.5	1 030.0	1 124.4	1 245.2
Investment in Money Market Instruments by:												
Central government	LSPI	–	0.5	0.9	–	–	–	–	2.4	2.3	4.9	5.5
Monetary financial institutions	HHZV	34.9	42.1	34.6	42.8	37.0	39.6	42.8	53.8	57.1	65.4	65.0
Insurance companies and pension funds	HBXX	1.3	1.1	1.4	1.5	2.1	3.5	3.0	3.1	3.8	4.0	3.9
Other financial intermediaries	JXG4	3.8	6.0	5.6	7.8	8.5	7.5	10.5	7.6	4.6	7.3	7.8
Private non-financial corporations	HFBN	3.0	4.9	6.0	9.8	10.4	11.4	16.2	6.4	1.3	2.9	4.9
Total investment in Money Market Instruments	HLYR	43.0	54.5	48.5	61.9	58.0	62.0	72.5	73.3	69.1	84.5	87.1
Total investment in debt securities	HHZX	476.8	532.8	538.1	563.9	636.8	743.8	837.7	940.8	1 099.1	1 208.9	1 332.3
Total	HHZZ	**906.1**	**937.4**	**844.0**	**935.8**	**1 092.1**	**1 360.9**	**1 531.0**	**1 689.7**	**1 664.3**	**1 875.3**	**2 076.1**

1 Includes pension funds managed by insurance companies.
2 The household sector includes non-profit institutions serving households.

8.5 Portfolio investment
Balance sheets valued at end of year

continued

£ billion

		2000	2001	2002	2003	2004	2005	2006	2007	2008	2009	2010
Portfolio investment in the UK (UK liabilities)												
Investment in equity securities (shares) issued by:												
Monetary financial institutions	HBQD	6.6	5.6	3.2	4.5	4.6	5.3	7.0	11.0	8.8	14.2	17.7
Other sectors[1]	HBQE	667.1	578.5	439.5	522.6	570.1	654.0	773.8	824.8	596.7	839.4	926.8
Total investment in equity securities	HLXX	673.7	584.1	442.7	527.1	574.7	659.3	780.8	835.8	605.5	853.6	944.6
Investment in debt securities												
Investment in bonds and notes												
Issues by central government												
UK foreign currency bonds and notes	HEWE	6.5	3.3	0.9	1.6	1.5	1.7	1.5	1.5	–	–	–
Investment in British government stocks (gilts) by:												
Foreign central banks (exchange reserves)	HCCH	18.1	18.7	17.3	15.9	21.0	21.0	25.2	29.2	36.4	49.1	61.2
Other foreign residents	HEQF	37.8	37.8	38.2	48.6	61.3	88.0	108.8	129.5	167.3	175.1	248.0
Total investment in British government stocks	HEWD	55.9	56.5	55.5	64.5	82.3	109.0	134.0	158.7	203.6	224.3	309.2
Total issues by central government	HHGF	62.4	59.9	56.4	66.1	83.8	110.7	135.5	160.2	203.6	224.3	309.2
Local authorities' bonds	HHGG	–	–	–	–	–	–	–	–	–	–	–
Public corporations' bonds	HEWM	–	–	–	–	–	–	–	–	–	–	–
Issues by monetary financial Institutions												
Bonds	HMBL	39.0	41.6	51.4	68.0	83.0	105.9	119.3	139.2	158.2	180.8	179.7
European medium term notes and other medium-term paper:	HHGI	38.4	42.5	43.6	53.7	70.9	95.5	114.9	166.9	200.2	208.0	204.0
Total monetary financial institutions	HMBF	77.4	84.1	95.0	121.7	154.0	201.3	234.1	306.2	358.4	388.8	383.7
Issues by other sectors[1]	HHGJ	121.3	129.5	160.1	211.7	258.3	329.3	371.3	433.4	559.4	630.0	626.4
Total investment in bonds and notes	HLXZ	261.1	273.4	311.5	399.5	496.1	641.3	740.8	899.8	1 121.4	1 243.1	1 319.2
Investment in Money Market Instruments												
Investment in treasury bills (issued by central government)												
Sterling treasury bills	ACQJ	–	0.1	0.2	1.9	3.8	2.8	3.5	7.2	21.0	19.4	27.9
Euro treasury bills	HHNX	–	–	–	–	–	–	–	–	–	–	–
Total treasury bills	HLYU	–	0.1	0.2	1.9	3.8	2.8	3.5	7.2	21.0	19.4	27.9
Investment in certificates of deposit issued by UK monetary financial institutions	HHGM	93.3	115.4	108.9	97.8	90.1	96.2	116.7	141.2	149.4	206.4	164.5
Investment in commercial paper												
Issued by UK monetary financial Institutions	HHGP	17.7	17.7	31.4	32.8	40.6	39.9	45.2	42.5	52.9	61.4	41.5
Issued by other sectors[1]	HLYQ	21.7	22.5	30.6	23.7	22.5	22.2	16.3	19.1	29.9	21.5	25.4
Total investment in commercial paper	HHGR	39.4	40.2	62.0	56.5	63.2	62.1	61.5	61.6	82.8	82.9	66.8
Total investment in Money Market Instruments	HLYB	132.7	155.7	171.1	156.3	157.1	161.1	181.8	210.0	253.2	308.7	259.3
Total investment in debt securities	HLXY	393.8	429.1	482.6	555.8	653.2	802.4	922.6	1 109.8	1 374.7	1 551.9	1 578.5
Total	HLXW	**1 067.6**	**1 013.2**	**925.3**	**1 082.9**	**1 227.9**	**1 461.7**	**1 703.5**	**1 945.7**	**1 980.2**	**2 405.5**	**2 523.1**

1 These series relate to non-governmental sectors other than monetary financial institutions.

8.5 Portfolio investment
Balance sheets valued at end of year

continued £ billion

		2000	2001	2002	2003	2004	2005	2006	2007	2008	2009	2010
Net international investment position												
(UK assets less UK liabilities)												
Equity securities	CGNE	–244.4	–179.4	–136.8	–155.1	–119.4	–42.1	–87.5	–86.9	–40.3	–187.2	–200.8
Debt securities												
Bonds and notes	LTNS	172.7	204.9	178.1	102.5	82.7	40.4	24.4	–32.3	–91.4	–118.8	–74.0
Money market instruments	LTNT	–89.8	–101.2	–122.6	–94.4	–99.1	–99.1	–109.3	–136.7	–184.1	–224.2	–172.1
Total debt securities	CGNF	82.9	103.7	55.5	8.1	–16.4	–58.6	–84.9	–169.0	–275.6	–343.0	–246.2
Total	CGNH	**–161.5**	**–75.7**	**–81.3**	**–147.0**	**–135.8**	**–100.8**	**–172.4**	**–255.9**	**–315.9**	**–530.2**	**–447.0**

8.6 Portfolio investment
Sector analysis
Balance sheets valued at end of year

Total CGNH –161.5 –75.7 –81.3 –147.0 –135.8 –100.8 –172.4 –255.9 –315.9 –530.2 –447.0

£ billion

		2000	2001	2002	2003	2004	2005	2006	2007	2008	2009	2010
Portfolio investment abroad												
(UK assets)												
Investment by:												
Monetary financial institutions	HHGQ	343.2	376.0	369.7	386.7	445.0	534.8	626.5	730.4	660.4	607.9	597.8
Central government	LOFC	–	0.5	0.9	–	–	0.2	0.2	2.6	2.5	5.3	5.8
Insurance companies and pension funds	HHHH	321.4	341.0	296.5	324.7	375.4	495.1	566.6	616.7	574.8	667.4	753.4
Other financial intermediaries	HHNH	204.3	184.0	144.5	183.7	225.5	266.8	263.8	273.6	371.6	538.4	658.9
Private non-financial corporations	AIMH	14.7	15.8	14.6	21.0	21.9	23.7	29.2	19.7	15.1	16.7	22.8
Household sector[1]	AINA	22.4	20.2	17.7	19.7	24.2	40.3	44.8	46.7	40.0	39.6	37.4
Total	HHZZ	**906.1**	**937.4**	**844.0**	**935.8**	**1 092.1**	**1 360.9**	**1 531.0**	**1 689.7**	**1 664.3**	**1 875.3**	**2 076.1**
Portfolio investment in the UK												
(UK liabilities)												
Investment in securities issued by:												
Monetary financial institutions	CGPC	195.0	222.8	238.6	256.8	289.3	342.7	403.1	500.9	569.5	670.9	607.4
Central government	HHGS	62.4	60.0	56.5	68.0	87.6	113.4	139.0	167.4	224.6	243.7	337.1
Local authorities	HHGG	–	–	–	–	–	–	–	–	–	–	–
Public corporations	HEWM	–	–	–	–	–	–	–	–	–	–	–
Other sectors	CGPG	810.2	730.5	630.2	758.0	851.0	1 005.5	1 161.4	1 277.4	1 186.0	1 490.9	1 578.6
Total	HLXW	**1 067.6**	**1 013.2**	**925.3**	**1 082.9**	**1 227.9**	**1 461.7**	**1 703.5**	**1 945.7**	**1 980.2**	**2 405.5**	**2 523.1**
Net international investment position												
(UK assets less UK liabilities)												
Monetary financial institutions	LTNU	148.3	153.2	131.1	129.8	155.7	192.1	223.4	229.5	90.8	–63.0	–9.6
Central government	ZPOH	–62.4	–59.5	–55.6	–68.0	–87.6	–113.3	–138.8	–164.7	–222.2	–238.4	–331.3
Local authorities	HHGG	–	–	–	–	–	–	–	–	–	–	–
Public corporations	-HEWM	–	–	–	–	–	–	–	–	–	–	–
Other sectors	LTNV	–247.3	–169.5	–156.7	–208.8	–203.9	–179.6	–257.1	–320.7	–184.6	–228.7	–106.1
Total	CGNH	**–161.5**	**–75.7**	**–81.3**	**–147.0**	**–135.8**	**–100.8**	**–172.4**	**–255.9**	**–315.9**	**–530.2**	**–447.0**

1 The household sector includes non-profit institutions serving households.

8.7 Other investment

Balance sheets valued at end of year

£ billion

		2000	2001	2002	2003	2004	2005	2006	2007	2008	2009	2010
Other investment abroad (UK assets)												
Trade credit												
Long-term												
Central government	ZPOC	–	–	–	–	–	–	–	–	–	–	–
Other sectors[1]	HCLK	–	–	–	–	–	–	–	–	–	–	–
Total long-term trade credit	HHGU	–	–	–	–	–	–	–	–	–	–	–
Short-term												
Other sectors[1]	HLXU	0.4	0.1	0.4	1.0	0.6	–0.7	0.6	0.7	0.8	0.7	0.7
Total trade credit	HLXP	0.4	0.1	0.4	1.0	0.6	–0.7	0.6	0.7	0.8	0.7	0.7
Loans												
Long-term												
Bank loans under ECGD[2] guarantee	HCFQ	4.8	5.1	3.8	3.7	3.7	4.1	3.3	3.2	4.4	4.1	4.5
Inter-government loans by the UK and other central government assets	HCFN	0.2	0.2	0.2	0.2	0.2	0.2	0.1	0.1	0.1	–	–
Loans by Commonwealth Development Corporation (public corporations)	HEWZ	0.5	0.4	0.4	0.4	0.3	0.3	0.3	0.3	0.3	0.3	0.3
Loans by the ECGD[2]	CY94	2.4	2.6	2.4	2.4	2.6	2.2	1.1	1.0	1.0	0.9	0.8
Loans by specialist leasing companies[1]	HGIH	–	–	–	–	–	–	–	–	–	–	–
Total long-term loans	HFAX	8.0	8.3	6.8	6.6	6.8	6.8	4.9	4.6	5.8	5.3	5.6
Short-term												
By monetary financial institutions												
Sterling loans	JXG7	27.5	32.2	37.4	40.2	47.4	66.9	87.7	113.1	117.8	96.6	103.4
Foreign currency loans	JXG8	252.4	290.9	290.9	358.3	448.9	575.1	621.3	842.8	1 010.0	806.9	867.9
Total monetary financial institutions	ZPOM	279.9	323.0	328.4	398.4	496.3	642.0	709.1	955.9	1 127.8	903.5	971.2
By other sectors	HLXI	0.5	0.5	0.5	0.5	0.5	0.5	0.5	0.5	1.3	0.5	0.5
Total short-term loans	VTUM	280.5	323.6	328.9	399.0	496.9	642.6	709.6	956.4	1 129.1	904.0	971.8
Total loans	HLXQ	288.5	331.9	335.7	405.6	503.7	649.4	714.5	961.1	1 134.8	909.4	977.4
Currency and deposits												
Foreign notes and coin												
Monetary financial institutions	TAAF	0.1	0.1	0.1	0.1	0.1	0.1	0.2	0.2	0.4	0.3	0.2
Other sectors[1]	CGML	0.4	0.4	0.4	0.5	0.5	0.5	0.5	0.6	0.6	0.5	0.5
Total foreign notes and coin	HEOX	0.5	0.5	0.5	0.6	0.6	0.6	0.7	0.8	0.9	0.8	0.7
Deposits abroad by UK residents												
Deposits by monetary financial institutions												
Sterling deposits	JXG9	97.4	104.7	96.6	114.9	112.0	146.1	193.3	304.8	279.1	210.4	185.1
Foreign currency deposits	JXH2	678.2	700.6	746.5	806.6	894.9	1 053.5	1 092.6	1 409.4	1 813.5	1 568.9	1 691.2
Total monetary financial institutions	VTWL	775.6	805.3	843.0	921.4	1 006.9	1 199.7	1 286.0	1 714.1	2 092.6	1 779.3	1 876.3
Deposits by securities dealers	HGUX	206.1	261.9	242.0	289.7	315.7	497.4	504.8	555.7	354.8	331.3	387.5
Deposits by other UK residents[1]	HHGW	98.9	112.3	112.4	183.9	279.3	356.5	397.6	497.1	577.5	474.2	528.3
Total deposits abroad	HBXS	1 080.6	1 179.5	1 197.4	1 395.0	1 602.0	2 053.5	2 188.3	2 767.0	3 024.9	2 584.7	2 792.1
Total currency and deposits	HBVS	1 081.1	1 180.0	1 198.0	1 395.6	1 602.6	2 054.1	2 189.0	2 767.7	3 025.9	2 585.5	2 792.7

1 These series relate to non-governmental sectors other than monetary financial institutions.
2 Export Credits Guarantee Department

8.7 Other investment
Balance sheets valued at end of year

continued

£ billion

		2000	2001	2002	2003	2004	2005	2006	2007	2008	2009	2010
Other investment abroad - *continued*												
(UK assets)												
Other assets												
Central government assets												
Central government subscriptions to international organisations												
International Development Association	HEXS	5.0	5.2	5.5	5.6	5.8	6.2	6.6	7.2	7.9	8.7	9.9
Regional development banks	HEXW	1.1	1.1	1.2	1.3	1.3	1.4	1.5	1.5	1.7	1.9	2.0
European Investment Bank (EIB)	HEXX	0.4	0.4	0.4	0.4	0.4	0.4	0.4	0.4	0.4	0.4	0.4
Other subscriptions	HEXZ	0.4	0.4	0.4	0.4	0.5	0.5	0.7	0.9	0.9	1.0	1.0
Total central government subscriptions	HLXO	6.8	7.1	7.5	7.7	8.0	8.5	9.2	10.0	11.0	12.0	13.3
Other long-term central government assets	XBJL	–	–	–	–	–	–	–	–	–	–	–
Other short-term central government assets	LOEM	1.8	1.7	2.3	2.5	1.9	2.4	2.6	3.0	5.6	6.1	6.3
Total central government	LOET	8.6	8.8	9.8	10.2	10.0	10.9	11.9	13.1	16.6	18.2	19.6
Other sectors assets												
Long-term assets[1]	HLXM	–	–	–	–	–	–	–	–	–	–	–
Short-term assets												
Public corporations assets abroad	HGJM	–	–	–	–	–	–	–	–	–	–	–
Other[1]	HHGY	1.1	1.1	1.4	1.3	1.1	1.1	0.6	1.9	2.5	3.3	3.9
Total short-term assets	HLXJ	1.1	1.1	1.4	1.3	1.1	1.1	0.6	1.9	2.5	3.3	3.9
Total other sectors	HLXN	1.1	1.1	1.4	1.3	1.1	1.1	0.6	1.9	2.5	3.3	3.9
Total other assets	HLXS	9.7	10.0	11.2	11.5	11.0	12.0	12.5	15.0	19.1	21.4	23.5
Total	HLXV	**1 379.7**	**1 521.9**	**1 545.2**	**1 813.7**	**2 118.0**	**2 714.8**	**2 916.6**	**3 744.5**	**4 180.6**	**3 517.1**	**3 794.3**

8.7 Other investment
Balance sheets valued at end of year

continued

£ billion

		2000	2001	2002	2003	2004	2005	2006	2007	2008	2009	2010
Other investment in the UK (UK liabilities)												
Trade credit												
Long-term[1]	HBWC	–	–	–	–	–	–	–	–	–	–	–
Short-term[1]	HCGB	1.1	1.1	1.0	0.9	0.9	1.0	0.8	0.8	1.1	1.0	1.0
Total trade credit	HLYL	1.1	1.1	1.0	0.9	0.9	1.0	0.8	0.8	1.1	1.0	1.0
Loans												
Long-term loans to:												
Central government	HHGZ	0.6	0.5	0.4	0.2	0.1	0.1	–	–	–	–	–
Local authorities	HHHA	0.8	0.8	0.9	1.1	1.7	1.9	2.1	2.1	2.5	3.0	3.2
Public corporations	HHHB	–	–	–	–	0.4	0.4	0.4	0.4	0.4	0.4	0.4
Other[1]	AQBX	–	–	–	–	–	–	–	–	–	–	–
Total long-term loans	HHHC	1.4	1.3	1.2	1.3	2.3	2.4	2.5	2.5	2.9	3.4	3.6
Short-term loans to:												
Central government	HHHD	–	–	–	–	–	–	–	–	–	–	–
Local authorities	HHHE	–	–	–	–	–	–	–	–	–	–	–
Securities dealers	HHHF	314.1	388.6	356.1	382.5	454.5	693.1	614.1	703.9	588.0	556.6	660.0
Other[1]	HHHG	55.5	82.8	83.7	130.6	184.0	195.1	259.0	246.3	314.3	240.2	298.5
Total short-term loans	HHHJ	369.6	471.3	439.7	513.1	638.5	888.1	873.1	950.2	902.3	796.9	958.6
Total loans	HLYI	371.0	472.6	441.0	514.4	640.8	890.5	875.6	952.7	905.2	800.3	962.2
Currency and deposits												
Sterling notes and coin												
Notes (issued by Bank of England)	HLVG	1.0	1.0	1.1	1.1	1.2	1.3	1.4	1.4	1.4	1.2	1.3
Coins (issued by central government)	HLVH	0.1	0.1	0.1	0.1	0.1	0.1	0.2	0.2	0.2	0.1	0.1
Total notes and coin	APME	1.1	1.1	1.2	1.3	1.4	1.4	1.5	1.5	1.5	1.4	1.4
Deposits from abroad with UK residents												
Deposits with monetary financial institutions												
Sterling deposits	JXH3	204.6	220.5	232.9	257.1	285.3	338.2	396.5	612.4	565.6	501.2	483.7
Foreign currency deposits	JXH4	1 060.0	1 152.4	1 206.5	1 348.1	1 570.0	1 861.6	1 974.2	2 531.0	3 031.5	2 475.1	2 584.9
Total deposits with UK monetary financial institutions	HDKG	1 264.6	1 372.9	1 439.4	1 605.3	1 855.2	2 199.8	2 370.7	3 143.4	3 597.2	2 976.3	3 068.6
Deposit liabilities of UK central government	HEYH	1.8	1.7	1.6	1.9	1.0	0.9	1.4	1.1	0.8	1.0	1.3
Total deposits from abroad with UK residents	HBYA	1 266.4	1 374.5	1 441.0	1 607.1	1 856.2	2 200.7	2 372.1	3 144.5	3 598.0	2 977.3	3 070.0
Total currency and deposits	HLVI	1 267.5	1 375.6	1 442.2	1 608.4	1 857.6	2 202.1	2 373.6	3 146.1	3 599.5	2 978.7	3 071.4
Other liabilities												
Long-term												
Net equity of foreign households in life assurance reserves and pension funds	VTUE	0.2	0.2	0.2	0.2	0.2	0.2	0.2	0.2	0.2	0.2	0.2
Prepayments of insurance premiums and reserves for oustanding claims	NQLR	10.8	10.7	12.6	10.2	11.5	14.2	18.6	14.4	10.5	10.2	10.4
Total long-term liabilities[1]	VTUF	11.0	10.9	12.9	10.4	11.7	14.4	18.8	14.6	10.7	10.4	10.6
Short-term	HBMV	1.1	1.6	1.0	1.0	0.9	1.0	1.1	1.3	1.5	1.6	2.4
Total other liabilities	HLYM	12.0	12.5	13.8	11.4	12.6	15.5	19.9	16.0	12.2	12.0	13.0
Total	HLYD	**1 651.6**	**1 861.9**	**1 898.0**	**2 135.2**	**2 511.8**	**3 109.0**	**3 270.0**	**4 115.6**	**4 518.1**	**3 792.0**	**4 047.6**

1 These series relate to non-governmental sectors other than monetary financial institutions.

8.7 Other investment

Balance sheets valued at end of year

continued

£ billion

		2000	2001	2002	2003	2004	2005	2006	2007	2008	2009	2010
Net international investment position												
(UK assets less UK liabilities)												
Trade credit	LTNW	–0.7	–1.0	–0.6	0.1	–0.2	–1.7	–0.2	–0.1	–0.4	–0.3	–0.4
Loans	LTNX	–82.5	–140.7	–105.3	–108.8	–137.1	–241.1	–161.1	8.4	229.6	109.1	15.2
Currency and deposits	LTNY	–186.5	–195.7	–244.2	–212.8	–254.9	–148.0	–184.6	–378.3	–573.7	–393.2	–278.7
Other	LTNZ	–2.3	–2.5	–2.7	0.1	–1.6	–3.5	–7.4	–1.0	6.9	9.4	10.5
Total	CGNG	**–271.9**	**–339.9**	**–352.8**	**–321.5**	**–393.9**	**–394.2**	**–353.4**	**–371.0**	**–337.5**	**–274.9**	**–253.4**

8.8 Other investment

Sector analysis

Balance sheets valued at end of year

£ billion

		2000	2001	2002	2003	2004	2005	2006	2007	2008	2009	2010
Other investment abroad												
(UK assets)												
Investment by:												
Monetary financial institutions	VTXD	1 060.5	1 133.5	1 175.3	1 323.6	1 507.1	1 845.9	1 998.5	2 673.4	3 225.2	2 687.2	2 852.2
Central government	CGEN	8.9	9.1	10.0	10.4	10.1	11.0	12.1	13.2	16.7	18.2	19.7
Public corporations	CGEO	2.9	3.0	2.8	2.8	2.9	2.5	1.4	1.3	1.3	1.2	1.0
Other sectors	CGGH	307.4	376.3	357.1	476.8	597.8	855.3	904.6	1 056.6	937.4	810.5	921.4
Total	HLXV	**1 379.7**	**1 521.9**	**1 545.2**	**1 813.7**	**2 118.0**	**2 714.8**	**2 916.6**	**3 744.5**	**4 180.6**	**3 517.1**	**3 794.3**
Other investment in the UK												
(UK liabilities)												
Investment in:												
Monetary financial institutions	CGHB	1 265.6	1 373.9	1 440.5	1 606.4	1 856.4	2 201.0	2 372.0	3 144.8	3 598.6	2 977.5	3 069.9
Central government	CGHG	3.2	3.4	2.6	2.8	1.7	1.8	2.3	2.2	2.1	2.4	3.5
Local authorities	CGHX	0.8	0.8	0.9	1.1	1.7	1.9	2.1	2.1	2.5	3.0	3.2
Public corporations	ZPOX	–	–	–	–	0.5	0.4	0.4	0.4	0.4	0.4	0.4
Other sectors	CGNC	382.1	483.8	454.1	524.8	651.5	903.9	893.2	966.0	914.5	808.7	970.6
Total	HLYD	**1 651.6**	**1 861.9**	**1 898.0**	**2 135.2**	**2 511.8**	**3 109.0**	**3 270.0**	**4 115.6**	**4 518.1**	**3 792.0**	**4 047.6**
Net international investment position												
(UK assets less UK liabilities)												
Monetary financial institutions	LTOC	–205.1	–240.3	–265.1	–282.8	–349.4	–355.1	–373.6	–471.4	–373.4	–290.3	–217.7
Central government	LTOD	5.7	5.7	7.4	7.6	8.4	9.3	9.8	11.0	14.6	15.8	16.1
Local authorities	-CGHX	–0.8	–0.8	–0.9	–1.1	–1.7	–1.9	–2.1	–2.1	–2.5	–3.0	–3.2
Public corporations	LTOE	2.9	3.0	2.8	2.8	2.5	2.1	1.0	0.9	0.9	0.8	0.6
Other sectors	LTOF	–74.6	–107.4	–96.9	–48.0	–53.6	–48.6	11.5	90.5	22.9	1.8	–49.2
Total	CGNG	**–271.9**	**–339.9**	**–352.8**	**–321.5**	**–393.9**	**–394.2**	**–353.4**	**–371.0**	**–337.5**	**–274.9**	**–253.4**

8.9 Reserve assets Central government sector

Balance sheets valued at end of year

£ billion

		2000	2001	2002	2003	2004	2005	2006	2007	2008	2009	2010
Monetary gold	HCGD	2.9	2.2	2.1	2.3	2.3	3.0	3.2	4.2	6.0	6.8	9.1
Special drawing rights	HCGE	0.2	0.2	0.2	0.2	0.2	0.2	0.2	0.2	0.3	8.9	9.1
Reserve position in the Fund	HCGF	2.9	3.5	3.8	3.5	2.9	1.0	0.7	0.5	1.6	2.1	3.2
Foreign exchange												
Currency and deposits												
With central banks	CGDE	0.1	0.1	0.2	0.1	0.1	0.1	0.1	0.1	0.4	0.3	0.3
With other banks	CGDF	3.7	2.8	1.9	1.3	0.3	0.8	0.4	0.4	0.4	0.3	0.3
Total currency and deposits	CGDD	3.7	2.9	2.1	1.4	0.4	1.0	0.5	0.5	0.9	0.7	0.6
Securities												
Bonds and notes	CGDH	16.7	14.4	16.8	16.2	17.1	17.5	15.3	18.2	24.4	21.0	27.0
Money market instruments	CGDL	2.3	2.2	0.2	0.2	0.3	1.7	3.0	3.1	3.1	0.7	0.6
Total securities	CGDG	19.0	16.6	17.0	16.4	17.4	19.2	18.3	21.3	27.5	21.7	27.6
Total foreign exchange	HCGG	22.7	19.4	19.1	17.7	17.8	20.2	18.8	21.7	28.4	22.3	28.2
Other claims	CGDM	0.1	0.4	0.2	–	0.1	0.4	–	0.1	–	–	0.1
Total	LTEB	**28.8**	**25.6**	**25.5**	**23.8**	**23.2**	**24.7**	**22.9**	**26.7**	**36.3**	**40.1**	**49.7**

8.10 External debt statement
End of period

£ billion

		2000	2001	2002	2003	2004	2005	2006	2007	2008	2009	2010
General Government												
Short-term												
Money market instruments	HLYU	–	0.1	0.2	1.9	3.8	2.8	3.5	7.2	21.0	19.4	27.9
Currency and deposits	HLVH	0.1	0.1	0.1	0.1	0.1	0.1	0.2	0.2	0.2	0.1	0.1
Other liabilities	VTZZ	1.8	1.7	1.6	1.9	1.0	0.9	1.4	1.1	0.8	1.0	1.3
Total short-term	ZAVF	2.0	1.9	1.9	3.9	4.9	3.8	5.1	8.5	22.0	20.6	29.4
Long-term												
Bonds and notes												
issued by central government	HHGF	62.4	59.9	56.4	66.1	83.8	110.7	135.5	160.2	203.6	224.3	309.2
Loans												
to central government	HHGZ	0.6	0.5	0.4	0.2	0.1	0.1	–	–	–	–	–
to local authorities	HHHA	0.8	0.8	0.9	1.1	1.7	1.9	2.1	2.1	2.5	3.0	3.2
Total long-term	ZAVG	63.7	61.2	57.6	67.4	85.7	112.6	137.6	162.2	206.1	227.3	312.4
Total General Government liabilities	ZAVH	65.7	63.0	59.5	71.4	90.6	116.4	142.6	170.7	228.1	247.9	341.7
Monetary Authorities												
Short-term												
Money market instruments	VTZS	0.2	1.4	2.8	3.5	3.4	3.6	2.4	2.5	3.3	2.6	2.6
Currency and deposits	VTZT	5.2	3.8	5.5	6.8	9.9	13.0	14.6	21.6	36.8	13.8	17.3
Total short-term	VTZY	5.5	5.2	8.3	10.3	13.3	16.5	16.9	24.0	40.2	16.4	20.0
Long-term												
Bonds and notes	VTZU	–	–	–	–	–	–	–	–	–	–	–
Total long-term	VTZV	–	–	–	–	–	–	–	–	–	–	–
Total Monetary Authorities liabilities	VTZW	5.5	5.2	8.3	10.3	13.3	16.5	16.9	24.0	40.2	16.4	20.0
Monetary financial institutions												
Short-term												
Money market instruments	ZAUX	110.7	131.7	137.5	127.1	127.4	132.6	159.6	181.2	199.0	265.2	203.4
Currency and deposits	JXI3	1 259.3	1 369.0	1 433.9	1 598.5	1 845.3	2 186.8	2 356.1	3 121.9	3 560.3	2 962.5	3 051.3
Total short-term	ZAVI	1 370.0	1 500.7	1 571.4	1 725.6	1 972.7	2 319.4	2 515.7	3 303.1	3 759.3	3 227.7	3 254.6
Long-term												
Bonds and notes	HMBF	77.4	84.1	95.0	121.7	154.0	201.3	234.1	306.2	358.4	388.8	383.7
Total long-term	ZPOK	77.4	84.1	95.0	121.7	154.0	201.3	234.1	306.2	358.4	388.8	383.7
Total monetary financial institutions liabilities	ZAVA	1 447.4	1 584.8	1 666.5	1 847.3	2 126.7	2 520.7	2 749.8	3 609.3	4 117.7	3 616.5	3 638.3
Other sectors												
Short-term												
Money market instruments	HLYQ	21.7	22.5	30.6	23.7	22.5	22.2	16.3	19.1	29.9	21.5	25.4
Loans	ZLBY	369.6	471.3	439.7	513.1	638.5	888.1	873.1	950.2	902.3	796.9	958.6
Trade credits	HCGB	1.1	1.1	1.0	0.9	0.9	1.0	0.8	0.8	1.1	1.0	1.0
Other liabilities	LSYR	1.1	1.6	1.0	1.0	0.9	1.0	1.1	1.3	1.5	1.6	2.4
Total short-term liabilities	ZAVB	393.5	496.6	472.3	538.8	662.7	912.3	891.3	971.5	934.9	821.0	987.4
Long-term												
Bond and notes	HHGJ	121.3	129.5	160.1	211.7	258.3	329.3	371.3	433.4	559.4	630.0	626.4
Loans	ZLBZ	–	–	–	–	0.4	0.4	0.4	0.4	0.4	0.4	0.4
Trade credits	HBWC	–	–	–	–	–	–	–	–	–	–	–
Other liabilities	VTUF	11.0	10.9	12.9	10.4	11.7	14.4	18.8	14.6	10.7	10.4	10.6
Total long-term liabilities	ZAUQ	132.3	140.3	173.0	222.1	270.5	344.2	390.5	448.5	570.5	640.8	637.4
Total other sectors liabilities	ZAUR	525.8	636.9	645.3	760.9	933.2	1 256.5	1 281.8	1 420.0	1 505.4	1 461.8	1 624.8
Direct investment												
Debt liabilities to affiliated enterprises	HHDJ	84.3	97.4	128.4	127.7	149.0	184.5	194.2	178.2	253.8	260.2	277.6
Debt liabilities to direct investors	HBVB	123.2	160.0	173.0	168.9	176.5	202.5	221.2	193.5	212.0	205.4	203.9
Total liabilities to direct investors	ZAUY	207.5	257.4	301.4	296.6	325.5	387.0	415.4	371.6	465.7	465.5	481.5
GROSS EXTERNAL DEBT	ZAUS	**2 251.9**	**2 547.4**	**2 681.0**	**2 986.5**	**3 489.3**	**4 297.1**	**4 606.6**	**5 595.6**	**6 357.1**	**5 808.2**	**6 106.3**

FD Financial derivatives[1]

Balance sheets valued at end of year

£ billion

		2000	2001	2002	2003	2004	2005	2006	2007	2008	2009	2010
Financial derivatives assets												
UK banks												
Sterling	ZPNP	49.8	43.5	56.7	44.1	46.1	51.3	62.9	84.2	180.2	112.0	157.6
Foreign currency	ZPNQ	340.6	481.0	626.2	579.3	663.3	768.8	790.9	1 294.0	3 859.9	2 064.4	2 094.5
Total UK banks	ZPNA	390.5	524.5	682.8	623.4	709.4	820.1	853.7	1 378.1	4 040.2	2 176.4	2 252.1
Other Financial Intermediaries												
UK securities dealers												
Sterling	RUVI	3.2	13.2	16.2	10.6	11.5	15.0	28.6	38.6	83.7	35.7	..
Foreign currency	RUVJ	52.6	51.9	70.9	144.0	104.7	186.5	234.5	400.6	849.4	456.9	..
Total UK securities dealers	KN8A	55.7	65.1	87.1	154.7	116.2	201.5	263.1	439.2	933.1	492.6	710.7
Other[2]	D4AG	0.5	0.6	0.7	1.1	0.4	0.5	0.2	1.9	2.6	2.6	..
Total Other Financial Intermediaries	D4AH	56.2	65.7	87.8	155.8	116.6	202.1	263.3	441.1	935.7	495.2	..
Insurance companies and pension funds												
Insurance companies[3]	D4AE	0.7	1.0	0.8	0.2	–	–	–	0.3	2.1	2.3	..
Pension funds[4]	GOJU	0.8	0.8	0.7	0.6	3.0	2.7	6.0	8.7	5.8	20.5	..
Total insurance companies and pension funds	D4AF	1.5	1.7	1.5	0.8	3.0	2.6	6.0	8.9	8.0	22.8	..
Total UK assets	ZPNC	448.2	592.0	772.1	780.0	828.9	1 024.8	1 123.0	1 828.2	4 983.8	2 694.4	..
Financial derivative liabilities												
UK banks												
Sterling	ZPNR	48.2	43.8	57.1	32.4	36.3	66.3	62.4	82.3	258.2	124.8	161.9
Foreign currency	ZPNS	351.8	485.8	631.5	600.0	678.8	764.8	828.1	1 309.9	3 657.0	1 972.0	2 032.3
Total UK banks	ZPNB	400.0	529.6	688.7	632.4	715.0	831.1	890.5	1 392.2	3 915.3	2 096.8	2 194.2
Other Financial Intermediaries												
UK securities dealers												
Sterling	RUXE	4.3	13.6	17.2	14.0	14.0	18.2	23.6	40.2	86.3	38.9	..
Foreign currency	RUXF	46.5	50.2	73.7	150.0	112.2	183.1	234.4	392.5	740.8	414.3	..
Total UK securities dealers	KN8B	50.9	63.8	90.9	163.9	126.2	201.3	258.0	432.6	827.1	453.2	700.8
Other[2]	D4AK	0.1	–	0.1	0.7	0.1	0.1	–	1.8	2.2	3.2	..
Total Other Financial Intermediaries	D4AL	51.0	63.8	91.0	164.6	126.3	201.4	258.0	434.5	829.3	456.4	..
Insurance companies and pension funds												
Insurance companies[3]	D4AI	0.3	0.2	0.5	0.2	0.1	–	–	0.4	2.3	1.1	..
Pension funds[4]	GKGR	0.6	0.7	0.4	0.4	3.1	2.8	7.0	11.3	6.3	41.1	..
Total insurance companies and pension funds	D4AJ	0.9	0.9	0.9	0.7	3.2	2.8	7.0	11.6	8.6	42.2	..
Total UK liabilities	ZPND	451.9	594.3	780.6	797.7	844.6	1 035.3	1 155.5	1 838.3	4 753.2	2 595.4	..
Net international investment position												
Banks	ZPNE	–9.5	–5.1	–5.8	–9.0	–5.6	–11.0	–36.8	–14.1	124.9	79.6	57.9
Other Financial Intermediaries												
Securities dealers	ZPNF	4.9	1.3	–3.8	–9.2	–10.0	0.2	5.1	6.6	106.0	39.4	10.0
Other[2]	D4AP	0.3	0.6	0.6	0.4	0.3	0.4	0.1	0.1	0.4	–0.6	..
Total Other Financial Intermediaries	D4AQ	5.2	1.9	–3.2	–8.8	–9.8	0.6	5.3	6.7	106.4	38.8	..
Insurance companies and pension funds												
Insurance companies[3]	D4AM	0.4	0.8	0.3	–	–0.1	–0.1	–	–0.1	–0.2	1.2	..
Pension funds[4]	D4AN	0.2	–	0.3	0.1	–0.1	–0.1	–1.0	–2.6	–0.5	–20.6	..
Total insurance companies and pension funds	D4AO	0.6	0.8	0.6	0.1	–0.3	–0.2	–1.0	–2.7	–0.7	–19.4	..
Total	ZPNG	–3.7	–2.4	–8.5	–17.7	–15.7	–10.6	–32.5	–10.1	230.6	98.9	..

1 The data in this table for 'other financial intermediaries' other than securities dealers and for insurance companies and pension funds are developmental and are not included in the main aggregates of the UK's international investment position. However, the data in this table for UK banks have now been included in the main aggregates of the international investment position from 2004 and the data for UK securites dealers have been included from 2010.

2 Includes unit and investment trusts and open-ended investment companies, finance leasing companies, credit grantors, factoring companies and building societies.

3 Includes both general and long-term insurance.

4 Includes self-administered pension funds only.

Geographical breakdown

Part 3

Geographical breakdown of current account

Chapter 9

9.1 Current account
Summary transactions in 2010

£ million

	Trade in goods	Trade in services	Income	Current transfers	**Current account**
Credits					
Europe					
European Union (EU)					
Austria	1 463	643	401	37	2 544
Belgium	13 377	2 888	2 440	217	18 922
Bulgaria	249	164	14	9	436
Cyprus	562	602	70	8	1 242
Czech Republic	1 827	452	–96	13	2 196
Denmark	2 757	2 910	1 124	46	6 837
Estonia	193	79	13	1	286
Finland	1 498	1 274	621	19	3 412
France	19 228	8 913	10 078	324	38 543
Germany	27 913	10 800	8 235	440	47 388
Greece	1 381	1 119	402	66	2 968
Hungary	1 082	472	102	9	1 665
Ireland	16 932	8 389	–5 426	182	20 077
Italy	8 853	5 151	3 693	171	17 868
Latvia	168	87	–56	7	206
Lithuania	225	96	14	20	355
Luxembourg	246	2 144	11 749	25	14 164
Malta	393	227	65	10	695
Netherlands	21 250	10 069	12 025	363	43 707
Poland	3 804	1 132	569	54	5 559
Portugal	1 837	779	582	25	3 223
Romania	781	359	114	6	1 260
Slovak Republic	466	291	52	9	818
Slovenia	220	92	–6	2	308
Spain	9 940	5 139	3 159	161	18 399
Sweden	5 563	2 911	3 220	91	11 785
European Central Bank	–	–	–	–	–
EU Institutions	–	758	513	6 870	8 141
Total EU27	142 208	67 940	53 671	9 185	273 004
European Free Trade Association (EFTA)					
Iceland	132	168	374	37	711
Liechtenstein	25	60	–4	2	83
Norway	3 114	2 383	977	106	6 580
Switzerland	5 214	8 981	6 965	96	21 256
Total EFTA	8 485	11 592	8 312	241	28 630
Other Europe					
Albania	21	12	2	1	36
Belarus	120	10	5	–	135
Croatia	173	82	23	3	281
Russia	3 595	1 665	2 049	23	7 332
Turkey	3 248	1 126	753	43	5 170
Ukraine	474	244	102	2	822
Serbia and Montenegro	97	59	–9	2	149
of which Serbia	*93*	*48*	*–10*	*2*	*133*
Montenegro	*4*	*11*	*1*	*–*	*16*
Other	810	3 322	4 842	43	9 017
Total Europe	**159 231**	**86 052**	**69 750**	**9 543**	**324 576**
Americas					
Argentina	357	233	277	12	879
Brazil	2 217	836	1 476	35	4 564
Canada	4 127	2 905	4 502	373	11 907
Chile	630	181	945	17	1 773
Colombia	230	200	289	15	734
Mexico	952	421	770	44	2 187
United States of America	37 925	34 286	37 348	2 315	111 874
Uruguay	79	20	7	1	107
Venezuela	273	354	153	11	791
Other Central American Countries	897	4 211	8 270	232	13 610
Other	394	277	45	17	733
Total Americas	**48 081**	**43 924**	**54 082**	**3 072**	**149 159**
Asia					
China	7 611	2 652	1 084	39	11 386
Hong Kong	4 456	1 606	4 791	39	10 892
India	4 068	2 060	1 851	40	8 019
Indonesia	461	325	420	17	1 223
Iran	307	128	43	2	480
Israel	1 387	682	148	30	2 247
Japan	4 334	4 315	3 883	125	12 657
Malaysia	1 272	701	895	29	2 897
Pakistan	461	302	207	9	979
Philippines	284	125	211	6	626
Saudi Arabia	2 488	2 925	432	455	6 300
Singapore	3 447	3 661	3 053	39	10 200
South Korea	2 344	1 123	1 533	23	5 023
Taiwan	1 116	1 145	850	8	3 119
Thailand	1 137	459	290	12	1 898
Residual Gulf Arabian Countries	6 590	4 007	1 037	189	11 823
Other Near & Middle Eastern Countries	1 316	610	1 842	278	4 046
Other	1 212	1 726	2 268	44	5 250
Total Asia	**44 291**	**28 552**	**24 838**	**1 384**	**99 065**
Australasia & Oceania					
Australia	3 362	5 025	7 890	352	16 629
New Zealand	414	452	492	61	1 419
Other	82	208	84	10	384
Total Australasia & Oceania	**3 858**	**5 685**	**8 466**	**423**	**18 432**
Africa					
Egypt	1 198	560	859	10	2 627
Morocco	565	137	27	8	737
South Africa	2 890	1 723	2 379	95	7 087
Other North Africa	907	504	121	13	1 545
Other	4 693	3 904	2 582	60	11 239
Total Africa	**10 253**	**6 828**	**5 968**	**186**	**23 235**
International Organisations	–	41	359	–	400
World Total	**265 714**	**171 082**	**163 463**	**14 608**	**614 867**

9.1 Current account
Summary transactions in 2010

continued

£ million

	Trade in goods	Trade in services	Income	Current transfers	**Current account**
Debits					
Europe					
European Union (EU)					
Austria	2 633	987	687	41	4 348
Belgium	17 081	2 319	1 995	83	21 478
Bulgaria	231	340	36	7	614
Cyprus	106	881	614	48	1 649
Czech Republic	3 988	434	62	21	4 505
Denmark	4 117	1 294	649	56	6 116
Estonia	166	30	1	6	203
Finland	2 164	451	449	20	3 084
France	21 572	9 636	11 595	419	43 222
Germany	46 415	9 127	13 911	718	70 171
Greece	701	1 951	1 869	81	4 602
Hungary	3 251	486	55	18	3 810
Ireland	12 873	4 150	6 907	688	24 618
Italy	13 940	4 350	2 518	220	21 028
Latvia	440	94	13	5	552
Lithuania	551	118	46	1	716
Luxembourg	937	1 411	6 189	18	8 555
Malta	170	326	117	39	652
Netherlands	26 449	3 898	7 857	225	38 429
Poland	6 106	1 361	163	77	7 707
Portugal	1 749	1 633	535	65	3 982
Romania	1 241	258	15	16	1 530
Slovak Republic	1 620	121	68	3	1 812
Slovenia	357	48	27	3	435
Spain	10 381	9 482	3 287	237	23 387
Sweden	6 809	1 614	1 247	53	9 723
European Central Bank	–	–	–	–	–
EU Institutions	–	2	2 466	15 987	18 455
Total EU27	186 048	56 802	63 378	19 155	325 383
European Free Trade Association (EFTA)					
Iceland	433	56	503	6	998
Liechtenstein	10	20	23	2	55
Norway	21 053	1 092	1 909	118	24 172
Switzerland	7 429	3 215	4 298	159	15 101
Total EFTA	28 925	4 383	6 733	285	40 326
Other Europe					
Albania	–	4	–	13	17
Belarus	37	9	4	–	50
Croatia	98	220	10	11	339
Russia	5 258	903	270	74	6 505
Turkey	5 351	1 623	81	54	7 109
Ukraine	283	217	91	27	618
Serbia and Montenegro	94	49	–	43	186
of which Serbia	*93*	*38*	–	*39*	*170*
Montenegro	1	11	–	4	16
Other	243	1 279	8 777	267	10 566
Total Europe	**226 337**	**65 489**	**79 344**	**19 929**	**391 099**
Americas					
Argentina	666	111	9	18	804
Brazil	3 111	447	79	64	3 701
Canada	5 770	1 477	2 321	575	10 143
Chile	584	50	140	21	795
Colombia	678	55	9	22	764
Mexico	1 032	398	35	46	1 511
United States of America	26 992	19 200	42 475	2 813	91 480
Uruguay	103	8	4	2	117
Venezuela	421	50	13	12	496
Other Central American Countries	1 146	2 267	–203	563	3 773
Other	364	123	24	68	579
Total Americas	**40 867**	**24 186**	**44 906**	**4 204**	**114 163**
Asia					
China	30 637	1 180	279	208	32 304
Hong Kong	8 172	1 056	2 267	189	11 684
India	5 812	2 292	204	1 006	9 314
Indonesia	1 388	119	20	132	1 659
Iran	206	66	20	24	316
Israel	1 566	415	115	46	2 142
Japan	8 107	3 627	5 187	147	17 068
Malaysia	1 837	260	287	75	2 459
Pakistan	809	443	28	333	1 613
Philippines	525	217	15	42	799
Saudi Arabia	766	249	559	68	1 642
Singapore	4 146	1 803	1 385	160	7 494
South Korea	2 563	351	258	24	3 196
Taiwan	3 118	247	78	8	3 451
Thailand	2 683	624	47	51	3 405
Residual Gulf Arabian Countries	5 387	1 782	835	392	8 396
Other Near & Middle Eastern Countries	297	230	86	103	716
Other	3 905	1 104	283	1 268	6 560
Total Asia	**81 924**	**16 065**	**11 953**	**4 276**	**114 218**
Australasia & Oceania					
Australia	2 315	2 194	1 327	560	6 396
New Zealand	844	354	64	126	1 388
Other	107	52	–277	30	–88
Total Australasia & Oceania	**3 266**	**2 600**	**1 114**	**716**	**7 696**
Africa					
Egypt	659	681	79	41	1 460
Morocco	343	248	13	15	619
South Africa	4 423	1 101	1 147	471	7 142
Other North Africa	2 851	432	182	19	3 484
Other	3 506	1 472	395	2 992	8 365
Total Africa	**11 782**	**3 934**	**1 816**	**3 538**	**21 070**
International Organisations	–	30	1 291	2 026	3 347
World total	**364 176**	**112 304**	**140 424**	**34 689**	**651 593**

9.1 Current account

Summary transactions in 2010

continued £ million

	Trade in goods	Trade in services	Income	Current transfers	**Current account**
Balances					
Europe					
European Union(EU)					
Austria	–1 170	–344	–286	–4	–1 804
Belgium	–3 704	569	445	134	–2 556
Bulgaria	18	–176	–22	2	–178
Cyprus	456	–279	–544	–40	–407
Czech Republic	–2 161	18	–158	–8	–2 309
Denmark	–1 360	1 616	475	–10	721
Estonia	27	49	12	–5	83
Finland	–666	823	172	–1	328
France	–2 344	–723	–1 517	–95	–4 679
Germany	–18 502	1 673	–5 676	–278	–22 783
Greece	680	–832	–1 467	–15	–1 634
Hungary	–2 169	–14	47	–9	–2 145
Ireland	4 059	4 239	–12 333	–506	–4 541
Italy	–5 087	801	1 175	–49	–3 160
Latvia	–272	–7	–69	2	–346
Lithuania	–326	–22	–32	19	–361
Luxembourg	–691	733	5 560	7	5 609
Malta	223	–99	–52	–29	43
Netherlands	–5 199	6 171	4 168	138	5 278
Poland	–2 302	–229	406	–23	–2 148
Portugal	88	–854	47	–40	–759
Romania	–460	101	99	–10	–270
Slovak Republic	–1 154	170	–16	6	–994
Slovenia	–137	44	–33	–1	–127
Spain	–441	–4 343	–128	–76	–4 988
Sweden	–1 246	1 297	1 973	38	2 062
European Central Bank	–	–	–	–	–
EU Institutions	–	756	–1 953	–9 117	–10 314
Total EU27	–43 840	11 138	–9 707	–9 970	–52 379
European Free Trade Association (EFTA)					
Iceland	–301	112	–129	31	–287
Liechtenstein	15	40	–27	–	28
Norway	–17 939	1 291	–932	–12	–17 592
Switzerland	–2 215	5 766	2 667	–63	6 155
Total EFTA	–20 440	7 209	1 579	–44	–11 696
Other Europe					
Albania	21	8	2	–12	19
Belarus	83	1	1	–	85
Croatia	75	–138	13	–8	–58
Russia	–1 663	762	1 779	–51	827
Turkey	–2 103	–497	672	–11	–1 939
Ukraine	191	27	11	–25	204
Serbia and Montenegro	3	10	–9	–41	–37
of which Serbia	*–*	*10*	*–10*	*–37*	*–37*
Montenegro	3	–	1	–4	–
Other	567	2 043	–3 935	–224	–1 549
Total Europe	**–67 106**	**20 563**	**–9 594**	**–10 386**	**–66 523**
Americas					
Argentina	–309	122	268	–6	75
Brazil	–894	389	1 397	–29	863
Canada	–1 643	1 428	2 181	–202	1 764
Chile	46	131	805	–4	978
Colombia	–448	145	280	–7	–30
Mexico	–80	23	735	–2	676
USA	10 933	15 086	–5 127	–498	20 394
Uruguay	–24	12	3	–1	–10
Venezuela	–148	304	140	–1	295
Other Central American Countries	–249	1 944	8 473	–331	9 837
Other America	30	154	21	–51	154
Total Americas	**7 214**	**19 738**	**9 176**	**–1 132**	**34 996**
Asia					
China	–23 026	1 472	805	–169	–20 918
Hong Kong	–3 716	550	2 524	–150	–792
India	–1 744	–232	1 647	–966	–1 295
Indonesia	–927	206	400	–115	–436
Iran	101	62	23	–22	164
Israel	–179	267	33	–16	105
Japan	–3 773	688	–1 304	–22	–4 411
Malaysia	–565	441	608	–46	438
Pakistan	–348	–141	179	–324	–634
Philippines	–241	–92	196	–36	–173
Saudi Arabia	1 722	2 676	–127	387	4 658
Singapore	–699	1 858	1 668	–121	2 706
South Korea	–219	772	1 275	–1	1 827
Taiwan	–2 002	898	772	–	–332
Thailand	–1 546	–165	243	–39	–1 507
Residual Gulf Arabian Countries	1 203	2 225	202	–203	3 427
Other Near & Middle Eastern Countries	1 019	380	1 756	175	3 330
Other	–2 693	622	1 985	–1 224	–1 310
Total Asia	**–37 633**	**12 487**	**12 885**	**–2 892**	**–15 153**
Australasia & Oceania					
Australia	1 047	2 831	6 563	–208	10 233
New Zealand	–430	98	428	–65	31
Other	–25	156	361	–20	472
Total Australasia & Oceania	**592**	**3 085**	**7 352**	**–293**	**10 736**
Africa					
Egypt	539	–121	780	–31	1 167
Morocco	222	–111	14	–7	118
South Africa	–1 533	622	1 232	–376	–55
Other North Africa	–1 944	72	–61	–6	–1 939
Other	1 187	2 432	2 187	–2 932	2 874
Total Africa	**–1 529**	**2 894**	**4 152**	**–3 352**	**2 165**
International Organisations	–	11	–932	–2 026	–2 947
World total	**–98 462**	**58 778**	**23 039**	**–20 081**	**–36 726**

THIS PAGE IS INTENTIONALLY BLANK

9.2 Current account

£ million

		2000	2001	2002	2003	2004	2005	2006	2007	2008	2009	2010
Credits												
Europe												
European Union (EU)												
Austria	CUGP	2 321	2 346	2 406	2 483	2 379	2 789	3 158	3 228	3 256	2 779	2 544
Belgium[1]	AA2Q	14 727	14 612	15 005	15 774	16 058	17 861	20 395	21 612	23 102	17 652	18 922
Bulgaria	ZWVI	166	248	288	294	323	350	393	413	498	435	436
Cyprus	AA2R	623	589	630	608	732	788	1 731	1 516	1 518	1 326	1 242
Czech Republic	LEPQ	1 225	1 459	1 370	1 477	1 539	1 585	1 972	2 132	2 003	1 835	2 196
Denmark	LEQR	4 625	4 668	4 666	4 435	4 559	5 333	7 936	6 594	7 016	6 480	6 837
Estonia	ZWVK	110	105	127	123	144	166	539	272	277	212	286
Finland	LEUD	3 034	3 156	2 876	2 978	2 858	2 965	3 515	4 236	4 104	3 361	3 412
France	LEUM	31 829	34 335	32 062	32 269	33 666	37 814	51 506	47 095	45 711	35 478	38 543
Germany	LEQI	39 992	42 306	39 510	37 346	39 870	44 387	51 590	53 578	58 773	47 210	47 388
Greece	LEUV	3 107	2 831	2 720	2 894	2 980	3 193	3 263	3 735	4 381	3 548	2 968
Hungary	BFKO	1 272	1 143	1 328	1 414	1 694	1 810	1 467	1 682	1 790	1 556	1 665
Ireland	BFLV	19 161	22 368	23 781	22 518	25 512	30 892	34 657	40 742	43 100	30 009	20 077
Italy	BFOD	17 647	17 771	16 441	16 623	16 639	17 732	19 159	20 777	20 693	17 577	17 868
Latvia	ZWVM	118	118	119	142	141	202	675	283	272	210	206
Lithuania	ZWVN	157	190	185	235	198	294	361	456	582	283	355
Luxembourg[1]	AA2U	4 362	4 645	4 143	3 803	5 082	7 344	13 264	13 919	20 456	16 366	14 164
Malta	AA2V	320	323	335	383	829	356	268	481	739	1 041	695
Netherlands	BFQF	32 861	36 418	34 817	34 485	28 815	31 468	40 396	44 464	52 101	42 957	43 707
Poland	BFRY	1 732	1 966	2 056	2 277	2 404	3 003	4 475	3 985	4 889	4 784	5 559
Portugal	BFSH	2 791	2 883	2 843	2 818	3 078	3 320	3 942	3 289	3 736	3 052	3 223
Romania	ZWVO	443	490	579	701	864	850	889	1 094	1 281	1 148	1 260
Slovak Republic	ZWVP	246	275	264	298	299	423	492	673	856	673	818
Slovenia	ZWVQ	229	296	302	291	312	269	299	318	369	285	308
Spain	LEST	13 213	13 118	13 259	14 212	15 797	19 527	23 775	23 760	25 255	20 801	18 399
Sweden	BFTI	8 029	7 987	7 568	7 371	8 446	9 151	10 442	11 360	12 854	11 253	11 785
European Central Bank	ZWVF	3	12	3	–	–	–	–	–	–	–	–
EU Institutions	CSFH	5 932	8 287	7 106	7 948	8 454	9 094	9 261	8 530	9 799	10 751	8 141
Total EU27	G970	210 275	224 945	216 789	216 200	223 672	252 966	309 820	320 224	349 411	283 062	273 004
European Free Trade Association (EFTA)												
Iceland	BFNH	334	286	265	307	348	468	638	1 412	1 608	768	711
Liechtenstein	BFPE	91	75	69	66	83	61	102	171	97	68	83
Norway	BFQO	4 185	3 933	4 006	4 134	4 435	6 112	6 181	8 152	8 171	6 645	6 580
Switzerland	LEOY	13 257	12 494	11 811	12 066	12 280	16 169	18 897	23 738	24 854	17 195	21 256
Total EFTA	CTFQ	17 867	16 788	16 151	16 573	17 146	22 810	25 819	33 473	34 730	24 676	28 630
Other Europe												
Albania	ZWVG	9	28	25	17	34	24	30	32	52	37	36
Belarus	ZWVH	63	37	43	49	59	68	76	91	117	89	135
Croatia	ZWVJ	128	148	180	233	218	236	299	294	419	383	281
Russia	BFSQ	1 382	1 916	2 248	2 717	3 655	5 357	6 783	7 822	9 752	6 264	7 332
Turkey	BFUJ	2 714	2 027	2 081	2 492	2 751	3 265	4 014	4 224	4 346	4 125	5 170
Ukraine	ZWVR	196	227	491	392	322	493	906	937	1 085	915	822
Serbia and Montenegro[2]	BFWC	138	94	93	111	86	72	148	185	202	171	149
of which Serbia	KNC9	..	..	..	..	..	..	..	171	189	152	133
Montenegro	KND2	..	..	..	..	..	..	..	14	13	19	16
Other	LEVW	4 932	4 327	4 641	6 353	8 162	10 110	12 881	13 897	11 485	7 758	9 017
Total Europe	LERA	237 704	250 537	242 742	245 137	256 105	295 401	360 776	381 179	411 599	327 480	324 576
Americas												
Argentina	ZWVT	971	832	322	409	581	553	908	815	840	777	879
Brazil	LENO	1 671	1 876	1 878	1 658	1 886	2 329	2 511	2 840	3 630	4 116	4 564
Canada	LEOP	7 284	7 362	6 561	6 976	7 573	8 481	10 456	10 632	6 193	7 060	11 907
Chile	ZWVU	475	436	449	517	1 064	1 451	1 178	1 215	1 196	1 284	1 773
Colombia	ZWVV	490	492	419	489	612	644	562	457	617	442	734
Mexico	BFPN	1 417	1 302	1 620	1 390	1 728	1 796	2 174	2 061	1 844	1 613	2 187
United States of America	BFVB	79 112	82 126	79 049	81 584	86 585	104 378	123 887	139 426	122 951	104 219	111 874
Uruguay	ZWVW	80	66	55	102	40	62	93	67	96	80	107
Venezuela	ZWVX	220	609	599	338	564	731	683	458	531	569	791
Other Central American Countries	JISS	7 993	8 316	8 864	9 173	10 343	14 794	19 944	22 781	21 369	14 284	13 610
Other	LEVE	479	411	389	409	769	179	1 356	–16	1 454	746	733
Total Americas	LESK	100 192	103 828	100 205	103 045	111 745	135 398	163 752	180 736	160 721	135 190	149 159
Asia												
China	LEPH	2 227	2 858	2 655	3 241	4 279	5 067	5 689	6 645	8 808	8 674	11 386
Hong Kong	BFJR	5 416	5 242	4 871	5 469	7 000	8 664	9 387	10 018	8 763	8 392	10 892
India	BFMY	3 104	2 955	3 039	3 661	3 853	4 805	5 624	6 412	7 850	6 311	8 019
Indonesia	BFKX	772	749	720	895	807	858	1 113	834	888	1 151	1 223
Iran	ZWWA	477	650	626	747	745	829	820	692	808	655	480
Israel	BFMP	2 038	1 961	1 930	1 839	1 889	2 039	1 964	1 937	2 051	1 895	2 247
Japan	BFOM	16 231	14 870	12 451	12 942	13 266	15 309	17 436	17 528	17 995	13 035	12 657
Malaysia	BFPW	1 807	1 830	1 884	2 109	2 274	2 356	2 209	2 292	2 450	2 588	2 897
Pakistan	BFRP	508	634	592	676	827	1 187	1 241	1 001	1 040	1 052	979
Philippines	BFRG	639	732	607	688	629	627	646	799	777	674	626
Saudi Arabia	BFSZ	4 724	4 405	4 060	4 827	4 852	4 684	5 183	5 138	5 240	5 582	6 300
Singapore	BFTR	5 498	5 434	4 521	4 873	6 133	8 201	9 123	8 385	10 082	9 872	10 200
South Korea	BFOV	2 174	2 200	2 692	2 608	3 201	3 650	4 025	4 326	5 248	4 201	5 023
Taiwan	BFUS	1 560	1 472	1 570	1 623	2 012	2 211	2 238	2 253	2 173	1 402	3 119
Thailand	BFUA	1 001	1 069	982	1 137	1 193	1 202	865	1 057	1 103	1 699	1 898
Residual Gulf Arabian Countries	JITT	5 386	5 121	4 856	5 556	6 768	10 502	9 340	9 816	12 145	11 278	11 823
Other Near & Middle Eastern Countries	ZWWC	1 102	1 299	1 147	1 269	1 562	1 872	2 443	3 057	3 872	2 854	4 046
Other	LEWF	1 814	1 733	1 770	1 627	1 893	1 889	3 267	4 428	3 797	4 804	5 250
Total Asia	LETC	56 478	55 214	50 973	55 787	63 183	75 952	82 613	86 618	95 090	86 119	99 065
Australasia & Oceania												
Australia	CWBG	6 955	6 883	6 941	7 052	8 982	9 921	10 571	12 195	12 909	13 392	16 629
New Zealand	BFQX	991	1 099	1 204	1 286	1 252	1 369	1 395	1 413	1 371	1 214	1 419
Other	LEVN	155	151	190	217	219	183	222	230	324	317	384
Total Australasia & Oceania	LETU	8 101	8 133	8 335	8 555	10 453	11 473	12 188	13 838	14 664	14 923	18 432
Africa												
Egypt	ZWWE	1 049	1 054	1 013	962	1 194	1 261	1 509	1 895	2 198	2 151	2 627
Morocco	ZWWF	498	480	419	425	407	323	434	422	644	500	737
South Africa	BFWU	3 667	4 076	4 708	4 849	6 053	7 513	5 898	6 568	6 102	5 371	7 087
Other North Africa	JIRU	787	783	665	991	905	–2 491	1 227	1 163	1 755	1 533	1 545
Other	LEWO	4 154	4 543	4 732	5 149	5 142	9 668	6 685	7 415	9 781	9 437	11 239
Total Africa	LERS	10 155	10 936	11 537	12 376	13 701	16 274	15 753	17 463	20 480	18 992	23 235
International Organisations	CTEY	501	578	560	539	503	583	626	673	521	437	400
World total	HBOE	413 131	429 226	414 352	425 439	455 690	535 081	635 708	680 507	703 075	583 141	614 867

1 Before 1999 only combined BLEU data is available under identifier CTFH.

2 Separate data for Serbia and Montenegro is available from 2007.

9.2 Current account

continued | £ million

		2000	2001	2002	2003	2004	2005	2006	2007	2008	2009	2010
Debits												
Europe												
European Union (EU)												
Austria	CUGW	2 508	3 108	3 801	4 093	3 762	4 161	4 793	4 678	4 397	4 035	4 348
Belgium[1]	AA34	14 129	15 315	16 184	16 265	17 055	19 383	21 069	22 289	23 819	19 780	21 478
Bulgaria	ZWWL	191	187	252	248	339	464	508	664	672	485	614
Cyprus	AA35	1 267	1 481	1 382	1 479	1 463	1 721	3 242	1 782	1 801	1 522	1 649
Czech Republic	LEPR	1 107	1 420	1 592	1 846	1 810	2 462	3 698	3 660	4 288	3 801	4 505
Denmark	LEQS	4 449	4 536	5 248	5 204	5 383	6 837	8 996	6 188	6 668	6 064	6 116
Estonia	ZWWN	376	318	342	302	433	425	2 198	312	220	168	203
Finland	LEUE	3 568	3 708	3 349	3 310	2 951	3 297	4 023	3 853	4 048	3 038	3 084
France	LEUN	34 140	35 012	34 493	36 719	38 960	44 350	51 895	48 934	48 546	48 506	43 222
Germany	LEQJ	44 988	44 176	44 582	49 808	54 128	63 807	70 259	78 723	74 991	58 373	70 171
Greece	LEUW	3 012	3 129	3 045	3 156	3 301	3 853	4 449	5 154	5 296	4 816	4 602
Hungary	BFKP	865	884	1 039	1 301	1 799	2 183	2 760	2 871	3 011	3 045	3 810
Ireland	BFLW	15 997	18 999	20 654	17 968	19 908	23 546	26 320	30 929	33 398	26 070	24 618
Italy	BFOE	15 421	16 030	15 756	17 255	18 364	20 064	20 464	22 087	22 852	18 442	21 028
Latvia	ZWWP	467	462	507	551	737	784	897	740	506	414	552
Lithuania	ZWWQ	286	272	316	313	299	377	402	450	485	489	716
Luxembourg[1]	AA38	3 089	3 581	3 603	3 923	4 938	5 483	8 780	8 334	9 813	6 268	8 555
Malta	AA39	412	462	469	515	556	584	562	707	872	615	652
Netherlands	BFQG	30 793	30 662	26 445	27 264	29 790	33 579	43 477	49 257	36 964	30 616	38 429
Poland	BFRZ	1 340	1 589	1 620	1 929	2 349	3 301	5 166	5 502	6 187	6 115	7 707
Portugal	BFSI	3 049	3 076	3 289	3 729	3 761	3 962	5 290	4 051	4 518	3 608	3 982
Romania	ZWWR	464	565	655	795	950	1 023	1 066	1 185	1 072	1 069	1 530
Slovak Republic	ZWWS	216	208	253	292	318	500	1 117	1 468	1 817	1 765	1 812
Slovenia	ZWWT	198	206	238	223	234	277	826	394	416	308	435
Spain	LESU	14 031	16 232	18 502	20 164	20 114	25 120	27 708	27 433	26 958	25 048	23 387
Sweden	BFTJ	7 233	6 904	6 506	6 748	7 325	8 112	9 382	8 830	10 556	9 047	9 723
European Central Bank	ZWWI	1	1	1	–	–	–	–	–	2	2	–
EU Institutions	CSFI	12 211	11 325	11 789	12 997	13 153	15 107	15 395	15 841	16 407	17 447	18 455
Total EU27	G97F	215 808	223 848	225 912	238 397	254 180	294 762	344 742	356 316	350 580	300 956	325 383
European Free Trade Association (EFTA)												
Iceland	BFNI	463	347	359	374	474	523	813	935	–741	790	998
Liechtenstein	BFPF	147	126	79	94	76	97	153	208	165	68	55
Norway	BFQP	6 920	7 103	7 497	8 097	10 357	14 830	17 905	18 503	25 391	19 375	24 172
Switzerland	LEOZ	18 877	16 179	13 203	11 769	11 537	15 377	19 041	20 294	4 262	9 911	15 101
Total EFTA	CTFR	26 407	23 755	21 138	20 334	22 444	30 827	37 912	39 940	29 077	30 144	40 326
Other Europe												
Albania	ZWWJ	41	28	26	24	27	15	20	35	32	23	17
Belarus	ZWWK	66	37	46	31	77	290	758	633	145	29	50
Croatia	ZWWM	136	159	155	152	168	250	320	331	378	296	339
Russia	BFSR	2 214	2 734	2 564	3 119	4 514	6 946	9 130	9 258	10 024	6 334	6 505
Turkey	BFUK	2 131	2 478	3 077	3 564	4 257	4 795	5 342	6 144	6 765	6 152	7 109
Ukraine	ZWWU	133	158	196	195	285	380	465	710	710	396	618
Serbia and Montenegro[2]	BFWD	141	110	100	110	108	100	194	208	205	177	186
of which *Serbia*	KND3	..	..	..	..	..	..	..	198	191	159	170
Montenegro	KND4	..	..	..	..	..	..	..	10	14	18	16
Other	LEVX	8 493	9 091	8 227	7 290	9 040	12 268	15 411	22 499	24 585	11 792	10 566
Total Europe	LERB	255 570	262 398	261 441	273 216	295 100	350 633	414 294	436 074	422 501	356 299	391 099
Americas												
Argentina	ZWWW	367	360	315	312	345	381	495	533	733	793	804
Brazil	LENP	1 533	1 734	1 770	1 801	1 926	2 257	2 447	2 551	3 101	2 967	3 701
Canada	LEOQ	6 862	6 283	6 519	6 396	7 745	8 027	10 006	9 330	7 117	8 464	10 143
Chile	ZWWX	530	574	560	499	600	623	657	674	753	743	795
Colombia	ZWWY	338	421	290	279	326	378	424	463	791	670	764
Mexico	BFPO	1 154	1 349	927	870	857	872	934	1 062	1 386	1 084	1 511
United States of America	BFVC	70 754	77 600	70 370	69 938	71 386	82 569	104 975	114 563	101 619	82 621	91 480
Uruguay	ZWWZ	63	55	73	56	54	72	94	96	130	146	117
Venezuela	ZWXA	279	248	255	176	265	468	743	634	742	506	496
Other Central American Countries	JIST	7 222	6 382	5 046	5 779	7 115	10 999	16 344	18 143	16 864	9 763	3 773
Other	LEVF	892	701	567	476	475	548	1 202	–3 036	19 646	9 058	579
Total Americas	LESL	89 994	95 707	86 692	86 582	91 094	107 194	138 321	145 013	152 882	116 815	114 163
Asia												
China	LEPI	5 692	6 739	7 774	9 279	11 557	14 428	16 945	20 882	25 513	26 217	32 304
Hong Kong	BFJS	10 248	9 901	8 323	7 703	8 111	9 392	11 049	12 046	13 463	11 497	11 684
India	BFMZ	3 172	3 536	3 420	3 668	4 398	5 509	6 589	7 395	8 272	7 794	9 314
Indonesia	BFKY	1 430	1 482	1 350	1 394	1 222	1 266	1 399	1 291	1 510	1 509	1 659
Iran	ZWXD	314	347	169	167	201	227	354	275	241	360	316
Israel	BFMQ	1 538	1 527	1 289	1 258	1 335	1 572	1 756	1 805	1 796	1 667	2 142
Japan	BFON	23 311	21 029	17 040	13 897	15 410	18 016	20 189	19 595	19 663	14 583	17 068
Malaysia	BFPX	2 966	2 488	2 133	2 193	2 440	2 356	2 709	2 587	2 701	2 460	2 459
Pakistan	BFRQ	879	936	1 176	1 166	1 243	1 250	1 364	1 292	1 411	1 431	1 613
Philippines	BFRH	1 506	1 354	1 134	933	833	948	1 067	1 012	940	652	799
Saudi Arabia	BFTA	2 470	2 568	2 417	2 164	2 400	3 106	3 124	3 211	3 439	1 717	1 642
Singapore	BFTS	5 654	5 202	4 342	4 668	5 705	7 198	8 090	9 272	9 116	7 110	7 494
South Korea	BFOW	3 694	3 147	3 034	2 776	3 184	3 627	3 740	3 808	4 416	3 489	3 196
Taiwan	BFUT	3 956	3 211	2 744	2 541	2 767	2 861	2 960	3 219	3 301	2 653	3 451
Thailand	BFUB	2 201	2 340	2 233	2 292	2 546	2 533	2 904	3 004	3 375	3 059	3 405
Residual Gulf Arabian Countries	JITU	3 001	3 280	2 764	3 133	3 710	4 494	5 734	6 297	6 929	6 015	8 396
Other Near & Middle Eastern Countries	ZWXF	577	569	540	515	514	704	1 371	942	977	756	716
Other	LEWG	3 004	3 031	3 129	3 251	3 985	4 080	4 854	4 894	5 673	6 065	6 560
Total Asia	LETD	75 613	72 687	65 011	62 998	71 561	83 567	96 198	102 827	112 736	99 034	114 218
Australasia & Oceania												
Australia	CWBO	3 617	3 786	4 312	4 756	4 950	6 184	6 368	7 377	7 282	7 668	6 396
New Zealand	BFQY	974	1 016	1 020	1 045	1 184	1 290	1 303	1 296	1 355	1 266	1 388
Other	LEVO	193	191	197	206	232	210	575	193	267	250	–88
Total Australasia & Oceania	LETV	4 784	4 993	5 529	6 007	6 366	7 684	8 246	8 866	8 904	9 184	7 696
Africa												
Egypt	ZWXH	1 049	1 070	913	932	1 012	1 198	1 682	1 504	1 681	1 514	1 460
Morocco	ZWXI	609	630	624	608	685	627	712	877	868	614	619
South Africa	BFWV	4 132	4 517	4 437	5 017	5 418	6 448	6 646	5 720	7 297	6 233	7 142
Other North Africa	JIRV	1 266	1 077	1 007	977	1 219	1 633	2 561	2 806	3 412	2 406	3 484
Other	LEWP	4 187	5 416	5 375	6 217	6 292	6 611	7 180	8 391	9 078	8 157	8 365
Total Africa	LERT	11 243	12 710	12 356	13 751	14 626	16 517	18 781	19 298	22 336	18 924	21 070
International Organisations	CTEZ	1 756	1 793	1 724	1 265	1 833	2 153	2 963	3 255	3 469	3 201	3 347
World total	HBOF	438 960	450 288	432 753	443 819	480 580	567 748	678 803	715 333	722 828	603 457	651 593

1 Before 1999 only combined BLEU data is available under identifier CTFI.

2 Separate data for Serbia and Montenegro is available from 2007.

9.2 Current account

continued £ million

		2000	2001	2002	2003	2004	2005	2006	2007	2008	2009	2010
Balances												
Europe												
European Union (EU)												
Austria	CUGX	–187	–762	–1 395	–1 610	–1 383	–1 372	–1 635	–1 450	–1 141	–1 256	–1 804
Belgium[1]	AA4H	598	–703	–1 179	–491	–997	–1 522	–674	–677	–717	–2 128	–2 556
Bulgaria	ZWXO	–25	61	36	46	–16	–114	–115	–251	–174	–50	–178
Cyprus	AA4I	–644	–892	–752	–871	–731	–933	–1 511	–266	–283	–196	–407
Czech Republic	LEPS	118	39	–222	–369	–271	–877	–1 726	–1 528	–2 285	–1 966	–2 309
Denmark	LEQT	176	132	–582	–769	–824	–1 504	–1 060	406	348	416	721
Estonia	ZWXQ	–266	–213	–215	–179	–289	–259	–1 659	–40	57	44	83
Finland	LEUF	–534	–552	–473	–332	–93	–332	–508	383	56	323	328
France	LEUO	–2 311	–677	–2 431	–4 450	–5 294	–6 536	–389	–1 839	–2 835	–13 028	–4 679
Germany	LEQK	–4 996	–1 870	–5 072	–12 462	–14 258	–19 420	–18 669	–25 145	–16 218	–11 163	–22 783
Greece	LEUX	95	–298	–325	–262	–321	–660	–1 186	–1 419	–915	–1 268	–1 634
Hungary	BFKQ	407	259	289	113	–105	–373	–1 293	–1 189	–1 221	–1 489	–2 145
Ireland	BFLX	3 164	3 369	3 127	4 550	5 604	7 346	8 337	9 813	9 702	3 939	–4 541
Italy	BFOF	2 226	1 741	685	–632	–1 725	–2 332	–1 305	–1 310	–2 159	–865	–3 160
Latvia	ZWXS	–349	–344	–388	–409	–596	–582	–222	–457	–234	–204	–346
Lithuania	ZWXT	–129	–82	–131	–78	–101	–83	–41	6	97	–206	–361
Luxembourg[1]	AA4L	1 273	1 064	540	–120	144	1 861	4 484	5 585	10 643	10 098	5 609
Malta	AA4M	–92	–139	–134	–132	273	–228	–294	–226	–133	426	43
Netherlands	BFQH	2 068	5 756	8 372	7 221	–975	–2 111	–3 081	–4 793	15 137	12 341	5 278
Poland	BFSA	392	377	436	348	55	–298	–691	–1 517	–1 298	–1 331	–2 148
Portugal	BFSJ	–258	–193	–446	–911	–683	–642	–1 348	–762	–782	–556	–759
Romania	ZWXU	–21	–75	–76	–94	–86	–173	–177	–91	209	79	–270
Slovak Republic	ZWXV	30	67	11	6	–19	–77	–625	–795	–961	–1 092	–994
Slovenia	ZWXW	31	90	64	68	78	–8	–527	–76	–47	–23	–127
Spain	LESV	–818	–3 114	–5 243	–5 952	–4 317	–5 593	–3 933	–3 673	–1 703	–4 247	–4 988
Sweden	BFTK	796	1 083	1 062	623	1 121	1 039	1 060	2 530	2 298	2 206	2 062
European Central Bank	ZWXL	2	11	2	–	–	–	–	–	–2	–2	–
EU Institutions	CSFJ	–6 279	–3 038	–4 683	–5 049	–4 699	–6 013	–6 134	–7 311	–6 608	–6 696	–10 314
Total EU27	G977	–5 533	1 097	–9 123	–22 197	–30 508	–41 796	–34 922	–36 092	–1 169	–17 894	–52 379
European Free Trade Association (EFTA)												
Iceland	BFNJ	–129	–61	–94	–67	–126	–55	–175	477	2 349	–22	–287
Liechtenstein	BFPG	–56	–51	–10	–28	7	–36	–51	–37	–68	–	28
Norway	BFQQ	–2 735	–3 170	–3 491	–3 963	–5 922	–8 718	–11 724	–10 351	–17 220	–12 730	–17 592
Switzerland	LEPA	–5 620	–3 685	–1 392	297	743	792	–144	3 444	20 592	7 284	6 155
Total EFTA	CTFS	–8 540	–6 967	–4 987	–3 761	–5 298	–8 017	–12 093	–6 467	5 653	–5 468	–11 696
Other Europe												
Albania	ZWXM	–32	–	–1	–7	7	9	10	–3	20	14	19
Belarus	ZWXN	–3	–	–3	18	–18	–222	–682	–542	–28	60	85
Croatia	ZWXP	–8	–11	25	81	50	–14	–21	–37	41	87	–58
Russia	BFSS	–832	–818	–316	–402	–859	–1 589	–2 347	–1 436	–272	–70	827
Turkey	BFUL	583	–451	–996	–1 072	–1 506	–1 530	–1 328	–1 920	–2 419	–2 027	–1 939
Ukraine	ZWXX	63	69	295	197	37	113	441	227	375	519	204
Serbia and Montenegro[2]	BFWE	–3	–16	–7	1	–22	–28	–46	–23	–3	–6	–37
of which *Serbia*	KND5	..	..	..	..	..	..	..	–27	–2	–7	–37
Montenegro	KND6	..	..	..	..	..	..	..	4	–1	1	–
Other	LEVY	–3 561	–4 764	–3 586	–937	–878	–2 158	–2 530	–8 602	–13 100	–4 034	–1 549
Total Europe	LERC	–17 866	–11 861	–18 699	–28 079	–38 995	–55 232	–53 518	–54 895	–10 902	–28 819	–66 523
Americas												
Argentina	ZWXZ	604	472	7	97	236	172	413	282	107	–16	75
Brazil	LENQ	138	142	108	–143	–40	72	64	289	529	1 149	863
Canada	LEOR	422	1 079	42	580	–172	454	450	1 302	–924	–1 404	1 764
Chile	ZWYA	–55	–138	–111	18	464	828	521	541	443	541	978
Colombia	ZWYB	152	71	129	210	286	266	138	–6	–174	–228	–30
Mexico	BFPP	263	–47	693	520	871	924	1 240	999	458	529	676
United States of America	BFVD	8 358	4 526	8 679	11 646	15 199	21 809	18 912	24 863	21 332	21 598	20 394
Uruguay	ZWYC	17	11	–18	46	–14	–10	–1	–29	–34	–66	–10
Venezuela	ZWYD	–59	361	344	162	299	263	–60	–176	–211	63	295
Other Central American Countries	JISU	771	1 934	3 818	3 394	3 228	3 795	3 600	4 638	4 505	4 521	9 837
Other	LEVG	–413	–290	–178	–67	294	–369	154	3 020	–18 192	–8 312	154
Total Americas	LESM	10 198	8 121	13 513	16 463	20 651	28 204	25 431	35 723	7 839	18 375	34 996
Asia												
China	LEPJ	–3 465	–3 881	–5 119	–6 038	–7 278	–9 361	–11 256	–14 237	–16 705	–17 543	–20 918
Hong Kong	BFJT	–4 832	–4 659	–3 452	–2 234	–1 111	–728	–1 662	–2 028	–4 700	–3 105	–792
India	BFNA	–68	–581	–381	–7	–545	–704	–965	–983	–422	–1 483	–1 295
Indonesia	BFKZ	–658	–733	–630	–499	–415	–408	–286	–457	–622	–358	–436
Iran	ZWYG	163	303	457	580	544	602	466	417	567	295	164
Israel	BFMR	500	434	641	581	554	467	208	132	255	228	105
Japan	BFOO	–7 080	–6 159	–4 589	–955	–2 144	–2 707	–2 753	–2 067	–1 668	–1 548	–4 411
Malaysia	BFPY	–1 159	–658	–249	–84	–166	–	–500	–295	–251	128	438
Pakistan	BFRR	–371	–302	–584	–490	–416	–63	–123	–291	–371	–379	–634
Philippines	BFRI	–867	–622	–527	–245	–204	–321	–421	–213	–163	22	–173
Saudi Arabia	BFTB	2 254	1 837	1 643	2 663	2 452	1 578	2 059	1 927	1 801	3 865	4 658
Singapore	BFTT	–156	232	179	205	428	1 003	1 033	–887	966	2 762	2 706
South Korea	BFOX	–1 520	–947	–342	–168	17	23	285	518	832	712	1 827
Taiwan	BFUU	–2 396	–1 739	–1 174	–918	–755	–650	–722	–966	–1 128	–1 251	–332
Thailand	BFUC	–1 200	–1 271	–1 251	–1 155	–1 353	–1 331	–2 039	–1 947	–2 272	–1 360	–1 507
Residual Gulf Arabian Countries	JITV	2 385	1 841	2 092	2 423	3 058	6 008	3 606	3 519	5 216	5 263	3 427
Other Near & Middle Eastern Countries	ZWYI	525	730	607	754	1 048	1 168	1 072	2 115	2 895	2 098	3 330
Other	LEWH	–1 190	–1 298	–1 359	–1 624	–2 092	–2 191	–1 587	–466	–1 876	–1 261	–1 310
Total Asia	LETE	–19 135	–17 473	–14 038	–7 211	–8 378	–7 615	–13 585	–16 209	–17 646	–12 915	–15 153
Australasia & Oceania												
Australia	CWJK	3 338	3 097	2 629	2 296	4 032	3 737	4 203	4 818	5 687	5 724	10 233
New Zealand	BFQZ	17	83	184	241	68	79	92	117	16	–52	31
Other	LEVP	–38	–40	–7	11	–13	–27	–353	37	57	67	472
Total Australasia & Oceania	LETW	3 317	3 140	2 806	2 548	4 087	3 789	3 942	4 972	5 760	5 739	10 736
Africa												
Egypt	ZWYK	–	–16	100	30	182	63	–173	391	517	637	1 167
Morocco	ZWYL	–111	–150	–205	–183	–278	–304	–278	–455	–224	–114	118
South Africa	BFWW	–465	–441	271	–168	635	1 065	–748	848	–1 195	–862	–55
Other North Africa	JIRW	–479	–294	–342	14	–314	–4 124	–1 334	–1 643	–1 657	–873	–1 939
Other	LEWQ	–33	–873	–643	–1 068	–1 150	3 057	–495	–976	703	1 280	2 874
Total Africa	LERU	–1 088	–1 774	–819	–1 375	–925	–243	–3 028	–1 835	–1 856	68	2 165
International Organisations	CTFA	–1 255	–1 215	–1 164	–726	–1 330	–1 570	–2 337	–2 582	–2 948	–2 764	–2 947
World total	HBOG	–25 829	–21 062	–18 401	–18 380	–24 890	–32 667	–43 095	–34 826	–19 753	–20 316	–36 726

1 Before 1999 only combined BLEU data is available under identifier CTFJ.

2 Separate data for Serbia and Montenegro is available from 2007.

THIS PAGE IS INTENTIONALLY BLANK

9.3 Trade in goods and services

£ million

		2000	2001	2002	2003	2004	2005	2006	2007	2008	2009	2010
Exports												
Europe												
European Union (EU)												
Austria	LGHT	1 549	1 632	1 688	1 686	1 528	1 851	2 242	2 080	2 256	2 034	2 106
Belgium[1]	A7RS	12 176	11 657	12 567	13 627	13 212	13 999	15 711	14 788	16 996	14 162	16 265
Bulgaria	ZWLR	127	155	208	219	233	314	343	379	445	401	413
Cyprus	A7RT	468	424	490	548	656	669	1 407	944	1 141	1 171	1 164
Czech Republic	LGIN	1 094	1 259	1 215	1 250	1 306	1 414	1 926	1 923	1 994	1 907	2 279
Denmark	LGHV	3 496	3 659	4 104	3 702	3 636	3 847	6 185	4 581	5 014	5 364	5 667
Estonia	ZWLX	108	97	121	115	135	152	528	264	270	183	272
Finland	LGHW	2 425	2 493	2 273	2 368	2 321	2 376	2 902	3 183	3 104	2 627	2 772
France	LGHX	24 015	25 327	24 778	25 122	25 175	26 390	36 388	26 534	28 018	25 955	28 141
Germany	LGHY	29 465	30 849	29 562	28 637	29 885	32 197	37 261	35 513	39 816	35 746	38 713
Greece	LGHZ	2 066	1 920	1 965	2 037	2 149	2 304	2 257	2 295	2 918	2 658	2 500
Hungary	XUXI	823	821	968	1 079	1 310	1 394	1 265	1 373	1 491	1 402	1 554
Ireland	LGIA	15 222	17 496	19 708	17 521	19 723	22 864	24 059	25 418	27 769	24 368	25 321
Italy	LGIB	11 120	11 307	11 527	11 623	11 814	12 501	13 233	13 461	13 935	13 344	14 004
Latvia	ZWMF	114	117	114	141	140	194	654	249	258	219	255
Lithuania	ZWME	148	182	181	231	197	279	340	432	560	265	321
Luxembourg[1]	A7RV	623	736	805	952	1 167	1 069	2 763	2 027	2 370	2 556	2 390
Malta	A7RW	269	267	286	329	336	310	411	485	635	684	620
Netherlands	LGIC	19 724	19 517	18 721	18 988	18 724	19 645	24 425	23 717	29 847	27 431	31 319
Poland	LGIO	1 585	1 634	1 707	1 870	1 927	2 455	3 809	3 391	4 092	3 851	4 936
Portugal	LGID	2 099	2 060	2 046	1 996	2 259	2 330	2 913	2 164	2 453	2 314	2 616
Romania	ZWMH	423	412	503	604	745	773	771	927	1 037	969	1 140
Slovak Republic	ZWMJ	195	244	230	270	269	358	389	525	761	620	757
Slovenia	ZWMI	181	195	229	202	212	231	269	276	316	259	312
Spain	LGIE	10 557	10 617	11 102	11 812	12 047	14 436	17 068	15 319	15 741	14 905	15 079
Sweden	LGIF	5 833	5 590	5 350	5 520	6 065	6 349	7 183	7 299	7 594	6 840	8 474
European Central Bank	ZWLL	3	12	3	–	–	–	–	–	–	–	–
EU Institutions	LGIG	248	544	544	513	578	602	609	627	685	673	758
Total EU27	GC8Q	146 156	151 223	152 995	152 962	157 749	171 303	207 311	190 174	211 516	192 908	210 148
European Free Trade Association (EFTA)												
Iceland	LGII	266	214	197	216	259	313	378	381	419	275	300
Liechtenstein	LGIJ	44	35	46	45	59	42	65	130	68	77	85
Norway	LGIK	3 103	2 856	3 239	3 272	3 528	4 075	4 119	5 272	5 309	5 263	5 497
Switzerland	LGIL	5 924	7 103	7 227	7 498	7 292	9 955	9 904	10 570	11 941	11 874	14 195
Total EFTA	LGIM	9 337	10 208	10 709	11 031	11 138	14 385	14 467	16 353	17 737	17 489	20 077
Other Europe												
Albania	ZWLP	9	28	25	17	34	24	30	30	46	31	33
Belarus	ZWLS	63	36	36	42	59	63	73	84	109	85	130
Croatia	ZWMC	111	121	149	188	168	162	245	257	338	328	255
Russia	LGIP	1 087	1 367	1 571	2 143	2 374	2 986	3 727	4 929	6 452	4 233	5 260
Turkey	LGIQ	2 193	1 589	1 729	2 097	2 331	2 711	3 033	3 110	3 333	3 293	4 374
Ukraine	ZWMK	195	224	473	364	269	373	487	647	840	766	718
Serbia and Montenegro[2]	ZWMN	135	92	90	105	87	58	131	170	168	173	156
of which Serbia	KN9Z	..	..	..	..	..	..	..	156	155	155	141
Montenegro	KNA2	..	..	..	..	..	..	..	14	13	18	15
Other	ZWLM	1 438	1 385	1 693	2 249	2 462	3 043	3 486	3 936	5 441	4 611	4 132
Total Europe	LGIS	160 724	166 273	169 470	171 198	176 671	195 108	232 990	219 690	245 980	223 917	245 283
Americas												
Argentina	ZWLQ	476	457	204	212	313	258	325	356	457	401	590
Brazil	LGIT	1 122	1 202	1 202	1 155	1 108	1 214	1 409	1 521	2 279	2 482	3 053
Canada	LGIU	4 862	4 831	4 630	4 809	5 090	5 009	5 901	5 786	5 921	6 029	7 032
Chile	ZWLT	209	230	200	200	217	237	316	361	439	707	811
Colombia	ZWLU	156	244	167	203	202	179	207	213	241	265	430
Mexico	LGIV	942	971	963	953	977	937	1 136	1 119	1 230	1 135	1 373
United States of America	LGIW	48 646	48 614	50 832	52 705	54 293	55 337	61 499	65 582	70 765	67 686	72 211
Uruguay	ZWML	64	53	35	93	41	50	59	53	83	75	99
Venezuela	ZWMM	300	423	402	241	286	322	306	308	345	375	627
Other Central American Countries	ZWLW	2 388	2 285	2 892	3 076	3 608	4 172	4 437	5 050	5 881	5 212	5 108
Other	ZWLZ	380	383	310	330	300	351	396	492	549	495	671
Total Americas	LGIY	59 545	59 693	61 837	63 977	66 435	68 066	75 991	80 841	88 190	84 862	92 005
Asia												
China	LGIZ	1 910	2 297	2 209	2 794	3 646	4 186	4 790	5 324	7 572	7 631	10 263
Hong Kong	LGJA	3 708	3 770	3 488	3 663	3 752	4 430	4 158	4 322	5 818	5 448	6 062
India	LGJB	2 599	2 438	2 379	2 988	3 233	3 954	4 346	4 665	5 886	4 660	6 128
Indonesia	LGJC	606	515	504	624	593	567	609	545	652	692	786
Iran	ZWMD	424	606	586	702	686	676	643	565	707	618	435
Israel	LGJD	1 957	1 867	1 849	1 729	1 798	1 903	1 763	1 723	1 863	1 730	2 069
Japan	LGJE	7 126	7 226	7 431	7 591	8 077	8 212	8 476	8 534	8 946	8 207	8 649
Malaysia	LGJF	1 293	1 403	1 278	1 444	1 547	1 546	1 383	1 402	1 661	1 726	1 973
Pakistan	LGJG	374	494	401	466	576	893	851	745	822	835	763
Philippines	LGJH	452	572	462	520	443	412	340	359	477	445	409
Saudi Arabia	LGJI	3 947	3 651	3 349	4 135	4 134	3 808	4 212	4 004	4 201	4 773	5 413
Singapore	LGJJ	2 704	2 882	2 605	3 219	3 867	4 719	5 331	6 025	6 410	6 959	7 108
South Korea	LGJK	1 742	1 687	1 984	1 948	2 392	2 413	2 609	2 832	3 664	3 088	3 467
Taiwan	LGJL	1 291	1 169	1 212	1 273	1 466	1 523	1 503	1 578	1 574	1 456	2 261
Thailand	LGJM	773	815	737	903	955	891	860	914	1 110	1 411	1 596
Residual Gulf Arabian Countries	ZWMA	3 715	3 817	3 920	4 702	5 782	9 042	7 473	7 350	9 773	9 640	10 597
Other Near & Middle Eastern Countries	ZWMB	619	803	748	878	1 103	1 175	1 414	1 180	1 632	1 743	1 926
Other	ZWLN	1 455	1 435	1 224	1 387	1 556	1 676	2 107	3 049	2 496	2 688	2 938
Total Asia	LGJO	36 695	37 447	36 366	40 966	45 606	52 026	52 868	55 116	65 264	63 750	72 843
Australasia & Oceania												
Australia	LGJP	4 281	4 262	3 947	4 308	4 743	5 292	5 338	5 889	7 160	7 139	8 387
New Zealand	LGJQ	611	605	586	650	797	828	781	793	817	776	866
Other	LGJR	131	141	154	185	177	143	198	176	240	224	290
Total Australasia & Oceania	LGJS	5 023	5 008	4 687	5 143	5 717	6 263	6 317	6 858	8 217	8 139	9 543
Africa												
Egypt	ZWLY	782	793	686	697	991	917	1 048	1 320	1 668	1 663	1 758
Morocco	ZWMG	467	449	377	406	397	298	395	387	617	478	702
South Africa	LGJT	2 383	2 654	2 590	2 843	2 955	3 203	3 548	3 627	4 209	3 754	4 613
Other North Africa	ZWLV	677	645	684	849	814	851	906	895	1 357	1 529	1 411
Other	ZWLO	3 367	3 749	3 672	4 055	3 974	4 275	4 986	5 251	7 312	7 457	8 597
Total Africa	LGJV	7 676	8 290	8 009	8 850	9 131	9 544	10 883	11 480	15 163	14 881	17 081
International Organisations	LGJW	51	64	85	73	52	60	42	47	50	39	41
World total	KTMW	269 714	276 775	280 454	290 207	303 612	331 067	379 091	374 032	422 864	395 588	436 796

1 Before 1999 only combined BLEU data is available under indentifier LGHU.

2 Separate data for Serbia and Montenegro available from 2007.

9.3 Trade in goods and services

continued £ million

		2000	2001	2002	2003	2004	2005	2006	2007	2008	2009	2010
Imports												
Europe												
European Union (EU)												
Austria	LGJY	1 894	2 391	3 083	3 436	3 112	3 340	3 667	3 311	3 318	3 188	3 620
Belgium[1]	A8EO	11 978	13 253	14 164	14 302	14 790	16 266	17 416	17 332	19 009	17 411	19 400
Bulgaria	ZWNX	125	152	213	230	324	427	438	572	609	448	571
Cyprus	A8EP	1 090	1 297	1 223	1 342	1 289	1 479	2 896	1 328	1 322	1 057	987
Czech Republic	LGKS	969	1 298	1 500	1 753	1 716	2 348	3 488	3 467	4 066	3 708	4 422
Denmark	LGKA	3 313	3 582	4 350	4 185	4 220	5 358	7 557	4 492	5 063	5 266	5 411
Estonia	ZWOD	345	307	340	299	427	418	2 188	293	206	157	196
Finland	LGKB	3 168	3 323	3 071	2 977	2 625	2 785	3 431	3 040	3 201	2 467	2 615
France	LGKC	26 207	27 665	28 651	28 655	28 668	31 000	36 335	31 827	33 206	29 723	31 208
Germany	LGKD	33 208	35 447	37 852	39 257	41 849	46 903	49 854	53 022	54 600	48 918	55 542
Greece	LGKE	2 069	2 372	2 503	2 625	2 635	2 719	2 821	2 888	2 809	2 670	2 652
Hungary	ZWOJ	775	833	975	1 269	1 767	2 136	2 699	2 746	2 880	2 958	3 737
Ireland	LGKF	12 548	14 528	15 535	12 497	13 195	13 849	14 212	15 312	16 464	16 685	17 023
Italy	LGKG	12 383	12 857	13 812	14 910	15 763	16 994	17 041	18 030	19 115	16 773	18 290
Latvia	ZWOM	432	450	495	546	728	762	880	718	488	395	534
Lithuania	ZWOL	250	245	300	312	289	351	367	405	446	471	669
Luxembourg[1]	A8ER	407	605	965	978	1 289	1 220	3 253	1 191	1 434	1 157	2 348
Malta	A8ES	351	401	408	465	502	522	461	483	517	433	496
Netherlands	LGKH	18 424	18 522	19 529	20 020	21 566	24 041	26 059	26 729	29 697	26 169	30 347
Poland	LGKT	1 095	1 367	1 453	1 770	2 133	2 880	4 623	4 914	5 624	5 924	7 467
Portugal	LGKI	2 755	2 740	2 970	3 334	3 325	3 463	4 603	3 211	3 666	2 938	3 382
Romania	ZWOO	400	529	603	772	918	971	997	1 119	1 025	1 024	1 499
Slovak Republic	ZWOQ	168	188	238	282	296	439	939	1 368	1 752	1 728	1 741
Slovenia	ZWOP	152	166	196	195	205	252	803	361	386	291	405
Spain	LGKJ	12 647	14 599	17 045	18 237	18 236	21 004	21 952	20 490	21 383	19 006	19 863
Sweden	LGKK	5 784	5 501	5 153	5 703	6 273	6 783	7 532	6 529	8 312	7 484	8 423
European Central Bank	ZWNR	1	1	1	–	–	–	–	–	2	2	–
EU Institutions	LGKL	3	5	14	17	4	4	2	–	5	5	2
Total EU27	GCU9	152 941	164 624	176 642	180 368	188 144	208 714	236 514	225 178	240 605	218 456	242 850
European Free Trade Association (EFTA)												
Iceland	LGKN	450	337	343	351	418	421	502	511	549	619	489
Liechtenstein	LGKO	29	33	27	36	22	20	45	61	42	34	30
Norway	LGKP	6 265	6 410	6 792	7 345	9 519	13 413	15 741	15 637	23 135	17 411	22 145
Switzerland	LGKQ	7 232	6 246	6 455	5 621	5 326	6 212	6 710	7 623	7 996	8 262	10 644
Total EFTA	LGKR	13 976	13 026	13 617	13 353	15 285	20 066	22 998	23 832	31 722	26 326	33 308
Other Europe												
Albania	ZWNV	7	9	15	17	20	8	13	22	20	13	4
Belarus	ZWNY	37	22	36	27	73	281	750	616	124	26	46
Croatia	ZWOI	69	108	117	120	138	193	243	228	318	275	318
Russia	LGKU	1 691	2 282	2 248	2 762	4 036	5 611	6 510	6 303	8 080	5 935	6 161
Turkey	LGKV	1 968	2 291	2 950	3 458	4 127	4 598	5 062	5 852	6 461	5 985	6 974
Ukraine	ZWOR	74	93	163	105	143	174	195	313	376	297	500
Serbia and Montenegro[2]	ZWOU	45	61	63	75	76	61	138	145	150	137	143
of which Serbia	KNA3	..	..	..	..	..	..	..	138	141	123	131
Montenegro	KNA4	..	..	..	..	..	..	..	7	9	14	12
Other	ZWNS	1 208	1 107	1 265	1 212	1 107	1 229	1 412	1 598	1 482	1 505	1 522
Total Europe	LGKX	172 016	183 623	197 116	201 497	213 149	240 935	273 835	264 087	289 338	258 955	291 826
Americas												
Argentina	ZWNW	245	273	293	295	328	360	461	511	697	769	777
Brazil	LGKY	1 303	1 529	1 634	1 677	1 800	2 039	2 199	2 332	3 002	2 889	3 558
Canada	LGKZ	5 080	4 823	4 612	4 667	5 221	5 305	6 262	7 165	7 253	5 743	7 247
Chile	ZWNZ	510	528	527	471	560	573	566	565	635	673	634
Colombia	ZWOA	277	349	250	256	300	341	347	405	732	634	733
Mexico	LGLA	890	1 067	827	789	764	730	701	914	1 239	1 022	1 430
United States of America	LGLB	41 673	43 364	38 643	37 871	37 432	38 350	42 195	43 677	45 577	43 445	46 192
Uruguay	ZWOS	43	46	69	47	46	65	78	77	120	140	111
Venezuela	ZWOT	250	197	214	146	234	425	636	525	653	470	471
Other Central American Countries	ZWOC	2 548	2 031	2 099	2 435	3 010	2 985	4 083	3 795	4 348	4 376	3 413
Other	ZWOF	544	448	392	353	347	395	428	411	525	475	487
Total Americas	LGLD	53 363	54 655	49 560	49 007	50 042	51 568	57 956	60 377	64 781	60 636	65 053
Asia												
China	LGLE	5 247	6 280	7 409	9 006	11 185	13 936	16 345	19 885	24 773	25 804	31 817
Hong Kong	LGLF	6 624	6 484	6 293	6 303	6 573	7 450	8 290	8 191	9 196	8 731	9 228
India	LGLG	2 314	2 640	2 617	2 897	3 388	4 077	4 725	5 527	6 789	6 560	8 104
Indonesia	LGLH	1 291	1 323	1 226	1 273	1 084	1 017	1 166	1 133	1 345	1 361	1 507
Iran	ZWOK	64	51	49	60	90	67	121	96	110	285	272
Israel	LGLI	1 276	1 233	1 062	1 052	1 146	1 245	1 253	1 348	1 483	1 448	1 981
Japan	LGLJ	11 788	10 906	9 518	9 826	9 769	10 866	10 585	10 827	12 217	9 976	11 734
Malaysia	LGLK	2 574	2 167	1 955	2 067	2 261	2 100	2 171	1 934	2 137	1 917	2 097
Pakistan	LGLL	666	706	872	907	987	955	995	903	1 031	1 091	1 252
Philippines	LGLM	1 385	1 270	1 068	881	776	864	921	877	833	577	742
Saudi Arabia	LGLN	1 559	1 584	1 990	1 793	1 974	2 402	1 970	1 635	1 275	905	1 015
Singapore	LGLO	2 769	2 482	2 404	3 124	4 092	4 607	4 653	5 026	5 434	5 136	5 949
South Korea	LGLP	3 523	2 930	2 902	2 739	3 315	3 289	3 310	3 311	3 913	3 226	2 914
Taiwan	LGLQ	3 809	3 011	2 628	2 419	2 587	2 572	2 598	2 727	2 982	2 538	3 365
Thailand	LGLR	2 025	2 114	2 108	2 192	2 439	2 360	2 645	2 711	3 127	2 951	3 307
Residual Gulf Arabian Countries	ZWOG	1 554	1 675	1 829	2 332	2 665	3 028	3 498	3 644	4 458	4 794	7 169
Other Near & Middle Eastern Countries	ZWOH	240	271	321	307	299	401	969	547	655	571	527
Other	ZWNT	2 208	2 159	2 250	2 606	3 109	2 896	3 492	3 512	4 145	4 623	5 009
Total Asia	LGLT	50 916	49 286	48 501	51 784	57 739	64 132	69 707	73 834	85 903	82 494	97 989
Australasia & Oceania												
Australia	LGLU	2 650	2 969	3 076	3 217	3 219	3 928	3 887	3 966	4 430	3 964	4 509
New Zealand	LGLV	799	829	854	894	1 012	1 087	1 043	1 088	1 119	1 102	1 198
Other	LGLW	154	119	131	154	181	179	206	164	245	223	159
Total Australasia & Oceania	LGLX	3 603	3 917	4 061	4 265	4 412	5 194	5 136	5 218	5 794	5 289	5 866
Africa												
Egypt	ZWOE	700	769	722	778	835	874	1 267	1 126	1 411	1 428	1 340
Morocco	ZWON	571	592	598	587	664	589	601	807	813	590	591
South Africa	LGLY	3 132	3 493	3 412	3 912	4 230	5 018	4 978	4 097	5 685	4 737	5 524
Other North Africa	ZWOB	1 080	878	874	855	1 093	1 356	2 013	2 105	2 804	2 196	3 283
Other	ZWNU	2 270	3 472	3 604	3 808	4 054	4 062	4 272	4 973	5 416	4 885	4 978
Total Africa	LGMA	7 753	9 204	9 210	9 940	10 876	11 899	13 131	13 108	16 129	13 836	15 716
International Organisations	LGMB	80	62	40	29	37	43	57	57	43	15	30
World total	KTMX	287 731	300 747	308 488	316 522	336 255	373 771	419 822	416 681	461 988	421 225	476 480

1 Before 1999 only combined BLEU data is available under identifier LGJZ.

2 Separate Serbia and Montenegro data available from 2007.

9.3 Trade in goods and services

continued

£ million

		2000	2001	2002	2003	2004	2005	2006	2007	2008	2009	2010
Balances												
Europe												
European Union (EU)												
Austria	LGMD	–345	–759	–1 395	–1 750	–1 584	–1 489	–1 425	–1 231	–1 062	–1 154	–1 514
Belgium[1]	A8HC	198	–1 596	–1 597	–675	–1 578	–2 267	–1 705	–2 544	–2 013	–3 249	–3 135
Bulgaria	ZWSK	2	3	–5	–11	–91	–113	–95	–193	–164	–47	–158
Cyprus	A8HD	–622	–873	–733	–794	–633	–810	–1 489	–384	–181	114	177
Czech Republic	LGMX	125	–39	–285	–503	–410	–934	–1 562	–1 544	–2 072	–1 801	–2 143
Denmark	LGMF	183	77	–246	–483	–584	–1 511	–1 372	89	–49	98	256
Estonia	ZWSQ	–237	–210	–219	–184	–292	–266	–1 660	–29	64	26	76
Finland	LGMG	–743	–830	–798	–609	–304	–409	–529	143	–97	160	157
France	LGMH	–2 192	–2 338	–3 873	–3 533	–3 493	–4 610	53	–5 293	–5 188	–3 768	–3 067
Germany	LGMI	–3 743	–4 598	–8 290	–10 620	–11 964	–14 706	–12 593	–17 509	–14 784	–13 172	–16 829
Greece	LGMJ	–3	–452	–538	–588	–486	–415	–564	–593	109	–12	–152
Hungary	ZWSW	48	–12	–7	–190	–457	–742	–1 434	–1 373	–1 389	–1 556	–2 183
Ireland	LGMK	2 674	2 968	4 173	5 024	6 528	9 015	9 847	10 106	11 305	7 683	8 298
Italy	LGML	–1 263	–1 550	–2 285	–3 287	–3 949	–4 493	–3 808	–4 569	–5 180	–3 429	–4 286
Latvia	ZWSZ	–318	–333	–381	–405	–588	–568	–226	–469	–230	–176	–279
Lithuania	ZWSY	–102	–63	–119	–81	–92	–72	–27	27	114	–206	–348
Luxembourg[1]	A8HF	216	131	–160	–26	–122	–151	–490	836	936	1 399	42
Malta	A8HG	–82	–134	–122	–136	–166	–212	–50	2	118	251	124
Netherlands	LGMM	1 300	995	–808	–1 032	–2 842	–4 396	–1 634	–3 012	150	1 262	972
Poland	LGMY	490	267	254	100	–206	–425	–814	–1 523	–1 532	–2 073	–2 531
Portugal	LGMN	–656	–680	–924	–1 338	–1 066	–1 133	–1 690	–1 047	–1 213	–624	–766
Romania	ZWTB	23	–117	–100	–168	–173	–198	–226	–192	12	–55	–359
Slovak Republic	ZWTD	27	56	–8	–12	–27	–81	–550	–843	–991	–1 108	–984
Slovenia	ZWTC	29	29	33	7	7	–21	–534	–85	–70	–32	–93
Spain	LGMO	–2 090	–3 982	–5 943	–6 425	–6 189	–6 568	–4 884	–5 171	–5 642	–4 101	–4 784
Sweden	LGMP	49	89	197	–183	–208	–434	–349	770	–718	–644	51
European Central Bank	ZWSE	2	11	2	–	–	–	–	–	–2	–2	–
EU Institutions	LGMQ	245	539	530	496	574	598	607	627	680	668	756
Total EU27	GD6Q	–6 785	–13 401	–23 647	–27 406	–30 395	–37 411	–29 203	–35 004	–29 089	–25 548	–32 702
European Free Trade Association (EFTA)												
Iceland	LGMS	–184	–123	–146	–135	–159	–108	–124	–130	–130	–344	–189
Liechtenstein	LGMT	15	2	19	9	37	22	20	69	26	43	55
Norway	LGMU	–3 162	–3 554	–3 553	–4 073	–5 991	–9 338	–11 622	–10 365	–17 826	–12 148	–16 648
Switzerland	LGMV	–1 308	857	772	1 877	1 966	3 743	3 194	2 947	3 945	3 612	3 551
Total EFTA	LGMW	–4 639	–2 818	–2 908	–2 322	–4 147	–5 681	–8 531	–7 479	–13 985	–8 837	–13 231
Other Europe												
Albania	ZWSI	2	19	10	–	14	16	17	8	26	18	29
Belarus	ZWSL	26	14	–	15	–14	–218	–677	–532	–15	59	84
Croatia	ZWSV	42	13	32	68	30	–31	2	29	20	53	–63
Russia	LGMZ	–604	–915	–677	–619	–1 662	–2 625	–2 783	–1 374	–1 628	–1 702	–901
Turkey	LGNA	225	–702	–1 221	–1 361	–1 796	–1 887	–2 029	–2 742	–3 128	–2 692	–2 600
Ukraine	ZWTE	121	131	310	259	126	199	292	334	464	469	218
Serbia and Montenegro[2]	ZWTH	90	31	27	30	11	–3	–7	25	18	36	13
of which Serbia	KNA5	..	..	..	..	..	..	..	18	14	32	10
Montenegro	KNA6	..	..	..	..	..	..	..	7	4	4	3
Other	ZWSF	230	278	428	1 037	1 355	1 814	2 074	2 338	3 959	3 106	2 610
Total Europe	LGNC	–11 292	–17 350	–27 646	–30 299	–36 478	–45 827	–40 845	–44 397	–43 358	–35 038	–46 543
Americas												
Argentina	ZWSJ	231	184	–89	–83	–15	–102	–136	–155	–240	–368	–187
Brazil	LGND	–181	–327	–432	–522	–692	–825	–790	–811	–723	–407	–505
Canada	LGNE	–218	8	18	142	–131	–296	–361	–1 379	–1 332	286	–215
Chile	ZWSM	–301	–298	–327	–271	–343	–336	–250	–204	–196	34	177
Colombia	ZWSN	–121	–105	–83	–53	–98	–162	–140	–192	–491	–369	–303
Mexico	LGNF	52	–96	136	164	213	207	435	205	–9	113	–57
United States of America	LGNG	6 973	5 250	12 189	14 834	16 861	16 987	19 304	21 905	25 188	24 241	26 019
Uruguay	ZWTF	21	7	–34	46	–5	–15	–19	–24	–37	–65	–12
Venezuela	ZWTG	50	226	188	95	52	–103	–330	–217	–308	–95	156
Other Central American Countries	ZWSP	–160	254	793	641	598	1 187	354	1 255	1 533	836	1 695
Other	ZWSS	–164	–65	–82	–23	–47	–44	–32	81	24	20	184
Total Americas	LGNI	6 182	5 038	12 277	14 970	16 393	16 498	18 035	20 464	23 409	24 226	26 952
Asia												
China	LGNJ	–3 337	–3 983	–5 200	–6 212	–7 539	–9 750	–11 555	–14 561	–17 201	–18 173	–21 554
Hong Kong	LGNK	–2 916	–2 714	–2 805	–2 640	–2 821	–3 020	–4 132	–3 869	–3 378	–3 283	–3 166
India	LGNL	285	–202	–238	91	–155	–123	–379	–862	–903	–1 900	–1 976
Indonesia	LGNM	–685	–808	–722	–649	–491	–450	–557	–588	–693	–669	–721
Iran	ZWSX	360	555	537	642	596	609	522	469	597	333	163
Israel	LGNN	681	634	787	677	652	658	510	375	380	282	88
Japan	LGNO	–4 662	–3 680	–2 087	–2 235	–1 692	–2 654	–2 109	–2 293	–3 271	–1 769	–3 085
Malaysia	LGNP	–1 281	–764	–677	–623	–714	–554	–788	–532	–476	–191	–124
Pakistan	LGNQ	–292	–212	–471	–441	–411	–62	–144	–158	–209	–256	–489
Philippines	LGNR	–933	–698	–606	–361	–333	–452	–581	–518	–356	–132	–333
Saudi Arabia	LGNS	2 388	2 067	1 359	2 342	2 160	1 406	2 242	2 369	2 926	3 868	4 398
Singapore	LGNT	–65	400	201	95	–225	112	678	999	976	1 823	1 159
South Korea	LGNU	–1 781	–1 243	–918	–791	–923	–876	–701	–479	–249	–138	553
Taiwan	LGNV	–2 518	–1 842	–1 416	–1 146	–1 121	–1 049	–1 095	–1 149	–1 408	–1 082	–1 104
Thailand	LGNW	–1 252	–1 299	–1 371	–1 289	–1 484	–1 469	–1 785	–1 797	–2 017	–1 540	–1 711
Residual Gulf Arabian Countries	ZWST	2 161	2 142	2 091	2 370	3 117	6 014	3 975	3 706	5 315	4 846	3 428
Other Near & Middle Eastern Countries	ZWSU	379	532	427	571	804	774	445	633	977	1 172	1 399
Other	ZWSG	–753	–724	–1 026	–1 219	–1 553	–1 220	–1 385	–463	–1 649	–1 935	–2 071
Total Asia	LGNY	–14 221	–11 839	–12 135	–10 818	–12 133	–12 106	–16 839	–18 718	–20 639	–18 744	–25 146
Australasia & Oceania												
Australia	LGNZ	1 631	1 293	871	1 091	1 524	1 364	1 451	1 923	2 730	3 175	3 878
New Zealand	LGOA	–188	–224	–268	–244	–215	–259	–262	–295	–302	–326	–332
Other	LGOB	–23	22	23	31	–4	–36	–8	12	–5	1	131
Total Australasia & Oceania	LGOC	1 420	1 091	626	878	1 305	1 069	1 181	1 640	2 423	2 850	3 677
Africa												
Egypt	ZWSR	82	24	–36	–81	156	43	–219	194	257	235	418
Morocco	ZWTA	–104	–143	–221	–181	–267	–291	–206	–420	–196	–112	111
South Africa	LGOD	–749	–839	–822	–1 069	–1 275	–1 815	–1 430	–470	–1 476	–983	–911
Other North Africa	ZWSO	–403	–233	–190	–6	–279	–505	–1 107	–1 210	–1 447	–667	–1 872
Other	ZWSH	1 097	277	68	247	–80	213	714	278	1 896	2 572	3 619
Total Africa	LGOF	–77	–914	–1 201	–1 090	–1 745	–2 355	–2 248	–1 628	–966	1 045	1 365
International Organisations	LGOG	–29	2	45	44	15	17	–15	–10	7	24	11
World total	KTMY	–18 017	–23 972	–28 034	–26 315	–32 643	–42 704	–40 731	–42 649	–39 124	–25 637	–39 684

1 Before 1999 only combined BLEU data is available under identifier LGME.
2 Separate Serbia and Montenegro data is available from 2007.

THIS PAGE IS INTENTIONALLY BLANK

9.4 Trade in goods

£ million

		2000	2001	2002	2003	2004	2005	2006	2007	2008	2009	2010
Exports												
Europe												
European Union (EU)												
Austria	QBRY	1 144	1 223	1 262	1 264	1 095	1 329	1 688	1 375	1 472	1 290	1 463
Belgium[1]	QDOH	10 088	9 606	10 184	11 078	10 255	11 181	13 119	11 822	13 429	10 882	13 377
Bulgaria	QAMF	85	120	133	152	155	220	226	202	252	197	249
Cyprus	QDNZ	319	289	271	314	321	355	1 047	415	537	620	562
Czech Republic	QDLF	926	1 074	1 034	1 007	977	1 078	1 577	1 401	1 550	1 441	1 827
Denmark	QBSE	2 316	2 269	2 730	2 180	2 045	2 317	3 860	2 177	2 594	2 477	2 757
Estonia	QAMN	96	83	100	93	106	115	471	228	220	140	193
Finland	QBSH	1 470	1 614	1 441	1 493	1 364	1 516	1 819	1 957	1 910	1 323	1 498
France	QDJA	18 572	19 249	18 757	18 886	18 568	19 926	29 077	18 085	18 095	17 204	19 228
Germany	QDJD	22 783	23 656	22 065	20 809	21 674	23 017	27 208	24 669	27 959	24 270	27 913
Greece	QDJG	1 230	1 111	1 200	1 250	1 407	1 369	1 473	1 355	1 661	1 621	1 381
Hungary	QDLI	617	616	750	854	938	833	839	861	1 009	850	1 082
Ireland	QDJJ	12 371	13 838	15 420	12 225	14 139	16 291	17 243	17 761	19 134	15 936	16 932
Italy	QDJM	8 427	8 406	8 509	8 606	8 405	8 789	9 486	9 174	9 401	8 348	8 853
Latvia	QAMO	84	84	76	112	91	101	587	145	169	109	168
Lithuania	QAMP	131	136	149	188	142	167	236	311	282	172	225
Luxembourg[1]	QDOK	234	293	369	300	260	212	1 631	271	202	193	246
Malta	QDOC	212	215	225	256	257	239	320	363	450	401	393
Netherlands	QDJP	15 167	14 603	14 012	13 599	12 027	12 711	16 663	15 079	19 920	18 205	21 250
Poland	QDLL	1 299	1 297	1 315	1 461	1 422	1 653	2 791	2 371	3 018	2 798	3 804
Portugal	QDJT	1 663	1 575	1 516	1 454	1 582	1 698	2 340	1 483	1 644	1 543	1 837
Romania	QAMQ	379	339	427	507	608	646	605	664	753	686	781
Slovak Republic	QAMR	156	201	200	234	223	259	275	380	454	378	466
Slovenia	QAMS	153	157	181	159	160	168	195	204	223	175	220
Spain	QDJW	8 301	8 365	8 490	8 945	9 101	10 672	12 557	10 035	10 278	9 224	9 940
Sweden	QDJZ	4 213	3 954	3 873	3 826	4 356	4 586	5 179	4 896	5 218	4 217	5 563
European Central Bank	QARP	–	–	–	–	–	–	–	–	–	–	–
EU Institutions	EOAY	–	–	–	–	–	–	–	–	–	–	–
Total EU27	LGCJ	112 436	114 373	114 689	111 252	111 678	121 448	152 512	127 684	141 834	124 700	142 208
European Free Trade Association (EFTA)												
Iceland	QDKW	193	151	133	144	170	178	189	201	188	128	132
Liechtenstein	EPOW	7	5	3	5	6	2	22	3	9	5	25
Norway	QDKZ	2 072	1 880	1 790	1 949	2 004	2 258	2 165	2 731	2 883	2 839	3 114
Switzerland	QDLC	3 140	3 615	3 260	2 887	2 937	5 087	4 254	3 829	4 712	3 979	5 214
Total EFTA	EPOT	5 412	5 651	5 186	4 985	5 117	7 525	6 630	6 764	7 792	6 951	8 485
Other Europe												
Albania	QAMC	7	23	19	11	12	16	17	19	16	18	21
Belarus	QAME	36	33	32	38	53	56	64	69	90	81	120
Croatia	QAMM	73	87	94	137	124	116	146	157	219	223	173
Russia	QDLO	672	897	990	1 413	1 473	1 859	2 048	2 793	4 268	2 402	3 595
Turkey	QDLR	1 842	1 191	1 357	1 696	1 963	2 200	2 465	2 346	2 600	2 369	3 248
Ukraine	QAMT	152	195	171	238	214	276	338	443	614	589	474
Serbia and Montenegro[2]	QAMW	32	51	62	65	66	23	89	106	130	102	97
of which Serbia	KN2P	..	..	..	..	..	..	..	98	120	98	93
Montenegro	KN2M	..	..	..	..	..	..	..	8	10	4	4
Other	BOQE	196	225	188	220	214	287	338	294	563	508	810
Total Europe	EPLM	120 858	122 726	122 788	120 055	120 914	133 806	164 647	140 675	158 126	137 943	159 231
Americas												
Argentina	QAOM	290	262	121	129	171	159	218	224	319	255	357
Brazil	QDLU	772	810	881	821	801	846	907	1 066	1 693	1 788	2 217
Canada	QATH	3 465	3 192	3 087	3 220	3 314	3 251	3 851	3 266	3 241	3 329	4 127
Chile	QAMG	113	127	113	121	134	149	187	183	264	514	630
Colombia	QAML	100	104	81	106	115	113	135	139	160	173	230
Mexico	QDLX	675	683	698	682	623	631	732	763	901	751	952
United States of America	J8V9	29 371	29 403	28 142	28 819	28 525	30 836	31 944	32 044	35 277	33 951	37 925
Uruguay	QAMU	57	48	30	33	31	37	42	36	65	60	79
Venezuela	QAMV	217	313	303	139	187	226	234	250	282	300	273
Other Central American Countries	BOQQ	969	681	683	700	622	685	850	862	1 018	757	897
Other	BOQT	159	164	160	173	153	157	172	188	245	234	394
Total Americas	EPLO	36 188	35 787	34 299	34 943	34 676	37 090	39 272	39 021	43 465	42 112	48 081
Asia												
China	QDMA	1 461	1 706	1 485	1 908	2 368	2 798	3 256	3 764	5 055	5 401	7 611
Hong Kong	QDMD	2 667	2 676	2 482	2 473	2 625	3 080	2 848	2 645	3 662	3 735	4 456
India	QDMG	2 046	1 763	1 744	2 269	2 235	2 791	2 689	2 952	4 117	2 949	4 068
Indonesia	QDMJ	414	310	330	460	403	379	317	294	396	367	461
Iran	QAON	300	437	401	478	444	460	427	400	443	405	307
Israel	QDMM	1 512	1 356	1 420	1 360	1 391	1 345	1 305	1 235	1 339	1 145	1 387
Japan	QAMJ	3 657	3 668	3 587	3 701	3 856	3 895	4 093	3 850	3 911	3 570	4 334
Malaysia	QDMP	903	1 027	874	1 023	993	1 081	879	948	1 130	1 052	1 272
Pakistan	QDMS	198	216	228	284	345	462	489	427	478	478	461
Philippines	QDMV	269	394	357	380	317	274	239	247	241	268	284
Saudi Arabia	QDMY	1 578	1 504	1 376	1 824	1 606	1 585	1 665	1 847	2 212	2 363	2 488
Singapore	QDNB	1 618	1 588	1 439	1 572	1 710	2 073	2 308	2 437	2 808	2 955	3 447
South Korea	QDNE	1 346	1 259	1 479	1 476	1 480	1 676	1 740	1 852	2 553	2 167	2 344
Taiwan	QDNH	1 010	874	842	892	951	940	909	932	887	795	1 116
Thailand	QDNK	579	596	530	570	636	632	564	598	758	914	1 137
Residual Gulf Arabian Countries	BOQW	2 612	2 703	2 588	3 372	4 017	7 051	5 150	4 503	6 027	5 773	6 590
Other Near & Middle Eastern Countries	QARJ	388	464	480	618	764	727	974	742	1 030	1 096	1 316
Other	BORB	644	551	497	591	599	564	672	1 585	846	982	1 212
Total Asia	EPLP	23 202	23 092	22 139	25 251	26 740	31 813	30 524	31 258	37 893	36 415	44 291
Australasia & Oceania												
Australia	QDNN	2 693	2 298	2 121	2 293	2 452	2 579	2 480	2 577	3 104	2 960	3 362
New Zealand	QDNQ	310	304	311	349	418	416	376	359	388	350	414
Other	EGIZ	47	46	57	70	47	80	75	66	102	91	82
Total Australasia & Oceania	EPLQ	3 050	2 648	2 489	2 712	2 917	3 075	2 931	3 002	3 594	3 401	3 858
Africa												
Egypt	QDNT	502	453	460	459	669	543	576	687	944	1 006	1 198
Morocco	QAOO	406	367	327	358	336	252	305	313	514	311	565
South Africa	QDNW	1 407	1 525	1 581	1 757	1 875	2 068	2 172	2 149	2 648	2 254	2 890
Other North Africa	BORU	412	426	462	563	526	476	498	506	812	959	907
Other	BOQH	1 801	1 978	1 898	2 143	2 133	2 375	2 639	2 736	3 981	3 725	4 693
Total Africa	EPLN	4 528	4 749	4 728	5 280	5 539	5 714	6 190	6 391	8 899	8 255	10 253
International Organisations	EPLR	–	–	–	–	–	–	–	–	–	–	–
World total	LQAD	187 826	189 002	186 443	188 241	190 786	211 498	243 564	220 347	251 977	228 126	265 714

1 Before 1999 only combined BLEU data is available under identifier QBSB.

2 Separate Serbia and Montenegro data is available from 2007.

9.4 Trade in goods

continued

£ million

		2000	2001	2002	2003	2004	2005	2006	2007	2008	2009	2010
Imports												
Europe												
European Union (EU)												
Austria	QBRZ	1 417	1 885	2 395	2 776	2 355	2 469	2 776	2 494	2 353	2 280	2 633
Belgium[1]	QDOI	10 486	11 636	12 339	12 343	12 786	14 113	15 281	15 016	16 441	15 005	17 081
Bulgaria	QAMZ	87	100	117	126	150	173	198	239	215	183	231
Cyprus	QDOA	205	238	246	253	208	273	1 712	196	155	123	106
Czech Republic	QDLG	801	1 099	1 250	1 416	1 290	1 880	2 952	2 987	3 601	3 336	3 988
Denmark	QBSF	2 639	2 927	3 604	3 402	3 367	4 416	6 522	3 448	3 937	3 837	4 117
Estonia	QAND	312	280	322	264	380	365	2 118	239	151	127	166
Finland	QBTG	2 764	2 963	2 789	2 663	2 340	2 432	3 068	2 620	2 799	2 113	2 164
France	QDJB	18 674	20 134	20 807	20 388	20 150	22 038	26 720	21 954	23 290	20 439	21 572
Germany	QDJE	28 502	30 206	32 450	33 674	35 407	39 176	41 920	44 657	44 891	39 984	46 415
Greece	QDJH	452	485	595	645	665	716	811	648	665	558	701
Hungary	QDLJ	680	707	846	1 118	1 581	1 862	2 358	2 379	2 541	2 540	3 251
Ireland	QDJK	10 286	12 190	13 218	9 919	10 141	10 409	10 716	11 349	12 289	12 430	12 873
Italy	QDJN	9 526	9 854	10 673	11 479	12 197	12 685	12 862	13 329	14 194	12 314	13 940
Latvia	QANE	407	430	476	517	690	718	798	627	420	339	440
Lithuania	QANF	244	229	263	287	270	279	283	309	359	370	551
Luxembourg[1]	QDOL	224	421	753	730	931	917	2 728	694	835	616	937
Malta	QDOD	128	145	170	186	184	179	167	179	136	106	170
Netherlands	QDJQ	15 397	15 393	16 148	16 698	18 212	20 463	22 441	23 198	25 979	21 945	26 449
Poland	QDLM	911	1 167	1 266	1 546	1 834	2 322	3 664	3 699	4 327	4 669	6 106
Portugal	QDJU	1 734	1 624	1 761	1 966	1 927	2 021	3 169	1 512	1 746	1 423	1 749
Romania	QANG	336	452	519	681	787	802	828	944	811	788	1 241
Slovak Republic	QANH	138	174	211	260	263	372	845	1 275	1 633	1 604	1 620
Slovenia	QANI	123	149	173	171	171	204	750	318	320	251	357
Spain	QDJX	6 150	7 365	9 196	9 254	9 126	11 528	12 011	10 499	10 821	9 570	10 381
Sweden	QDKA	4 954	4 669	4 323	4 567	5 123	5 465	6 176	5 305	6 888	5 726	6 809
European Central Bank	QARQ	–	–	–	–	–	–	–	–	–	–	–
EU Institutions	EOBS	–	–	–	–	–	–	–	–	–	–	–
Total EU27	LGDB	117 577	126 922	136 910	137 329	142 535	158 277	183 874	170 114	181 797	162 676	186 048
European Free Trade Association (EFTA)												
Iceland	QDKX	375	293	301	305	361	350	404	419	467	489	433
Liechtenstein	EPOX	23	26	26	25	18	16	39	38	34	21	10
Norway	QDLA	5 728	5 763	5 526	6 635	8 748	12 437	14 725	14 588	21 973	16 212	21 053
Switzerland	QDLD	5 599	4 658	4 778	3 826	3 495	3 857	4 347	4 802	5 329	5 319	7 429
Total EFTA	EPOU	11 725	10 740	10 631	10 791	12 622	16 660	19 515	19 847	27 803	22 041	28 925
Other Europe												
Albania	QAMX	2	–	2	3	–	–	–	–	–	–	–
Belarus	QAMY	35	18	33	23	72	273	729	594	104	20	37
Croatia	QANC	42	53	70	47	55	54	67	72	91	80	98
Russia	QDLP	1 503	2 064	1 952	2 459	3 537	5 062	5 783	5 439	6 984	4 649	5 258
Turkey	QDLS	1 447	1 722	2 246	2 670	3 315	3 559	3 967	4 687	4 955	4 665	5 351
Ukraine	QANJ	60	60	138	82	101	79	119	119	147	145	283
Serbia and Montenegro[2]	QANM	23	23	30	34	38	18	65	74	90	74	94
of which *Serbia*	KN2Q	..	..	..	..	..	..	..	74	88	74	93
Montenegro	KN2N	..	..	..	..	..	..	..	–	2	–	1
Other	BOQF	118	148	143	156	147	229	183	194	214	257	243
Total Europe	EPMM	132 532	141 750	152 155	153 594	162 422	184 211	214 302	201 140	222 185	194 607	226 337
Americas												
Argentina	QAOP	170	199	238	247	259	273	346	420	568	669	666
Brazil	QDLV	1 129	1 298	1 383	1 501	1 583	1 777	1 934	2 060	2 658	2 566	3 111
Canada	QATI	3 975	3 630	3 522	3 664	4 172	4 142	4 916	5 791	5 725	4 464	5 770
Chile	QANA	475	480	479	428	488	492	527	497	586	600	584
Colombia	QANB	238	318	215	224	277	301	301	368	701	583	678
Mexico	QDLY	607	669	491	477	399	431	427	555	782	757	1 032
United States of America	J8VA	28 465	29 855	25 234	23 000	22 121	22 049	25 416	25 608	25 540	24 222	26 992
Uruguay	QANK	37	37	46	43	41	58	66	71	116	114	103
Venezuela	QANL	204	155	179	112	208	391	605	488	615	428	421
Other Central American Countries	BOQR	1 075	624	786	1 020	1 128	1 211	1 411	1 165	1 371	1 249	1 146
Other	BOQU	286	301	268	224	236	224	301	251	369	352	364
Total Americas	EPMO	36 661	37 566	32 841	30 940	30 912	31 349	36 250	37 274	39 031	36 004	40 867
Asia												
China	QDMB	4 955	5 905	6 913	8 543	10 626	13 240	15 534	18 881	23 447	24 627	30 637
Hong Kong	QDME	6 053	5 878	5 669	5 588	5 852	6 691	7 446	6 989	8 169	7 757	8 172
India	QDMH	1 650	1 823	1 801	2 079	2 299	2 770	3 127	3 735	4 533	4 618	5 812
Indonesia	QDMK	1 166	1 202	1 090	976	984	920	1 029	1 010	1 219	1 240	1 388
Iran	QAOQ	21	14	20	15	29	25	60	55	69	211	206
Israel	QDMN	1 010	919	860	839	913	996	958	1 046	1 172	1 099	1 566
Japan	QAMK	10 124	9 089	8 068	8 086	8 065	8 607	7 834	7 910	8 547	6 670	8 107
Malaysia	QDMQ	2 347	1 976	1 762	1 897	2 053	1 829	1 917	1 702	1 893	1 665	1 837
Pakistan	QDMT	366	426	474	521	556	483	508	493	637	702	809
Philippines	QDMW	1 179	1 188	968	726	667	722	748	720	637	396	525
Saudi Arabia	QDMZ	1 006	941	687	728	1 195	1 836	1 277	893	688	610	766
Singapore	QDNC	2 433	2 087	1 976	2 699	3 431	3 877	3 788	4 086	4 044	3 589	4 146
South Korea	QDNF	3 382	2 751	2 717	2 553	3 069	3 035	3 056	2 990	3 509	2 862	2 563
Taiwan	QDNI	3 652	2 862	2 445	2 239	2 385	2 262	2 379	2 414	2 631	2 268	3 118
Thailand	QDNL	1 640	1 656	1 587	1 679	1 798	1 747	1 960	2 021	2 454	2 321	2 683
Residual Gulf Arabian Countries	BOQX	1 140	1 124	1 218	1 571	1 737	2 010	2 238	2 137	2 398	2 821	5 387
Other Near & Middle Eastern Countries	QARK	115	116	170	156	91	202	749	376	435	343	297
Other	BORD	1 575	1 622	1 692	1 958	2 207	2 049	2 463	2 643	3 158	3 626	3 905
Total Asia	EPMP	43 814	41 579	40 117	42 853	47 957	53 301	57 071	60 101	69 640	67 425	81 924
Australasia & Oceania												
Australia	QDNO	1 459	1 717	1 645	1 740	1 829	2 059	2 081	2 190	2 384	2 225	2 315
New Zealand	QDNR	535	542	517	547	578	586	602	657	750	819	844
Other	HFKF	129	99	98	126	127	131	130	116	169	168	107
Total Australasia & Oceania	EPMQ	2 123	2 358	2 260	2 413	2 534	2 776	2 813	2 963	3 303	3 212	3 266
Africa												
Egypt	QDNU	410	402	409	428	491	335	662	536	647	687	659
Morocco	QAOR	457	445	457	446	515	414	362	428	440	336	343
South Africa	QDNX	2 604	2 895	2 728	2 990	3 321	4 001	3 952	3 143	4 794	3 854	4 423
Other North Africa	BORW	757	529	611	589	763	1 007	1 727	1 702	2 375	1 839	2 851
Other	BOQJ	1 498	2 658	2 532	2 519	2 810	2 888	2 994	3 665	3 743	3 014	3 506
Total Africa	EPMN	5 726	6 929	6 737	6 972	7 900	8 645	9 697	9 474	11 999	9 730	11 782
International Organisations	EPMR	–	–	–	–	–	–	–	–	–	–	–
World total	LQBL	220 856	230 182	234 110	236 772	251 725	280 282	320 133	310 952	346 158	310 978	364 176

1 Before 1999 only combined BLEU data is available under indentifier QBSC.

2 Separate Serbia and Montenegro data is available from 2007.

9.4 Trade in goods

continued

£ million

		2000	2001	2002	2003	2004	2005	2006	2007	2008	2009	2010
Balances												
Europe												
European Union (EU)												
Austria	QBSA	–273	–662	–1 133	–1 512	–1 260	–1 140	–1 088	–1 119	–881	–990	–1 170
Belgium[1]	QDOJ	–398	–2 030	–2 155	–1 265	–2 531	–2 932	–2 162	–3 194	–3 012	–4 123	–3 704
Bulgaria	QANP	–2	20	16	26	5	47	28	–37	37	14	18
Cyprus	QDOB	114	51	25	61	113	82	–665	219	382	497	456
Czech Republic	QDLH	125	–25	–216	–409	–313	–802	–1 375	–1 586	–2 051	–1 895	–2 161
Denmark	QBSG	–323	–658	–874	–1 222	–1 322	–2 099	–2 662	–1 271	–1 343	–1 360	–1 360
Estonia	QANT	–216	–197	–222	–171	–274	–250	–1 647	–11	69	13	27
Finland	QBTL	–1 294	–1 349	–1 348	–1 170	–976	–916	–1 249	–663	–889	–790	–666
France	QDJC	–102	–885	–2 050	–1 502	–1 582	–2 112	2 357	–3 869	–5 195	–3 235	–2 344
Germany	QDJF	–5 719	–6 550	–10 385	–12 865	–13 733	–16 159	–14 712	–19 988	–16 932	–15 714	–18 502
Greece	QDJI	778	626	605	605	742	653	662	707	996	1 063	680
Hungary	QDLK	–63	–91	–96	–264	–643	–1 029	–1 519	–1 518	–1 532	–1 690	–2 169
Ireland	QDJL	2 085	1 648	2 202	2 306	3 998	5 882	6 527	6 412	6 845	3 506	4 059
Italy	QDJO	–1 099	–1 448	–2 164	–2 873	–3 792	–3 896	–3 376	–4 155	–4 793	–3 966	–5 087
Latvia	QANU	–323	–346	–400	–405	–599	–617	–211	–482	–251	–230	–272
Lithuania	QANV	–113	–93	–114	–99	–128	–112	–47	2	–77	–198	–326
Luxembourg[1]	QDOM	10	–128	–384	–430	–671	–705	–1 097	–423	–633	–423	–691
Malta	QDOE	84	70	55	70	73	60	153	184	314	295	223
Netherlands	QDJR	–230	–790	–2 136	–3 099	–6 185	–7 752	–5 778	–8 119	–6 059	–3 740	–5 199
Poland	QDLN	388	130	49	–85	–412	–669	–873	–1 328	–1 309	–1 871	–2 302
Portugal	QDJV	–71	–49	–245	–512	–345	–323	–829	–29	–102	120	88
Romania	QAOD	43	–113	–92	–174	–179	–156	–223	–280	–58	–102	–460
Slovak Republic	QAOG	18	27	–11	–26	–40	–113	–570	–895	–1 179	–1 226	–1 154
Slovenia	QAOH	30	8	8	–12	–11	–36	–555	–114	–97	–76	–137
Spain	QDJY	2 151	1 000	–706	–309	–25	–856	546	–464	–543	–346	–441
Sweden	QDKV	–741	–715	–450	–741	–767	–879	–997	–409	–1 670	–1 509	–1 246
European Central Bank	QARR	–	–	–	–	–	–	–	–	–	–	–
EU Institutions	EOCM	–	–	–	–	–	–	–	–	–	–	–
Total EU27	LGCF	–5 141	–12 549	–22 221	–26 077	–30 857	–36 829	–31 362	–42 430	–39 963	–37 976	–43 840
European Free Trade Association (EFTA)												
Iceland	QDKY	–182	–142	–168	–161	–191	–172	–215	–218	–279	–361	–301
Liechtenstein	EPOY	–16	–21	–23	–20	–12	–14	–17	–35	–25	–16	15
Norway	QDLB	–3 656	–3 883	–3 736	–4 686	–6 744	–10 179	–12 560	–11 857	–19 090	–13 373	–17 939
Switzerland	QDLE	–2 459	–1 043	–1 518	–939	–558	1 230	–93	–973	–617	–1 340	–2 215
Total EFTA	EPOV	–6 313	–5 089	–5 445	–5 806	–7 505	–9 135	–12 885	–13 083	–20 011	–15 090	–20 440
Other Europe												
Albania	QANN	5	23	17	8	12	16	17	19	16	18	21
Belarus	QANO	1	15	–1	15	–19	–217	–665	–525	–14	61	83
Croatia	QANS	31	34	24	90	69	62	79	85	128	143	75
Russia	QDLQ	–831	–1 167	–962	–1 046	–2 064	–3 203	–3 735	–2 646	–2 716	–2 247	–1 663
Turkey	QDLT	395	–531	–889	–974	–1 352	–1 359	–1 502	–2 341	–2 355	–2 296	–2 103
Ukraine	QAOI	92	135	33	156	113	197	219	324	467	444	191
Serbia and Montenegro[2]	QAOL	9	28	32	31	28	5	24	32	40	28	3
of which Serbia	KN2O	..	..	..	..	..	..	..	24	32	24	–
Montenegro	KN2L	..	..	..	..	..	..	..	8	8	4	3
Other	BOQG	78	77	45	64	67	58	155	100	349	251	567
Total Europe	EPNM	–11 674	–19 024	–29 367	–33 539	–41 508	–50 405	–49 655	–60 465	–64 059	–56 664	–67 106
Americas												
Argentina	QAOS	120	63	–117	–118	–88	–114	–128	–196	–249	–414	–309
Brazil	QDLW	–357	–488	–502	–680	–782	–931	–1 027	–994	–965	–778	–894
Canada	QBRV	–510	–438	–435	–444	–858	–891	–1 065	–2 525	–2 484	–1 135	–1 643
Chile	QANQ	–362	–353	–366	–307	–354	–343	–340	–314	–322	–86	46
Colombia	QANR	–138	–214	–134	–118	–162	–188	–166	–229	–541	–410	–448
Mexico	QDLZ	68	14	207	205	224	200	305	208	119	–6	–80
United States of America	J8VB	906	–452	2 908	5 819	6 404	8 787	6 528	6 436	9 737	9 729	10 933
Uruguay	QAOJ	20	11	–16	–10	–10	–21	–24	–35	–51	–54	–24
Venezuela	QAOK	13	158	124	27	–21	–165	–371	–238	–333	–128	–148
Other Central American Countries	BOQS	–106	57	–103	–320	–506	–526	–561	–303	–353	–492	–249
Other	BOQV	–127	–137	–108	–51	–83	–67	–129	–63	–124	–118	30
Total Americas	EPNO	–473	–1 779	1 458	4 003	3 764	5 741	3 022	1 747	4 434	6 108	7 214
Asia												
China	QDMC	–3 494	–4 199	–5 428	–6 635	–8 258	–10 442	–12 278	–15 117	–18 392	–19 226	–23 026
Hong Kong	QDMF	–3 386	–3 202	–3 187	–3 115	–3 227	–3 611	–4 598	–4 344	–4 507	–4 022	–3 716
India	QDMI	396	–60	–57	190	–64	21	–438	–783	–416	–1 669	–1 744
Indonesia	QDML	–752	–892	–760	–516	–581	–541	–712	–716	–823	–873	–927
Iran	QAOT	279	423	381	463	415	435	367	345	374	194	101
Israel	QDMO	502	437	560	521	478	349	347	189	167	46	–179
Japan	QBRR	–6 467	–5 421	–4 481	–4 385	–4 209	–4 712	–3 741	–4 060	–4 636	–3 100	–3 773
Malaysia	QDMR	–1 444	–949	–888	–874	–1 060	–748	–1 038	–754	–763	–613	–565
Pakistan	QDMU	–168	–210	–246	–237	–211	–21	–19	–66	–159	–224	–348
Philippines	QDMX	–910	–794	–611	–346	–350	–448	–509	–473	–396	–128	–241
Saudi Arabia	QDNA	572	563	689	1 096	411	–251	388	954	1 524	1 753	1 722
Singapore	QDND	–815	–499	–537	–1 127	–1 721	–1 804	–1 480	–1 649	–1 236	–634	–699
South Korea	QDNG	–2 036	–1 492	–1 238	–1 077	–1 589	–1 359	–1 316	–1 138	–956	–695	–219
Taiwan	QDNJ	–2 642	–1 988	–1 603	–1 347	–1 434	–1 322	–1 470	–1 482	–1 744	–1 473	–2 002
Thailand	QDNM	–1 061	–1 060	–1 057	–1 109	–1 162	–1 115	–1 396	–1 423	–1 696	–1 407	–1 546
Residual Gulf Arabian Countries	BORA	1 472	1 579	1 370	1 801	2 280	5 041	2 912	2 366	3 629	2 952	1 203
Other Near & Middle Eastern Countries	QARL	273	348	310	462	673	525	225	366	595	753	1 019
Other	BORE	–931	–1 071	–1 195	–1 367	–1 608	–1 485	–1 791	–1 058	–2 312	–2 644	–2 693
Total Asia	EPNP	–20 612	–18 487	–17 978	–17 602	–21 217	–21 488	–26 547	–28 843	–31 747	–31 010	–37 633
Australasia & Oceania												
Australia	QDNP	1 234	581	476	553	623	520	399	387	720	735	1 047
New Zealand	QDNS	–225	–238	–206	–198	–160	–170	–226	–298	–362	–469	–430
Other	HFKK	–82	–53	–41	–56	–80	–51	–55	–50	–67	–77	–25
Total Australasia & Oceania	EPNQ	927	290	229	299	383	299	118	39	291	189	592
Africa												
Egypt	QDNV	92	51	51	31	178	208	–86	151	297	319	539
Morocco	QAOU	–51	–78	–130	–88	–179	–162	–57	–115	74	–25	222
South Africa	QDNY	–1 197	–1 370	–1 147	–1 233	–1 446	–1 933	–1 780	–994	–2 146	–1 600	–1 533
Other North Africa	BORX	–345	–103	–149	–26	–237	–531	–1 229	–1 196	–1 563	–880	–1 944
Other	BOQK	303	–680	–634	–376	–677	–513	–355	–929	238	711	1 187
Total Africa	EPNN	–1 198	–2 180	–2 009	–1 692	–2 361	–2 931	–3 507	–3 083	–3 100	–1 475	–1 529
International Organisations	EPNR	–	–	–	–	–	–	–	–	–	–	–
World total	LQCT	–33 030	–41 180	–47 667	–48 531	–60 939	–68 784	–76 569	–90 605	–94 181	–82 852	–98 462

1 Before 1999 only combined BLEU data is available under identifier QBSD.

2 Separate Serbia and Montenegro data is available from 2007.

THIS PAGE IS INTENTIONALLY BLANK

9.5 Trade in services

£ million

		2000	2001	2002	2003	2004	2005	2006	2007	2008	2009	2010
Exports												
Europe												
European Union (EU)												
Austria	FYVC	405	409	426	422	433	522	554	705	784	744	643
Belgium[1]	A7RX	2 088	2 051	2 383	2 549	2 957	2 818	2 592	2 966	3 567	3 280	2 888
Bulgaria	ZWKO	42	35	75	67	78	94	117	177	193	204	164
Cyprus	A7RY	149	135	219	234	335	314	360	529	604	551	602
Czech Republic	FYVW	168	185	181	243	329	336	349	522	444	466	452
Denmark	FYVE	1 180	1 390	1 374	1 522	1 591	1 530	2 325	2 404	2 420	2 887	2 910
Estonia	ZWKU	12	14	21	22	29	37	57	36	50	43	79
Finland	FYVF	955	879	832	875	957	860	1 083	1 226	1 194	1 304	1 274
France	FYVG	5 443	6 078	6 021	6 236	6 607	6 464	7 311	8 449	9 923	8 751	8 913
Germany	FYVH	6 682	7 193	7 497	7 828	8 211	9 180	10 053	10 844	11 857	11 476	10 800
Greece	FYVI	836	809	765	787	742	935	784	940	1 257	1 037	1 119
Hungary	GYWV	206	205	218	225	372	561	426	512	482	552	472
Ireland	FYVJ	2 851	3 658	4 288	5 296	5 584	6 573	6 816	7 657	8 635	8 432	8 389
Italy	FYVK	2 693	2 901	3 018	3 017	3 409	3 712	3 747	4 287	4 534	4 996	5 151
Latvia	ZWLC	30	33	38	29	49	93	67	104	89	110	87
Lithuania	ZWLB	17	46	32	43	55	112	104	121	278	93	96
Luxembourg[1]	A7S2	389	443	436	652	907	857	1 132	1 756	2 168	2 363	2 144
Malta	A7S3	57	52	61	73	79	71	91	122	185	283	227
Netherlands	FYVL	4 557	4 914	4 709	5 389	6 697	6 934	7 762	8 638	9 927	9 226	10 069
Poland	FYVX	286	337	392	409	505	802	1 018	1 020	1 074	1 053	1 132
Portugal	FYVM	436	485	530	542	677	632	573	681	809	771	779
Romania	ZWLE	44	73	76	97	137	127	166	263	284	283	359
Slovak Republic	ZWLG	39	43	30	36	46	99	114	145	307	242	291
Slovenia	ZWLF	28	38	48	43	52	63	74	72	93	84	92
Spain	FYVN	2 256	2 252	2 612	2 867	2 946	3 764	4 511	5 284	5 463	5 681	5 139
Sweden	FYVO	1 620	1 636	1 477	1 694	1 709	1 763	2 004	2 403	2 376	2 623	2 911
European Central Bank	KNWZ	3	12	3	–	–	–	–	–	–	–	–
EU Institutions	FYVP	248	544	544	513	578	602	609	627	685	673	758
Total EU27	GC8R	33 720	36 850	38 306	41 710	46 071	49 855	54 799	62 490	69 682	68 208	67 940
European Free Trade Association (EFTA)												
Iceland	FYVR	73	63	64	72	89	135	189	180	231	147	168
Liechtenstein	FYVS	37	30	43	40	53	40	43	127	59	72	60
Norway	FYVT	1 031	976	1 449	1 323	1 524	1 817	1 954	2 541	2 426	2 424	2 383
Switzerland	FYVU	2 784	3 488	3 967	4 611	4 355	4 868	5 650	6 741	7 229	7 895	8 981
Total EFTA	FYVV	3 925	4 557	5 523	6 046	6 021	6 860	7 837	9 589	9 945	10 538	11 592
Other Europe												
Albania	ZWKM	2	5	6	6	22	8	13	11	30	13	12
Belarus	ZWKP	27	3	4	4	6	7	9	15	19	4	10
Croatia	ZWKZ	38	34	55	51	44	46	99	100	119	105	82
Russia	FYVY	415	470	581	730	901	1 127	1 679	2 136	2 184	1 831	1 665
Turkey	FYVZ	351	398	372	401	368	511	568	764	733	924	1 126
Ukraine	ZWLH	43	29	302	126	55	97	149	204	226	177	244
Serbia and Montenegro[2]	ZWLK	103	41	28	40	21	35	42	64	38	71	59
of which *Serbia*	JOA2	..	..	..	..	..	..	..	58	35	57	48
Montenegro	JO9Y	..	..	..	..	..	..	..	6	3	14	11
Other	ZWKJ	1 242	1 160	1 505	2 029	2 248	2 756	3 148	3 642	4 878	4 103	3 322
Total Europe	FYWB	39 866	43 547	46 682	51 143	55 757	61 302	68 343	79 015	87 854	85 974	86 052
Americas												
Argentina	ZWKN	186	195	83	83	142	99	107	132	138	146	233
Brazil	FYWC	350	392	321	334	307	368	502	455	586	694	836
Canada	FYWD	1 397	1 639	1 543	1 589	1 776	1 758	2 050	2 520	2 680	2 700	2 905
Chile	ZWKQ	96	103	87	79	83	88	129	178	175	193	181
Colombia	ZWKR	56	140	86	97	87	66	72	74	81	92	200
Mexico	FYWE	267	288	265	271	354	306	404	356	329	384	421
United States of America	FYWF	19 275	19 211	22 690	23 886	25 768	24 501	29 555	33 538	35 488	33 735	34 286
Uruguay	ZWLI	7	5	5	60	10	13	17	17	18	15	20
Venezuela	ZWLJ	83	110	99	102	99	96	72	58	63	75	354
Other Central American Countries	ZWKT	1 419	1 604	2 209	2 376	2 986	3 487	3 587	4 188	4 863	4 455	4 211
Other	ZWKW	221	219	150	157	147	194	224	304	304	261	277
Total Americas	FYWH	23 357	23 906	27 538	29 034	31 759	30 976	36 719	41 820	44 725	42 750	43 924
Asia												
China	FYWI	449	591	724	886	1 278	1 388	1 534	1 560	2 517	2 230	2 652
Hong Kong	FYWJ	1 041	1 094	1 006	1 190	1 127	1 350	1 310	1 677	2 156	1 713	1 606
India	FYWK	553	675	635	719	998	1 163	1 657	1 713	1 769	1 711	2 060
Indonesia	FYWL	192	205	174	164	190	188	292	251	256	325	325
Iran	ZWLA	124	169	185	224	242	216	216	165	264	213	128
Israel	FYWM	445	511	429	369	407	558	458	488	524	585	682
Japan	FYWN	3 469	3 558	3 844	3 890	4 221	4 317	4 383	4 684	5 035	4 637	4 315
Malaysia	FYWO	390	376	404	421	554	465	504	454	531	674	701
Pakistan	FYWP	176	278	173	182	231	431	362	318	344	357	302
Philippines	FYWQ	183	178	105	140	126	138	101	112	236	177	125
Saudi Arabia	FYWR	2 369	2 147	1 973	2 311	2 528	2 223	2 547	2 157	1 989	2 410	2 925
Singapore	FYWS	1 086	1 294	1 166	1 647	2 157	2 646	3 023	3 588	3 602	4 004	3 661
South Korea	FYWT	396	428	505	472	912	737	869	980	1 111	921	1 123
Taiwan	FYWU	281	295	370	381	515	583	594	646	687	661	1 145
Thailand	FYWV	194	219	207	333	319	259	296	316	352	497	459
Residual Gulf Arabian Countries	ZWKX	1 103	1 114	1 332	1 330	1 765	1 991	2 323	2 847	3 746	3 867	4 007
Other Near & Middle Eastern Countries	ZWKY	231	339	268	260	339	448	440	438	602	647	610
Other Asian Countries	ZWKK	811	884	727	796	957	1 112	1 435	1 464	1 650	1 706	1 726
Total Asia	FYWX	13 493	14 355	14 227	15 715	18 866	20 213	22 344	23 858	27 371	27 335	28 552
Australasia & Oceania												
Australia	FYWY	1 588	1 964	1 826	2 015	2 291	2 713	2 858	3 312	4 056	4 179	5 025
New Zealand	FYWZ	301	301	275	301	379	412	405	434	429	426	452
Other	FYXA	84	95	97	115	130	63	123	110	138	133	208
Total Australasia & Oceania	FYXB	1 973	2 360	2 198	2 431	2 800	3 188	3 386	3 856	4 623	4 738	5 685
Africa												
Egypt	ZWKV	280	340	226	238	322	374	472	633	724	657	560
Morocco	ZWLD	61	82	50	48	61	46	90	74	103	167	137
South Africa	FYXC	976	1 129	1 009	1 086	1 080	1 135	1 376	1 478	1 561	1 500	1 723
Other North Africa	ZWKS	265	219	222	286	288	375	408	389	545	570	504
Other	ZWKL	1 566	1 771	1 774	1 912	1 841	1 900	2 347	2 515	3 331	3 732	3 904
Total Africa	FYXE	3 148	3 541	3 281	3 570	3 592	3 830	4 693	5 089	6 264	6 626	6 828
International Organisations	FYXF	51	64	85	73	52	60	42	47	50	39	41
World total	KTMQ	81 888	87 773	94 011	101 966	112 826	119 569	135 527	153 685	170 887	167 462	171 082

1 Before 1999 only combined BLEU data is available under indentifier FYVD. 2 Separate Serbia and Montenegro data available from 2007.

9.5 Trade in services

continued

£ million

		2000	2001	2002	2003	2004	2005	2006	2007	2008	2009	2010
Imports												
Europe												
European Union (EU)												
Austria	GGOR	477	506	688	660	757	871	891	817	965	908	987
Belgium[1]	A8ET	1 492	1 617	1 825	1 959	2 004	2 153	2 135	2 316	2 568	2 406	2 319
Bulgaria	ZWMU	38	52	96	104	174	254	240	333	394	265	340
Cyprus	A8EU	885	1 059	977	1 089	1 081	1 206	1 184	1 132	1 167	934	881
Czech Republic	GGPL	168	199	250	337	426	468	536	480	465	372	434
Denmark	GGOT	674	655	746	783	853	942	1 035	1 044	1 126	1 429	1 294
Estonia	ZWNA	33	27	18	35	47	53	70	54	55	30	30
Finland	GGOU	404	360	282	314	285	353	363	420	402	354	451
France	GGOV	7 533	7 531	7 844	8 267	8 518	8 962	9 615	9 873	9 916	9 284	9 636
Germany	GGOW	4 706	5 241	5 402	5 583	6 442	7 727	7 934	8 365	9 709	8 934	9 127
Greece	GGOX	1 617	1 887	1 908	1 980	1 970	2 003	2 010	2 240	2 144	2 112	1 951
Hungary	GYXH	95	126	129	151	186	274	341	367	339	418	486
Ireland	GGOY	2 262	2 338	2 317	2 578	3 054	3 440	3 496	3 963	4 175	4 255	4 150
Italy	GGOZ	2 857	3 003	3 139	3 431	3 566	4 309	4 179	4 701	4 921	4 459	4 350
Latvia	ZWNI	25	20	19	29	38	44	82	91	68	56	94
Lithuania	ZWNH	6	16	37	25	19	72	84	96	87	101	118
Luxembourg[1]	A8EW	183	184	212	248	358	303	525	497	599	541	1 411
Malta	A8EX	223	256	238	279	318	343	294	304	381	327	326
Netherlands	GGPA	3 027	3 129	3 381	3 322	3 354	3 578	3 618	3 531	3 718	4 224	3 898
Poland	GGPM	184	200	187	224	299	558	959	1 215	1 297	1 255	1 361
Portugal	GGPB	1 021	1 116	1 209	1 368	1 398	1 442	1 434	1 699	1 920	1 515	1 633
Romania	ZWNK	64	77	84	91	131	169	169	175	214	236	258
Slovak Republic	ZWNM	30	14	27	22	33	67	94	93	119	124	121
Slovenia	ZWNL	29	17	23	24	34	48	53	43	66	40	48
Spain	GGPC	6 497	7 234	7 849	8 983	9 110	9 476	9 941	9 991	10 562	9 436	9 482
Sweden	GGPD	830	832	830	1 136	1 150	1 318	1 356	1 224	1 424	1 758	1 614
European Central Bank	KOFJ	1	1	1	–	–	–	–	–	2	2	–
EU Institutions	GGPE	3	5	14	17	4	4	2	–	5	5	2
Total EU27	GCV2	35 364	37 702	39 732	43 039	45 609	50 437	52 640	55 064	58 808	55 780	56 802
European Free Trade Association (EFTA)												
Iceland	GGPG	75	44	42	46	57	71	98	92	82	130	56
Liechtenstein	GGPH	6	7	1	11	4	4	6	23	8	13	20
Norway	GGPI	537	647	1 266	710	771	976	1 016	1 049	1 162	1 199	1 092
Switzerland	GGPJ	1 633	1 588	1 677	1 795	1 831	2 355	2 363	2 821	2 667	2 943	3 215
Total EFTA	GGPK	2 251	2 286	2 986	2 562	2 663	3 406	3 483	3 985	3 919	4 285	4 383
Other Europe												
Albania	ZWMS	5	9	13	14	20	8	13	22	20	13	4
Belarus	ZWMV	2	4	3	4	1	8	21	22	20	6	9
Croatia	ZWNF	27	55	47	73	83	139	176	156	227	195	220
Russia	GGPN	188	218	296	303	499	549	727	864	1 096	1 286	903
Turkey	GGPO	521	569	704	788	812	1 039	1 095	1 165	1 506	1 320	1 623
Ukraine	ZWNN	14	33	25	23	42	95	76	194	229	152	217
Serbia and Montenegro[2]	ZWNQ	22	38	33	41	38	43	73	71	60	63	49
of which Serbia	JOB2	..	..	..	..	..	..	..	64	53	49	38
Montenegro	JOA8	..	..	..	..	..	..	..	7	7	14	11
Other	ZWMP	1 090	959	1 122	1 056	960	1 000	1 229	1 404	1 268	1 248	1 279
Total Europe	GGPQ	39 484	41 873	44 961	47 903	50 727	56 724	59 533	62 947	67 153	64 348	65 489
Americas												
Argentina	ZWMT	75	74	55	48	69	87	115	91	129	100	111
Brazil	GGPR	174	231	251	176	217	262	265	272	344	323	447
Canada	GGPS	1 105	1 193	1 090	1 003	1 049	1 163	1 346	1 374	1 528	1 279	1 477
Chile	ZWMW	35	48	48	43	72	81	39	68	49	73	50
Colombia	ZWMX	39	31	35	32	23	40	46	37	31	51	55
Mexico	GGPT	283	398	336	312	365	299	274	359	457	265	398
United States of America	GGPU	13 208	13 509	13 409	14 871	15 311	16 301	16 779	18 069	20 037	19 223	19 200
Uruguay	ZWNO	6	9	23	4	5	7	12	6	4	26	8
Venezuela	ZWNP	46	42	35	34	26	34	31	37	38	42	50
Other Central American Countries	ZWMZ	1 473	1 407	1 313	1 415	1 882	1 774	2 672	2 630	2 977	3 127	2 267
Other	ZWNC	258	147	124	129	111	171	127	160	156	123	123
Total Americas	GGPW	16 702	17 089	16 719	18 067	19 130	20 219	21 706	23 103	25 750	24 632	24 186
Asia												
China	GGPX	292	375	496	463	559	696	811	1 004	1 326	1 177	1 180
Hong Kong	GGPY	571	606	624	715	721	759	844	1 202	1 027	974	1 056
India	GGPZ	664	817	816	818	1 089	1 307	1 598	1 792	2 256	1 942	2 292
Indonesia	GGQA	125	121	136	297	100	97	137	123	126	121	119
Iran	ZWNG	43	37	29	45	61	42	61	41	41	74	66
Israel	GGQB	266	314	202	213	233	249	295	302	311	349	415
Japan	GGQC	1 664	1 817	1 450	1 740	1 704	2 259	2 751	2 917	3 670	3 306	3 627
Malaysia	GGQD	227	191	193	170	208	271	254	232	244	252	260
Pakistan	GGQE	300	280	398	386	431	472	487	410	394	389	443
Philippines	GGQF	206	82	100	155	109	142	173	157	196	181	217
Saudi Arabia	GGQG	553	643	1 303	1 065	779	566	693	742	587	295	249
Singapore	GGQH	336	395	428	425	661	730	865	940	1 390	1 547	1 803
South Korea	GGQI	141	179	185	186	246	254	254	321	404	364	351
Taiwan	GGQJ	157	149	183	180	202	310	219	313	351	270	247
Thailand	GGQK	385	458	521	513	641	613	685	690	673	630	624
Residual Gulf Arabian Countries	ZWND	414	551	611	761	928	1 018	1 260	1 507	2 060	1 973	1 782
Other Near & Middle Eastern Countries	ZWNE	125	155	151	151	208	199	220	171	220	228	230
Other	ZWMQ	633	537	558	648	902	847	1 029	869	987	997	1 104
Total Asia	GGQM	7 102	7 707	8 384	8 931	9 782	10 831	12 636	13 733	16 263	15 069	16 065
Australasia & Oceania												
Australia	GGQN	1 191	1 252	1 431	1 477	1 390	1 869	1 806	1 776	2 046	1 739	2 194
New Zealand	GGQO	264	287	337	347	434	501	441	431	369	283	354
Other	GGQP	25	20	33	28	54	48	76	48	76	55	52
Total Australasia & Oceania	GGQQ	1 480	1 559	1 801	1 852	1 878	2 418	2 323	2 255	2 491	2 077	2 600
Africa												
Egypt	ZWNB	290	367	313	350	344	539	605	590	764	741	681
Morocco	ZWNJ	114	147	141	141	149	175	239	379	373	254	248
South Africa	GGQR	528	598	684	922	909	1 017	1 026	954	891	883	1 101
Other North Africa	ZWMY	323	349	263	266	330	349	286	403	429	357	432
Other	ZWMR	772	814	1 072	1 289	1 244	1 174	1 278	1 308	1 673	1 871	1 472
Total Africa	GGQT	2 027	2 275	2 473	2 968	2 976	3 254	3 434	3 634	4 130	4 106	3 934
International Organisations	GGQU	80	62	40	29	37	43	57	57	43	15	30
World total	KTMR	66 875	70 565	74 378	79 750	84 530	93 489	99 689	105 729	115 830	110 247	112 304

1 Before 1999 only combined BLEU data is available under identifier GGOS.
2 Separate Serbia and Montenegro data is available from 2007.

9.5 Trade in services

continued

£ million

		2000	2001	2002	2003	2004	2005	2006	2007	2008	2009	2010
Balances												
Europe												
European Union (EU)												
Austria	GGQW	-72	-97	-262	-238	-324	-349	-337	-112	-181	-164	-344
Belgium[1]	A8HH	596	434	558	590	953	665	457	650	999	874	569
Bulgaria	ZWTO	4	-17	-21	-37	-96	-160	-123	-156	-201	-61	-176
Cyprus	A8HI	-736	-924	-758	-855	-746	-892	-824	-603	-563	-383	-279
Czech Republic	GGRQ	–	-14	-69	-94	-97	-132	-187	42	-21	94	18
Denmark	GGQY	506	735	628	739	738	588	1 290	1 360	1 294	1 458	1 616
Estonia	ZWTU	-21	-13	3	-13	-18	-16	-13	-18	-5	13	49
Finland	GGQZ	551	519	550	561	672	507	720	806	792	950	823
France	GGRA	-2 090	-1 453	-1 823	-2 031	-1 911	-2 498	-2 304	-1 424	7	-533	-723
Germany	GGRB	1 976	1 952	2 095	2 245	1 769	1 453	2 119	2 479	2 148	2 542	1 673
Greece	GGRC	-781	-1 078	-1 143	-1 193	-1 228	-1 068	-1 226	-1 300	-887	-1 075	-832
Hungary	GYXT	111	79	89	74	186	287	85	145	143	134	-14
Ireland	GGRD	589	1 320	1 971	2 718	2 530	3 133	3 320	3 694	4 460	4 177	4 239
Italy	GGRE	-164	-102	-121	-414	-157	-597	-432	-414	-387	537	801
Latvia	ZWUC	5	13	19	–	11	49	-15	13	21	54	-7
Lithuania	ZWUB	11	30	-5	18	36	40	20	25	191	-8	-22
Luxembourg[1]	A8HK	206	259	224	404	549	554	607	1 259	1 569	1 822	733
Malta	A8HL	-166	-204	-177	-206	-239	-272	-203	-182	-196	-44	-99
Netherlands	GGRF	1 530	1 785	1 328	2 067	3 343	3 356	4 144	5 107	6 209	5 002	6 171
Poland	GGRR	102	137	205	185	206	244	59	-195	-223	-202	-229
Portugal	GGRG	-585	-631	-679	-826	-721	-810	-861	-1 018	-1 111	-744	-854
Romania	ZWUE	-20	-4	-8	6	6	-42	-3	88	70	47	101
Slovak Republic	ZWUG	9	29	3	14	13	32	20	52	188	118	170
Slovenia	ZWUF	-1	21	25	19	18	15	21	29	27	44	44
Spain	GGRH	-4 241	-4 982	-5 237	-6 116	-6 164	-5 712	-5 430	-4 707	-5 099	-3 755	-4 343
Sweden	GGRI	790	804	647	558	559	445	648	1 179	952	865	1 297
European Central Bank	ZWTI	2	11	2	–	–	–	–	–	-2	-2	–
EU Institutions	GGRJ	245	539	530	496	574	598	607	627	680	668	756
Total EU27	GD6R	-1 644	-852	-1 426	-1 329	462	-582	2 159	7 426	10 874	12 428	11 138
European Free Trade Association (EFTA)												
Iceland	GGRL	-2	19	22	26	32	64	91	88	149	17	112
Liechtenstein	GGRM	31	23	42	29	49	36	37	104	51	59	40
Norway	GGRN	494	329	183	613	753	841	938	1 492	1 264	1 225	1 291
Switzerland	GGRO	1 151	1 900	2 290	2 816	2 524	2 513	3 288	3 920	4 562	4 952	5 766
Total EFTA	GGRP	1 674	2 271	2 537	3 484	3 358	3 454	4 354	5 604	6 026	6 253	7 209
Other Europe												
Albania	ZWTM	-3	-4	-7	-8	2	–	–	-11	10	–	8
Belarus	ZWTP	25	-1	1	–	5	-1	-12	-7	-1	-2	1
Croatia	ZWTZ	11	-21	8	-22	-39	-93	-77	-56	-108	-90	-138
Russia	GGRS	227	252	285	427	402	578	952	1 272	1 088	545	762
Turkey	GGRT	-170	-171	-332	-387	-444	-528	-527	-401	-773	-396	-497
Ukraine	ZWUH	29	-4	277	103	13	2	73	10	-3	25	27
Serbia and Montenegro[2]	ZWUK	81	3	-5	-1	-17	-8	-31	-7	-22	8	10
of which Serbia	JOB9	..	..	..	..	..	..	..	-6	-18	8	10
Montenegro	JOB8	..	..	..	..	..	..	..	-1	-4	–	–
Other	ZWTJ	152	201	383	973	1 288	1 756	1 919	2 238	3 610	2 855	2 043
Total Europe	GGRV	382	1 674	1 721	3 240	5 030	4 578	8 810	16 068	20 701	21 626	20 563
Americas												
Argentina	ZWTN	111	121	28	35	73	12	-8	41	9	46	122
Brazil	GGRW	176	161	70	158	90	106	237	183	242	371	389
Canada	GGRX	292	446	453	586	727	595	704	1 146	1 152	1 421	1 428
Chile	ZWTQ	61	55	39	36	11	7	90	110	126	120	131
Colombia	ZWTR	17	109	51	65	64	26	26	37	50	41	145
Mexico	GGRY	-16	-110	-71	-41	-11	7	130	-3	-128	119	23
United States of America	GGRZ	6 067	5 702	9 281	9 015	10 457	8 200	12 776	15 469	15 451	14 512	15 086
Uruguay	ZWUI	1	-4	-18	56	5	6	5	11	14	-11	12
Venezuela	ZWUJ	37	68	64	68	73	62	41	21	25	33	304
Other Central American Countries	ZWTT	-54	197	896	961	1 104	1 713	915	1 558	1 886	1 328	1 944
Other	ZWTW	-37	72	26	28	36	23	97	144	148	138	154
Total Americas	GGSB	6 655	6 817	10 819	10 967	12 629	10 757	15 013	18 717	18 975	18 118	19 738
Asia												
China	GGSC	157	216	228	423	719	692	723	556	1 191	1 053	1 472
Hong Kong	GGSD	470	488	382	475	406	591	466	475	1 129	739	550
India	GGSE	-111	-142	-181	-99	-91	-144	59	-79	-487	-231	-232
Indonesia	GGSF	67	84	38	-133	90	91	155	128	130	204	206
Iran	ZWUA	81	132	156	179	181	174	155	124	223	139	62
Israel	GGSG	179	197	227	156	174	309	163	186	213	236	267
Japan	GGSH	1 805	1 741	2 394	2 150	2 517	2 058	1 632	1 767	1 365	1 331	688
Malaysia	GGSI	163	185	211	251	346	194	250	222	287	422	441
Pakistan	GGSJ	-124	-2	-225	-204	-200	-41	-125	-92	-50	-32	-141
Philippines	GGSK	-23	96	5	-15	17	-4	-72	-45	40	-4	-92
Saudi Arabia	GGSL	1 816	1 504	670	1 246	1 749	1 657	1 854	1 415	1 402	2 115	2 676
Singapore	GGSM	750	899	738	1 222	1 496	1 916	2 158	2 648	2 212	2 457	1 858
South Korea	GGSN	255	249	320	286	666	483	615	659	707	557	772
Taiwan	GGSO	124	146	187	201	313	273	375	333	336	391	898
Thailand	GGSP	-191	-239	-314	-180	-322	-354	-389	-374	-321	-133	-165
Residual Gulf Arabian Countries	ZWTX	689	563	721	569	837	973	1 063	1 340	1 686	1 894	2 225
Other Near & Middle Eastern Countries	ZWTY	106	184	117	109	131	249	220	267	382	419	380
Other	ZWTK	178	347	169	148	55	265	406	595	663	709	622
Total Asia	GGSR	6 391	6 648	5 843	6 784	9 084	9 382	9 708	10 125	11 108	12 266	12 487
Australasia & Oceania												
Australia	GGSS	397	712	395	538	901	844	1 052	1 536	2 010	2 440	2 831
New Zealand	GGST	37	14	-62	-46	-55	-89	-36	3	60	143	98
Other	GGSU	59	75	64	87	76	15	47	62	62	78	156
Total Australasia & Oceania	GGSV	493	801	397	579	922	770	1 063	1 601	2 132	2 661	3 085
Africa												
Egypt	ZWTV	-10	-27	-87	-112	-22	-165	-133	43	-40	-84	-121
Morocco	ZWUD	-53	-65	-91	-93	-88	-129	-149	-305	-270	-87	-111
South Africa	GGSW	448	531	325	164	171	118	350	524	670	617	622
Other North Africa	ZWTS	-58	-130	-41	20	-42	26	122	-14	116	213	72
Other	ZWTL	794	957	702	623	597	726	1 069	1 207	1 658	1 861	2 432
Total Africa	GGSY	1 121	1 266	808	602	616	576	1 259	1 455	2 134	2 520	2 894
International Organisations	GGSZ	-29	2	45	44	15	17	-15	-10	7	24	11
World total	KTMS	15 013	17 208	19 633	22 216	28 296	26 080	35 838	47 956	55 057	57 215	58 778

1 Before 1999 only combined BLEU data is available under identifier GGQX..

2 Separate Serbia and Montenegro data is available from 2007.

THIS PAGE IS INTENTIONALLY BLANK

9.6 Income

£ million

		2000	2001	2002	2003	2004	2005	2006	2007	2008	2009	2010
Credits												
Europe												
European Union (EU)												
Austria	CUGY	742	683	685	746	815	900	871	1 114	966	708	401
Belgium[1]	AA2K	2 342	2 753	2 208	1 930	2 619	3 620	4 447	6 609	5 890	3 280	2 440
Bulgaria	ZWYR	37	93	72	74	89	28	40	19	38	24	14
Cyprus	AA2L	153	163	137	56	72	115	315	569	373	150	70
Czech Republic	LEPT	125	198	152	195	210	155	9	192	–9	–80	–96
Denmark	LEQU	1 101	979	521	705	883	1 441	1 692	1 980	1 960	1 068	1 124
Estonia	ZWYT	2	8	6	8	9	14	11	8	7	26	13
Finland	LEUG	585	648	587	517	520	572	589	1 035	980	714	621
France	LEUP	7 535	8 680	6 948	6 954	8 159	11 105	14 747	20 288	17 375	9 201	10 078
Germany	LEQL	10 136	11 065	9 504	8 330	9 528	11 691	13 774	17 623	18 486	11 034	8 235
Greece	LEUY	1 002	871	707	817	782	834	949	1 399	1 412	842	402
Hungary	BFKR	448	321	352	334	383	411	196	296	286	144	102
Ireland	BFLY	3 824	4 710	3 918	4 884	5 619	7 862	10 399	15 167	15 145	5 447	–5 426
Italy	BFOG	6 426	6 347	4 791	4 900	4 647	5 051	5 697	7 190	6 596	4 078	3 693
Latvia	ZWYU	2	–	–	–	–	1	18	30	9	–17	–56
Lithuania	ZWYV	9	7	4	4	1	8	8	10	8	8	14
Luxembourg[1]	AA2O	3 724	3 894	3 321	2 836	3 896	6 254	10 473	11 878	18 070	13 795	11 749
Malta	AA2P	51	55	48	53	491	44	–145	–7	99	352	65
Netherlands	BFQI	12 814	16 586	15 722	15 205	9 738	11 446	15 619	20 432	21 931	15 143	12 025
Poland	BFSB	144	329	335	400	440	441	537	472	669	896	569
Portugal	BFSK	664	808	776	807	797	970	1 001	1 107	1 263	707	582
Romania	ZWYW	20	78	65	96	117	70	109	159	235	165	114
Slovak Republic	ZWYX	51	29	31	28	30	52	41	131	77	44	52
Slovenia	ZWYY	48	101	68	89	99	37	27	41	52	23	–6
Spain	LESW	2 564	2 403	2 052	2 314	3 623	4 954	6 535	8 318	9 377	5 763	3 159
Sweden	BFTL	2 108	2 307	2 121	1 767	2 273	2 695	3 140	3 974	5 162	4 321	3 220
European Central Bank	ZWYO	–	–	–	–	–	–	–	–	–	–	–
EU Institutions	CSFK	370	468	657	747	522	516	533	516	563	640	513
Total EU27	GNF6	57 027	64 584	55 788	54 796	56 362	71 287	91 632	120 550	127 020	78 476	53 671
European Free Trade Association (EFTA)												
Iceland	BFNQ	35	38	33	27	55	121	220	997	1 155	460	374
Liechtenstein	BFPH	45	39	21	20	23	19	32	40	27	–10	–4
Norway	BFQR	1 022	1 017	687	796	832	1 950	1 959	2 809	2 776	1 301	977
Switzerland	LEPB	7 274	5 326	4 504	4 505	4 903	6 109	8 843	13 107	12 831	5 230	6 965
Total EFTA	CTFT	8 376	6 420	5 245	5 348	5 813	8 199	11 054	16 953	16 789	6 981	8 312
Other Europe												
Albania	ZWYP	–	–	–	–	–	–	–	2	6	6	2
Belarus	ZWYQ	–	–	7	–	–	4	3	7	8	4	5
Croatia	ZWYS	15	26	29	43	48	74	45	28	71	45	23
Russia	BFST	285	537	661	563	1 262	2 347	3 006	2 877	3 278	2 013	2 049
Turkey	BFUM	493	408	318	365	383	515	920	1 083	978	797	753
Ukraine	ZWYZ	–	3	18	21	34	118	417	282	237	149	102
Serbia and Montenegro[2]	BFWF	1	1	1	1	–2	14	12	12	30	–3	–9
of which Serbia	KNA7	..	..	..	..	..	..	..	12	30	–4	–10
Montenegro	KNA8	..	..	..	..	..	..	..	–	–	1	1
Other	LEVZ	3 484	2 915	2 932	4 088	5 691	7 053	9 366	9 920	6 001	3 108	4 842
Total Europe	LERD	69 681	74 894	64 999	65 225	69 591	89 611	116 455	151 714	154 418	91 576	69 750
Americas												
Argentina	ZWZB	487	365	107	190	260	290	566	454	372	366	277
Brazil	LENR	539	660	660	492	766	1 103	1 065	1 309	1 335	1 616	1 476
Canada	LEOS	2 248	2 334	1 722	2 007	2 240	3 205	4 287	4 663	12	765	4 502
Chile	ZWZC	259	196	240	310	838	1 204	835	847	745	567	945
Colombia	ZWZD	320	224	235	261	395	450	319	235	358	164	289
Mexico	BFPQ	457	312	629	416	724	827	941	923	585	452	770
United States of America	BFVE	29 284	31 117	26 524	27 662	30 743	44 855	59 034	71 715	49 446	33 815	37 348
Uruguay	ZWZE	16	13	20	9	–1	12	32	14	13	5	7
Venezuela	ZWZF	–88	176	185	89	265	394	350	144	174	184	153
Other Central American Countries	JISP	5 465	5 886	5 791	5 962	6 521	10 364	14 997	17 583	15 260	8 868	8 270
Other	LEVH	91	18	66	66	456	–187	929	–515	891	238	45
Total Americas	LESN	39 078	41 301	36 179	37 464	43 207	62 517	83 355	97 372	69 191	47 040	54 082
Asia												
China	LEPK	308	551	433	438	620	869	863	1 311	1 219	1 024	1 084
Hong Kong	BFJU	1 659	1 418	1 343	1 777	3 211	4 198	5 182	5 674	2 908	2 906	4 791
India	BFNB	490	494	635	660	593	821	1 203	1 732	1 943	1 621	1 851
Indonesia	BFLP	149	215	192	227	196	273	431	277	212	441	420
Iran	ZWZG	50	42	37	43	56	149	168	125	98	35	43
Israel	BFMS	52	63	46	77	59	102	152	189	150	133	148
Japan	BFOP	9 008	7 535	4 890	5 256	5 065	6 960	8 688	8 906	8 921	4 712	3 883
Malaysia	BFPZ	497	404	585	617	706	789	788	874	767	839	895
Pakistan	BFRS	131	136	187	181	247	291	377	251	212	212	207
Philippines	BFRJ	179	150	134	161	177	205	289	435	289	219	211
Saudi Arabia	BFTC	292	260	223	193	237	386	461	656	573	342	432
Singapore	BFTU	2 785	2 537	1 901	1 641	2 243	3 454	3 762	2 345	3 650	2 885	3 053
South Korea	BFOY	423	501	688	650	787	1 209	1 360	1 490	1 574	1 103	1 533
Taiwan	BFUV	262	293	343	328	534	673	708	669	589	–63	850
Thailand	BFUD	223	249	236	228	230	301	–15	139	–13	279	290
Residual Gulf Arabian Countries	JITQ	1 509	1 139	764	686	809	1 281	1 637	2 300	2 202	1 466	1 037
Other Near & Middle Eastern Countries	ZWZH	189	197	104	97	166	398	718	1 587	1 959	832	1 842
Other	LEWI	305	236	502	202	296	172	1 091	1 335	1 250	2 066	2 268
Total Asia	LETF	18 511	16 420	13 243	13 462	16 232	22 531	27 863	30 295	28 503	21 052	24 838
Australasia & Oceania												
Australia	CXAT	2 516	2 452	2 791	2 579	3 995	4 361	5 012	6 114	5 578	6 012	7 890
New Zealand	BFRA	327	436	560	585	391	481	546	565	495	380	492
Other	LEVQ	21	8	33	30	36	35	17	51	80	89	84
Total Australasia & Oceania	LETX	2 864	2 896	3 384	3 194	4 422	4 877	5 575	6 730	6 153	6 481	8 466
Africa												
Egypt	ZWZJ	264	259	323	239	196	335	442	571	525	484	859
Morocco	ZWZK	29	30	40	17	8	24	32	33	24	19	27
South Africa	BFWX	1 203	1 334	2 035	1 937	3 002	4 205	2 232	2 883	1 804	1 527	2 379
Other North Africa	JIRR	100	128	–32	122	77	–3 357	304	258	388	–7	121
Other	LEWR	754	758	1 018	1 059	1 125	5 348	1 601	2 116	2 411	1 919	2 582
Total Africa	LERV	2 350	2 509	3 384	3 374	4 408	6 555	4 611	5 861	5 152	3 942	5 968
International Organisations	CTFB	450	514	475	466	451	523	584	626	471	398	359
World total	HMBQ	132 934	138 534	121 664	123 185	138 311	186 614	238 443	292 598	263 888	170 489	163 463

1 Before 1999 only combined BLEU data is available under identifier CTFK.

2 Separate Serbia and Montenegro data is available from 2007.

9.6 Income

continued £ million

		2000	2001	2002	2003	2004	2005	2006	2007	2008	2009	2010
Debits												
Europe												
European Union (EU)												
Austria	CUGZ	591	696	694	632	621	787	1 087	1 336	1 043	811	687
Belgium[1]	AA2W	2 081	1 980	1 933	1 869	2 164	3 038	3 588	4 890	4 727	2 291	1 995
Bulgaria	ZWZP	54	27	25	11	11	33	60	87	59	31	36
Cyprus	AA2X	159	165	132	111	142	207	307	424	449	430	614
Czech Republic	LEPU	129	113	81	81	81	100	191	177	201	81	62
Denmark	LEQV	1 099	922	862	989	1 121	1 425	1 379	1 657	1 552	749	649
Estonia	ZWZR	31	11	2	2	2	3	6	15	14	7	1
Finland	LEUH	378	371	264	320	309	495	567	798	829	554	449
France	LEUQ	7 665	7 059	5 509	7 797	9 972	12 999	15 138	16 770	14 928	18 384	11 595
Germany	LEQM	11 486	8 441	6 364	10 235	11 878	16 449	19 922	25 322	19 944	8 861	13 911
Greece	LEUZ	894	712	496	485	607	1 069	1 562	2 205	2 408	2 076	1 869
Hungary	BFKS	74	39	45	22	21	35	46	112	117	70	55
Ireland	BFLZ	2 978	4 029	4 643	4 965	6 154	9 086	11 481	15 033	16 280	8 711	6 907
Italy	BFOH	2 905	3 034	1 794	2 214	2 423	2 863	3 180	3 900	3 534	1 465	2 518
Latvia	ZWZS	33	11	10	4	8	22	11	21	16	18	13
Lithuania	ZWZT	35	12	2	1	2	17	31	41	35	17	46
Luxembourg[1]	AA32	2 674	2 965	2 627	2 934	3 636	4 249	5 506	7 136	8 369	5 103	6 189
Malta	AA33	46	44	43	31	32	39	77	200	326	148	117
Netherlands	BFQJ	12 182	11 996	6 738	7 117	8 048	9 333	17 270	22 363	7 042	4 265	7 857
Poland	BFSC	187	176	117	107	160	362	477	528	495	112	163
Portugal	BFSL	246	300	279	354	390	452	629	794	799	614	535
Romania	ZWZU	50	25	32	13	20	40	51	54	41	30	15
Slovak Republic	ZWZV	43	17	9	7	21	55	177	99	64	36	68
Slovenia	ZWZW	46	35	38	28	28	24	20	32	29	16	27
Spain	LESX	1 259	1 507	1 316	1 776	1 707	3 944	5 559	6 758	5 360	5 824	3 287
Sweden	BFTM	1 416	1 369	1 314	1 010	1 009	1 288	1 796	2 273	2 198	1 508	1 247
European Central Bank	ZWZM	–	–	–	–	–	–	–	–	–	–	–
EU Institutions	CSFL	1 489	1 763	1 678	1 495	1 644	2 005	2 368	2 781	3 068	2 663	2 466
Total EU27	G97L	50 230	47 819	37 047	44 610	52 211	70 419	92 486	115 806	93 927	64 875	63 378
European Free Trade Association (EFTA)												
Iceland	BFNR	9	8	10	21	54	101	304	422	–1 293	168	503
Liechtenstein	BFPI	116	92	50	57	53	77	103	146	121	33	23
Norway	BFQS	599	634	642	698	766	1 340	2 075	2 784	2 152	1 870	1 909
Switzerland	LEPC	11 551	9 842	6 624	6 058	6 090	9 019	12 149	12 574	–3 865	1 505	4 298
Total EFTA	CTFU	12 275	10 576	7 326	6 834	6 963	10 537	14 631	15 926	–2 885	3 576	6 733
Other Europe												
Albania	ZWZN	28	10	–1	–	–	–	3	4	3	–	–
Belarus	ZWZO	29	9	–1	1	2	7	8	17	21	3	4
Croatia	ZWZQ	59	46	32	27	24	46	61	89	47	6	10
Russia	BFSU	433	397	293	308	418	1 273	2 520	2 901	1 911	327	270
Turkey	BFUN	135	153	86	74	86	149	211	259	263	125	81
Ukraine	ZWZX	29	11	18	62	101	164	248	371	310	75	91
Serbia and Montenegro[2]	BFWG	29	11	6	5	5	10	23	31	19	–	–
of which *Serbia*	KNA9	..	..	..	..	..	..	..	31	18	–	–
Montenegro	KNB2	..	..	..	..	..	..	..	–	1	–	–
Other	LEWA	7 159	7 835	6 806	5 889	7 765	10 859	13 805	20 676	22 864	10 037	8 777
Total Europe	LERE	70 406	66 867	51 612	57 810	67 575	93 464	123 996	156 080	116 480	79 024	79 344
Americas												
Argentina	ZWZZ	106	70	4	3	1	6	8	8	14	5	9
Brazil	LENS	194	160	79	89	88	177	188	189	70	42	79
Canada	LEOT	1 517	1 180	1 592	1 453	2 156	2 316	3 348	1 827	–574	2 285	2 321
Chile	ZXAA	8	35	20	18	27	36	60	98	101	56	140
Colombia	ZXAB	38	43	18	9	5	16	37	43	33	15	9
Mexico	BFPR	239	260	69	60	65	109	135	126	113	34	35
United States of America	BFVF	27 660	31 683	29 836	30 618	32 109	39 748	59 176	68 444	52 861	36 128	42 475
Uruguay	ZXAC	19	8	3	8	7	6	13	18	9	5	4
Venezuela	ZXAD	20	40	28	21	17	27	79	102	76	24	13
Other Central American Countries	JISQ	4 245	3 950	2 521	2 979	3 649	7 504	11 478	13 918	11 993	4 865	–203
Other	LEVI	268	157	79	59	60	85	707	–3 502	19 069	8 521	24
Total Americas	LESO	34 314	37 586	34 249	35 317	38 184	50 030	75 229	81 271	83 765	51 980	44 906
Asia												
China	LEPL	363	373	240	196	236	355	447	854	586	235	279
Hong Kong	BFJV	3 507	3 296	1 897	1 274	1 391	1 787	2 584	3 705	4 086	2 589	2 267
India	BFNC	369	362	246	268	389	721	1 130	1 072	560	290	204
Indonesia	BFLQ	85	114	73	54	55	67	76	62	38	21	20
Iran	ZXAE	230	279	101	90	90	137	205	157	108	51	20
Israel	BFMT	229	258	185	171	149	284	445	424	264	175	115
Japan	BFOQ	11 428	10 019	7 390	3 972	5 509	7 002	9 330	8 669	7 301	4 479	5 187
Malaysia	BFQA	347	277	129	80	126	195	459	597	494	478	287
Pakistan	BFRT	69	68	71	76	60	84	118	123	66	26	28
Philippines	BFRK	91	51	31	19	20	44	98	98	63	29	15
Saudi Arabia	BFTD	870	942	376	323	374	655	1 088	1 524	2 100	744	559
Singapore	BFTV	2 809	2 644	1 850	1 454	1 504	2 473	3 318	4 136	3 554	1 835	1 385
South Korea	BFOZ	160	204	111	27	–154	309	374	492	492	253	258
Taiwan	BFUW	140	189	101	113	168	274	335	486	309	104	78
Thailand	BFUE	147	196	85	69	70	123	208	252	202	59	47
Residual Gulf Arabian Countries	JITR	1 373	1 522	847	608	720	1 124	1 877	2 359	2 217	866	835
Other Near & Middle Eastern Countries	ZXAF	270	221	142	135	124	207	308	322	261	96	86
Other	LEWJ	392	334	270	116	136	330	400	439	421	264	283
Total Asia	LETG	22 879	21 349	14 145	9 045	10 967	16 171	22 800	25 771	23 122	12 594	11 953
Australasia & Oceania												
Australia	CXCM	750	577	961	1 275	1 386	1 857	2 128	3 068	2 446	3 281	1 327
New Zealand	BFRB	109	112	86	72	80	102	151	103	118	46	64
Other	LEVR	28	62	43	30	25	4	341	9	6	2	–277
Total Australasia & Oceania	LETY	887	751	1 090	1 377	1 491	1 963	2 620	3 180	2 570	3 329	1 114
Africa												
Egypt	ZXAH	325	278	164	128	141	285	369	341	235	52	79
Morocco	ZXAI	30	31	18	12	12	29	96	59	43	10	13
South Africa	BFWY	743	738	716	792	842	1 066	1 283	1 271	1 197	1 062	1 147
Other North Africa	JIRS	176	186	119	96	106	256	527	685	590	193	182
Other	LEWS	649	624	408	322	344	540	824	1 119	1 214	463	395
Total Africa	LERW	1 923	1 857	1 425	1 350	1 445	2 176	3 099	3 475	3 279	1 780	1 816
International Organisations	CTFC	562	699	640	516	620	924	1 187	1 452	1 536	1 385	1 291
World total	HMBR	130 971	129 109	103 161	105 415	120 282	164 728	228 931	271 229	230 752	150 092	140 424

1 Before 1999 only combined BLEU data is available under identifier CTFL. 2 Separate Serbia and Montenegro data is available from 2007.

9.6 Income

continued £ million

		2000	2001	2002	2003	2004	2005	2006	2007	2008	2009	2010
Balances												
Europe												
European Union (EU)												
Austria	CUHA	151	−13	−9	114	194	113	−216	−222	−77	−103	−286
Belgium[1]	AA3A	261	773	275	61	455	582	859	1 719	1 163	989	445
Bulgaria	ZXAN	−17	66	47	63	78	−5	−20	−68	−21	−7	−22
Cyprus	AA3B	−6	−2	5	−55	−70	−92	8	145	−76	−280	−544
Czech Republic	LEPV	−4	85	71	114	129	55	−182	15	−210	−161	−158
Denmark	LEQW	2	57	−341	−284	−238	16	313	323	408	319	475
Estonia	ZXAP	−29	−3	4	6	7	11	5	−7	−7	19	12
Finland	LEUI	207	277	323	197	211	77	22	237	151	160	172
France	LEUR	−130	1 621	1 439	−843	−1 813	−1 894	−391	3 518	2 447	−9 183	−1 517
Germany	LEQN	−1 350	2 624	3 140	−1 905	−2 350	−4 758	−6 148	−7 699	−1 458	2 173	−5 676
Greece	LEVA	108	159	211	332	175	−235	−613	−806	−996	−1 234	−1 467
Hungary	BFKT	374	282	307	312	362	376	150	184	169	74	47
Ireland	BFML	846	681	−725	−81	−535	−1 224	−1 082	134	−1 135	−3 264	−12 333
Italy	BFOI	3 521	3 313	2 997	2 686	2 224	2 188	2 517	3 290	3 062	2 613	1 175
Latvia	ZXAQ	−31	−11	−10	−4	−8	−21	7	9	−7	−35	−69
Lithuania	ZXAR	−26	−5	2	3	−1	−9	−23	−31	−27	−9	−32
Luxembourg[1]	AA3E	1 050	929	694	−98	260	2 005	4 967	4 742	9 701	8 692	5 560
Malta	AA3F	5	11	5	22	459	5	−222	−207	−227	204	−52
Netherlands	BFQK	632	4 590	8 984	8 088	1 690	2 113	−1 651	−1 931	14 889	10 878	4 168
Poland	BFSD	−43	153	218	293	280	79	60	−56	174	784	406
Portugal	BFSM	418	508	497	453	407	518	372	313	464	93	47
Romania	ZXAS	−30	53	33	83	97	30	58	105	194	135	99
Slovak Republic	ZXAT	8	12	22	21	9	−3	−136	32	13	8	−16
Slovenia	ZXAU	2	66	30	61	71	13	7	9	23	7	−33
Spain	LESY	1 305	896	736	538	1 916	1 010	976	1 560	4 017	−61	−128
Sweden	BFTN	692	938	807	757	1 264	1 407	1 344	1 701	2 964	2 813	1 973
European Central Bank	ZXAK	–	–	–	–	–	–	–	–	–	–	–
EU Institutions	CSFM	−1 119	−1 295	−1 021	−748	−1 122	−1 489	−1 835	−2 265	−2 505	−2 023	−1 953
Total EU27	G97D	6 797	16 765	18 741	10 186	4 151	868	−854	4 744	33 093	13 601	−9 707
European Free Trade Association (EFTA)												
Iceland	BFNU	26	30	23	6	1	20	−84	575	2 448	292	−129
Liechtenstein	BFPJ	−71	−53	−29	−37	−30	−58	−71	−106	−94	−43	−27
Norway	BFQT	423	383	45	98	66	610	−116	25	624	−569	−932
Switzerland	LEPD	−4 277	−4 516	−2 120	−1 553	−1 187	−2 910	−3 306	533	16 696	3 725	2 667
Total EFTA	CTFV	−3 899	−4 156	−2 081	−1 486	−1 150	−2 338	−3 577	1 027	19 674	3 405	1 579
Other Europe												
Albania	ZXAL	−28	−10	1	–	–	–	−3	−2	3	6	2
Belarus	ZXAM	−29	−9	8	−1	−2	−3	−5	−10	−13	1	1
Croatia	ZXAO	−44	−20	−3	16	24	28	−16	−61	24	39	13
Russia	BFSV	−148	140	368	255	844	1 074	486	−24	1 367	1 686	1 779
Turkey	BFUO	358	255	232	291	297	366	709	824	715	672	672
Ukraine	ZXAV	−29	−8	–	−41	−67	−46	169	−89	−73	74	11
Serbia and Montenegro,[2]	BFWH	−28	−10	−5	−4	−7	4	−11	−19	11	−3	−9
of which *Serbia*	KNB3	..	..	..	..	..	..	..	−19	12	−4	−10
Montenegro	KNB4	..	..	..	..	..	..	..	–	−1	1	1
Other	LEWB	−3 675	−4 920	−3 874	−1 801	−2 074	−3 806	−4 439	−10 756	−16 863	−6 929	−3 935
Total Europe	LERF	−725	8 027	13 387	7 415	2 016	−3 853	−7 541	−4 366	37 938	12 552	−9 594
Americas												
Argentina	ZXAX	381	295	103	187	259	284	558	446	358	361	268
Brazil	LENT	345	500	581	403	678	926	877	1 120	1 265	1 574	1 397
Canada	LEOU	731	1 154	130	554	84	889	939	2 836	586	−1 520	2 181
Chile	ZXAY	251	161	220	292	811	1 168	775	749	644	511	805
Colombia	ZXAZ	282	181	217	252	390	434	282	192	325	149	280
Mexico	BFPS	218	52	560	356	659	718	806	797	472	418	735
United States of America	BFVG	1 624	−566	−3 312	−2 956	−1 366	5 107	−142	3 271	−3 415	−2 313	−5 127
Uruguay	ZXBA	−3	5	17	1	−8	6	19	−4	4	–	3
Venezuela	ZXBB	−108	136	157	68	248	367	271	42	98	160	140
Other Central American Countries	JISR	1 220	1 936	3 270	2 983	2 872	2 860	3 519	3 665	3 267	4 003	8 473
Other	LEVJ	−177	−139	−13	7	396	−272	222	2 987	−18 178	−8 283	21
Total Americas	LESP	4 764	3 715	1 930	2 147	5 023	12 487	8 126	16 101	−14 574	−4 940	9 176
Asia												
China	LEPM	−55	178	193	242	384	514	416	457	633	789	805
Hong Kong	BFJW	−1 848	−1 878	−554	503	1 820	2 411	2 598	1 969	−1 178	317	2 524
India	BFND	121	132	389	392	204	100	73	660	1 383	1 331	1 647
Indonesia	BFLR	64	101	119	173	141	206	355	215	174	420	400
Iran	ZXBC	−180	−237	−64	−47	−34	12	−37	−32	−10	−16	23
Israel	BFMU	−177	−195	−139	−94	−90	−182	−293	−235	−114	−42	33
Japan	BFOR	−2 420	−2 484	−2 500	1 284	−444	−42	−642	237	1 620	233	−1 304
Malaysia	BFQB	150	127	456	537	580	594	329	277	273	361	608
Pakistan	BFRU	62	68	116	105	187	207	259	128	146	186	179
Philippines	BFRL	88	99	103	142	157	161	191	337	226	190	196
Saudi Arabia	BFTE	−578	−682	−153	−130	−137	−269	−627	−868	−1 527	−402	−127
Singapore	BFTW	−24	−107	51	187	739	981	444	−1 791	96	1 050	1 668
South Korea	BFPA	263	297	577	623	941	900	986	998	1 082	850	1 275
Taiwan	BFUX	122	104	242	215	366	399	373	183	280	−167	772
Thailand	BFUF	76	53	151	159	160	178	−223	−113	−215	220	243
Residual Gulf Arabian Countries	JITS	136	−383	−83	78	89	157	−240	−59	−15	600	202
Other Near & Middle Eastern Countries	ZXBD	−81	−24	−38	−38	42	191	410	1 265	1 698	736	1 756
Other	LEWK	−87	−98	232	86	160	−158	691	896	829	1 802	1 985
Total Asia	LETH	−4 368	−4 929	−902	4 417	5 265	6 360	5 063	4 524	5 381	8 458	12 885
Australasia & Oceania												
Australia	CYAA	1 766	1 875	1 830	1 304	2 609	2 504	2 884	3 046	3 132	2 731	6 563
New Zealand	BFRC	218	324	474	513	311	379	395	462	377	334	428
Other	LEVS	−7	−54	−10	–	11	31	−324	42	74	87	361
Total Australasia & Oceania	LETZ	1 977	2 145	2 294	1 817	2 931	2 914	2 955	3 550	3 583	3 152	7 352
Africa												
Egypt	ZXBF	−61	−19	159	111	55	50	73	230	290	432	780
Morocco	ZXBG	−1	−1	22	5	−4	−5	−64	−26	−19	9	14
South Africa	BFWZ	460	596	1 319	1 145	2 160	3 139	949	1 612	607	465	1 232
Other North Africa	JIRT	−76	−58	−151	26	−29	−3 613	−223	−427	−202	−200	−61
Other	LEWT	105	134	610	737	781	4 808	777	997	1 197	1 456	2 187
Total Africa	LERX	427	652	1 959	2 024	2 963	4 379	1 512	2 386	1 873	2 162	4 152
International Organisations	CTFD	−112	−185	−165	−50	−169	−401	−603	−826	−1 065	−987	−932
World total	HMBP	1 963	9 425	18 503	17 770	18 029	21 886	9 512	21 369	33 136	20 397	23 039

1 Before 1999 only combined BLEU data is available under identifier CTFM.
2 Separate Serbia and Montenegro data is available from 2007.

THIS PAGE IS INTENTIONALLY BLANK

9.7 Current transfers

£ million

		2000	2001	2002	2003	2004	2005	2006	2007	2008	2009	2010
Credits												
Europe												
European Union (EU)												
Austria	GXVQ	30	31	33	51	36	38	45	34	34	37	37
Belgium[1]	A7PL	209	202	230	217	227	242	237	215	216	210	217
Bulgaria	KOLZ	2	–	8	1	1	8	10	15	15	10	9
Cyprus	A7PM	2	2	3	4	4	4	9	3	4	5	8
Czech Republic	GXWK	6	2	3	32	23	16	37	17	18	8	13
Denmark	GXVS	28	30	41	28	40	45	59	33	42	48	46
Estonia	LWMG	–	–	–	–	–	–	–	–	–	3	1
Finland	GXVT	24	15	16	93	17	17	24	18	20	20	19
France	GXVU	279	328	336	193	332	319	371	273	318	322	324
Germany	GXVV	391	392	444	379	457	499	555	442	471	430	440
Greece	GXVW	39	40	48	40	49	55	57	41	51	48	66
Hungary	HZXT	1	1	8	1	1	5	6	13	13	10	9
Ireland	GXVX	115	162	155	113	170	166	199	157	186	194	182
Italy	GXVY	101	117	123	100	178	180	229	126	162	155	171
Latvia	LWWC	2	1	5	1	1	7	3	4	5	8	7
Lithuania	LYTR	–	1	–	–	–	7	13	14	14	10	20
Luxembourg[1]	A7PO	15	15	17	15	19	21	28	14	16	15	25
Malta	A7PP	–	1	1	1	2	2	2	3	5	5	10
Netherlands	GXVZ	323	315	374	292	353	377	352	315	323	383	363
Poland	GXWL	3	3	14	7	37	107	129	122	128	37	54
Portugal	GXWA	28	15	21	15	22	20	28	18	20	31	25
Romania	HZXV	–	–	11	1	2	7	9	8	9	14	6
Slovak Republic	HZXX	–	2	3	–	–	13	62	17	18	9	9
Slovenia	HZXY	–	–	5	–	1	1	3	1	1	3	2
Spain	GXWB	92	98	105	86	127	137	172	123	137	133	161
Sweden	GXWC	88	90	97	84	108	107	119	87	98	92	91
European Central Bank	KNWK	–	–	–	–	–	–	–	–	–	–	–
EU Institutions	GXWD	5 314	7 275	5 905	6 688	7 354	7 976	8 119	7 387	8 551	9 438	6 870
Total EU27	GC84	7 092	9 138	8 006	8 442	9 561	10 376	10 877	9 500	10 875	11 678	9 185
European Free Trade Association (EFTA)												
Iceland	GXWF	33	34	35	64	34	34	40	34	34	33	37
Liechtenstein	GXWG	2	1	2	1	1	–	5	1	2	1	2
Norway	GXWH	60	60	80	66	75	87	103	71	86	81	106
Switzerland	GXWI	59	65	80	63	85	105	150	61	82	91	96
Total EFTA	GXWJ	154	160	197	194	195	226	298	167	204	206	241
Other Europe												
Albania	HZXP	–	–	–	–	–	–	–	–	–	–	1
Belarus	HZXQ	–	1	–	7	–	1	–	–	–	–	–
Croatia	HZXR	2	1	2	2	2	–	9	9	10	10	3
Russia	GXWM	10	12	16	11	19	24	50	16	22	18	23
Turkey	GXWN	28	30	34	30	37	39	61	31	35	35	43
Ukraine	HZYA	1	–	–	7	19	2	2	8	8	–	2
Serbia and Montenegro[2]	LTVE	2	1	2	5	1	–	5	3	4	1	2
of which Serbia	KN4L	..	..	..	..	..	..	..	3	4	1	2
Montenegro	KN4K	..	..	..	..	..	..	..	–	–	–	–
Other	HKJF	10	27	16	16	9	14	29	41	43	39	43
Total Europe	GXWP	7 299	9 370	8 273	8 714	9 843	10 682	11 331	9 775	11 201	11 987	9 543
Americas												
Argentina	HZYJ	8	10	11	7	8	5	17	5	11	10	12
Brazil	GXWQ	10	14	16	11	12	12	37	10	16	18	35
Canada	GXWR	174	197	209	160	243	267	268	183	260	266	373
Chile	HZYL	7	10	9	7	9	10	27	7	12	10	17
Colombia	HZYM	14	24	17	25	15	15	36	9	18	13	15
Mexico	GXWS	18	19	28	21	27	32	97	19	29	26	44
United States of America	GXWT	1 182	2 395	1 693	1 217	1 549	4 186	3 354	2 129	2 740	2 718	2 315
Uruguay	HZYN	–	–	–	–	–	–	2	–	–	–	1
Venezuela	HZYO	8	10	12	8	13	15	27	6	12	10	11
Other Central American Countries	HZYG	140	145	181	135	214	258	510	148	228	204	232
Other	HZYI	8	10	13	13	13	15	31	7	14	13	17
Total Americas	GXWV	1 569	2 834	2 189	1 604	2 103	4 815	4 406	2 523	3 340	3 288	3 072
Asia												
China	GXWW	9	10	13	9	13	12	36	10	17	19	39
Hong Kong	GXWX	49	54	40	29	37	36	47	22	37	38	39
India	GXWY	15	23	25	13	27	30	75	15	21	30	40
Indonesia	GXWZ	17	19	24	44	18	18	73	12	24	18	17
Iran	HZYQ	3	2	3	2	3	4	9	2	3	2	2
Israel	GXXA	29	31	35	33	32	34	49	25	38	32	30
Japan	GXXB	97	109	130	95	124	137	272	88	128	116	125
Malaysia	GXXC	17	23	21	48	21	21	38	16	22	23	29
Pakistan	GXXD	3	4	4	29	4	3	13	5	6	5	9
Philippines	GXXE	8	10	11	7	9	10	17	5	11	10	6
Saudi Arabia	GXXF	485	494	488	499	481	490	510	478	466	467	455
Singapore	GXXG	9	15	15	13	23	28	30	15	22	28	39
South Korea	GXXH	9	12	20	10	22	28	56	4	10	10	23
Taiwan	GXXI	7	10	15	22	12	15	27	6	10	9	8
Thailand	GXXJ	5	5	9	6	8	10	20	4	6	9	12
Residual Gulf Arabian Countries	HZYS	162	165	172	168	177	179	230	166	170	172	189
Other Near & Middle Eastern Countries	HZYU	294	299	295	294	293	299	311	290	281	279	278
Other	HZVR	54	62	44	38	41	41	69	44	51	50	44
Total Asia	GXXL	1 272	1 347	1 364	1 359	1 345	1 395	1 882	1 207	1 323	1 317	1 384
Australasia & Oceania												
Australia	GXXM	158	169	203	165	244	268	221	192	231	241	352
New Zealand	GXXN	53	58	58	51	64	60	68	55	59	58	61
Other	GXXO	3	2	3	2	6	5	7	3	4	4	10
Total Australasia & Oceania	GXXP	214	229	264	218	314	333	296	250	294	303	423
Africa												
Egypt	LZDN	3	2	4	26	7	9	19	4	5	4	10
Morocco	HICY	2	1	2	2	2	1	7	2	3	3	8
South Africa	GXXQ	81	88	83	69	96	105	118	58	89	90	95
Other North Africa	HICX	10	10	13	20	14	15	17	10	10	11	13
Other	HZUI	33	36	42	35	43	45	98	48	58	61	60
Total Africa	GXXS	129	137	144	152	162	175	259	122	165	169	186
International Organisations	GXXT	–	–	–	–	–	–	–	–	–	–	–
World total	KTND	10 483	13 917	12 234	12 047	13 767	17 400	18 174	13 877	16 323	17 064	14 608

1 Before 1999 only combined data is available under identifier GXVR.

2 Separate Serbia and Montenegro data is available from 2007.

9.7 Current transfers

continued £ million

		2000	2001	2002	2003	2004	2005	2006	2007	2008	2009	2010
Debits												
Europe												
European Union (EU)												
Austria	GXXV	23	21	24	25	29	34	39	31	36	36	41
Belgium[1]	A8BV	70	82	87	94	101	79	65	67	83	78	83
Bulgaria	LTQA	12	8	14	7	4	4	10	5	4	6	7
Cyprus	A8BW	18	19	27	26	32	35	39	30	30	35	48
Czech Republic	GXYP	9	9	11	12	13	14	19	16	21	12	21
Denmark	GXXX	37	32	36	30	42	54	60	39	53	49	56
Estonia	LWQY	–	–	–	1	4	4	4	4	–	4	6
Finland	GXXY	22	14	14	13	17	17	25	15	18	17	20
France	GXXZ	268	288	333	267	320	351	422	337	412	399	419
Germany	GXYA	294	288	366	316	401	455	483	379	447	594	718
Greece	GXYB	49	45	46	46	59	65	66	61	79	70	81
Hungary	HIEC	16	12	19	10	11	12	15	13	14	17	18
Ireland	GXYC	471	442	476	506	559	611	627	584	654	674	688
Italy	GXYD	133	139	150	131	178	207	243	157	203	204	220
Latvia	LYON	2	1	2	1	1	–	6	1	2	1	5
Lithuania	LYYJ	1	15	14	–	8	9	4	4	4	1	1
Luxembourg[1]	A8BY	8	11	11	11	13	14	21	7	10	8	18
Malta	A8BZ	15	17	18	19	22	23	24	24	29	34	39
Netherlands	GXYE	187	144	178	127	176	205	148	165	225	182	225
Poland	GXYQ	58	46	50	52	56	59	66	60	68	79	77
Portugal	GXYF	48	36	40	41	46	47	58	46	53	56	65
Romania	HIEE	14	11	20	10	12	12	18	12	6	15	16
Slovak Republic	HIEG	5	3	6	3	1	6	1	1	1	1	3
Slovenia	HIEH	–	5	4	–	1	1	3	1	1	1	3
Spain	GXYG	125	126	141	151	171	172	197	185	215	218	237
Sweden	GXYH	33	34	39	35	43	41	54	28	46	55	53
European Central Bank	KOEJ	–	–	–	–	–	–	–	–	–	–	–
EU Institutions	GXYI	10 719	9 557	10 097	11 485	11 505	13 098	13 025	13 060	13 334	14 779	15 987
Total EU27	GCR2	12 637	11 405	12 223	13 419	13 825	15 629	15 742	15 332	16 048	17 625	19 155
European Free Trade Association (EFTA)												
Iceland	GXYK	4	2	6	2	2	1	7	2	3	3	6
Liechtenstein	GXYL	2	1	2	1	1	–	5	1	2	1	2
Norway	GXYM	56	59	63	54	72	77	89	82	104	94	118
Switzerland	GXYN	94	91	124	90	121	146	182	97	131	144	159
Total EFTA	GXYO	156	153	195	147	196	224	283	182	240	242	285
Other Europe												
Albania	HIDY	6	9	12	7	7	7	4	9	9	10	13
Belarus	HIDZ	–	6	11	3	2	2	–	–	–	–	–
Croatia	HIEA	8	5	6	5	6	11	16	14	13	15	11
Russia	GXYR	90	55	23	49	60	62	100	54	33	72	74
Turkey	GXYS	28	34	41	32	44	48	69	33	41	42	54
Ukraine	HIEJ	30	54	15	28	41	42	22	26	24	24	27
Serbia and Montenegro[2]	LWHC	67	38	31	30	27	29	33	32	36	40	43
of which *Serbia*	KN4N	..	..	..	..	..	..	..	29	32	36	39
Montenegro	KN4M	..	..	..	..	..	..	..	3	4	4	4
Other	HZWJ	126	149	156	189	168	180	194	225	239	250	267
Total Europe	GXYU	13 148	11 908	12 713	13 909	14 376	16 234	16 463	15 907	16 683	18 320	19 929
Americas												
Argentina	HIES	16	17	18	14	16	15	26	14	22	19	18
Brazil	GXYV	36	45	57	35	38	41	60	30	29	36	64
Canada	GXYW	265	280	315	276	368	406	396	338	438	436	575
Chile	HIEU	12	11	13	10	13	14	31	11	17	14	21
Colombia	HIEV	23	29	22	14	21	21	40	15	26	21	22
Mexico	GXYX	25	22	31	21	28	33	98	22	34	28	46
United States of America	GXYY	1 421	2 553	1 891	1 449	1 845	4 471	3 604	2 442	3 181	3 048	2 813
Uruguay	HIEW	1	1	1	1	1	1	3	1	1	1	2
Venezuela	HIEX	9	11	13	9	14	16	28	7	13	12	12
Other Central American Countries	HIEP	429	401	426	365	456	510	783	430	523	522	563
Other	HIER	80	96	96	64	68	68	67	55	52	62	68
Total Americas	GXZA	2 317	3 466	2 883	2 258	2 868	5 596	5 136	3 365	4 336	4 199	4 204
Asia												
China	GXZB	82	86	125	77	136	137	153	143	154	178	208
Hong Kong	GXZC	117	121	133	126	147	155	175	150	181	177	189
India	GXZD	489	534	557	503	621	711	734	796	923	944	1 006
Indonesia	GXZE	54	45	51	67	83	182	157	96	127	127	132
Iran	HIEZ	20	17	19	17	21	23	28	22	23	24	24
Israel	GXZF	33	36	42	35	40	43	58	33	49	44	46
Japan	GXZG	95	104	132	99	132	148	274	99	145	128	147
Malaysia	GXZH	45	44	49	46	53	61	79	56	70	65	75
Pakistan	GXZI	144	162	233	183	196	211	251	266	314	314	333
Philippines	GXZJ	30	33	35	33	37	40	48	37	44	46	42
Saudi Arabia	GXZK	41	42	51	48	52	49	66	52	64	68	68
Singapore	GXZL	76	76	88	90	109	118	119	110	128	139	160
South Korea	GXZM	11	13	21	10	23	29	56	5	11	10	24
Taiwan	GXZN	7	11	15	9	12	15	27	6	10	11	8
Thailand	GXZO	29	30	40	31	37	50	51	41	46	49	51
Residual Gulf Arabian Countries	HIFB	74	83	88	193	325	342	359	294	254	355	392
Other Near & Middle Eastern Countries	HIFD	67	77	77	73	91	96	94	73	61	89	103
Other	HZWN	404	538	609	529	740	854	962	943	1 107	1 178	1 268
Total Asia	GXZQ	1 818	2 052	2 365	2 169	2 855	3 264	3 691	3 222	3 711	3 946	4 276
Australasia & Oceania												
Australia	GXZR	217	240	275	264	345	399	353	343	406	423	560
New Zealand	GXZS	66	75	80	79	92	101	109	105	118	118	126
Other	GXZT	11	10	23	22	26	27	28	20	16	25	30
Total Australasia & Oceania	GXZU	294	325	378	365	463	527	490	468	540	566	716
Africa												
Egypt	LZIF	24	23	27	26	36	39	46	37	35	34	41
Morocco	HIYZ	8	7	8	9	9	9	15	11	12	14	15
South Africa	GXZV	257	286	309	313	346	364	385	352	415	434	471
Other North Africa	HIYX	10	13	14	26	20	21	21	16	18	17	19
Other	HZUA	1 268	1 320	1 363	2 087	1 894	2 009	2 084	2 299	2 448	2 809	2 992
Total Africa	GXZX	1 567	1 649	1 721	2 461	2 305	2 442	2 551	2 715	2 928	3 308	3 538
International Organisations	GXZY	1 114	1 032	1 044	720	1 176	1 186	1 719	1 746	1 890	1 801	2 026
World total	KTNE	20 258	20 432	21 104	21 882	24 043	29 249	30 050	27 423	30 088	32 140	34 689

1 Before 1999 only combined BLEU data is available under indentifier GXXW.
2 Separate Serbia and Montenegro data is available from 2007.

9.7 Current transfers

continued £ million

		2000	2001	2002	2003	2004	2005	2006	2007	2008	2009	2010
Balances												
Europe												
European Union (EU)												
Austria	GZDU	7	10	9	26	7	4	6	3	-2	1	-4
Belgium[1]	A8H2	139	120	143	123	126	163	172	148	133	132	134
Bulgaria	ZWRH	-10	-8	-6	-6	-3	4	–	10	11	4	2
Cyprus	A8H3	-16	-17	-24	-22	-28	-31	-30	-27	-26	-30	-40
Czech Republic	GZCJ	-3	-7	-8	20	10	2	18	1	-3	-4	-8
Denmark	GZDW	-9	-2	5	-2	-2	-9	-1	-6	-11	-1	-10
Estonia	ZWRN	–	–	–	-1	-4	-4	-4	-4	–	-1	-5
Finland	GZDX	2	1	2	80	–	–	-1	3	2	3	-1
France	GZDY	11	40	3	-74	12	-32	-51	-64	-94	-77	-95
Germany	GZDZ	97	104	78	63	56	44	72	63	24	-164	-278
Greece	GZEA	-10	-5	2	-6	-10	-10	-9	-20	-28	-22	-15
Hungary	GYWH	-15	-11	-11	-9	-10	-7	-9	–	-1	-7	-9
Ireland	GZEB	-356	-280	-321	-393	-389	-445	-428	-427	-468	-480	-506
Italy	GZEC	-32	-22	-27	-31	–	-27	-14	-31	-41	-49	-49
Latvia	ZWRV	–	–	3	–	–	7	-3	3	3	7	2
Lithuania	ZWRU	-1	-14	-14	–	-8	-2	9	10	10	9	19
Luxembourg[1]	A8H5	7	4	6	4	6	7	7	7	6	7	7
Malta	A8H6	-15	-16	-17	-18	-20	-21	-22	-21	-24	-29	-29
Netherlands	GZED	136	171	196	165	177	172	204	150	98	201	138
Poland	GZCK	-55	-43	-36	-45	-19	48	63	62	60	-42	-23
Portugal	GZEE	-20	-21	-19	-26	-24	-27	-30	-28	-33	-25	-40
Romania	ZWRX	-14	-11	-9	-9	-10	-5	-9	-4	3	-1	-10
Slovak Republic	ZWRZ	-5	-1	-3	-3	-1	7	61	16	17	8	6
Slovenia	ZWRY	–	-5	1	–	–	–	–	–	–	2	-1
Spain	GZEF	-33	-28	-36	-65	-44	-35	-25	-62	-78	-85	-76
Sweden	GYRO	55	56	58	49	65	66	65	59	52	37	38
European Central Bank	ZWRB	–	–	–	–	–	–	–	–	–	–	–
EU Institutions	GYRP	-5 405	-2 282	-4 192	-4 797	-4 151	-5 122	-4 906	-5 673	-4 783	-5 341	-9 117
Total EU27	GD6K	-5 545	-2 267	-4 217	-4 977	-4 264	-5 253	-4 865	-5 832	-5 173	-5 947	-9 970
European Free Trade Association (EFTA)												
Iceland	GXEL	29	32	29	62	32	33	33	32	31	30	31
Liechtenstein	GXEM	–	–	–	–	–	–	–	–	–	–	–
Norway	GXEN	4	1	17	12	3	10	14	-11	-18	-13	-12
Switzerland	GZCH	-35	-26	-44	-27	-36	-41	-32	-36	-49	-53	-63
Total EFTA	GZCI	-2	7	2	47	-1	2	15	-15	-36	-36	-44
Other Europe												
Albania	ZWRF	-6	-9	-12	-7	-7	-7	-4	-9	-9	-10	-12
Belarus	ZWRI	–	-5	-11	4	-2	-1	–	–	–	–	–
Croatia	ZWRS	-6	-4	-4	-3	-4	-11	-7	-5	-3	-5	-8
Russia	GZCL	-80	-43	-7	-38	-41	-38	-50	-38	-11	-54	-51
Turkey	GZCM	–	-4	-7	-2	-7	-9	-8	-2	-6	-7	-11
Ukraine	ZWSA	-29	-54	-15	-21	-22	-40	-20	-18	-16	-24	-25
Serbia and Montenegro[2]	ZWSD	-65	-37	-29	-25	-26	-29	-28	-29	-32	-39	-41
of which *Serbia*	KN4P	..	..	..	..	..	..	..	-26	-28	-35	-37
Montenegro	KN4O	..	..	..	..	..	..	..	-3	-4	-4	-4
Other	ZWRC	-116	-122	-140	-173	-159	-166	-165	-184	-196	-211	-224
Total Europe	GZCO	-5 849	-2 538	-4 440	-5 195	-4 533	-5 552	-5 132	-6 132	-5 482	-6 333	-10 386
Americas												
Argentina	ZWRG	-8	-7	-7	-7	-8	-10	-9	-9	-11	-9	-6
Brazil	GZCP	-26	-31	-41	-24	-26	-29	-23	-20	-13	-18	-29
Canada	GZCQ	-91	-83	-106	-116	-125	-139	-128	-155	-178	-170	-202
Chile	ZWRJ	-5	-1	-4	-3	-4	-4	-4	-4	-5	-4	-4
Colombia	ZWRK	-9	-5	-5	11	-6	-6	-4	-6	-8	-8	-7
Mexico	GZCR	-7	-3	-3	–	-1	-1	-1	-3	-5	-2	-2
United States of America	GZCS	-239	-158	-198	-232	-296	-285	-250	-313	-441	-330	-498
Uruguay	ZWSB	-1	-1	-1	-1	-1	-1	-1	-1	-1	-1	-1
Venezuela	ZWSC	-1	-1	-1	-1	-1	-1	-1	-1	-1	-2	-1
Other Central American Countries	ZWRM	-289	-256	-245	-230	-242	-252	-273	-282	-295	-318	-331
Other	ZWRP	-72	-86	-83	-51	-55	-53	-36	-48	-38	-49	-51
Total Americas	GZCU	-748	-632	-694	-654	-765	-781	-730	-842	-996	-911	-1 132
Asia												
China	GZCV	-73	-76	-112	-68	-123	-125	-117	-133	-137	-159	-169
Hong Kong	GZCW	-68	-67	-93	-97	-110	-119	-128	-128	-144	-139	-150
India	GZCX	-474	-511	-532	-490	-594	-681	-659	-781	-902	-914	-966
Indonesia	GZCY	-37	-26	-27	-23	-65	-164	-84	-84	-103	-109	-115
Iran	ZWRT	-17	-15	-16	-15	-18	-19	-19	-20	-20	-22	-22
Israel	GZCZ	-4	-5	-7	-2	-8	-9	-9	-8	-11	-12	-16
Japan	GZDA	2	5	-2	-4	-8	-11	-2	-11	-17	-12	-22
Malaysia	GZDB	-28	-21	-28	2	-32	-40	-41	-40	-48	-42	-46
Pakistan	GZDC	-141	-158	-229	-154	-192	-208	-238	-261	-308	-309	-324
Philippines	GZDD	-22	-23	-24	-26	-28	-30	-31	-32	-33	-36	-36
Saudi Arabia	GZDE	444	452	437	451	429	441	444	426	402	399	387
Singapore	GZDF	-67	-61	-73	-77	-86	-90	-89	-95	-106	-111	-121
South Korea	GZDG	-2	-1	-1	–	-1	-1	–	-1	-1	–	-1
Taiwan	GZDH	–	-1	–	13	–	–	–	–	–	-2	–
Thailand	GZDI	-24	-25	-31	-25	-29	-40	-31	-37	-40	-40	-39
Residual Gulf Arabian Countries	ZWRQ	88	82	84	-25	-148	-163	-129	-128	-84	-183	-203
Other Near & Middle Eastern Countries	ZWRR	227	222	218	221	202	203	217	217	220	190	175
Other	ZWRD	-350	-476	-565	-491	-699	-813	-893	-899	-1 056	-1 128	-1 224
Total Asia	GZDK	-546	-705	-1 001	-810	-1 510	-1 869	-1 809	-2 015	-2 388	-2 629	-2 892
Australasia & Oceania												
Australia	GZDL	-59	-71	-72	-99	-101	-131	-132	-151	-175	-182	-208
New Zealand	GZDM	-13	-17	-22	-28	-28	-41	-41	-50	-59	-60	-65
Other	GZDN	-8	-8	-20	-20	-20	-22	-21	-17	-12	-21	-20
Total Australasia & Oceania	GZDO	-80	-96	-114	-147	-149	-194	-194	-218	-246	-263	-293
Africa												
Egypt	ZWRO	-21	-21	-23	–	-29	-30	-27	-33	-30	-30	-31
Morocco	ZWRW	-6	-6	-6	-7	-7	-8	-8	-9	-9	-11	-7
South Africa	GZDP	-176	-198	-226	-244	-250	-259	-267	-294	-326	-344	-376
Other North Africa	ZWRL	–	-3	-1	-6	-6	-6	-4	-6	-8	-6	-6
Other	ZWRE	-1 235	-1 284	-1 321	-2 052	-1 851	-1 964	-1 986	-2 251	-2 390	-2 748	-2 932
Total Africa	GZDR	-1 438	-1 512	-1 577	-2 309	-2 143	-2 267	-2 292	-2 593	-2 763	-3 139	-3 352
International Organisations	GZDS	-1 114	-1 032	-1 044	-720	-1 176	-1 186	-1 719	-1 746	-1 890	-1 801	-2 026
World total	KTNF	-9 775	-6 515	-8 870	-9 835	-10 276	-11 849	-11 876	-13 546	-13 765	-15 076	-20 081

1 Before 1999 only combined BLEU data is available under identifier GZDV.

2 Separate Serbia and Montenegro data is available froom 2007.

THIS PAGE IS INTENTIONALLY BLANK

9.8 Current account

Transactions with Europe and USA[1,2]

£ million

		2000	2001	2002	2003	2004	2005	2006	2007	2008	2009	2010
Credits												
Exports of goods												
EMU members	QATL	102 386	104 484	104 202	100 965	100 944	109 847	136 612	114 656	126 989	111 753	125 752
EU members	LGCJ	112 436	114 373	114 689	111 252	111 678	121 448	152 512	127 684	141 834	124 700	142 208
Total Europe	EPLM	120 858	122 726	122 788	120 055	120 914	133 806	164 647	140 675	158 126	137 943	159 231
USA	J8V9	29 371	29 403	28 142	28 819	28 525	30 836	31 944	32 044	35 277	33 951	37 925
Exports of services												
EMU members	K9HU	29 876	32 354	33 896	36 868	40 669	43 835	47 614	54 337	61 357	59 264	58 599
EU members	GC8R	33 720	36 850	38 306	41 710	46 071	49 855	54 799	62 490	69 682	68 208	67 940
Total Europe	FYWB	39 866	43 547	46 682	51 143	55 757	61 302	68 343	79 015	87 854	85 974	86 052
USA	FYWF	19 275	19 211	22 690	23 886	25 768	24 501	29 555	33 538	35 488	33 735	34 286
Income												
EMU members	KHS4	50 534	57 703	50 070	49 159	49 765	63 405	84 781	112 965	115 423	69 777	48 153
EU members	GNF6	57 027	64 584	55 788	54 796	56 362	71 287	91 632	120 550	127 020	78 476	53 671
Total Europe	LERD	69 681	74 894	64 999	65 225	69 591	89 611	116 455	151 714	154 418	91 576	69 750
USA	BFVE	29 284	31 117	26 524	27 662	30 743	44 855	59 034	71 715	49 446	33 815	37 348
Current transfers												
EMU members	K9GG	1 648	1 735	1 914	1 599	1 994	2 091	2 373	1 800	1 982	2 003	2 060
EU members	GC84	7 092	9 138	8 006	8 442	9 561	10 376	10 877	9 500	10 875	11 678	9 185
Total Europe	GXWP	7 299	9 370	8 273	8 714	9 843	10 682	11 331	9 775	11 201	11 987	9 543
USA	GXWT	1 182	2 395	1 693	1 217	1 549	4 186	3 354	2 129	2 740	2 718	2 315
TOTAL CREDITS												
EMU members	KHS7	184 444	196 276	190 082	188 591	193 372	219 178	271 380	283 758	305 751	242 797	234 564
EU members	G970	210 275	224 945	216 789	216 200	223 672	252 966	309 820	320 224	349 411	283 062	273 004
Total Europe	LERA	237 704	250 537	242 742	245 137	256 105	295 401	360 776	381 179	411 599	327 480	324 576
USA	BFVB	79 112	82 126	79 049	81 584	86 585	104 378	123 887	139 426	122 951	104 219	111 874
Debits												
Imports of goods												
EMU members	QBRM	106 518	115 142	124 246	123 669	127 443	140 360	160 095	150 177	158 698	140 888	159 314
EU members	LGDB	117 577	126 922	136 910	137 329	142 535	158 277	183 874	170 114	181 797	162 676	186 048
Total Europe	EPMM	132 532	141 750	152 155	153 594	162 422	184 211	214 302	201 140	222 185	194 607	226 337
USA	J8VA	28 465	29 855	25 234	23 000	22 121	22 049	25 416	25 608	25 540	24 222	26 992
Imports of services												
EMU members	K9OH	33 276	35 519	37 339	40 142	42 330	46 334	47 836	50 039	53 387	49 883	50 801
EU members	GCV2	35 364	37 702	39 732	43 039	45 609	50 437	52 640	55 064	58 808	55 780	56 802
Total Europe	GGPQ	39 484	41 873	44 961	47 903	50 727	56 724	59 533	62 947	67 153	64 348	65 489
USA	GGPU	13 208	13 509	13 409	14 871	15 311	16 301	16 779	18 069	20 037	19 223	19 200
Income												
EMU members	KHS5	43 484	41 314	31 206	39 205	46 819	63 682	86 205	108 016	86 166	59 972	58 626
EU members	G97L	50 230	47 819	37 047	44 610	52 211	70 419	92 486	115 806	93 927	64 875	63 378
Total Europe	LERE	70 406	66 867	51 612	57 810	67 575	93 464	123 996	156 080	116 480	79 024	79 344
USA	BFVF	27 660	31 683	29 836	30 618	32 109	39 748	59 176	68 444	52 861	36 128	42 475
Current transfers												
EMU members	K9MG	1 736	1 680	1 921	1 777	2 130	2 326	2 465	2 094	2 496	2 611	2 914
EU members	GCR2	12 637	11 405	12 223	13 419	13 825	15 629	15 742	15 332	16 048	17 625	19 155
Total Europe	GXYU	13 148	11 908	12 713	13 909	14 376	16 234	16 463	15 907	16 683	18 320	19 929
USA	GXYY	1 421	2 553	1 891	1 449	1 845	4 471	3 604	2 442	3 181	3 048	2 813
TOTAL DEBITS												
EMU members	KHS8	185 014	193 655	194 712	204 793	218 722	252 702	296 601	310 326	300 747	253 354	271 655
EU members	G97F	215 808	223 848	225 912	238 397	254 180	294 762	344 742	356 316	350 580	300 956	325 383
Total Europe	LERB	255 570	262 398	261 441	273 216	295 100	350 633	414 294	436 074	422 501	356 299	391 099
USA	BFVC	70 754	77 600	70 370	69 938	71 386	82 569	104 975	114 563	101 619	82 621	91 480
Balances												
Trade in goods												
EMU members	QBRX	−4 132	−10 658	−20 044	−22 704	−26 499	−30 513	−23 483	−35 521	−31 709	−29 135	−33 562
EU members	LGCF	−5 141	−12 549	−22 221	−26 077	−30 857	−36 829	−31 362	−42 430	−39 963	−37 976	−43 840
Total Europe	EPNM	−11 674	−19 024	−29 367	−33 539	−41 508	−50 405	−49 655	−60 465	−64 059	−56 664	−67 106
USA	J8VB	906	−452	2 908	5 819	6 404	8 787	6 528	6 436	9 737	9 729	10 933
Trade in services												
EMU members	K9TG	−3 400	−3 165	−3 443	−3 274	−1 661	−2 499	−222	4 298	7 970	9 381	7 798
EU members	GD6R	−1 644	−852	−1 426	−1 329	462	−582	2 159	7 426	10 874	12 428	11 138
Total Europe	GGRV	382	1 674	1 721	3 240	5 030	4 578	8 810	16 068	20 701	21 626	20 563
USA	GGRZ	6 067	5 702	9 281	9 015	10 457	8 200	12 776	15 469	15 451	14 512	15 086
Income												
EMU members	KHS6	7 050	16 389	18 864	9 954	2 946	−277	−1 424	4 949	29 257	9 805	−10 473
EU members	G97D	6 797	16 765	18 741	10 186	4 151	868	−854	4 744	33 093	13 601	−9 707
Total Europe	LERF	−725	8 027	13 387	7 415	2 016	−3 853	−7 541	−4 366	37 938	12 552	−9 594
USA	BFVG	1 624	−566	−3 312	−2 956	−1 366	5 107	−142	3 271	−3 415	−2 313	−5 127
Current transfers												
EMU members	K9SZ	−88	55	−7	−178	−136	−235	−92	−294	−514	−608	−854
EU members	GD6K	−5 545	−2 267	−4 217	−4 977	−4 264	−5 253	−4 865	−5 832	−5 173	−5 947	−9 970
Total Europe	GZCO	−5 849	−2 538	−4 440	−5 195	−4 533	−5 552	−5 132	−6 132	−5 482	−6 333	−10 386
USA	GZCS	−239	−158	−198	−232	−296	−285	−250	−313	−441	−330	−498
CURRENT BALANCE												
EMU members	KHS9	−570	2 621	−4 630	−16 202	−25 350	−33 524	−25 221	−26 568	5 004	−10 557	−37 091
EU members	G977	−5 533	1 097	−9 123	−22 197	−30 508	−41 796	−34 922	−36 092	−1 169	−17 894	−52 379
Total Europe	LERC	−17 866	−11 861	−18 699	−28 079	−38 995	−55 232	−53 518	−54 895	−10 902	−28 819	−66 523
USA	BFVD	8 358	4 526	8 679	11 646	15 199	21 809	18 912	24 863	21 332	21 598	20 394

1 EMU Members: Austria, Belgium, Cyprus, Estonia, Finland, France, Germany, Greece, Irish Republic, Italy, Luxembourg, Malta, Netherlands, Portugal, Slovakia, Slovenia and Spain.

2 EU and Europe include transactions with European Union institutions.

9.9 UK official transactions with institutions of the EU

£ million

		2000	2001	2002	2003	2004	2005	2006	2007	2008	2009	2010
Credits												
Exports of services												
UK charge for collecting duties and levies(net)[1]	QWUE	217	525	487	489	543	565	583	603	660	661	733
Current transfers												
Other sectors												
Agricultural Guarantee Fund[2]	EBGL	2 571	2 336	2 381	2 691	3 315	3 408	3 221	2 952	3 051	3 411	3 032
European Social Fund	HDIZ	659	370	412	427	433	900	1 305	795	608	609	777
European Coal & Steel Community Grant	FJKP	–	1	–	–	2	–	–	–	–	–	–
Central government												
Fontainebleau abatement	FKKL	2 084	4 560	3 099	3 560	3 592	3 655	3 570	3 523	4 862	5 392	3 046
Other EU receipts	GCSD	–	8	13	10	12	13	24	117	30	26	15
Capital transfers												
Other sectors												
Agricultural Fund for Regional Development[3]	FJXL	82	26	–	2	49	80	50	150	417	215	431
European Regional Development Fund	HBZA	989	543	296	622	1 062	1 402	618	707	972	640	609
Other capital transfers from EU Institutions[2]	EBGO	–	322	–	–	–	–	–	–	–	–	–
Total credits	GCSL	**6 602**	**8 691**	**6 688**	**7 801**	**9 008**	**10 023**	**9 371**	**8 847**	**10 600**	**10 954**	**8 643**
Debits												
Current transfers												
Other sectors												
Customs duties and agricultural levies[4]	FJWD	2 086	2 069	1 919	1 937	2 145	2 237	2 329	2 412	2 636	2 645	2 933
Sugar levies[4]	GTBA	44	31	25	18	25	24	–	–	–	–	–
European Coal & Steel Community production levy[4]	GTBB	–	–	–	–	–	–	–	–	–	–	–
VAT based contribution[5]	HCML	4 104	3 624	2 720	2 775	1 764	1 980	2 165	2 293	2 255	1 733	2 172
VAT adjustment[5]	FSVL	100	–49	88	–35	25	19	2	26	15	–140	81
Central government												
GNP fourth resource[6]	HCSO	4 243	3 859	5 259	6 622	7 565	8 597	8 358	7 996	8 628	10 692	10 718
GNP adjustments[6]	HCSM	136	–1	76	150	–16	135	163	327	–205	–137	101
Total GNP based fourth own resource contribution	NMFH	4 379	3 858	5 335	6 772	7 549	8 732	8 521	8 323	8 423	10 555	10 819
Inter-government agreements	HCBW	–	–	–	–	–	–	–	–	–	–	–
EU non-budget (miscellaneous)	HRTM	–	–	–	–	–	–	–	–	–	–	–
Other current transfers to EU institutions	GVEG	6	24	10	18	–3	106	8	6	5	–14	–18
Total debits	GCSM	**10 719**	**9 557**	**10 097**	**11 485**	**11 505**	**13 098**	**13 025**	**13 060**	**13 334**	**14 779**	**15 987**
Balance (UK net contribution to the EU)	BLZS	**–4 117**	**–866**	**–3 409**	**–3 684**	**–2 497**	**–3 075**	**–3 654**	**–4 213**	**–2 734**	**–3 825**	**–7 344**

1 Before 1989 this is netted off the VAT contribution but cannot be identified separately.
2 Other capital transfers from EU institutions are included indistiguishably with Agricultural Guarantee Fund receipts before 1996.
3 Up to 2006 this series includes the European Agricultural Guidance Fund.
4 EU traditional own resource.
5 Third own resource contribution.
6 Fourth own resource contribution.

9.10 Trade in services

By type of service 2009

£ million

	Transport-ation	Travel	Commun-ications	Cons-truction	Insu-rance	Finan-cial	Computer and infor-mation	Royal-ties and license fees	Other busi-ness services	Personal, cultural and recrea-tional	Govern-ment	Total services
Exports												
European Union (EU27) total	**8 206**	**9 010**	**2 632**	**406**	**725**	**19 167**	**3 850**	**3 252**	**19 031**	**1 050**	**879**	**68 208**
Belgium	366	244	69	..	24	983	170	59	1 310	19	..	3 280
Luxembourg	7	19	48	–	10	1 451	58	8	761	1	–	2 363
Denmark	1 126	286	44	6	32	394	99	133	744	16	7	2 887
France	927	1 094	298	35	139	3 271	438	346	2 120	60	23	8 751
Germany	872	1 107	515	31	114	3 867	959	376	3 420	183	32	11 476
Ireland	712	983	266	265	74	1 603	967	965	2 523	62	12	8 432
Italy	605	1 420	340	22	118	1 059	155	246	807	206	18	4 996
Netherlands	925	671	343	10	69	2 960	339	240	3 473	184	12	9 226
Russia	127	164	42	13	22	919	49	43	421	21	10	1 831
Spain	1 614	945	304	8	40	1 508	181	220	749	97	15	5 681
Switzerland	338	360	93	9	67	1 921	1 195	756	3 085	68	3	7 895
Turkey	164	151	30	10	17	241	36	33	224	9	9	924
Argentina	14	50	20	..	11	12	4	7	22	..	..	146
Brazil	110	200	46	12	22	101	29	15	152	1	6	694
Canada	337	404	45	12	259	691	64	46	816	9	17	2 700
Chile	42	6	7	11	14	12	..	..	93	..	..	193
Mexico	66	66	11	..	36	92	12	29	66	..	..	384
United States of America	3 121	2 157	790	..	3 303	9 626	2 059	1 751	9 763	703	..	33 735
China	737	600	48	13	17	204	34	43	436	85	13	2 230
Hong Kong	280	265	44	2	29	694	28	41	300	27	3	1 713
India	417	416	60	6	21	232	70	44	349	12	84	1 711
Iran	20	61	18	12	3	13	4	..	63	–	..	213
Japan	525	376	46	2	108	2 138	83	308	975	72	4	4 637
Malaysia	41	191	19	3	17	88	32	35	230	15	3	674
Philippines	34	39	..	..	12	12	11	..	56	..	..	177
Saudi Arabia	176	320	56	14	18	303	26	12	..	7	..	2 410
Singapore	592	123	39	5	28	501	48	..	780	144	..	4 004
South Korea	260	91	14	1	12	222	18	51	245	1	6	921
Taiwan	110	123	6	2	12	211	..	24	67	..	20	661
Thailand	74	141	17	..	9	81	11	11	114	..	6	497
Australia	1 321	819	76	79	157	706	110	93	748	57	13	4 179
South Africa	272	234	66	3	48	207	110	127	368	52	13	1 500
Other	3 455	5 227	..	..	779	10 185	..	..	..	..	..	36 341
Global total	**19 787**	**19 353**	**5 111**	**1 561**	**5 641**	**46 508**	**8 488**	**8 829**	**47 399**	**2 601**	**2 184**	**167 462**
Imports												
European Union (EU27) total	**10 793**	**18 656**	**2 039**	**518**	**519**	**3 857**	**1 962**	**1 210**	**13 122**	**510**	**2 594**	**55 780**
Belgium	396	364	66	8	42	452	57	161	829	6	25	2 406
Luxembourg	45	16	98	..	..	142	25	61	148	..	..	541
Denmark	578	137	28	127	..	82	27	68	283	76	..	1 429
France	1 470	3 823	240	33	99	579	244	153	2 477	56	110	9 284
Germany	930	753	691	120	111	819	518	212	2 711	86	1 983	8 934
Ireland	597	1 007	216	117	38	535	402	122	1 129	65	27	4 255
Italy	1 254	1 457	221	46	33	274	68	29	968	60	49	4 459
Netherlands	642	579	152	19	61	404	172	282	1 861	25	27	4 224
Russia	158	118	28	..	12	290	10	2	631	..	11	1 286
Spain	2 317	5 668	125	10	26	232	58	25	795	21	159	9 436
Switzerland	422	527	42	11	16	382	..	318	833	33	..	2 943
Turkey	347	816	22	14	12	19	–	4	70	..	..	1 320
Argentina	15	48	..	..	..	2	..	2	22	..	3	100
Brazil	59	89	7	8	7	..	5	6	82	..	12	323
Canada	190	380	63	12	14	120	50	88	296	5	61	1 279
Chile	42	15	..	..	..	–	..	..	9	..	..	73
Mexico	45	170	5	–	2	9	..	6	18	..	4	265
United States of America	1 524	3 128	439	102	109	3 461	912	2 810	5 635	286	817	19 223
China	359	248	44	12	65	33	24	4	375	..	..	1 177
Hong Kong	146	130	36	–	20	307	10	2	316	3	4	974
India	291	672	83	1	12	49	433	3	351	41	6	1 942
Iran	14	35	..	..	..	..	..	..	16	..	..	74
Japan	300	129	31	..	18	883	24	676	1 203	25	..	3 306
Malaysia	47	111	13	..	..	11	19	4	40	..	..	252
Philippines	36	94	..	..	..	..	11	..	26	..	..	181
Saudi Arabia	34	95	11	..	..	13	2	..	..	..	3	295
Singapore	134	144	22	..	9	205	..	12	922	12	..	1 547
South Korea	51	29	8	..	8	76	10	..	176	..	..	364
Taiwan	46	16	6	..	6	..	..	1	107	..	2	270
Thailand	84	472	13	–	..	12	7	..	31	..	..	630
Australia	336	721	57	..	8	109	50	63	315	11	..	1 739
South Africa	141	400	31	..	14	37	18	..	204	25	..	883
Other	4 979	9 797	..	..	..	..	..	..	..	..	..	24 833
Global total	**18 029**	**32 188**	**4 402**	**1 346**	**1 007**	**10 958**	**4 002**	**5 374**	**27 742**	**1 133**	**4 066**	**110 247**

Symbols used in this table:
.. Indicates that data might be disclosive and have therefore been omitted
- Indicates that the data is nil or less than £500,000

9.11 Trade in services

By type of service 2010

£ million

	Transportation	Travel	Communications	Construction	Insurance	Financial	Computer and information	Royalties and license fees	Other business services	Personal, cultural and recreational	Government	Total services
Exports												
European Union (EU27) total	**8 118**	**9 645**	**2 384**	**331**	**750**	**17 010**	**4 068**	**3 396**	**19 575**	**1 745**	**918**	**67 940**
Belgium	334	410	57	18	23	708	122	59	1 123	21	13	2 888
Luxembourg	6	24	93	..	17	1 464	41	..	472	15	..	2 144
Denmark	1 060	260	38	2	31	340	111	208	833	23	4	2 910
France	1 029	1 195	299	18	131	2 801	442	264	2 524	191	19	8 913
Germany	947	1 252	394	25	111	3 080	1 097	402	3 088	372	32	10 800
Ireland	805	913	287	232	49	1 651	950	891	2 498	105	8	8 389
Italy	601	1 675	239	6	121	798	200	260	916	323	12	5 151
Netherlands	803	856	419	7	78	3 286	355	272	3 795	191	7	10 069
Russia	99	239	37	8	25	686	42	56	385	78	10	1 665
Spain	1 509	853	209	8	54	1 038	233	253	808	165	9	5 139
Switzerland	344	375	694	4	75	1 793	1 067	591	3 980	55	3	8 981
Turkey	177	197	35	5	23	250	40	43	329	19	8	1 126
Argentina	29	59	14	..	7	41	3	19	..	5	4	233
Brazil	116	174	48	4	40	139	67	18	221	..	..	836
Canada	379	562	126	17	382	638	91	40	647	9	14	2 905
Chile	63	16	10	9	20	8	..	..	46	..	..	181
Mexico	73	50	12	–	51	114	15	32	66	..	..	421
United States of America	3 584	2 354	658	39	2 497	9 115	2 020	1 755	11 029	936	299	34 286
China	729	813	51	7	27	218	68	47	609	69	14	2 652
Hong Kong	253	240	42	..	30	598	48	28	345	..	..	1 606
India	436	582	42	3	27	216	67	26	569	10	82	2 060
Iran	13	42	9	–	2	12	4	5	25	..	..	128
Japan	495	213	..	..	109	1 811	96	280	1 166	101	..	4 315
Malaysia	39	185	15	4	24	95	24	23	231	..	..	701
Philippines	34	16	5	–	5	10	8	4	42	–	1	125
Saudi Arabia	118	290	43	51	19	282	38	22	..	35	..	2 925
Singapore	497	194	28	4	43	449	62	..	785	96	..	3 661
South Korea	281	116	13	..	26	208	30	42	396	..	..	1 123
Taiwan	130	112	6	..	7	556	83	29	200	..	..	1 145
Thailand	58	154	18	–	11	75	16	6	100	..	..	459
Australia	1 732	982	75	120	295	719	80	89	810	111	12	5 025
South Africa	285	219	60	2	63	243	151	157	431	98	14	1 723
Other	3 271	5 347	..	..	842	8 720	..	..	..	..	..	36 397
Global total	**20 329**	**20 969**	**5 340**	**1 218**	**5 265**	**42 162**	**8 742**	**8 678**	**52 162**	**4 012**	**2 205**	**171 082**
Imports												
European Union (EU27) total	**10 764**	**18 035**	**2 504**	**551**	**625**	**3 807**	**1 915**	**1 232**	**13 798**	**870**	**2 701**	**56 802**
Belgium	413	330	65	13	49	413	66	109	844	6	11	2 319
Luxembourg	21	29	770	..	..	248	..	24	198	..	1	1 411
Denmark	604	99	26	17	15	87	35	77	294	31	9	1 294
France	1 424	3 789	186	61	95	574	221	145	2 834	126	181	9 636
Germany	905	797	640	212	139	867	485	228	2 916	99	1 839	9 127
Ireland	578	862	199	87	58	448	488	198	1 145	47	40	4 150
Italy	1 167	1 345	192	59	42	153	43	18	999	268	64	4 350
Netherlands	636	587	151	23	79	528	143	278	1 352	87	34	3 898
Russia	154	86	24	..	17	89	13	3	493	10	..	903
Spain	2 334	5 425	91	13	31	232	75	27	930	68	256	9 482
Switzerland	381	546	184	..	25	453	220	326	1 034	33	..	3 215
Turkey	438	1 016	9	8	16	36	..	4	79	5	..	1 623
Argentina	18	49	4	..	..	2	..	..	24	5	2	111
Brazil	63	131	8	–	11	..	5	3	107	21	..	447
Canada	199	412	140	17	41	133	32	80	361	6	56	1 477
Chile	9	14	..	..	..	..	..	..	18	..	..	50
Mexico	72	254	5	–	..	14	..	1	29	2	3	398
United States of America	1 664	3 455	409	72	322	3 356	844	2 416	5 471	318	873	19 200
China	362	281	44	14	78	41	33	1	315	4	7	1 180
Hong Kong	134	170	..	..	26	358	13	1	301	5	2	1 056
India	405	702	56	9	17	65	539	3	481	7	8	2 292
Iran	14	44	..	–	..	–	..	..	..	..	1	66
Japan	295	114	34	..	33	775	16	987	1 339	19	..	3 627
Malaysia	42	115	13	..	7	14	9	1	57	..	..	260
Philippines	49	93	..	..	..	..	16	1	50	..	..	217
Saudi Arabia	39	84	10	..	..	16	..	..	53	..	2	249
Singapore	127	115	18	–	13	198	28	..	1 237	10	..	1 803
South Korea	49	23	6	..	10	88	12	..	156	..	..	351
Taiwan	37	27	..	–	8	72	..	..	91	..	1	247
Thailand	92	458	13	–	8	..	5	1	23	..	1	624
Australia	476	800	57	..	24	131	108	63	420	19	..	2 194
South Africa	149	419	48	1	20	55	27	8	358	13	3	1 101
Other	5 360	9 689	..	..	..	..	..	..	..	..	..	23 946
Global total	**18 710**	**32 360**	**4 396**	**1 229**	**1 561**	**10 667**	**3 968**	**5 281**	**28 472**	**1 511**	**4 149**	**112 304**

Symbols used in this table:
.. Indicates that data might be disclosive and have therefore been omitted
- Indicates that the data is nil or less than £500,000

9.12 Trade in goods and services

Top fifty UK trading partners

Exports						Imports					
Goods (£266 bn in 2010)			Services (£171bn in 2010)			Goods (£364bn in 2010)			Services (£112bn in 2010)		
	10	09		10	09		10	09		10	09
USA[1]	1	1	USA[1]	1	1	Germany	1	1	USA[1]	1	1
Germany	2	2	Germany	2	2	China	2	3	France	2	3
Netherlands	3	3	Netherlands	3	3	USA[1]	3	2	Spain	3	2
France	4	4	Switzerland	4	6	Netherlands	4	4	Germany	4	4
Irish Republic	5	5	France	5	4	France	5	5	Italy	5	5
Belgium-Lux	6	6	Ireland	6	5	Norway	6	6	Ireland	6	6
Spain	7	7	Italy	7	8	Belgium-Lux	7	7	Netherlands	7	7
Italy	8	8	Spain	8	7	Italy	8	9	Japan	8	8
China	9	9	Australia	9	10	Irish Republic	9	8	Switzerland	9	9
Sweden	10	10	Japan	10	9	Spain	10	10	Belgium	10	10
Switzerland	11	11	Singapore	11	11	Hong Kong	11	11	India	11	12
Hong Kong	12	12	Saudi Arabia	12	18	Japan	12	12	Australia	12	14
Japan	13	14	Sweden	13	16	Switzerland	13	14	Greece	13	11
Canada	14	15	Denmark	14	14	Sweden	14	13	Singapore	14	15
India	15	18	Canada	15	15	Poland	15	15	Portugal	15	16
United Arab Emirates[2]	16	13	Belgium	16	13	India	16	18	Turkey	16	19
Poland	17	20	The Channel Islands	17	12	Canada	17	19	Sweden	17	13
Russia	18	22	China	18	20	Turkey	18	17	Canada	18	22
Singapore	19	16	Norway	19	17	Russia	19	16	Luxembourg	19	34
Australia	20	17	United Arab Emirates[2]	20	22	South Africa	20	21	Poland	20	23
Turkey	21	23	Luxembourg	21	19	Singapore	21	22	Denmark	21	18
Norway	22	19	India	22	25	Denmark	22	20	China	22	25
South Africa	23	25	South Africa	23	26	Czech Republic	23	23	United Arab Emirates[2]	23	20
Denmark	24	21	Russia	24	23	Hungary	24	25	South Africa	24	30
Saudi Arabia	25	24	Cayman Islands	25	21	Taiwan	25	29	Norway	25	24
South Korea	26	26	Hong Kong	26	24	Brazil	26	26	Bermuda	26	17
Brazil	27	27	Nigeria	27	27	Thailand	27	27	The Channel Islands	27	26
Portugal	28	29	Finland	28	28	Austria	28	28	Hong Kong	28	27
Czech Rep	29	30	Taiwan	29	40	South Korea	29	24	Austria	29	29
Finland	30	31	Poland	30	29	Qatar	30	43	Russia	30	21
Austria	31	33	Turkey	31	31	Australia	31	30	Cyprus	31	28
Nigeria	32	32	South Korea	32	32	Finland	32	31	Egypt	32	31
Israel	33	34	Greece	33	30	Malaysia	33	32	Thailand	33	32
Greece	34	28	Virgin Islands, British	34	35	Portugal	34	34	Hungary	34	35
Malaysia	35	35	Brazil	35	38	United Arab Emirates[2]	35	37	Finland	35	41
Egypt	36	36	Angola	36	48	Slovakia	36	33	Brazil	36	44
Thailand	37	37	Portugal	37	36	Israel	37	39	Pakistan	37	37
Taiwan	38	40	Malaysia	38	39	Libya	38	42	Czech Republic	38	39
Hungary	39	38	Bermuda	39	33	Indonesia	39	35	Israel	39	42
Qatar	40	39	Israel	40	43	Vietnam	40	36	Afghanistan	40	–
Mexico	41	41	Austria	41	37	Romania	41	41	Mexico	41	50
Romania	42	42	Cyprus	42	45	Bangladesh	42	38	New Zealand	42	45
Chile	43	45	Kazakhstan	43	34	Kuwait	43	46	South Korea	43	40
Angola	44	–	Egypt	44	41	Mexico	44	44	Bulgaria	44	49
Morocco	45	–	Qatar	45	49	Nigeria	45	50	Malta	45	43
Cyprus	46	43	Kuwait	46	–	New Zealand	46	40	Barbados	46	38
Kuwait	47	47	Hungary	47	44	Pakistan	47	47	Nigeria	47	33
Senegal	48	–	Thailand	48	47	Saudi Arabia	48	–	Malaysia	48	–
Ukraine	49	44	Czech Republic	49	50	Sri Lanka	49	45	Romania	49	–
Slovakia	50	–	New Zealand	50	–	Algeria	50	–	Saudi Arabia	50	45

1 USA includes Puerto Rico
2 United Arab Emirates includes Abu Dhabi, Dubai, Sharjah, Ajman, Umm al Qaiwain, Ras al Khaimah and Fujairah

THIS PAGE IS INTENTIONALLY BLANK

9.13 Trade in services

Trading partners ranked[1]

£ million

Exports

	2010	2009		2010	2009		2010	2009
USA	34 286	33 735	Kenya	200	178	Belize	17	18
Germany	10 800	11 476	Bangladesh	198	169	Cuba	17	20
Netherlands	10 069	9 226	Viet Nam	192	239	Guinea	17	22
Switzerland	8 981	7 895	Bahamas	186	164	Somalia	17	5
France	8 913	8 751	Chile	181	193	Armenia	16	6
Ireland	8 389	8 432	Iceland	168	147	Bosnia & Herzegovina	16	9
Italy	5 151	4 996	Bulgaria	164	204	Andorra	15	15
Spain	5 139	5 681	Oman	164	148	Macao	14	9
Australia	5 025	4 179	Isle of Man	156	202	Seychelles	14	33
Japan	4 315	4 637	Morocco	137	167	Macedonia	13	15
Singapore	3 661	4 004	Sri Lanka	135	83	Rwanda	13	7
Saudi Arabia	2 925	2 410	Algeria	133	147	Albania	12	13
Sweden	2 911	2 623	Iran	128	213	Mali	12	18
Denmark	2 910	2 887	Philippines	125	177	Mongolia	12	10
Canada	2 905	2 700	Lebanon	124	106	Uzbekistan	12	7
Belgium	2 888	3 280	Jordan	123	131	Cambodia	11	11
The Channel Islands	2 834	3 334	Trinidad &Tobago	116	147	Montenegro	11	14
China	2 652	2 230	Panama	115	67	Turkmenistan	11	7
Norway	2 383	2 424	Tunisia	115	165	Aruba	10	12
United Arab Emirates2	2 166	1 916	Cameroon	113	108	Belarus	10	4
Luxembourg	2 144	2 363	Peru	106	124	Democratic Republic Congo	9	11
India	2 060	1 711	Lithuania	96	93	Guatemala	9	8
South Africa	1 723	1 500	Slovenia	92	84	Maldives	9	11
Russia	1 665	1 831	Latvia	87	110	Micronesia,	9	4
Cayman Islands	1 643	1 950	Barbados	84	98	Moldova	9	10
Hong Kong	1 606	1 713	Zambia	84	47	Solomon Islands	9	6
Nigeria	1 280	1 323	Croatia	82	105	Togo	9	9
Finland	1 274	1 304	Mozambique	80	86	Benin	8	10
Taiwan	1 145	661	Estonia	79	43	Cape Verde	8	9
Poland	1 132	1 053	Sudan	78	58	Mauritania	8	10
Turkey	1 126	924	Papua New Guinea	75	83	Nicaragua	8	12
South Korea	1 123	921	Congo	72	62	North Korea	8	15
Greece	1 119	1 037	Equatorial Guinea	66	72	Saint Lucia	8	4
Virgin Islands, British	1 115	799	Senegal	65	55	America Samoa	7	2
Brazil	836	694	Netherlands Antilles	63	65	Guam	7	2
Angola	781	496	Uganda	62	74	Kyrgyzstan	7	18
Portugal	779	771	Liechtenstein	60	72	Turks & Caicos Islands	7	13
Malaysia	701	674	Brunei Darussalam	54	47	Tajikistan	7	5
Bermuda	695	913	Georgia	53	43	Vanuatu	7	1
Israel	682	585	Marshall Islands	53	17	Burundi	6	1
Austria	643	744	Tanzania	52	54	Gambia	6	9
Cyprus	602	551	Gabon	50	45	Myanmar	6	4
Kazakhstan	590	806	Syrian Arab Republic	50	65	Tonga	6	5
Egypt	560	657	Serbia	48	57	Antigua & Barbuda	5	4
Qatar	504	489	Botswana	47	52	Lesotho	5	8
Kuwait	485	626	Guyana	45	36	San Marino	5	1
Hungary	472	552	Ethiopia	39	45	Burkina Faso	4	7
Thailand	459	497	Cote d`Ivoire	36	76	Djibouti	4	1
Czech Republic	452	466	Ecuador	35	21	El Salvador	4	9
New Zealand	452	426	Dominican Republic	34	49	Haiti	4	4
Afghanistan	432	244	Malawi	34	30	Honduras	4	10
Mexico	421	384	Jamaica	33	44	Kiribati	4	3
Iraq	413	346	Yemen	29	40	Palau	4	1
Romania	359	283	Suriname	28	27	Swaziland	4	29
Venezuela	354	75	Zimbabwe	28	40	Comoros	3	1
Indonesia	325	325	Namibia	27	27	Eritrea	3	2
Pakistan	302	357	Fiji	26	9	Grenada	3	3
Slovakia	291	242	Nepal	25	16	St Vincent & the Grenadines	3	4
Gibraltar	273	516	Liberia	24	12	Virgin Islands,U.S.	3	3
Libyan Arab Jamahiriya	256	258	Falkland Islands (Malvinas)	23	15	Guinea-Bissau	2	1
Bahrain	246	302	Sierra Leone	23	48	Democratic Republic Lao	2	3
Azerbaijan	244	296	Chad	23	25	St Kitts & Nevis	2	4
Ukraine	244	177	Costa Rica	22	30	St Helena	2	8
Mauritius	240	159	Madagascar	22	22	Anguilla	1	1
Argentina	233	146	Bolivia	21	24	Bhutan	1	1
Malta	227	283	Niger	21	5	Holy see (Vatican City State)	1	1
Ghana	203	331	Uruguay	20	15			
Colombia	200	92	Paraguay	19	14			

1 Any country not included in this table is estimated having Trade in Services of less than £500,000

2 United Arab Emirates includes Abu Dhabi, Dubai, Sharjah, Ajman, Umm al Qaiwain, Ras al Khaimah and Fujairah

9.13 Trade in services

Trading partners ranked[1]

continued

£ million

Imports

	2010	2009
USA	19 200	19 223
France	9 636	9 284
Spain	9 482	9 436
Germany	9 127	8 934
Italy	4 350	4 459
Ireland	4 150	4 255
Netherlands	3 898	4 224
Japan	3 627	3 306
Switzerland	3 215	2 943
Belgium	2 319	2 406
India	2 292	1 942
Australia	2 194	1 739
Greece	1 951	2 112
Singapore	1 803	1 547
Portugal	1 633	1 515
Turkey	1 623	1 320
Sweden	1 614	1 758
Canada	1 477	1 279
Luxembourg	1 411	541
Poland	1 361	1 255
Denmark	1 294	1 429
China	1 180	1 177
United Arab Emirates2	1 150	1 303
South Africa	1 101	883
Norway	1 092	1 199
Bermuda	1 069	1 498
The Channel Islands	1 059	1 052
Hong Kong	1 056	974
Austria	987	908
Russia	903	1 286
Cyprus	881	934
Egypt	681	741
Thailand	624	630
Hungary	486	418
Finland	451	354
Brazil	447	323
Pakistan	443	389
Czech Republic	434	372
Israel	415	349
Afghanistan	399	238
Mexico	398	265
New Zealand	354	283
South Korea	351	364
Bulgaria	340	265
Malta	326	327
Barbados	311	373
Nigeria	293	596
Malaysia	260	252
Romania	258	236
Saudi Arabia	249	295
Morocco	248	254
Taiwan	247	270
Tunisia	233	178
Angola	230	265
Croatia	220	195
Philippines	217	181
Ukraine	217	152
Mauritius	213	165
Jamaica	193	395
Kuwait	193	135
Iraq	192	235
Cuba	172	157
Kenya	171	190
Gibraltar	144	89
Kazakhstan	139	236
Sri Lanka	133	103

	2010	2009
Libyan Arab Jamahiriya	129	110
Bangladesh	122	136
Slovakia	121	124
Indonesia	119	121
Maldives	119	138
Lithuania	118	101
Virgin Islands, British	115	165
Argentina	111	100
Viet Nam	97	78
Latvia	94	56
Bahrain	93	67
Ghana	90	95
Qatar	89	167
Azerbaijan	85	117
Algeria	70	69
Dominican Republic	69	120
Tanzania	69	63
Iran	66	74
Peru	64	67
Antigua & Barbuda	61	56
Lebanon	57	33
Iceland	56	130
Colombia	55	51
Chile	50	73
Venezuela	50	42
Zimbabwe	49	45
Slovenia	48	40
Oman	46	47
Jordan	44	46
Nepal	43	35
Seychelles	43	23
Zambia	42	56
Cayman Islands	41	36
Ecuador	38	30
Serbia	38	49
Saint Lucia	36	61
Isle of Man	34	18
Estonia	30	30
Guatemala	30	22
Syrian Arab Republic	30	20
Trinidad &Tobago	30	48
Uganda	28	53
Bahamas	27	61
Grenada	26	43
Costa Rica	25	37
Andorra	23	37
Papua New Guinea	22	42
Sierra Leone	22	35
Cameroon	20	21
Ethiopia	20	34
Liechtenstein	20	13
Sudan	20	28
Aruba	19	6
Yemen	19	19
Fiji	18	10
Botswana	16	17
Gambia	15	33
Turks & Caicos Islands	15	10
Togo	14	5
Congo	13	16
Georgia	12	9
Panama	12	16
Uzbekistan	12	5
Macedonia	11	4
Montenegro	11	14
Malawi	10	16

	2010	2009
Belarus	9	6
Gabon	9	3
Guyana	9	8
Myanmar	9	2
Brunei Darussalam	8	3
Democratic Republic Congo	8	8
Cote d`Ivoire	8	10
Democratic Republic Lao	8	5
Namibia	8	15
Uruguay	8	26
Eritrea	7	6
Marshall Islands	7	1
Mauritania	7	1
Senegal	7	11
Madagascar	6	11
Turkmenistan	6	2
Anguilla	5	1
Bosnia & Herzegovina	5	38
Mozambique	5	16
Swaziland	5	2
Albania	4	13
Benin	4	1
Bolivia	4	11
Burkina Faso	4	1
Falkland Islands	4	4
Honduras	4	1
Paraguay	4	2
Belize	3	12
Cape Verde	3	2
Mali	3	4
Moldova	3	10
North Korea	3	6
Armenia	2	3
America Samoa	2	–
Cambodia	2	6
Djibouti	2	5
Guam	2	
Kyrgyzstan	2	1
Liberia	2	3
Netherlands Antilles	2	4
Rwanda	2	5
Antartica	1	–
Dominica	1	2
Equatorial Guinea	1	1
Guinea	1	3
Macao	1	1
Mongolia	1	1
Niger	1	1
Solomon Islands	1	2
Somalia	1	4
St Vincent & the Grenadines	1	1

1 Any country not included in this table is estimated having Trade in Services of less than £500,000

2 United Arab Emirates includes Abu Dhabi, Dubai, Sharjah, Ajman, Umm al Qaiwain, Ras al Khaimah and Fujairah

9.14 World total and G7 countries trade in services[1]

	US$ million										%	
											The UK as a percentage of:	
	World	US	Canada	Japan	France	Germany	Italy	Russia	UK[2]	G8 total	*World*	*G8*
Exports												
2000	1 508 491	283 778	40 230	69 238	82 703	83 150	56 556	9 565	124 159	749 379	*8.2*	*16.6*
2001	1 513 727	271 488	38 804	64 516	82 227	88 714	57 676	11 441	126 393	741 259	*8.3*	*17.1*
2002	1 632 231	277 692	40 481	65 712	88 734	103 144	60 439	13 611	141 261	791 074	*8.7*	*17.9*
2003	1 881 426	288 348	44 242	77 621	101 585	123 873	71 767	16 229	166 674	890 339	*8.9*	*18.7*
2004	2 274 137	335 211	50 286	97 611	114 629	147 498	84 524	20 595	206 697	1 057 051	*9.1*	*19.6*
2005	2 538 158	368 343	55 829	110 210	122 221	166 593	89 216	24 970	217 580	1 154 962	*8.6*	*18.8*
2006	2 874 551	413 168	60 353	117 298	128 943	194 788	98 984	31 102	249 763	1 294 399	*8.7*	*19.3*
2007	3 453 213	484 210	65 338	129 117	149 595	229 156	112 213	39 257	307 647	1 516 533	*8.9*	*20.3*
2008	3 883 444	530 102	68 011	148 755	167 639	261 374	120 183	51 132	316 619	1 663 815	*8.2*	*19.0*
2009	3 423 629	497 869	59 077	128 338	143 474	231 262	102 637	41 524	262 095	1 466 276	*7.7*	*17.9*
Imports												
2000	1 527 751	218 252	44 118	116 864	65 509	137 256	55 601	16 230	101 396	755 226	*6.6*	*13.4*
2001	1 544 343	216 264	43 843	108 249	67 053	141 916	57 753	20 572	101 614	757 264	*6.6*	*13.4*
2002	1 642 178	225 644	45 069	107 940	73 211	145 154	63 166	23 497	111 760	795 441	*6.8*	*14.1*
2003	1 873 877	243 478	52 454	111 528	87 565	173 059	74 332	27 122	130 359	899 897	*7.0*	*14.5*
2004	2 222 657	281 592	58 776	135 514	99 687	196 756	83 246	33 287	154 859	1 043 717	*7.0*	*14.8*
2005	2 464 172	301 649	65 749	134 256	106 962	211 563	90 081	38 745	170 122	1 119 127	*6.9*	*15.2*
2006	2 749 115	335 749	72 760	135 556	113 410	226 253	100 511	44 716	183 717	1 212 672	*6.7*	*15.1*
2007	3 248 241	366 164	82 788	150 367	129 872	261 298	121 874	58 145	211 648	1 382 156	*6.5*	*15.3*
2008	3 706 398	397 226	89 139	169 544	142 013	291 342	130 539	75 468	214 610	1 509 881	*5.8*	*14.2*
2009	3 305 784	369 200	78 727	148 718	127 416	254 881	116 663	61 287	172 548	1 329 440	*5.2*	*13.0*
Balances												
2000		65 526	–3 888	–47 626	17 194	–54 106	955	–6 665	22 763	–5 847		
2001		55 224	–5 039	–43 733	15 174	–53 202	–77	–9 131	24 779	–16 005		
2002		52 048	–4 588	–42 228	15 523	–42 010	–2 727	–9 886	29 501	–4 367		
2003		44 870	–8 212	–33 907	14 020	–49 186	–2 565	–10 893	36 315	–9 558		
2004		53 619	–8 490	–37 903	14 942	–49 258	1 278	–12 692	51 838	13 334		
2005		66 694	–9 920	–24 046	15 259	–44 970	–865	–13 775	47 458	35 835		
2006		77 419	–12 407	–18 258	15 533	–31 465	–1 527	–13 614	66 046	81 727		
2007		118 046	–17 450	–21 250	19 723	–32 142	–9 661	–18 888	95 999	134 377		
2008		132 876	–21 128	–20 789	25 626	–29 968	–10 356	–24 336	102 009	153 934		
2009		128 669	–19 650	–20 380	16 058	–23 619	–14 026	–19 763	89 547	136 836		

1 G8 country data is not yet available for 2010
2 The analysis of UK data is based on the all accounts totals shown in table 3.1

Sources: G8 and world data provided by IMF; UK data provided by ONS

Chapter 10

Geographical breakdown of the UK international investment position

10.1 International Investment Position: by type of investment
Balance sheets valued at end of year
2009

£ billion

	Assets					Liabilities				
	Type of Investment					Type of Investment				
	Direct	Portfolio	Other	Derivatives [1]	Total	Direct	Portfolio	Other	Derivatives [1]	Total
Belgium	10.5	16.4	84.6	43.9	155.4	5.1	22.5	96.2	36.5	160.4
France	41.0	119.6	317.5	246.9	725.1	73.8	174.7	215.5	230.5	694.5
Germany	29.4	154.8	290.9	323.1	798.1	68.8	147.3	411.2	310.5	937.8
Ireland	29.1	117.3	224.0	64.9	435.4	12.1	249.0	191.1	58.0	510.2
Italy	11.7	80.3	110.5	45.2	247.7	7.3	51.4	59.4	31.3	149.3
Luxembourg	126.1	55.2	67.2	17.2	265.7	30.7	156.3	68.9	22.0	278.0
Netherlands	154.8	101.6	230.4	106.9	593.7	110.6	94.0	275.3	97.5	577.4
Spain	32.9	55.0	185.3	32.8	306.0	28.0	37.6	73.1	28.6	167.2
Total EU27	**482.4**	**777.4**	**1 671.4**	**968.0**	**3 899.2**	**352.0**	**1 145.2**	**1 546.9**	**900.4**	**3 944.5**
Norway	5.3	12.4	20.4	5.4	43.5	1.7	57.6	18.7	6.3	84.4
Switzerland	20.4	37.3	130.9	73.1	261.8	27.1	44.1	182.7	66.3	320.2
Total EFTA	**26.2**	**54.9**	**161.0**	**78.7**	**320.8**	**29.9**	**102.3**	**205.5**	**72.8**	**410.6**
Russia	10.1	6.7	18.7	1.8	37.2	0.8	1.1	15.6	1.1	18.6
Total Europe	**553.1**	**879.4**	**1 991.2**	**1 065.0**	**4 488.6**	**406.2**	**1 329.9**	**2 151.9**	**990.3**	**4 878.3**
Brazil	5.0	22.2	4.9	3.3	35.4	–	–	3.4	3.1	6.5
Canada	29.5	25.0	64.8	30.2	149.5	18.4	30.8	43.8	27.6	120.5
USA	252.3	498.4	792.0	870.2	2 412.9	158.7	672.9	836.3	887.2	2 555.1
Total Americas	**347.1**	**634.1**	**1 090.6**	**949.5**	**3 021.3**	**193.4**	**725.4**	**1 102.6**	**960.7**	**2 982.1**
China	4.5	15.0	9.5	1.9	30.9	0.6	–	9.6	0.7	10.9
Hong Kong	29.4	19.7	23.0	10.9	82.9	6.9	60.9	64.0	9.8	141.6
India	9.3	10.4	13.8	2.0	35.5	1.8	0.1	9.0	1.6	12.5
Japan	3.0	88.0	156.7	76.0	323.8	21.3	131.2	128.2	67.7	348.3
Singapore	5.2	8.8	46.7	12.7	73.4	3.0	35.3	65.4	12.2	115.8
Total Asia	**84.8**	**201.6**	**346.0**	**118.9**	**751.3**	**38.9**	**243.3**	**429.2**	**104.3**	**815.7**
Australia	16.1	55.8	45.2	28.2	145.4	12.3	25.0	36.4	24.6	98.3
Total Australasia and Oceania	**19.2**	**58.6**	**49.0**	**30.6**	**157.4**	**12.5**	**26.3**	**38.2**	**26.6**	**103.6**
South Africa	14.3	6.8	8.9	6.3	36.3	0.5	34.6	13.2	5.5	53.8
Total Africa	**29.4**	**5.3**	**26.7**	**7.6**	**69.0**	**1.1**	**35.4**	**63.8**	**6.8**	**107.2**
International Organisations	–	13.2	13.5	4.9	31.6	–	45.2	6.3	8.2	59.6
World Total	**1 033.6**	**1 875.3**	**3 517.1**	**2 176.4**	**8 642.5**	**652.3**	**2 405.5**	**3 792.0**	**2 096.8**	**8 946.6**

1 Derivatives geographical data is only available from 2006.

10.2 Geographical breakdown of International Investment Position: UK assets

Balance sheets valued at end of year

£ million

		2001	2002	2003	2004	2005	2006	2007	2008	2009
Europe										
European Union (EU)										
Austria	HCZI	15 013	13 839	17 825	27 802	28 034	29 438	31 653	49 021	33 872
Belgium	A54T	57 216	59 068	72 219	103 614	140 890	128 563	165 322	215 231	155 447
Bulgaria	HCZU	1 102	364	436	612	940	1 203	1 018	2 117	1 745
Cyprus	A3OB	2 209	1 648	1 678	2 028	4 192	5 463	7 817	8 458	8 465
Czech Republic	HDFF	2 642	2 050	2 200	2 970	4 054	4 106	5 117	6 795	5 419
Denmark	HDRV	18 996	19 550	24 521	40 959	55 160	50 964	61 103	82 776	55 026
Estonia	HDSA	265	196	238	384	123	93	63	93	57
Finland	HDSJ	19 475	16 755	15 625	22 674	27 878	27 323	35 538	57 598	48 124
France	HDSL	224 478	213 594	233 014	346 282	419 895	526 953	746 104	985 181	725 094
Germany	HDQJ	276 726	267 203	297 359	442 383	476 344	499 203	610 933	1 072 699	798 092
Greece	HDSM	17 860	19 957	22 241	26 695	24 919	32 765	39 067	43 860	33 542
Hungary	HDXA	4 193	4 759	4 582	6 949	6 531	7 776	8 491	10 500	8 083
Ireland	HDZG	93 637	91 255	120 039	158 462	257 983	293 965	374 774	568 169	435 385
Italy	HEGT	132 842	127 829	148 566	165 626	178 206	175 328	202 615	250 038	247 680
Latvia	HFHZ	102	120	70	127	187	391	1 086	1 074	616
Lithuania	HFHY	156	166	117	152	957	65	146	–58	277
Luxembourg	A5BW	111 247	105 816	147 451	177 177	204 835	155 298	221 111	357 448	265 701
Malta	A3OC	589	719	956	2 511	583	2 696	5 151	6 995	3 360
Netherlands	HFID	299 006	307 486	324 626	386 697	388 252	416 711	577 820	689 905	593 701
Poland	HFII	5 336	6 224	7 279	8 356	8 958	8 712	10 643	18 001	15 196
Portugal	HFIJ	19 872	20 653	25 843	23 875	28 319	27 278	29 202	34 079	39 443
Romania	HFIX	558	714	1 032	1 580	2 149	1 851	3 271	6 368	4 799
Slovak Republic	HFJI	436	592	817	483	769	669	1 155	2 408	1 511
Slovenia	HFJH	496	309	426	717	992	893	1 039	1 529	535
Spain	HDSC	59 757	55 974	85 285	124 321	196 040	206 370	234 167	341 563	306 021
Sweden	HFJA	50 748	38 078	45 071	58 415	76 629	79 303	85 188	99 811	83 425
European Central Bank	HBKQ	–	–	–	–	–	–	–	–	–
EU Institutions	HBKP	17 654	20 983	21 845	24 507	26 396	27 853	26 330	53 716	28 557
Total EU27	GB6F	**1 432 611**	**1 395 901**	**1 621 361**	**2 156 358**	**2 560 215**	**2 711 233**	**3 485 924**	**4 965 375**	**3 899 173**
European Free Trade Association (EFTA)										
Iceland	HDZZ	1 128	909	1 519	2 808	4 575	6 981	20 120	11 596	14 668
Liechtenstein	HFCE	841	819	960	563	702	898	1 094	858	773
Norway	HFIE	17 900	19 290	23 254	32 134	45 281	59 308	68 033	108 609	43 520
Switzerland	HCZZ	153 198	147 300	171 774	167 484	189 226	172 154	316 318	359 403	261 846
Total EFTA	HBKW	**173 067**	**168 318**	**197 507**	**202 989**	**239 784**	**239 341**	**405 565**	**480 466**	**320 807**
Other Europe										
Albania	HBLA	–	–8	1	20	25	27	79	395	397
Belarus	HCZX	1	1	1	1	–	29	119	204	42
Croatia	HDWZ	635	1 053	1 184	1 155	1 531	1 101	1 050	1 813	2 141
Russia	HFIY	7 619	8 395	12 058	17 043	40 340	35 036	54 557	55 278	37 219
Turkey	HFJK	7 004	8 126	6 576	8 654	16 056	19 655	24 996	29 268	29 752
Ukraine	HFJM	106	167	243	850	3 633	4 160	6 116	5 785	4 578
Serbia and Montenegro[1]	HFJQ	49	51	37	45	250	272	697	1 335	1 224
of which Serbia	KI3Z	..	..	..	..	..	..	697	1 335	1 117
Montenegro	KI44	..	..	..	..	..	..	..	–	107
Other	HFIP	83 795	96 939	109 993	144 822	187 603	238 329	271 411	246 636	193 274
Total Europe	HDRW	**1 704 887**	**1 678 943**	**1 948 961**	**2 531 937**	**3 049 437**	**3 249 183**	**4 250 514**	**5 786 555**	**4 488 607**
Americas										
Argentina	HCPD	5 199	3 108	3 292	3 598	6 805	5 298	5 830	5 535	3 538
Brazil	HCZW	11 780	9 219	8 810	11 184	14 147	17 947	26 860	24 072	35 407
Canada	HCZY	45 615	49 275	43 014	55 377	78 447	100 249	132 927	212 406	149 468
Chile	HDER	3 362	3 401	3 311	4 123	5 212	2 895	3 293	3 952	3 556
Colombia	HDEZ	2 113	2 656	2 943	2 904	3 220	2 629	2 983	3 683	3 160
Mexico	HFIB	10 165	7 790	7 961	10 726	16 148	13 668	13 385	15 819	13 293
United States of America	HFJN	699 158	625 857	716 945	1 038 828	1 348 945	1 548 597	1 889 860	3 205 169	2 412 862
Uruguay	HFJO	301	324	243	477	774	698	660	268	222
Venezuela	HFJP	1 807	1 733	1 077	1 658	3 966	1 634	1 089	1 556	1 456
Other Central American Countries	HFIR	106 271	119 271	146 435	205 742	291 620	309 568	381 523	436 968	396 015
Other	HFIV	912	1 427	1 741	3 453	4 548	4 416	1 190	1 862	2 337
Total Americas	HDRZ	**886 683**	**824 061**	**935 772**	**1 338 070**	**1 773 832**	**2 007 599**	**2 459 600**	**3 911 290**	**3 021 314**
Asia										
China	HDES	5 943	6 484	7 029	9 589	12 396	15 463	32 265	25 006	30 895
Hong Kong	HDSN	39 310	30 365	35 746	47 470	61 456	72 879	80 920	96 495	82 935
India	HDZX	5 541	4 993	6 979	9 738	14 814	17 478	35 566	32 414	35 511
Indonesia	HDZD	3 038	2 592	2 958	3 333	4 144	4 656	5 483	4 102	5 762
Iran	HDZY	1 115	1 591	2 496	3 430	4 729	3 307	2 894	1 861	1 392
Israel	HDZK	1 672	2 301	2 463	2 916	3 109	3 791	3 819	6 099	6 173
Japan	HEIC	198 151	212 085	212 204	282 793	294 018	263 473	288 476	399 386	323 829
Malaysia	HFIC	4 941	5 234	5 361	6 827	7 253	7 539	8 312	7 254	6 350
Pakistan	HFIH	1 228	847	944	1 225	1 491	1 808	2 022	2 107	2 141
Philippines	HFIG	2 221	2 492	3 316	2 573	3 746	3 625	4 128	3 935	2 607
Saudi Arabia	HFIZ	6 028	5 830	5 736	5 205	7 299	6 685	13 511	16 914	15 007
Singapore	HFJG	48 384	39 117	43 991	47 824	52 172	52 223	78 250	117 948	73 383
South Korea	HEJH	11 502	14 890	17 460	23 020	32 574	28 920	39 453	44 918	41 396
Taiwan	HFJL	7 460	5 189	11 476	21 456	26 543	21 519	21 319	15 831	20 229
Thailand	HFJJ	3 054	3 731	4 417	4 858	5 024	5 152	5 656	5 262	5 144
Residual Gulf Arabian Countries	HFIS	19 999	20 184	20 840	29 222	36 840	37 085	61 435	97 221	78 142
Other Near & Middle Eastern Countries	HDSG	1 122	1 092	616	1 523	1 633	2 915	4 630	7 259	7 167
Other	HFIT	5 771	3 834	3 890	3 960	5 929	8 541	9 165	11 123	13 265
Total Asia	HDSF	**366 480**	**362 851**	**387 922**	**506 962**	**575 170**	**557 059**	**697 304**	**895 135**	**751 328**
Australasia & Oceania										
Australia	HCZT	44 908	48 186	52 888	78 323	95 690	101 359	126 468	174 099	145 380
New Zealand	HFIF	5 136	5 971	5 773	8 563	7 238	7 675	8 641	12 542	10 002
Other	HFIU	368	407	320	329	340	304	331	1 932	2 028
Total Australasia & Oceania	HDSH	**50 412**	**54 564**	**58 981**	**87 215**	**103 268**	**109 338**	**135 440**	**188 573**	**157 410**
Africa										
Egypt	HDSB	2 254	1 917	1 520	2 013	3 515	5 547	5 731	5 194	3 165
Morocco	HFIA	574	323	473	647	781	730	580	399	434
South Africa	HFJR	11 357	16 598	18 770	25 354	31 808	25 841	28 587	38 214	36 254
Other North Africa	HFIW	601	1 428	1 020	1 075	874	1 221	1 472	1 979	2 975
Other	HFIQ	8 262	7 795	9 047	12 099	14 081	13 422	17 949	26 743	26 187
Total Africa	HDRY	**23 048**	**28 061**	**30 830**	**41 188**	**51 059**	**46 761**	**54 319**	**72 529**	**69 015**
International Organisations	HBKR	18 593	21 134	21 230	27 052	29 150	31 872	32 664	40 906	31 613
Unallocated	G972	26 182	56 794	56 961	65 103	19 747	32 681	82 298	58 877	83 104
Reserve Assets	LTEB	25 649	25 469	23 794	23 250	24 739	22 931	26 685	36 283	40 144
World total	HBQA	**3 101 934**	**3 051 877**	**3 464 451**	**4 620 777**	**5 626 402**	**6 057 424**	**7 738 824**	**10 990 148**	**8 642 535**

1 Separate data for Serbia or Montenegro is only available from 2007.

10.3 Geographical breakdown of International Investment Position: UK liabilities

Balance sheets valued at end of year

£ million

		2001	2002	2003	2004	2005	2006	2007	2008	2009
Europe										
European Union (EU)										
Austria	HFMW	17 268	17 581	18 452	27 762	29 792	34 069	39 162	53 629	44 899
Belgium	A56Z	53 143	62 333	71 151	100 534	112 954	109 463	135 841	206 270	160 375
Bulgaria	HFMY	522	513	507	669	1 110	1 464	1 596	473	1 511
Cyprus	A3SB	3 376	3 237	3 102	3 840	6 555	8 165	10 593	17 316	23 461
Czech Republic	HFNG	3 419	2 175	2 030	2 822	4 419	4 891	5 339	6 952	5 511
Denmark	HFNJ	21 138	20 075	28 699	43 189	46 666	48 211	73 410	89 220	54 635
Estonia	HFNO	125	310	232	351	392	402	452	338	390
Finland	HFOA	6 025	6 907	11 854	20 175	22 362	24 917	29 529	52 360	47 253
France	HFOB	162 393	185 427	197 228	314 318	426 604	424 772	568 450	921 657	694 480
Germany	HFNI	253 307	290 223	349 591	538 256	592 905	637 567	781 962	1 206 389	937 784
Greece	HFOD	13 981	17 847	18 814	24 559	33 922	36 710	46 796	79 363	77 104
Hungary	HFOG	741	1 259	929	2 501	3 143	2 763	3 769	4 721	3 232
Ireland	HFOI	110 211	133 012	162 583	223 016	292 418	331 035	422 701	550 904	510 222
Italy	HFOO	69 476	74 606	78 704	93 803	98 259	100 950	108 181	144 871	149 325
Latvia	HFOX	190	323	254	423	363	386	594	505	398
Lithuania	HFOW	104	180	133	293	216	345	490	140	85
Luxembourg	A5E4	82 117	83 907	116 495	136 316	155 447	189 584	222 380	312 537	277 979
Malta	A3SC	1 166	1 379	1 542	1 112	1 917	2 479	6 450	12 075	7 780
Netherlands	HFPD	200 347	195 951	218 718	324 840	439 416	530 676	655 676	756 328	577 364
Poland	HFPN	4 500	3 160	3 120	5 061	6 488	6 625	9 373	8 740	4 291
Portugal	HFPO	6 668	9 682	11 101	13 772	16 963	18 507	20 801	22 078	28 121
Romania	HFQB	533	422	615	800	1 075	1 426	1 088	749	785
Slovak Republic	HFQH	405	154	559	1 559	1 236	1 247	1 317	722	2 567
Slovenia	HFQG	1 008	938	764	256	452	354	600	160	745
Spain	HFNR	35 732	45 361	54 600	74 894	95 167	129 814	151 629	166 690	167 228
Sweden	HFQE	30 084	26 333	32 555	47 678	50 129	57 506	69 954	70 839	62 966
European Central Bank	HFMP	–	–	–	–	–	–	–	–	–
EU Institutions	HFMO	38 386	39 056	40 457	47 684	58 813	63 421	69 680	124 898	104 023
Total EU27	GB9A	**1 116 365**	**1 222 351**	**1 424 789**	**2 050 483**	**2 499 183**	**2 767 749**	**3 437 813**	**4 810 924**	**3 944 514**
European Free Trade Association (EFTA)										
Iceland	HFOM	488	294	826	1 897	3 725	5 397	6 717	6 614	3 696
Liechtenstein	HFOU	2 026	2 233	2 213	2 444	2 867	2 438	3 362	3 493	2 318
Norway	HFPG	16 574	20 341	27 246	32 262	54 490	66 972	79 096	124 842	84 407
Switzerland	HFNC	231 765	240 193	266 310	274 396	307 278	245 577	420 872	413 499	320 160
Total EFTA	HFMT	**250 853**	**263 061**	**296 595**	**310 999**	**368 360**	**320 384**	**510 047**	**548 448**	**410 581**
Other Europe										
Albania	HFMU	89	54	60	93	58	179	153	83	71
Belarus	HFNA	71	72	139	231	446	345	781	802	398
Croatia	HFOF	849	1 387	1 476	1 549	1 614	1 648	2 147	579	598
Russia	HFQC	9 567	13 967	17 348	24 555	55 951	64 805	72 569	31 223	18 620
Turkey	HFQJ	3 150	2 574	2 620	4 085	6 588	6 874	8 101	9 986	7 472
Ukraine	HFQL	213	1 262	1 496	2 712	7 464	7 622	9 470	8 198	5 844
Serbia and Montenegro[1]	HFQP	218	469	360	462	292	978	716	215	73
of which Serbia	KI42	..	..	..	..	..	..	716	199	61
Montenegro	KI45	..	..	..	..	..	..	–	16	12
Other	HFPT	212 461	222 135	225 221	285 156	350 103	403 050	498 266	557 331	490 154
Total Europe	HFNK	**1 593 836**	**1 727 332**	**1 970 104**	**2 680 325**	**3 290 059**	**3 573 634**	**4 540 063**	**5 967 789**	**4 878 325**
Americas										
Argentina	HFMV	475	256	232	316	448	471	485	614	305
Brazil	HFMZ	3 293	2 754	4 347	7 609	8 840	7 622	7 775	6 471	6 539
Canada	HFNB	41 486	35 548	43 058	62 211	72 930	88 896	104 909	160 078	120 507
Chile	HFND	985	797	1 083	1 594	1 615	2 689	4 303	4 869	8 648
Colombia	HFNF	1 344	589	818	1 070	1 193	1 857	1 549	2 126	1 522
Mexico	HFPB	5 802	2 645	2 839	4 799	5 800	4 851	5 524	12 555	3 805
United States of America	HFQM	875 866	738 838	850 406	1 150 494	1 430 918	1 627 593	1 937 995	3 050 567	2 555 087
Uruguay	HFQN	176	116	806	466	714	592	789	429	640
Venezuela	HFQO	1 056	1 040	1 130	1 319	1 623	2 598	3 273	2 344	1 535
Other Central American Countries	HFPV	119 863	107 560	156 136	212 527	284 710	272 670	367 645	426 899	280 241
Other	HFPZ	4 084	2 571	2 934	2 959	3 358	4 021	3 075	3 813	3 315
Total Americas	HFNN	**1 054 430**	**892 714**	**1 063 789**	**1 445 364**	**1 812 149**	**2 013 860**	**2 437 322**	**3 670 765**	**2 982 144**
Asia										
China	HFNE	8 287	9 407	7 234	10 807	12 836	14 512	25 586	16 224	10 871
Hong Kong	HFOE	84 118	71 722	80 077	92 099	103 404	106 945	154 793	188 952	141 626
India	HFOK	7 921	7 849	11 337	19 008	23 613	29 296	15 255	20 214	12 526
Indonesia	HFOH	3 127	2 847	2 729	2 332	2 365	1 835	1 544	1 999	1 705
Iran	HFOL	6 130	3 695	3 418	3 252	3 468	3 549	2 895	2 319	2 045
Israel	HFOJ	6 910	6 451	6 065	6 527	9 495	11 098	10 550	9 179	7 743
Japan	HFOP	225 644	206 255	178 025	237 768	242 513	254 289	313 646	479 874	348 320
Malaysia	HFPC	6 160	4 345	4 419	8 239	4 084	7 841	10 108	5 199	5 772
Pakistan	HFPM	2 254	3 497	3 790	2 791	2 727	3 305	3 106	1 832	3 110
Philippines	HFPJ	1 209	1 059	594	1 025	2 410	2 389	3 584	2 214	1 998
Saudi Arabia	HFQD	16 496	16 071	14 068	17 131	28 411	33 303	61 451	79 798	61 574
Singapore	HFQF	67 828	68 850	67 144	82 955	84 384	90 539	120 921	166 917	115 833
South Korea	HFOS	4 316	4 122	5 585	8 267	12 865	10 649	17 843	27 783	15 708
Taiwan	HFQK	4 217	3 073	7 221	11 138	11 306	7 977	14 559	11 160	7 275
Thailand	HFQI	4 135	1 348	3 521	3 339	5 275	5 465	7 394	5 717	3 267
Residual Gulf Arabian Countries	HFPW	39 603	32 233	27 239	37 376	43 338	53 642	66 025	72 546	53 432
Other Near & Middle Eastern Countries	HFNX	5 301	5 807	6 472	6 594	8 178	8 099	8 965	10 365	11 943
Other	HFPX	3 893	3 759	4 253	5 065	7 843	9 207	11 065	11 372	10 966
Total Asia	HFNT	**497 549**	**452 390**	**433 191**	**555 713**	**608 515**	**653 940**	**849 290**	**1 113 664**	**815 714**
Australasia & Oceania										
Australia	HFMX	26 538	26 904	32 469	64 878	67 095	69 579	94 752	132 970	98 266
New Zealand	HFPH	2 644	2 569	2 289	4 196	5 211	4 716	5 851	8 734	5 273
Other	HFPY	182	181	177	212	277	167	442	224	110
Total Australasia & Oceania	HFNZ	**29 364**	**29 654**	**34 935**	**69 286**	**72 583**	**74 462**	**101 045**	**141 928**	**103 649**
Africa										
Egypt	HFNQ	6 778	6 220	6 462	6 356	11 361	9 561	7 633	7 076	5 889
Morocco	HFOZ	897	754	831	944	1 712	2 366	1 784	1 246	1 449
South Africa	HFQQ	19 870	21 719	29 131	34 269	36 641	36 512	39 078	49 985	53 820
Other North Africa	HFQA	4 583	3 955	4 364	5 549	11 036	15 815	17 559	16 607	14 182
Other	HFPU	14 711	14 277	13 644	14 824	18 880	23 773	30 374	37 366	31 839
Total Africa	HFNM	**46 839**	**46 925**	**54 432**	**61 942**	**79 630**	**88 027**	**96 428**	**112 280**	**107 179**
International Organisations	HFMQ	16 461	14 867	17 150	25 478	33 080	37 315	43 112	67 522	59 579
World total	HBQB	**3 238 479**	**3 163 882**	**3 573 601**	**4 838 108**	**5 896 016**	**6 441 238**	**8 067 260**	**11 073 948**	**8 946 590**

1 Separate data for Serbia or Montenegro is only available from 2007.

10.4 Geographical breakdown of International Investment Position: Net

Balance sheets valued at end of year

£ million

		2001	2002	2003	2004	2005	2006	2007	2008	2009
Europe										
European Union (EU)										
Austria	IDBU	−2 255	−3 742	−627	40	−1 758	−4 631	−7 509	−4 608	−11 027
Belgium	A58F	4 073	−3 265	1 068	3 080	27 936	19 100	29 481	8 961	−4 928
Bulgaria	IDBW	580	−149	−71	−57	−170	−261	−578	1 644	234
Cyprus	A3V5	−1 167	−1 589	−1 424	−1 812	−2 363	−2 702	−2 776	−8 858	−14 996
Czech Republic	IDCE	−777	−125	170	148	−365	−785	−222	−157	−92
Denmark	IDCH	−2 142	−525	−4 178	−2 230	8 494	2 753	−12 307	−6 444	391
Estonia	IDCM	140	−114	6	33	−269	−309	−389	−245	−333
Finland	IDCS	13 450	9 848	3 771	2 499	5 516	2 406	6 009	5 238	871
France	IDCT	62 085	28 167	35 786	31 964	−6 709	102 181	177 654	63 524	30 614
Germany	IDCG	23 419	−23 020	−52 232	−95 873	−116 561	−138 364	−171 029	−133 690	−139 692
Greece	IDCU	3 879	2 110	3 427	2 136	−9 003	−3 945	−7 729	−35 503	−43 562
Hungary	IDCX	3 452	3 500	3 653	4 448	3 388	5 013	4 722	5 779	4 851
Ireland	IDCZ	−16 574	−41 757	−42 544	−64 554	−34 435	−37 070	−47 927	17 265	−74 837
Italy	IDDE	63 366	53 223	69 862	71 823	79 947	74 378	94 434	105 167	98 355
Latvia	IDDJ	−88	−203	−184	−296	−176	5	492	569	218
Lithuania	IDDI	52	−14	−16	−141	741	−280	−344	−198	192
Luxembourg	A5FI	29 130	21 909	30 956	40 861	49 388	−34 286	−1 269	44 911	−12 278
Malta	A3V6	−577	−660	−586	1 399	−1 334	217	−1 299	−5 080	−4 420
Netherlands	IDDN	98 659	111 535	105 908	61 857	−51 164	−113 965	−77 856	−66 423	16 337
Poland	IDDS	836	3 064	4 159	3 295	2 470	2 087	1 270	9 261	10 905
Portugal	IDDT	13 204	10 971	14 742	10 103	11 356	8 771	8 401	12 001	11 322
Romania	IDEC	25	292	417	780	1 074	425	2 183	5 619	4 014
Slovak Republic	IDEI	31	438	258	−1 076	−467	−578	−162	1 686	−1 056
Slovenia	IDEH	−512	−629	−338	461	540	539	439	1 369	−210
Spain	IDCO	24 025	10 613	30 685	49 427	100 873	76 556	82 538	174 873	138 793
Sweden	IDEF	20 664	11 745	12 516	10 737	26 500	21 797	15 234	28 972	20 459
European Central Bank	IDBN	–	–	–	–	–	–	–	–	–
EU Institutions	IDBM	−20 732	−18 073	−18 612	−23 177	−32 417	−35 568	−43 350	−71 182	−75 466
Total EU27	GC25	**316 246**	**173 550**	**196 572**	**105 875**	**61 032**	**−56 516**	**48 111**	**154 451**	**−45 341**
European Free Trade Association (EFTA)										
Iceland	IDDD	640	615	693	911	850	1 584	13 403	4 982	10 972
Liechtenstein	IDDH	−1 185	−1 414	−1 253	−1 881	−2 165	−1 540	−2 268	−2 635	−1 545
Norway	IDDO	1 326	−1 051	−3 992	−128	−9 209	−7 664	−11 063	−16 233	−40 887
Switzerland	IDCA	−78 567	−92 893	−94 536	−106 912	−118 052	−73 423	−104 554	−54 096	−58 314
Total EFTA	IDBR	**−77 786**	**−94 743**	**−99 088**	**−108 010**	**−128 576**	**−81 043**	**−104 482**	**−67 982**	**−89 774**
Other Europe										
Albania	IDBS	−89	−62	−59	−73	−33	−152	−74	312	326
Belarus	IDBY	−70	−71	−138	−230	−446	−316	−662	−598	−356
Croatia	IDCW	−214	−334	−292	−394	−83	−547	−1 097	1 234	1 543
Russia	IDED	−1 948	−5 572	−5 290	−7 512	−15 611	−29 769	−18 012	24 055	18 599
Turkey	IDEK	3 854	5 552	3 956	4 569	9 468	12 781	16 895	19 282	22 280
Ukraine	IDEM	−107	−1 095	−1 253	−1 862	−3 831	−3 462	−3 354	−2 413	−1 266
Serbia and Montenegro[1]	IDEQ	−169	−418	−323	−417	−42	−706	−19	1 120	1 151
of which Serbia	KI43	..	..	..	..	..	..	−19	1 136	1 056
Montenegro	KI46	..	..	..	..	..	..	–	−16	95
Other	IDDU	−128 666	−125 196	−115 228	−140 334	−162 500	−164 721	−226 855	−310 695	−296 880
Total Europe	IDCI	**111 051**	**−48 389**	**−21 143**	**−148 388**	**−240 622**	**−324 451**	**−289 549**	**−181 234**	**−389 718**
Americas										
Argentina	IDBT	4 724	2 852	3 060	3 282	6 357	4 827	5 345	4 921	3 233
Brazil	IDBX	8 487	6 465	4 463	3 575	5 307	10 325	19 085	17 601	28 868
Canada	IDBZ	4 129	13 727	−44	−6 834	5 517	11 353	28 018	52 328	28 961
Chile	IDCB	2 377	2 604	2 228	2 529	3 597	206	−1 010	−917	−5 092
Colombia	IDCD	769	2 067	2 125	1 834	2 027	772	1 434	1 557	1 638
Mexico	IDDL	4 363	5 145	5 122	5 927	10 348	8 817	7 861	3 264	9 488
United States of America	IDEN	−176 708	−112 981	−133 461	−111 666	−81 973	−78 996	−48 135	154 602	−142 225
Uruguay	IDEO	125	208	−563	11	60	106	−129	−161	−418
Venezuela	IDEP	751	693	−53	339	2 343	−964	−2 184	−788	−79
Other Central American Countries	IDDW	−13 592	11 711	−9 701	−6 785	6 910	36 898	13 878	10 069	115 774
Other	IDEA	−3 172	−1 144	−1 193	494	1 190	395	−1 885	−1 951	−978
Total Americas	IDCL	**−167 747**	**−68 653**	**−128 017**	**−107 294**	**−38 317**	**−6 261**	**22 278**	**240 525**	**39 170**
Asia										
China	IDCC	−2 344	−2 923	−205	−1 218	−440	951	6 679	8 782	20 024
Hong Kong	IDCV	−44 808	−41 357	−44 331	−44 629	−41 948	−34 066	−73 873	−92 457	−58 691
India	IDDB	−2 380	−2 856	−4 358	−9 270	−8 799	−11 818	20 311	12 200	22 985
Indonesia	IDCY	−89	−255	229	1 001	1 779	2 821	3 939	2 103	4 057
Iran	IDDC	−5 015	−2 104	−922	178	1 261	−242	−1	−458	−653
Israel	IDDA	−5 238	−4 150	−3 602	−3 611	−6 386	−7 307	−6 731	−3 080	−1 570
Japan	IDDF	−27 493	5 830	34 179	45 025	51 505	9 184	−25 170	−80 488	−24 491
Malaysia	IDDM	−1 219	889	942	−1 412	3 169	−302	−1 796	2 055	578
Pakistan	IDDR	−1 026	−2 650	−2 846	−1 566	−1 236	−1 497	−1 084	275	−969
Philippines	IDDQ	1 012	1 433	2 722	1 548	1 336	1 236	544	1 721	609
Saudi Arabia	IDEE	−10 468	−10 241	−8 332	−11 926	−21 112	−26 618	−47 940	−62 884	−46 567
Singapore	IDEG	−19 444	−29 733	−23 153	−35 131	−32 212	−38 316	−42 671	−48 969	−42 450
South Korea	IDDG	7 186	10 768	11 875	14 753	19 709	18 271	21 610	17 135	25 688
Taiwan	IDEL	3 243	2 116	4 255	10 318	15 237	13 542	6 760	4 671	12 954
Thailand	IDEJ	−1 081	2 383	896	1 519	−251	−313	−1 738	−455	1 877
Residual Gulf Arabian Countries	IDDX	−19 604	−12 049	−6 399	−8 154	−6 498	−16 557	−4 590	24 675	24 710
Other Near & Middle Eastern Countries	IDCQ	−4 179	−4 715	−5 856	−5 071	−6 545	−5 184	−4 335	−3 106	−4 776
Other	IDDY	1 878	75	−363	−1 105	−1 914	−666	−1 900	−249	2 299
Total Asia	IDCP	**−131 069**	**−89 539**	**−45 269**	**−48 751**	**−33 345**	**−96 881**	**−151 986**	**−218 529**	**−64 386**
Australasia & Oceania										
Australia	IDBV	18 370	21 282	20 419	13 445	28 595	31 780	31 716	41 129	47 114
New Zealand	IDDP	2 492	3 402	3 484	4 367	2 027	2 959	2 790	3 808	4 729
Other	IDDZ	186	226	143	117	63	137	−111	1 708	1 918
Total Australasia & Oceania	IDCR	**21 048**	**24 910**	**24 046**	**17 929**	**30 685**	**34 876**	**34 395**	**46 645**	**53 761**
Africa										
Egypt	IDCN	−4 524	−4 303	−4 942	−4 343	−7 846	−4 014	−1 902	−1 882	−2 724
Morocco	IDDK	−323	−431	−358	−297	−931	−1 636	−1 204	−847	−1 015
South Africa	IDER	−8 513	−5 121	−10 361	−8 915	−4 833	−10 671	−10 491	−11 771	−17 566
Other North Africa	IDEB	−3 982	−2 527	−3 344	−4 474	−10 162	−14 594	−16 087	−14 628	−11 207
Other	IDDV	−6 449	−6 482	−4 597	−2 725	−4 799	−10 351	−12 425	−10 623	−5 652
Total Africa	IDCK	**−23 791**	**−18 864**	**−23 602**	**−20 754**	**−28 571**	**−41 266**	**−42 109**	**−39 751**	**−38 164**
International Organisations	IDBO	2 132	6 267	4 080	1 574	−3 930	−5 443	−10 448	−26 616	−27 966
Unallocated	G972	26 182	56 794	56 961	65 103	19 747	32 681	82 298	58 877	83 104
Reserve Assets	LTEB	25 649	25 469	23 794	23 250	24 739	22 931	26 685	36 283	40 144
World total	HBQC	**−136 545**	**−112 005**	**−109 150**	**−217 331**	**−269 614**	**−383 814**	**−328 436**	**−83 800**	**−304 055**

1 Separate data for Serbia or Montenegro is only available from 2007.

Part 4

Supplementary information

Balance of payments and the relationship to national accounts

This section is intended to help users of the Pink Book gain a better understanding of how the data fit within the broader economic accounts framework. It can be read as a standalone, although it makes several references to Blue Book tables and so readers are advised to have access to these if possible.

Introduction

Conceptually, the balance of payments, including the international investment position, form part of the broader system of the UK National Accounts. The National Accounts provide a comprehensive and systematic set of statistics for the UK economy, with information on economic transactions, other changes in the levels of assets and liabilities, and the levels of assets and liabilities themselves. The UK National Accounts have generally been compiled according to the *European System of Accounts (ESA95)*. Linkages between the UK balance of payments and National Accounts are reinforced by the fact that the UK balance of payments are compiled at the same time as the National Accounts, as a component of the sector accounts and using many common data sources.

The National Accounts are a closed system in which both ends of every transaction involving a resident economic entity are recorded. A set of accounts is introduced to capture transactions that involve economic relationships with non-resident entities. These accounts are known as the 'rest of the world accounts' and are presented from the perspective of non-residents rather than residents. Consequently, entries in the balance of payments (which show transactions from the perspective of residents) are reversed in the presentation of the rest of the world accounts. The accounts for resident entities, which consist of the production, income and accumulation accounts, are described in more detail below.

Two important accounting differences occur when comparing the balance of payments and the National Accounts. First, each transaction is recorded twice in the balance of payments (double entry) and four times in the National Accounts (quadruple entry). This is because in the balance of payments the activity of only one transactor is recorded, that of the resident entity (with a non-resident entity), whereas in the National Accounts the activity of both transactors is recorded (that is, the activity of either two residents or a resident and a non-resident). Second, in the balance of payments, transactions are shown from the perspective of the resident entity; whereas in the National Accounts, transactions are shown from the perspective of the resident in the production, income and accumulation accounts, and from the perspective of the non-resident in the rest of the world account.

Relationship between National Accounts and balance of payments concepts and classifications

Because the balance of payments, including the international investment position, forms an integral part of the National Accounts, there is complete concordance between them in concept and classification, although the extent of cross-classifications may differ between the two systems.

The balance of payments and National Accounts identify resident producers and consumers identically, and both invoke the same concepts of economic territory and centre of economic interest. Both use market prices as the primary concept of valuation of transactions and they adopt identical concepts of accrual accounting. The systems use identical conversion procedures to convert transactions which take place in foreign currency to UK currency.

While for some purposes it would be convenient if classifications used in the rest of the world accounts and the balance of payments accounts were identical, differences between the two are justifiable because on occasion they serve different purposes. For example, in the balance of payments financial account, precedence is given to classification of transactions by type of investment (that is, direct, portfolio, other, financial derivatives and reserve assets), whereas in the rest of the world financial account the instrument of investment is the primary classification. More important is the fact that concepts, definitions and classifications are consistent between the two systems.

The production, income and capital accounts of the National Accounts

The National Accounts tables reflect the basic aspects of economic life (production, income, consumption, accumulation and wealth). For many analysts, Gross Domestic Product (GDP) is the key economic aggregate as it measures the total value added for the UK economy in any period. GDP may be measured as:

- the total value of output less the cost of goods and services used in the production process (intermediate consumption). This is referred to as the **output (or production) approach**
- the value of income accruing from the production process to each of the

factors of production (plus net taxes on production and imports). This is referred to as the **income approach**

- total final expenditure on goods and services during the period, referred to as the **expenditure approach**

Conceptually these measures are equal, but because different and imperfect data sources are used to measure each approach, the measures may differ in practice. This difference is reflected in the statistical discrepancy item. The National Accounts are regularly benchmarked to balanced annual supply and use (input-output) tables. This ensures that, except for the latest year, the three measures of GDP are equal on an annual basis, though there will still be a statistical discrepancy between the quarterly estimates based on the three approaches.

Blue Book Table 1.2 presents the Gross Domestic Product Account for the whole economy, the derivation of GDP using the expenditure approach and the income approach. Table 1.7.1, the Production Account, shows the derivation of GDP using the production approach.

- The expenditure-based measure of GDP is derived as final consumption expenditure by government and households, plus investment in fixed capital formation and changes in inventories, plus exports minus imports of goods and services, plus (or minus) the statistical discrepancy. Exports and imports are the same as the balance of payments components, exports and imports of goods and services
- The income-based measure of GDP shows the components of factor income, namely compensation of employees, gross operating surplus and mixed incomes, plus taxes less subsidies on production and imports
- The production-based measure of GDP is shown as total gross output at purchasers' prices less intermediate consumption

For the purpose of discussion here, all values are in current prices.

Blue Book Tables 1.7.3, 1.7.4 and 1.7.6 present the National Income, Secondary Distribution of Income and Use of Income Accounts, showing the derivation of gross national income, gross disposable income and use of gross disposable income. Gross national income is equivalent to GDP plus property income receivable from non-residents, less property income payable to non-residents.

These primary income items are the same as the balance of payments income components which are used in the derivation of gross saving (gross disposable income less consumption) and net saving (gross saving less consumption of fixed capital). Tables 1.7.3 and 1.7.4 illustrate how the various balance of payments income and current transfers components affect the nation's saving. To derive gross disposable income, net secondary income receivable from non-residents is added to gross national income; secondary income items are equivalent to the net current transfer components in the balance of payments.

Table 1.7.6 deals with use of gross disposable income and shows the derivation of gross saving (gross disposable income less consumption) and net saving (gross saving less consumption of fixed capital).

Blue Book Table 1.7.7, the National Capital Account, shows the link between gross saving and net lending/borrowing (to/from the rest of the world). The latter is derived as gross saving plus net capital transfers from non-residents less investment in fixed capital and inventories and the net acquisitions of non-produced, non-financial assets from non-residents. The items net capital transactions and net acquisitions of non-produced non-financial assets are both sourced from the balance of payments capital account. The capital account was introduced into the balance of payments to emphasise this clear relationship between the balance of payments and the National Accounts.

The financial account and balance sheet of the National Accounts

Net lending/borrowing is also the balance shown in *Blue Book* Table 1.7.8, the Financial Account. The financial account shows how the net lending/borrowing is financed through a combination of transactions in financial assets and liabilities. Table 1.7.8 is the UK's Financial Account and includes transactions for all sectors. Financial transactions between all resident sectors can be offset and eliminated. This results in the UK's Financial Account for the total economy being equal to the inverse of the financial account for the rest of the world sector and equivalent to the balance of payments financial account.

However, there are some important differences in classification emphasis between Table 1.7.8 and the balance of payments financial account. In Table 1.7.8 the emphasis is on instrument of investment (such as currency and deposits, securities, loans, and equity), while in the balance of payments financial account, the emphasis is on type of investment (direct investment, portfolio investment, financial derivatives, other investment and reserve assets). Both presentations give emphasis to the asset and liability classification.

Blue Book Table 1.7.9, the UK's Financial Balance Sheet, shows the UK's financial assets, and liabilities and net worth at the end of the period. Financial assets and liabilities measure financial claims and liabilities between all sectors of the economy. Claims and liabilities between resident sectors can be offset and eliminated. This results in the UK's Financial Balance Sheet being the equivalent of the international investment position statement for the UK.

Again, there are some important classification differences between Table 1.7.9 and the international investment position statement. In Table 1.7.9 the emphasis is on instrument of investment, while in the international investment position statement the emphasis is on type of investment. Both presentations give emphasis to the asset and liability classification.

Rest of the world accounts of the National Accounts

There are five accounts for the rest of the world in the National Accounts shown in the *Blue Book*. These are:

- Table 7.1.0, the External account of goods and services
- Table 7.1.2, the External account of primary incomes and current transfers
- Table 7.1.7, the External capital account
- Table 7.1.8, the External Financial Account
- Table 7.1.9, the External Balance Sheet Accounts

The external accounts are published quarterly in *UK Economic Accounts*. As mentioned earlier, these accounts are required to close the system of National Accounts and, while essentially the same as the balance of payments accounts and international investment position statement, they are compiled from the perspective of the non-resident transactor. Table 7.1.2 is essentially the current account of the balance of payments, Table 7.1.7 the capital account, Table 7.1.8 the financial account, and Table 7.1.9 the international investment position. The reader should be able to readily identify the counterpart entries in all of these tables.

Transactions with the EU

Blue Book Table 12.1 shows UK official transactions with institutions of the EU from a UK National Accounts perspective. It has been recreated in the *Pink Book* as Table 9.9 using balance of payments terminology.

Methodological notes

Trade in goods (chapter 2)

Introduction

The IMF *Balance of Payments Manual*, 5th edition (BPM5) defines trade in goods as covering general merchandise, goods for processing, repairs on goods, goods procured in ports by carriers, and non-monetary gold.

General merchandise (with some exceptions) refers to moveable goods for which real or imputed changes of ownership occur between UK residents and the rest of the world.

Goods for processing: this covers goods that are exported or imported for processing on the basis of a contract and for a fee, where there is no change of ownership. There is a corresponding import or export (respectively) when the goods return to the originator. The inclusion of these transactions on a gross basis is an exception to the change of ownership principle. The value of the good before and after processing is recorded. This is included in total trade in goods but cannot be separately identified.

Repairs on goods: this covers repairs that involve work performed by residents on movable goods owned by non-residents (or vice versa). Examples of such goods are ships, aircraft and other transport equipment. The value recorded is the value of the repairs (fee paid or received) rather than the value of the goods before and after repair.

Goods procured in ports: this covers goods such as fuels, provisions, stores and supplies procured by UK resident carriers abroad or by non-resident carriers in the UK.

Non-monetary gold: this is defined as all gold not held as reserve assets (monetary gold) by the authorities. Non-monetary gold can be subdivided into gold held as a store of value and other (industrial) gold – for further information see Glossary.

Coverage and other adjustments

The balance of payments statistics of trade in goods compiled by the ONS are derived principally from data published by HM Revenue & Customs (HMRC) on the physical goods exported from and imported to the UK. However, this information is on a different basis to that required for balance of payments statistics. In order to conform to the IMF definitions, ONS has to make various adjustments to include certain transactions which are not reported to HMRC, and to exclude certain transactions which are reported to them but where there is no change of ownership. In addition, the value required for balance of payments purposes is the value of goods at the point of export (that is, the customs border of the exporting country), rather than the value of goods as they arrive in the UK. Therefore, the freight and insurance costs of transporting the goods to the UK needs to be deducted from the values recorded by HMRC. Table 2.4 summarises this transition onto a balance of payments basis for each of the last 11 years.

Overseas trade statistics compiled by HM Revenue & Customs (HMRC)

Statistics of the UK's overseas trade in goods have been collected for over 300 years by HMRC, formerly HM Customs and Excise (HMCE). Since 1993 these data comprise statistics of UK imports from, and exports to, countries outside the EU, and statistics on trade with other EU member states collected via the Intrastat survey. Data are compiled from declarations made to HMRC by importers, exporters or their agents, and statistics of UK arrivals (imports) from and dispatches (exports) to other member states of the EU compiled from the Intrastat returns submitted by traders or their agents to HMRC.

Prior to 1993 statistics of UK imports from, and exports to, all countries in the world were compiled from declarations made to HMRC by importers, exporters or their agents.

Information on trade with EU countries

The Intrastat system has applied since 1993, with minor variations, in all EU member states. In the UK all VAT registered businesses are required to complete two additional boxes on their VAT returns, which are normally submitted quarterly. These show the total value of exports of goods to customers in other member states (dispatches) and the total value of imports of goods from suppliers in other member states (arrivals).

Traders whose annual value of arrivals and/or dispatches exceeds given thresholds are required to provide an Intrastat declaration each month, showing full details of their arrivals and dispatches during the month. These thresholds are reviewed annually. For the calendar years 2010 and 2011 the threshold for arrivals has been set at £600,000, to capture a reduced coverage of 95 per cent of trade by value. The threshold for dispatches has been set at £250,000 for this period to maintain coverage at 97 per cent.

Link with VAT

The information on the VAT returns serves three purposes:

- to establish a register of traders and to determine which exceed the thresholds
- to provide a cross-check with the Intrastat declarations, and
- to provide an estimate of the total value of trade carried out by traders below the Intrastat thresholds

Traders not registered for VAT and private individuals who move goods within the EU have no obligations under the Intrastat system and their trade is therefore not included in the statistics. Examples of commodities where this trade can be significant are works of art and racehorses.

Below threshold trade

The total values of arrivals and dispatches by traders below the Intrastat thresholds are available from their VAT returns, although the coverage is slightly different. The figures are included in the month in which the VAT return is received by HMRC, although the VAT return itself may relate to a period of more than one month. Detailed information on below-threshold trade is not available from the VAT data. However, it has been established that the pattern of that trade before the Intrastat system was introduced on 1 January 1993 was similar to that of traders just above the thresholds. Thus estimates enabling detailed allocations of below-threshold trade can be made on this basis by HMRC.

Late response

Traders who have a legal responsibility to provide Intrastat declarations are required to do so by the end of the calendar month following the month to which the declaration relates. However, where traders have failed to provide returns to Intrastat by the due date, estimates of the total value of such trade are included. These are based on the trade reported by these traders in a previous period, and the growth rate since that period experienced by comparable traders who have provided returns for the current month. From January 2010 HMRC included an estimate for those traders who have only partially declared their trade for a given month.

Late declarations of trade with EU countries are subsequently incorporated into the month's figures to which they relate with a corresponding reassessment of the initial estimates for late response.

EU Gas and Electricity

The methodology used to collect EU (Intrastat) data on natural gas and electricity was amended by the Commission of the European Communities (EC regulation no 1982/2004). As a result, from January 2005 HMRC has changed to collecting information relating to the trade in natural gas and electricity directly from the pipeline and grid operators. This has removed the need for individual companies to submit Intrastat (EU) import and export declarations for these goods. The new methodology records the physical flow of natural gas and electricity between the UK and the last country at the point the goods cross the border into the UK.

Value data are estimated using the relevant market prices for gas and electricity.

Information on trade with non-EU countries

In general the figures for trade with non-EU countries show: the trade as declared by importers and exporters or their agents, and for which documentation has been received and processed by HMRC during the calendar month.

Importers are usually required to present a Customs declaration before they can obtain Customs clearance and remove the goods. The great majority of imports are cleared immediately by a computerised system. Import statistics may include documents received by HMRC up to the third working day after the end of the month. Therefore the import figures correspond fairly closely to goods actually imported during the calendar month.

Under the procedures for the control of exports, the principle is the same – namely that goods cannot be cleared for export until a Customs declaration has been made. Traders can, if they wish, submit a simplified declaration so that the goods can be exported. This has to be followed within 14 days after date of shipment with a complete export declaration. The processing of these complete export documents begins three working days before the end of the calendar month (two working days for December). Thus the export statistics compiled for a month (which are based on the date of receipt of the complete export documents) do not correspond with goods actually shipped in the calendar month.

HMRC's New Export System (NES), which replaced manual (paper) Customs declarations with electronic submissions, requires electronic messages from the trader once the goods have been exported in order to provide the departure date. The new system has led to greater efficiency; improving processing and thereby speeding up the flow of information. This means that, in terms of the value of trade, the proportion allocated to the correct month has increased from September 2003 onwards.

A further improvement in the allocation of trade was introduced in 2011 (starting with February 2011 data) with the processing of export documents being fully aligned to calendar months removing the early close down and processing before the end of the month. This means that more export documents are processed and allocated to the correct calendar month than previously.

Basis of valuation

For statistical purposes the UK adopts the valuation bases recommended in the International Merchandise Trade Statistics Concepts & Definitions published by the United Nations.

The valuation of exports (and dispatches) is on a free on board (f.o.b.) basis, that is, the cost of goods to the purchaser abroad, including:

- packaging
- inland and coastal transport in the UK
- dock dues
- loading charges
- all other costs such as profits, charges and expenses (for example, insurance) accruing up to the point where the goods are deposited on board the exporting vessel or aircraft or at the land boundary of Northern Ireland

The valuation of imports (and arrivals) is on a cost, insurance and freight (c.i.f.) basis including:

- the cost of the goods
- charges for freight and insurance
- all other related expenses in moving the goods to the point of entry into the UK (but excluding any duty or tax chargeable in the UK)

When goods are re-imported after process or repair abroad, the value includes the cost of the process or repair as well as the value of the goods when exported.

Arrivals from and dispatches to EU countries

As part of the simplification procedure to reduce the burden on business, in the UK most traders are permitted to provide a valuation for trade in goods with EU countries based on the invoice value. Large traders, those who have more than £16 million of trade in the year, are required to supply information on their delivery terms. Regular sample surveys to all traders are conducted by HMRC to establish conversion factors to adjust the invoice values to produce the valuation basis required for statistical purposes. Separate factors are imputed for a range of different delivery terms and for trade with each member state.

The value recorded for arrivals and dispatches includes any duties or levies that have been applied to goods originating in non-EU countries but which have since cleared EU Customs procedures in one EU country prior to moving on to other EU countries.

Imports from and exports to non-EU countries

The statistical value of imports from and exports to non-EU countries is the same as the value for Customs purposes. This value is arrived at by the use of specific methods of valuation in the following order of preference:

- the transaction value of the goods (that is, the price paid or payable on the goods)
- the transaction value of identical goods
- the customs value of similar goods
- the 'deductive method' – value derived from the selling price in the country of importation
- computed value based on the built-up cost of the imported goods
- the 'fall-back' method by adopting the above methods flexibly to fit unusual circumstances

Imported goods are valued at the point where the goods are introduced into the Customs territory of the EU. This means that costs for delivery of the imported goods to that point have to be included in the Customs value.

For all other goods (that is, goods free or exempted from duty and goods subject to a specific duty) the statistical value is determined in relation to the point at which the goods enter the UK.

An amount expressed in foreign currency is converted to sterling by the importer using a system of 'period rates of exchange' published by HMRC. These rates are normally operative for a four-weekly period unless there is a significant movement in the exchange rate.

Treatment of taxes

As described above, the value of all goods moving into and out of the UK is based on the transaction value recorded for Customs purposes or, in the case of trade in goods with EU countries, the invoice or contract value. In line with this principle, the values recorded exclude VAT. For trade in goods with non-EU countries, all other taxes such as duties and levies applied to goods after arrival in the UK are excluded. For trade in goods with EU countries, the value recorded for imports and exports includes any duties or levies that have been applied to goods originating in non-EU countries but which have since cleared Customs procedures prior to moving on to other EU countries. However excise duties are excluded from the value recorded for trade.

Balance of payments statistics for trade compiled by ONS

Table 2.4 summarises the transition from trade in goods statistics on an Overseas Trade Statistics basis (compiled and published by HMRC) to those on a Balance of Payments basis (compiled by ONS).

Valuation adjustments

Freight: the cost of freight services for the sea legs of dry cargo imports is estimated by applying freight rates (derived from the rates for a large sample of individual commodities imported from various countries) to tonnages of goods arriving by sea. For the land legs, estimates of freight rates per tonne-kilometre for different commodities and estimated distances are used. Estimates of rail freight through the Channel Tunnel are estimated from data provided by Le Shuttle and freight operators. The cost of freight on imports arriving by air is derived from information on the earnings of UK airlines on UK imports and the respective tonnages landed by UK and foreign airlines at UK airports. Pending investigations of an alternative methodology, the cost of freight and insurance on oil and gas imports is projected from data formerly supplied by the Department of Trade and Industry.

Sources: tonnages from HMRC; information on freight rates from Chamber of Shipping, Civil Aviation Authority and road hauliers; information from Eurotunnel

Insurance: the cost of insurance premiums on non-oil imports is estimated as a fixed percentage of the value of imports.

Source: ONS estimate

Coverage adjustments

Second-hand ships: to include purchases and sales of second-hand ships not included in the Overseas Trade Statistics.

Source: inquiries to UK ship owners conducted by the Department for Transport until late 2005. Estimates are now made by ONS where possible

New ships delivered abroad: to include deliveries of new ships built abroad for UK owners while the vessel is still in a foreign port.

Source: inquiries to UK ship owners conducted by the Department for Transport until late 2005. Data now provided by HMRC are when the change of ownership/sale takes place

North Sea installations: to include goods (including drilling rigs) directly exported from and imported to the UK production sites in the North Sea. This adjustment is also used when there is a redistribution of the resources of fields which lie in both UK and non-UK territorial waters (for example, the Frigg, Murchison and Statfjord). In these circumstances the contribution to (or reimbursement of) a proportion of the development costs has been treated as a purchase (or sale) of fixed assets at the date of the re-determination and appears as an adjustment to imports (exports) of goods.

Source: ONS surveys to the petroleum and natural gas industry

NAAFI: to exclude goods exported by the Navy, Army and Air Force Institute for the use of UK forces abroad since these are regarded as sales to UK residents (this adjustment ceased with effect from 2004). These exports are not now included in the Overseas Trade Statistics.

Source: quarterly returns from NAAFI

Goods not changing ownership: the Overseas Trade Statistics exclude temporary trade (that is, goods that are to be returned to the original country within two years and there is no change of ownership). However, goods which may well have originally been recorded as 'genuine' trade may subsequently be returned to the original country. Examples of these 'returned goods' are goods traded on a 'sale or return' basis, goods damaged in transit and returned for replacement or repair, and contractor's plant. The same amount is deducted from both imports and exports for the month in which the return movement is declared to Customs.

Source: HMRC (non-EU trade in goods identified by reference to Customs Procedure codes (CPCs) and by 'Nature of Transaction Code' on Intrastat submissions)

Gold: trade in gold (that is, gold bullion, gold coin, unwrought or semi-manufactured gold and scrap) is reported to HMRC but it is excluded from the statistics of total exports and imports published in the Overseas Trade Statistics. However, trade in ores and concentrates, and finished manufactures of gold (for example, jewellery) are included in total exports and imports.

For balance of payments purposes, all trade in non-monetary gold should be included under trade in goods. Non-monetary gold is defined as all gold not held as reserve assets (monetary gold) by the authorities. Non-monetary gold can be subdivided into gold held as a store of value and other (industrial) gold. The UK currently makes adjustments to include industrial gold. In exports, the adjustment reflects the value added in refining gold and producing proof coins. In imports, the adjustment reflects the value of gold used in finished manufactures (such as jewellery and dentistry).

Within the transactions of the London Bullion Market, the UK cannot currently distinguish between monetary gold and non-monetary gold held as a store of value. Accordingly, the UK has obtained an exemption from adopting IMF recommendations, as specified in BPM5 and for the time being these transactions are included in the Financial Account.

The treatment of non-monetary gold is being reviewed as part of the worldwide process to revise the IMF *Balance of Payments Manual*. UK BoP will continue current practice until the treatments defined in the revised manual are implemented. HMRC is currently working in conjunction with Eurostat to agree future treatment of non-monetary gold in the *Overseas Trade Statistics*.

Source: ONS estimate

Letter post: to include exports by letter post which are not included in the Overseas Trade Statistics.

Sources: books – ONS estimate based on historic information from publishers and booksellers; other items – ONS estimate based on historic sample inquiry made by the former Post Office

Additions and alterations to ships: to include work carried out abroad on UK-owned ships and work carried out in UK yards on foreign-owned ships.

Sources: Inquiries to UK ship owners conducted by the Department for Transport, (imports) until late 2005, then HMRC data, (exports)

Repairs to aircraft: to include the value of repairs carried out in the UK on foreign-owned aircraft.

Source: ONS estimate

Goods procured in ports: to include fuels, provisions, stores and supplies purchased for commercial use in ships, aircraft and vehicles. (Estimates of goods dispatched are recorded by HMRC.)

Sources: Chamber of Shipping and Civil Aviation Authority for goods procured in foreign ports by UK transport companies (imports); UK oil companies, Civil Aviation Authority, BAA, municipal airports and port authorities for goods procured in UK ports by overseas transport companies (exports)

Smuggling of alcohol and tobacco: Customs provide volume figures for smuggled goods entering the UK based on published estimates of revenue loss and revenue evasion through smuggling. This information is supplemented by information on the average prices for alcohol and tobacco goods in France and Belgium, from the published sources of the statistical and banking institutions in those countries, in order to estimate the value of smuggled alcohol and tobacco entering the UK.

Sources: HMRC, INSEE and National Bank of Belgium

Territorial coverage adjustment: for the purposes of the Overseas Trade Statistics, 'UK' is defined as Great Britain, Northern Ireland, the Isle of Man, the Channel Islands, and the Continental Shelf (UK part). Therefore the Overseas Trade Statistics exclude trade between these different parts of the UK but include their trade with other countries.

For balance of payments purposes the Channel Islands and the Isle of Man are not considered part of the UK economic territory. Adjustments are made to exports to include UK exports to those islands and to exclude their exports to other countries; and to imports to include UK imports from those islands and to exclude their imports from other countries.

Source: ONS estimate

Other adjustments

Diamonds: much of the world's trade in rough (uncut) diamonds is controlled from London by the Diamond Trading Company, part of De Beers. Prior to 2001, in order not to distort the trade statistics, all imports into and exports from the UK of uncut diamonds which remain in the ownership of foreign principles are excluded from the Overseas Trade Statistics by HMRC. In addition the value of diamonds imported into the UK can be reassessed after the diamonds have been cleared by Customs. Prior to 2001, this adjustment reflects these changes in valuation. From 2001 the procedure for recording movements of diamonds was changed so that all trade was included in the Overseas Trade Statistics by HMRC. From 2001 this adjustment removes movements of diamonds where no change of ownership has taken place.

Source: Diamond Trading Company

Adjustments to imports for the impact of VAT Missing Trader Intra-Community (MTIC) fraud: VAT missing trader intra-Community fraud is a systematic, criminal attack on the VAT system, which has been detected in many EU member states. In essence, fraudsters obtain VAT registration to acquire goods VAT-free from other member states. They then sell on the goods, at VAT inclusive prices, and disappear without paying over the VAT from their customers to the tax authorities. The fraud is often carried out very quickly, with the fraudsters disappearing by the time the tax authorities follow up the registration with their regular assurance activities.

Acquisition fraud is where the goods are imported from the EU into the UK by a trader who then goes missing without completing a VAT return or Intrastat declaration. The 'missing trader' therefore has a VAT- free supply of goods, as they make no payment of the VAT monies due on the goods. The trader sells the goods to a buyer in the UK and the goods are available on the home market for consumption.

Carousel fraud is similar to acquisition fraud in the early stages, but the goods are not sold for consumption on the home market. Rather, they are sold through a series of companies in the UK and then re-exported to another country. Goods may be imported and exported several times, hence the goods moving in a circular pattern or 'carousel'.

The VAT system (and therefore the Intrastat collection of trade statistics) picks up the exports of any 'carouselled' goods, but does not always pick up the associated import at the time the carouselled goods entered the UK. As a consequence, UK import statistics have been under reported.

Originally, most carousel chains only involved EU member states. From the beginning of 2004, there was an increase in carousel chains that involve non-EU countries, for example, Dubai and Switzerland. However, the MTIC trade adjustments are added to the EU import estimates as it is this part of the trading chain that is not recorded. Changes to the pattern of trading associated with MTIC fraud can therefore make it difficult to analyse trade by commodity group and by country. In particular, adjustments affect trade in capital goods and intermediate goods – these categories include mobile phones and computer components (now covered by the UK's reverse charge derogation).

HMRC estimates for the impact of MTIC on the trade statistics. The method used relies heavily on information uncovered during HMRC's operational activity and, as such cannot be detailed for risk of prejudicing current activity (including criminal investigations and prosecutions) and, more generally, undermining HMRC's ability to tackle the fraud effectively. The method specifically excludes adjustments for the acquisition variant of the fraud which cannot be quantified at present. To take account of mutations in the fraud. HMRC regularly reviews the methodology for producing the estimates of the MTIC impact on the trade statistics. Estimates may change as the analysis of the fraud continues. The UK was the first member state to make adjustments in their trade statistics for this type of fraud.

Source: HMRC estimate

Adjustment for under-recording and for currency and other valuation errors: these adjustments compensate for the following types of error:

- failure on the part of traders or their agents to submit details of shipments
- incorrect valuations recorded
- declarations wrongly given in foreign currency instead of sterling

Regular reviews show the adjustments for non-EU trade remaining broadly constant over time. Those for EU trade have reduced since the early days of the Intrastat system. The adjustments, expressed as percentages of total trade excluding oil and erratics, are shown in Table 1.

Adjustments to estimates for late response: a review of the introduction of the Intrastat system carried out in 1994 identified a number of issues in the initial monthly estimates of trade with EU countries provided by HMRC. The following describes the adjustments made by ONS to cope with these difficulties.

The HMRC method of estimation for late response relies on linking the values of trade reported by traders in the current period with previous periods. Issues can arise when traders change their VAT registration (perhaps as a result of an internal reorganisation, mergers or sales), or when a trader starts submitting returns for the first time. If the trader then becomes a late responder there may be no history of previous trade upon which to base an estimate. The current HMRC adjustments make an allowance for this, but recent changes in the overall trader profile, with an increasing proportion of smaller traders, means the current methodology needs to be revised. In the meantime, ONS and HMRC have agreed that ONS makes an initial monthly adjustment of +£30 million to both exports and imports (reducing to zero over the following two months).

Furthermore, some traders may submit first declarations for a month that do not include all their trade in that month. Later declarations are then received for the rest of their trade. The pattern of receipt at HMRC of these partial returns is analysed to enable ONS to make initial adjustments to both exports and imports to anticipate these later declarations. These initial adjustments are progressively reduced in subsequent months as late declarations are processed.

When Intrastat was introduced it was envisaged that the vast majority of declarations in respect of any particular month would be made within six months of the end of that month. As a consequence, HMRC computer programs were designed to recalculate its initial estimates for late response for six months after those estimates first appear in the Overseas Trade Statistics. However the reality is that some declarations (around half a per cent) are still being received and processed after that six-month period. These are being included as additions to the value of reported trade with no corresponding reduction in the value of monthly estimated trade (until the annual HMRC closedown of the trade year). ONS therefore, in order to eliminate this element of double counting on a monthly basis, makes a negative adjustment to the value of estimated trade equal to the value of these late amendments. Note that where the value of late amendments exceeds the value of estimated trade the level of estimated trade is set to zero.

It should be noted that this methodology has changed with effect from January 2010. At this point, HMRC began to systematically adjust for partial response in their monthly estimates of trade with EU countries. This is set out in the following paper: https://www.uktradeinfo.com/pagecontent/documents/Partial_Estimates_Briefing_Paper.pdf

The profile of these adjustments prior to 2010 are shown in Table 2.

Source: ONS estimate

Price and volume indices

Any difference between time periods in the total value of trade reflects changes in prices as well as changes in the levels of the underlying economic activity (for example, the physical amounts of goods exported or imported). Separation of these changes greatly enhances the interpretation of the data and, for this reason, ONS compiles separate data measuring changes in price and changes in volume. These data are presented in index number form.

Classifications and definitions

From October 2011, Balance of Payments basis data have been compiled under the United Nations Standard International Trade Classification Revision 4 (SITC R4). This may remove some discontinuities at detailed levels between 2006 and 2007, particularly between capital and intermediate goods. It is also possible that volume and price changes may have been improved for this period.

Table 1

	Exports to:		Imports from:	
	EU	non-EU	EU	non-EU
Under-recording	+¼%	+1½%	+¼%	0
Currency errors	0	–½%	0	0
Other valuation errors	0	–¼%	0	0

Source: ONS estimates based on historic quality surveys conducted by HMRC

Table 2: Late declaration adjustments made to HMRC before 2010 £ million

	Exports	Imports
First published estimates	+600	+650
Second estimates	+250	+250
Third estimates	+120	+150
Fourth estimates	+50	+70
Fifth estimates	+10	+20
All subsequent estimates	0	0

Source: ONS (derived from HMRC estimates)

References

Aggregate estimates of trade in goods, seasonally adjusted and on a balance of payments basis, are published monthly by ONS in a Statistical Bulletin. More detailed figures are available from the Time Series Data Service and are also contained in the *Monthly Review of External Trade Statistics*. This is available, free of charge, in electronic format as a PDF on the ONS website.

The latest *UK Trade Statistical Bulletin* can be found at: http://www.ons.gov.uk/ons/search/index.html?pageSize=50&newquery=uk+trade

The *Monthly Review of External Trade Statistics*, previously published as MM24, can be found at: http://www.ons.gov.uk/ons/search/index.html?pageSize=50&newquery=mm24

An article describing MTIC fraud and its effect on Balance of Payments Statistics and the UK National Accounts was published in *Economic Trends* No. 597, August 2003. A copy of the article can be found at: http://www.ons.gov.uk/ons/rel/elmr/economic-trends--discontinued-/no--598--august-2003/vat-missing-trader-intra-community-fraud--the-effect-on-balance-of-payments-statistics---uk-national-accounts-.pdf

A follow-up report was published on 17 February 2005 which summarised the work carried out since July 2003 to review the estimates of the impact on the trade figures; a copy can be found at http://www.ons.gov.uk/ons/rel/uktrade/uk-trade/report-on-impact-of-mtic-on-uk-trade-statistics/report-on-impact-of-mtic-on-uk-trade-statistics-.pdf

A fuller version of these methodological notes appears in *Statistics on Trade in Goods* (Government Statistical Service Methodological Series 36). It also describes the methodology employed to derive volume and price indices and is available on the Office for National Statistics website at: http://www.ons.gov.uk/ons/guide-method/method-quality/specific/gss-methodology-series/gss-methodology-series--36--statistics-on-trade-in-goods.pdf

A full version of the *Overseas Trade Statistics* methodology is available on the dedicated HMRC trade data website at:

www.uktradeinfo.com/pagecontent/documents/GSSMethodspaperv4.pdf

Trade in services (Chapter 3)

Introduction

Trade in services covers the provision of services by UK residents to non-residents and vice versa. Trade in services are disaggregated into 11 broad categories of services, as follows:

- Transportation (Sea, Air and Other) – Passenger, freight and other
- Travel (Business and Personal)
- Communications services
- Construction services
- Insurance services
- Financial services
- Computer and information services
- Royalties and licence fees
- Other business services (Merchanting and other trade-related services; operational leasing services; miscellaneous business, professional and technical services)
- Personal, cultural and recreational services (Audio-visual and related services; other cultural and recreational services)
- Government services

Separate tables appear at chapter 3 of this publication for each of the above categories except construction services, which are shown in the trade in services summary Table 3.1.

Trade in services data has been compiled and presented on a product rather than an industry basis since the 1998 Pink Book, when the BPM5 changes were implemented. This change was facilitated by the introduction of the International Trade in Services (ITIS) survey in 1996. A full product-based dataset is available from this date. Account totals, and some additional product estimates have been constructed back to 1991 or 1992, based on the relationship between the ITIS data and the previous industry-based data. For the transport, travel, royalties and government services accounts, there were only small changes from the industry-based data, and it was possible to construct longer time series.

The latest year's data for trade in services, which is compiled from the ITIS survey, are provisional as these figures are subject to annual benchmarking after publication. The latest data when available can be found at: http://www.ons.gov.uk/ons/search/index.html?newquery=itis

Construction services (shown within Table 3.1)

Construction services covers work done on construction projects and installations by employees of an enterprise in locations outside the resident economic territory of the enterprise. The source of information is the International Trade in Services (ITIS) survey. For construction services, where a permanent base is established which is intended to operate for over a year, the enterprise becomes part of the host economy and its transactions are excluded from the trade in services account. Transactions where a permanent base is established are recorded under direct investment, within investment income.

Transportation services (Table 3.2)

The transportation account covers sea, air and other (that is, rail, land, and pipeline) transport. It includes the movement of passengers and freight, and other related transport services, including chartering of ships or aircraft with crew, cargo handling, storage and warehousing, towing, pilotage and navigation, maintenance and cleaning, and commission and agents' fees associated with passenger/freight transportation.

Freight and the valuation of UK trade in goods

The trade in goods estimates included in the balance of payments value imports as they arrive in the UK free on board (f.o.b.) at the frontiers of the exporting country. This is net of the cost of freight to the UK border and any loss and damage incurred in transit to the UK. For UK importers who purchase goods f.o.b. and arrange transport themselves, their payment for the goods at the exporting countries' frontiers comprises:

(i) the value included in the trade in goods estimates (which is net of subsequent loss and damage);

(ii) the value of loss and damage incurred in transit.

In addition, such importers bear the costs of:

(iii) freight services outside the exporting countries;

(iv) insurance services (the excess of insurance premiums paid for the journeys over claims made).

Where importers purchase goods cost, insurance and freight (c.i.f.) on arrival in the UK, items (ii) to (iv) are paid by the foreign exporters in the first instance. The c.i.f. prices are set accordingly, however, and the UK importers are regarded as bearing the costs of items (i) to (iv).

Therefore, irrespective of the payment basis, items (ii) to (iv) represent costs to UK importers additional to the trade in goods entries, item (i). Item (ii), the value of loss and damage, is part of the price paid to the foreign exporter and so always represents a debit entry in the balance of payments accounts. Items (iii) and (iv), freight and insurance services also represent debit entries when provided by non-residents; where such services are provided by UK residents there is no balance of payments entry. The debit entries above relating to freight are included in imports of transportation services.

The estimates of trade in goods cover exports valued f.o.b. The valuation of exports at the UK frontier must, by definition, include any subsequent loss or damage en route to the importer. Therefore, unlike imports, there is no need to make an explicit adjustment for loss and damage to exports. However, foreign importers must additionally bear the costs of freight and insurance services for the journeys outside the UK and where such services are provided by UK residents this gives rise to credit entries in the services accounts.

The f.o.b. value for UK imports includes the cost of transport within the exporting country. Where this service is provided by a UK operator then the trade valuation of imports overstates the balance of payments effect and an offsetting credit entry is therefore included under 'Road transport'. Similarly, an offsetting debit entry is included for foreign operators' carriage of UK exports within the UK.

Sea transport

Exports by UK operators consist of freight services on UK exports (but not imports – see 'Freight and the valuation of UK trade in goods', above) and on cross-trades, the carriage of non-resident passengers and the provision to them of services, and the chartering of ships to non-residents. Exports also include port charges and other services purchased in the UK by non-resident operators. Conversely, imports comprise services purchased abroad by UK operators, their chartering of ships from non-residents, and the carriage by non-resident operators of UK imports (but not exports) and goods on UK coastal routes and UK passengers.

Statistics relating to UK operators are provided by the Chamber of Shipping (CoS), which conducts inquiries into its members' participation in foreign trade. Until 1995, inquiries covering all CoS members were made every four years, with sample surveys for intervening years. Since 1995, the CoS has surveyed all its members annually. The data from the CoS are uplifted to account for UK sea transport companies who are not members using estimates for the gross tonnage of the UK fleet for different types of ship.

Exports

Passenger revenue: the value of services provided to non-resident passengers comprises fares and passengers' expenditure on board. Since UK operators are not able to distinguish between fares received from UK residents and non-residents, fares collected abroad are assumed to represent fares received from non-residents (passenger revenue collected abroad from UK residents is thought to be small and is likely to be counter-balanced by that collected in the UK from foreign residents). An estimate of passengers' expenditure on board is added. It is assumed that the non-residents' proportion of this is the same as for fares.

Freight: earnings consist of freight services on UK exports and are based on data supplied to the Chamber of Shipping. Time charter receipts include receipts for charters with crew. Time charters without crew are included within the operational leasing component of 'Other business services' (Table 3.9).

Disbursements: estimates of disbursements in the UK by foreign operators are formed from a variety of sources. UK income from port charges, towage, handling costs and other port-related services was collected in 1996 from a survey of port authorities and has been projected forward from this. Crews' expenditure is estimated from information on numbers of visiting seamen, supplied by the Home Office. Regular returns are received on light dues from Trinity House. Estimates of expenditure on ships stores and on bunkers are included within the trade in goods data. Time charter payments made to UK residents are included under 'Ships owned or chartered-in by UK residents'.

Imports

Passenger revenue: estimates of passenger fares paid to non-resident operators are derived mainly from the results of the International Passenger Survey, which is described in the notes below on 'Travel'. A further allowance is made for on-board sales of goods and services. However, 'Travel' imports includes, but does not separately identify, passenger fares paid to non-resident operators for fly-cruises, together with other expenditure by UK passengers aboard non-resident shipping.

Freight: estimates of freight services on UK imports provided by non-resident operators are compiled as follows; the estimates of total freight services (provided by all operators) on the sea legs of UK imports of goods are taken as the starting point, as described in the methodological notes to Table 2.4. Estimates of the element provided by UK-operated ships, based on data from the Chamber of Shipping are then deducted to obtain the non-resident operators' element, which is then used in the transportation account. Charter payments cover payments for charters with crew.

Disbursements: disbursements abroad include payments for canal dues, the maintenance of shore establishments, port charges, agency fees, handling charges, crews' expenditure, pilotage and towage, light dues, and other miscellaneous port expenditure abroad. Payments for bunkers, ships stores and other goods purchased are included within the trade in goods data.

Air transport

The exports of UK airlines comprise the carriage of non-resident passengers to, from or outside the UK; the carriage of UK exports of goods (but not imports – see 'Freight and the valuation of UK trade in goods', above); and cross-trades and the chartering of aircraft to non-residents. Exports also include airport charges and services purchased in the UK by foreign airlines. Purchases of fuel and other goods are included within trade in goods.

Imports include for example, expenditure abroad by UK airlines on airport charges, crews' expenses, and charter payments. They also include payments to foreign airlines for the carriage of UK imports of goods (but not exports) and of UK mail, and for the carriage of UK passengers on flights covered by tickets for journeys to or from the UK. The carriage of UK passengers on other non-resident flights is included under 'Travel'.

The transactions of UK airlines are derived from returns supplied by the airlines to the Civil Aviation Authority.

Exports

Passenger revenue: this relates to all tickets sold outside the UK and used on UK aircraft, together with receipts from carrying passengers' excess baggage. An exercise by British Airways plc demonstrated that the value of tickets sold abroad to UK residents is roughly counterbalanced by sales in the UK to non-residents.

Freight: this consists of freight services on UK exports and the carriage of non-resident airmails, and is based on data supplied to the Civil Aviation Authority.

Disbursements and other revenue: these comprise expenditure in the UK by non-resident airlines on landing fees, other airport charges, handling charges, crews' expenses, office rentals and expenses, salaries and wages of staff at UK offices, commissions to agents and advertising. The estimates are based on returns from the Civil Aviation Authority, National Air Traffic Services, BAA plc and municipal airports on their receipts from non-resident airlines for air traffic control, landing fees and other airport charges; and survey information collected from large non-resident airlines operating in the UK on their other UK expenses. Purchases of fuel and other goods are included within trade in goods.

Also included are receipts from the charter or hire of aircraft and gross receipts of sums due from non-resident airlines under pooling arrangements and for services such as consultancy and engine overhaul.

Imports

Passenger: the information on fares paid by UK passengers to non-resident airlines is derived from the International Passenger Survey; see notes on 'Travel' below.

Freight: estimates of non-resident airlines' freight on UK imports are derived by subtracting from the estimates of total freight on imports of goods arriving by air (see the methodological notes to Table 2.4) – the element provided by UK airlines, the residual being the freight services supplied by non-resident airlines. Other imports comprise payments to non-resident airlines for carrying UK airmails as reported by the Royal Mail Group to the Civil Aviation Authority.

Disbursements and other payments: disbursements abroad include airport landing fees; other airport charges; charter payments; crews' expenses; the operating costs of overseas offices; agents' commissions; advertising; settlements with non-resident airlines under pooling arrangements; and miscellaneous expenditure abroad. Purchases of fuel and other goods are included within trade in goods.

Other Transport

This covers the movement of passengers and freight, and other related transport services, by rail, road and pipeline.

Rail: this consists primarily of expenditure on fares and rail freight through the Channel Tunnel. Passenger revenue estimates are based on numbers of passengers through the tunnel and average fare information. Estimates of rail freight through the tunnel are based on data provided by Eurotunnel and freight operators.

As the tunnel operators are a joint UK/French enterprise, half of passenger and freight transactions are taken to accrue to the UK part of the business. All tickets sold in France are assumed to be sold to non-UK residents (likewise, all tickets sold in the UK are assumed sold to UK residents). Of these, 50 per cent are assumed to accrue to the UK as they represent exports of rail transport services.

Road: exports comprise the earnings of UK road hauliers for the carriage outside the UK of UK exports of goods and the carriage within the exporting countries of UK imports (although such earnings from lorries leaving the UK via the Northern Ireland land boundary are only included from 2002). Estimates of numbers of journeys to various countries are derived from the International Road Haulage Survey, and rates for each journey are estimated from trade and other sources.

Imports include payments to all non-resident land transport operators for the carriage of UK imports of goods between the frontiers of the exporting countries and the foreign sea ports.

Estimates are made by subtracting from the estimate of total freight on imports for land legs (see the methodological notes to Table 2.4) an estimate of the element earned by UK operators (derived as for exports). Imports also include the earnings of non-resident road hauliers for carrying UK exports and imports within the UK, although estimates of the trade with the Republic of Ireland are only included from 1996. These are estimated from the statistics of ferry movements of foreign-registered lorries, average loads, and average lengths of haul within the UK and estimated freight rates. The disbursements abroad by UK road hauliers, and in the UK by non-resident road hauliers, are included within 'Travel'.

Pipeline: this covers the cost of transport of oil freight via undersea pipelines. Data are derived from a survey of North Sea oil and gas companies.

Travel (Table 3.3)

Travel covers goods and services provided to UK residents during trips of less than one year abroad and provided to non-residents during similar trips in the UK. Transport to and from the UK is excluded and shown as passenger services under transportation (see above). Internal transport within the country being visited is included within travel.

A traveller is defined as an individual staying for less than one year in an economy of which he/she is not a resident. The exceptions are those military and diplomatic personnel, whose expenditure is recorded under government services. The one-year rule does not apply to students and medical patients, who remain residents of their country of origin, even if the length of stay in another economy is more than a year.

The estimates are based primarily on the International Passenger Survey (IPS), which is a frontier sample survey which collects information on the expenditure of non-resident visitors leaving the UK, and of UK residents returning from abroad. For package tourists, estimates of the transport elements are deducted from the reported total package costs. Estimates of the expenditure of UK residents visiting the Republic of Ireland and of Irish residents visiting the UK have been covered by the survey since the second quarter of 1999. Prior to this, data were derived from statistics published by the Irish Central Statistics Office.

Business travel

Business travel is divided into expenditure by seasonal and border workers (individuals who work some or all of the time in economic territories that differ from their resident households) and other business travel. Estimates are based on the IPS.

Personal travel

Personal travel covers holidays, visits to friends and relatives, the expenditures of people visiting for education and health reasons, and miscellaneous purposes. Visits for more than one purpose, where none is distinguished as the main purpose, are classified as other.

Education related travel exports cover the tuition fees and other expenditure of students who are funded from abroad and studying in the UK (imports cover the expenditure of UK students studying abroad). The figures also include the fees and other expenditure of pupils in UK private schools and students at other colleges and language schools. Income received direct from abroad by examining bodies and correspondence course colleges is included within personal, cultural and recreational services.

Fees and other expenditure paid by non-resident students for higher education are collected via a special IPS trailer which commenced in 1997.

Health-related travel covers the cost of medical and other expenses of those travelling abroad for medical treatment. Estimates are based on information supplied to the IPS.

Communication services (Table 3.4)

Communication services covers two main categories of international transactions: telecommunications (telephone, telex, fax, email, satellite, cable and business network services) and postal and courier services. Information is obtained through the ONS International Trade in Services survey (ITIS) and direct from the Royal Mail Group.

Insurance services (Table 3.5)

Insurance services covers the provision of various types of insurance to non-residents by resident insurance enterprises and vice versa. Insurance services include freight insurance on goods being imported or exported, direct insurance (such as, life, accident, fire, marine, and aviation) and reinsurance. The amounts recorded in the accounts reflect the service charge earned on the provision of insurance services. This is equal to net premiums from abroad (premiums less claims), plus property income attributed to policy holders, less the change in the reserves for foreign business, less foreign expenses. The figures for UK insurance companies' and brokers' underwriting activities are derived from annual surveys conducted by ONS. Lloyd's of London underwriting activity is based on data supplied by the Corporation of Lloyd's; they also include receipts for management services provided to overseas members of Lloyd's syndicates.

Life insurance and pension funds

Life insurance covers underwriting services associated with long-term policies. Data are collected in the ONS inquiry into insurance companies. Pension fund services include service charges relating to occupational and other pension schemes, but not compulsory social security services.

Freight

Treatment of freight insurance is consistent with the f.o.b. valuation of trade in goods (see 'Freight and the valuation of trade in goods', above). That is, non-resident importers pay for freight and insurance on journeys outside the UK. Where such services are provided by UK residents to foreign enterprises, this gives rise to a credit entry.

Other direct insurance

Other direct insurance covers accident and health insurance; marine, aviation and other transport insurance; fire and property insurance; pecuniary loss insurance; general liability insurance; and other (such as travel insurance and insurance related to loans and credit cards).

Reinsurance

Reinsurance represents subcontracting parts of risks, often to specialised operators, in return for a proportionate share of the premium income. Reinsurance may relate to packages which mix several types of risks. Exports of services are estimated as the balance of flows between resident reinsurers and non-resident insurers. Imports are estimated as the balance of flows between resident insurers and non-resident reinsurers.

Auxiliary insurance services

This covers insurance broking and agency services; insurance and pension consultancy services; evaluation and adjustment services; actuarial services; salvage administration services; regulatory and monitoring services on indemnities and recovery services. These are measured by net brokerage earnings on business written in foreign currencies, and sterling business known to relate to non-residents. The main source of information on auxiliary insurance services is the ITIS survey.

Financial services (Table 3.6)

Financial services cover financial intermediary and auxiliary services other than those of insurance companies and pension funds. They include services provided in connection with transactions in financial instruments, as well as other services related to financial activity, such as advisory, custody and asset management services. These services may be charged for explicitly, for example through fees and commissions or implicitly, for example in the price spread offered in market making and foreign currency transactions. From the 2008 edition of the Pink Book, financial services also include financial intermediation services indirectly measured (FISIM). FISIM represents the implicit charge for the services related to borrowing and lending that are provided by monetary financial institutions and paid for by the interest differential between borrowing and lending rather than by fees and commissions. FISIM is exported by UK monetary financial institutions and imported by UK insurance companies and pension funds, private non-financial corporations and households. Prior to the 2008 edition of the Pink Book, the data for FISIM imports and exports were implicitly included as part of earnings on other investment debits and credits within income.

Estimates of financial services are based on returns from the Bank of England (for monetary financial institutions), ITIS, ONS's security dealers survey and directly from other sources including the Baltic Exchange.

From the 2001 edition of the Pink Book, the service earnings of financial institutions are presented on a gross exports and imports basis.

This treatment is consistent with the BPM5 edition of the accounts. Trade in services transactions covered by type of financial institution are detailed below:

Monetary financial institutions (banks and building societies)

This covers UK banking services giving rise to:

- commissions for credit and bill transactions such as advising, opening and confirming documentary credits, and collection of bills
- financial intermediation services indirectly measured (FISIM)
- spread earnings (net service earnings through spreads on market making) including those on transactions in foreign exchange, securities and derivatives
- fees and commissions on foreign exchange dealing
- commission on new issues of securities, investment management and securities transactions
- commission on derivatives transactions
- banking charges, income arising from lending activities, fees and commissions in respect of current account operations, overdraft facilities, executor and trustee services, guarantees, securities transactions and similar services

Estimates are based on surveys carried out annually from 1986 to 1990 and for some earlier years. A quarterly survey was run in 1991. A new survey was introduced in 1992 to collect data on UK banks' current account transactions including services. A further new survey was introduced in 2004, which enabled the collection of spread earnings on foreign exchange, securities and derivatives transactions – the data prior to 2004 are estimated by the Bank of England largely on the basis of information on the volumes of transactions and movements in spreads. The survey is completed quarterly by a selected sample of banks and annually by a larger sample of the UK banking population. From 2008 the Bank of England additionally included a sample of UK building societies in the quarterly reporting population.

FISIM is calculated by assuming the existence of an interest rate that represents the pure costs of borrowing funds, known as the reference rate. When monetary financial institutions lend money, FISIM is the difference between the interest they actually charge on the loan and the amount that would be charged if this reference rate were used. When financial institutions accept deposits (or borrow money), FISIM is the difference between the amount of interest they actually pay on the deposit (or loan) and the amount that would be paid if the reference rate were used. Exports of FISIM from 1992 onwards have been estimated by the Bank of England based on survey information relating to UK monetary financial institutions balance sheet data for loans and deposits with non-residents and their interest receipts and payments on loans and deposits with non-residents. The reference rate used in these calculations is the average of the implied rates of return for loans and deposits. The implied rates of return are calculated by dividing the annualised amounts of interest paid or received in a quarter by the balance sheet level. FISIM on loans is calculated by multiplying the balance sheet level for loans by the quarterly reference rate and subtracting the result from the actual interest receipts on loans. FISIM on deposits is calculated by subtracting the actual interest paid on deposits from the result of multiplying the balance sheet level for deposits by the quarterly reference rate. Separate reference rates and FISIM estimates are calculated for sterling and foreign currency loans and deposits. As the information on interest receipts and payments with non-residents is not available before 1992, exports of FISIM have been estimated by ONS using balance sheet levels and interest rates based on LIBOR and the spread between implied rates of return on loans and deposits in the period for which data are available.

Fund management companies

From 2001, information on investment management fees and fees generated from advisory and other related functions has been collected via the ITIS survey. Earlier estimates were derived from a survey of companies whose main activity is fund management. Earnings are net of any foreign expenses by the institutions concerned. They exclude earnings of insurance companies, which are covered by separate returns made to ONS (see above, under 'Insurance Services').

Securities Dealers

The earnings of securities dealers are derived from a survey run by ONS. From the 1998 edition of the Pink Book, security dealers' spread earnings (service earnings through market making activities) are included as part of securities dealers' overseas earnings. This treatment is consistent with the domestic accounts as described in the European System of Accounts (1995). Estimates of these spread earnings are based on information on acquisitions and realisations of various classes of securities derived from ONS surveys, together with the bid and offer prices for certain international bonds.

Baltic Exchange

This covers the brokerage and other service earnings of members of the Exchange for chartering, sales and purchases of ships and other associated activities. Estimates are based on a survey of Exchange members.

Other

This includes commissions and other earnings received from abroad by UK residents (other than monetary financial institutions and oil companies, whose earnings are included elsewhere) for dealings in physical goods and in futures and options contracts. From 1990 to 2004 ONS carried out an annual survey of dealers in physical commodities. This data is now collected via the ITIS survey. The foreign earnings of financial futures and options dealers are assumed to have moved in line with the corresponding total earnings of such dealers reported in statutory returns to supervisory bodies.

This component also includes those financial services not included elsewhere, including financial service transactions (exports and imports) picked up from the ITIS survey, service charges on purchases of IMF resources and estimates of imports of net spread earnings, which are based on the UK's share of world turnover data for cross-border foreign exchange and derivatives transactions and the UK's share of global imports of financial services.

Imports of FISIM are included under this section as well. Estimates are made for imports of FISIM by UK insurance companies and pension funds, non-financial corporations and households. These estimates are based on Bank for International Settlements (BIS) balance sheet data for UK private sector loans from and deposits with non-resident banks, described in more detail in the methodological notes for tables 8.7 and 8.8. FISIM is calculated separately for each sector's loans and deposits by multiplying the sectorised balance sheet data from the BIS by a fixed margin, which represents the difference between the reference rate and the interest rate paid or received on loans or deposits. The margins used are based on the margins observed in the calculation of exports.

Computer and information services (Table 3.7)

Computer and information services covers computer, news agency and other information provision related service transactions. Examples of these services include data processing; hardware consultancy; software implementation; maintenance and repair of computers and peripheral equipment; the provision of news, photographs and feature articles to the media; database development, storage and dissemination both through the internet and through magnetic, optical or printed media; and direct, non-bulk subscriptions to newspapers and periodicals. Information is obtained from the ITIS survey. Excluded from computer services are the provision of packaged non-customised software on magnetic media, which are included in trade in goods.

Royalties and license fees (Table 3.8)

Royalties and licence fees cover the exchange of payments and receipts for the authorised use of intangible, non-produced, non-financial assets and proprietary rights (such as patents, copyrights, trademarks, industrial processes, and franchises) and with the use, through licensing agreements, of produced originals or prototypes (such as manuscripts and films).

The heading includes royalties, licenses to use patents, trade marks, designs, copyrights; manufacturing rights and the use of technical 'know-how'; amounts payable or receivable in respect of mineral royalties; and royalties on printed matter, sound recordings and performing rights. Data are obtained through the ITIS survey. Film royalties from the ONS Films and TV (FTV) inquiry are also included prior to 2009. From 2009 the FTV inquiry was discontinued and data from the FTV businesses was collected via the ITIS survey. Royalties incorporated in the contract prices of UK exports and imports of goods are recorded under 'Trade in Goods'. The outright sale of a copyright is treated as a sale of a non-produced, nonfinancial asset and is recorded within the Capital Account (Table 6.1).

Other business services (Table 3.9)

'Other business services' covers a range of services including merchanting and other trade-related services, operational leasing (rental) without operators and miscellaneous business, professional and technical services.

Merchanting and other trade related services

Merchanting is defined as the purchase of a good by a resident from a non-resident, and the subsequent resale of the good to another non-resident without the good entering the compiling economy. The difference between the purchase and sale price is recorded as the value of merchanting services provided. Other trade related services covers commissions on cross-border goods and service transactions paid to, for example, merchants, commodity brokers, commission agents and auction houses.

Estimates of the net profits of UK firms from third country trade in goods are derived from ONS surveys. From 1990 to 2004, ONS carried out a specific sample survey of export houses, but information from these institutions is now collected via the ITIS survey, which has always collected information from other institutions on merchanting and trade related services. This component also covers fees charged for ship classifications and other related services, including information supplied by Lloyd's Register of Shipping.

Operational leasing

Operational leasing covers leasing (other than financial leasing) and charters of ships, aircraft and other transportation equipment without crews. Operational leasing data are derived from the ITIS survey and from the Chamber of Shipping.

Miscellaneous business, professional and technical services

Miscellaneous business, professional and technical services include legal, accounting, management consulting, recruitment and training and public relations; advertising and market research and development; architectural, engineering and other technical services; agricultural, mining and on-site processing services associated with agricultural crops (protection against disease or insects), forestry, mining (analysis of ores); and other services such as placement of personnel, security and investigative services, translation, and photographic. This item includes data from a number of different data sources, the most important of which is the ITIS survey.

Estimates of the earnings of solicitors are based on surveys held in respect of 1980 and annually since 1986 by the Law Society (in which amounts forwarded to barristers are included).

From the 2000 edition of the Pink Book, earnings of solicitors are collected as part of the ITIS survey. Other legal services also include estimates of the overseas earnings of UK barristers as supplied by the Commercial Bar Association.

Estimates of monetary financial institutions' and securities dealers' non-financial service transactions appear in the other business services account.

Personal, cultural and recreational services (Table 3.10)

Personal, cultural and recreational services are divided into audio-visual and related services and other. The first category covers services and associated fees relating to the production of motion pictures (on film or video tape), radio and television programmes (live or on tape), and musical recordings. It includes rentals; and fees received by actors, directors and producers. The second category covers all other personal, cultural and recreational services including those associated with museums, libraries, archives, and provision of correspondence courses by teachers or doctors. Income received direct from abroad by examining bodies and correspondence course colleges is also included. Most of the information is obtained from the ITIS survey but there was a separate ONS survey for the film and television industry (FTV) prior to 2009. From 2009 the FTV inquiry was discontinued and data from the FTV businesses was collected via the ITIS survey.

Government services (Table 3.11)

Government services include all transactions by embassies, consulates, military units and defence agencies with residents of staff or military personnel in the economies in which they are located. Other services included are transactions by other official entities such as aid missions and services, government tourist information and promotion offices, and the provision of joint military arrangements and peacekeeping forces (for example, United Nations). Information comes directly from government departments (including the Ministry of Defence and the Foreign and Commonwealth Office), foreign embassies and United States Air Force bases in the UK.

Exports

Expenditure by foreign embassies/consulates in the UK: this comprises the cost of operating and maintaining Commonwealth High Commission offices, foreign embassies and consulates in the UK, including the personal expenditure of diplomatic staff, but excluding the salaries of locally engaged staff, which are included within income; and similar expenditure by the UK offices of non-territorial organisations. In 1993 ONS conducted an inquiry to all high commission offices, embassies, consulates and international organisations in the UK. This figure has been updated for subsequent years using information obtained from several key high commissions and embassies and information on the number of diplomats in the UK.

Military units and agencies: this includes expenditure by the United States Air Force (USAF) in the UK (excluding the pay of locally engaged staff which is included within compensation of employees), together with receipts for services provided by UK military units in the UK and elsewhere to non-residents, such as military training schemes, which is sourced from the Defence Analytical Services Agency (DASA).

European Union institutions exports: these are services of the UK Government in collecting the UK contributions to the EU Budget, and services provided at the site of the EU's Joint European Torus project in Oxfordshire.

Other: this comprises goods and services which the government provides to non-residents under its economic aid programmes (these are offset under 'Bilateral aid' transfer debits) and miscellaneous goods and services supplied by the UK Government to foreign countries, including the reimbursement from other member states of the EU for treatment given by the National Health Service to their nationals.

Imports

Expenditure abroad by UK embassies and consulates: goods and services provided by local residents to UK embassies, high commission offices, consulates and the British Council account for most of this heading. It also includes the goods and services provided by local residents to UK diplomatic and other non-military personnel stationed abroad, excluding the salaries of locally engaged staff. The source for this information is the Foreign and Commonwealth Office.

Expenditure abroad by UK military units and agencies: this includes expenditure on food, equipment, fuel and services purchased locally. These items are recorded partly on a net basis – that is, after deducting receipts arising locally. The source for this information is DASA.

Other: this includes goods and services provided by local residents to the UK Government, excluding military and diplomatic expenditure. It covers expenditure abroad of the British Council and the reimbursement to other member states of the EU for medical treatment given to UK nationals.

References

United Kingdom Trade in Services, UKA1

UKA1 has been discontinued as a separate publication. All of the tables that were in Section A of UKA1 are now included in the Pink Book. New tables that were formerly in UKA1 but not in the Pink Book have been added to chapter 9. The tables that were formerly in Sections B and C of UKA1 are now in a web-only publication which focuses on the results of the ITIS survey.

The publication containing the ITIS survey results can be found at the following web address:

http://www.ons.gov.uk/ons/search/index.html?newquery=itis

Sea transport

An annual analysis describing the international activities of the UK shipping industry is published by the Department for Transport, in Transport Statistics Great Britain (The Stationery Office).

Transport Statistics Great Britain, 2009 edition can be found at: www.dft.gov.uk/pgr/statistics/datatablespublications/tsgb/

Air transport

Information relating to passenger expenditure is published by the Civil Aviation Authority in CAA Monthly and Annual Statistics.

CAA statistics are available at: www.caa.co.uk/

Travel

Details are published regularly in National Statistics monthly Statistical Bulletins (previously First Releases) and quarterly Business Monitors (MQ6), both titled *Overseas Travel and Tourism*, and in the annual publication *Travel Trends*.

Overseas Travel and Tourism Statistical Bulletins can be found at: http://www.ons.gov.uk/ons/search/index.html?newquery=overseas+travel+and+tourism

MQ6 can be found at: http://www.ons.gov.uk/ons/search/index.html?pageSize=50&newquery=mq6

Travel Trends can be found at: http://www.ons.gov.uk/ons/search/index.html?pageSize=50&newquery=travel+trends

Income (Chapter 4)

The income account covers compensation of employees and investment income. For compensation of employees, estimates for total credits, debits and the balance appear in Table 4.1 but no detailed breakdown of the account is available. Investment income is broken down into four main categories: direct investment, portfolio investment, other investment, and reserve assets.

Compensation of employees (Table 4.1)

Compensation of employees comprises wages, salaries, and other benefits paid by employers, in cash or in kind, to individuals who work in economies other than those in which they are residents. Employees, in this context, include seasonal or other short term workers (who stay for less than one year) and workers who cross international borders to get to their regular place of work. Compensation of employees also includes pay received by local (host country) staff of embassies, international organisations, consulates and military bases, as such entities are considered non-resident of the host economy.

Personal expenditure made by non-resident seasonal and border workers in the economies in which they are employed is recorded under travel within trade in services. Wages and salaries are recorded gross, with taxes paid recorded under current transfers.

Credits

There are three components:

- Wages, salaries and other benefits earned by UK seasonal and border workers, together with employers' contributions. These are estimated using data from the International Passenger Survey on the number of UK resident seasonal and border workers working abroad and average earnings data
- Wages and salaries earned by UK employees in US military bases in the UK. Information has been supplied to ONS by US military bases
- Wages and salaries earned by UK employees of foreign embassies in the UK. In 1993, ONS conducted an inquiry to all high commission offices, embassies, consulates and international organisations in the UK, asking for information on expenditure – including that on locally employed staff. This figure has been updated for subsequent years using information from a small sample of key embassies

Debits

There are two components:

- Wages, salaries and other benefits earned by non-resident workers employed in the UK for less than one year. These are estimated using data from the International Passenger Survey on the number of foreign resident seasonal and border workers working in the UK and average earnings data
- Wages, salaries and other benefits earned by foreign workers working in UK embassies and military bases abroad. Information on pay of locally engaged staff in UK embassies and military bases abroad is obtained from HM Treasury's Combined Online Information System (COINS), the Foreign and Commonwealth Office (FCO) and the Ministry of Defence (MOD)

International investment (Chapters 4, 7 and 8)

International investment comprises investment between resident and non-resident economies. Five functional categories of investment are distinguished in the international investment accounts:

- Direct investment
- Portfolio investment
- Financial derivatives
- Other investment
- Reserve assets

The international investment accounts measure investment income (chapter 4), transactions in financial assets and liabilities (chapter 7) and the international investment position (chapter 8).

Investment income (Chapter 4)

The investment income account covers earnings (for example, profits, dividends and interest payments and receipts) arising from foreign investment in financial assets and liabilities. Credits are the earnings of UK residents from their investments abroad and other foreign assets. Debits are the earnings of foreign residents from their investments in the UK and other UK liabilities. The flow of investment in the financial account is recorded separately from the earnings, although reinvested earnings of companies with foreign affiliates are a component of both. The total value of UK assets and liabilities held at any time is also recorded separately under the international investment position. The presentation of these three sections is almost identical, although there are small differences in coverage in some cases, mainly because complete information is not available for all items.

Earnings on the credit side of the account cover such items as interest on UK residents' deposits with banks abroad, profits earned by UK companies from their foreign affiliates, and dividends and interest received by UK investors on their portfolio investments in foreign companies' securities. Similarly, debits cover earnings by foreign investors on deposits held with UK monetary financial institutions, profits of foreign companies from their investments in their affiliates in the UK, and dividends and interest paid to foreign investors on their holdings of UK bonds and shares, including British government stocks.

Earnings on assets and liabilities are defined to include all profits earned and interest and dividends paid to UK residents from non-residents or to non-residents by UK residents. They are, where possible, measured net of income or corporation taxes payable without penalty during the recording period by the enterprise to the economy in which that enterprise operates and, in the case of profits, after allowing for depreciation. Dividends are recorded when they are paid (on a cash basis), whereas interest is recorded on an accruals basis.

Profits and dividends include the (credit) earnings from foreign affiliates of UK registered companies and the (debit) earnings of profits and dividends by UK-based affiliates of foreign-based companies. Conceptually, stock appreciation and other holding gains and losses should be excluded from the income flows entered in the balance of payments accounts because they represent only valuation changes. However, data on these are included in banking sector statistics provided by the Bank of England. Profits retained abroad by foreign affiliates or retained in the UK by affiliates of foreign companies are included in the flows of earnings and offset in the financial account. All interest flows between UK residents and non-residents are in principle included.

Interest on loans extended by and deposits with UK monetary financial institutions are now presented net of FISIM (Financial Intermediation Services Indirectly Measured). Likewise, UK non-bank loans from and deposits with banks abroad are also presented net of FISIM. FISIM is an estimate of the value of the services provided by financial intermediaries, such as banks, for which no explicit charges are made; instead these services are paid for as part of the margin between rates applied to savers and borrowers. The supposition is that savers would receive a higher interest rate and borrowers pay a lower interest rate if all financial services had explicit charges. FISIM received by UK monetary financial institutions is now recorded as an export of financial services while FISIM paid by UK non-banks is now recorded as an import of financial services. Information on the estimation of FISIM is included in the methodological notes for 'Trade in services'.

Financial account (Chapter 7)

The financial account covers transactions which result in a change of ownership of financial assets and liabilities between UK residents and non-residents. The financial account is broken down into five main categories: direct investment, portfolio investment, financial derivatives, other investment, and reserve assets.

In the balance of payments accounts, the term 'investment' has a wide coverage. It refers not only to the creation of physical assets but also, for example, to the purchase (or sale) of paper assets, such as shares, bonds and other securities. Investment also covers the financing of trade movements and other financial transactions between related companies in the UK and abroad. These 'other financial transactions' consist mainly of borrowing and lending by banks, both transactions by UK banks with non-residents and transactions of banks abroad with UK residents. Such borrowing and lending may be associated with UK trade in goods. For example, a non-resident may borrow from a UK bank to pay a UK exporter; alternatively he may use money already on deposit with the bank. Such borrowing or use of deposits will be included in the appropriate item in the financial account offsetting the entry under trade in goods.

Banking transactions may also arise from the financing of other financial transactions. For example, a UK company may borrow from a foreign bank in order to finance investment ('direct investment') in one of its subsidiary companies abroad. In this case, both the bank borrowing and the investment would be recorded in this section of the accounts and the two entries would offset each other; the investment would increase UK assets abroad while the borrowing would increase UK liabilities to foreign residents.

The total value of assets and liabilities held at the end of each year is recorded separately under the international investment position (see chapter 8) and the income earned from them is recorded under investment income within the income account (see chapter 4). The presentations of these sections are almost identical although there are small differences in coverage in some cases, mainly because full information is not available for all items. The financial account tables appearing at chapter 7 show net debits (UK assets) above net credits (UK liabilities), in order to allow easier read across with the investment income and international investment position tables which appear at chapters 4 and 8.

International investment position (Chapter 8)

The international investment position brings together the available estimates of the levels of identified UK external assets (foreign assets owned by UK residents) and identified UK external liabilities (UK assets owned by foreign residents) at the end of each calendar year.

The presentation of the international investment position is almost identical to the presentation of investment income, within the income account (see chapter 4) and the financial account (see chapter 7) although there are small differences in coverage in some cases, mainly because full information is not available for all items.

Changes in balance sheet levels will reflect not only transactions in the corresponding assets and liabilities but also changes in valuation and certain other changes. Changes in valuation will occur in the following circumstances:

- where assets and liabilities are denominated in foreign currencies, their equivalent sterling value may change because of changes in foreign exchange rates
- where assets and liabilities are regularly bought and sold (for example, British government stocks, UK and foreign company securities), the current market value may be different from the value at which they were acquired
- where the holders of assets and liabilities change their values in preparing their accounts to reflect what is thought to represent the current position (for example, bad debts may be written off and direct investment assets may be written up or down in the books of the investing company)

In addition to changes in the valuation of identical underlying assets and liabilities, changes in recorded levels of external assets and liabilities will also reflect some changes in coverage which introduce discontinuities in the series.

Assessment of the international investment position

Due to the very varied data sources used to derive the estimates for the international investment position, there are some inconsistencies between the different figures in the tables, resulting particularly from different methods of valuation. Wherever possible, figures are at market values. However, for significant items such as direct investment, the figures are at own funds of book value and are subject to all the limitations of data taken from accounting balance sheets as a reflection of current market values. To the extent that the conventional valuation basis for direct investment is own funds at book value or, in the case of monetary financial institutions, often historical cost values, an up-to-date valuation closer to market values is likely to be higher.

In addition, some assets and liabilities are measured very imperfectly (for example, for a number of items, levels of assets and liabilities are not directly reported but derived from cumulating recent identified transactions and allowing for estimated valuation changes). The balance between the estimates of identified external assets and liabilities has always been an imperfect measure of the UK's debtor/creditor position with the rest of the world.

To the extent that net errors and omissions reflect unrecorded or misrecorded financial transactions, the external balance sheet will tend to fail to capture the corresponding levels of assets and liabilities, although much will depend on the categories of assets and liabilities concerned:

- where both levels and transactions are reported (for example, portfolio investment by most financial intermediaries), there may be similar deficiencies to estimates of both levels and transactions, although levels may tend to be more accurate to the extent they are derived from annual accounting data
- where only levels are reported and transactions are derived from changes in levels, allowing as far as possible for valuation changes, (for example, non-portfolio transactions of UK and foreign monetary financial institutions), there may be errors in the estimates of transactions (for example, in allowing for valuation changes) with no corresponding error in levels
- where only transactions are reported and levels are calculated by cumulating transactions and allowing for valuation changes (for example, inward portfolio investment in UK company bonds), errors in recording transactions will lead to corresponding errors in levels. Thus if part of the net errors and omissions represents such missing portfolio investment inflows, the identified net assets figures will be overstated

Allocation of Special Drawing Rights

These are issued to the UK by the IMF but are not regarded as a liability of the UK and do not form part of total external liabilities in the summary table (Table 8.1).

Direct investment

Introduction

A direct investment relationship exists if the investor has an equity holding in an enterprise, resident in another country, of 10 per cent or more of the ordinary shares or voting stock. The direct investment relationship extends to branches, subsidiaries and other businesses where the enterprise has significant shareholding. Equity investment in which the investor does not have an effective voice in the management of the enterprise (that is, the investor has less than 10 per cent of the voting shares) is regarded as portfolio investment. The estimates of direct investment include the investor's share of the reinvested earnings of the subsidiary or associated company, the net acquisition of equity capital, changes in inter-company accounts and changes in branch/head office indebtedness. Further details are given in the Glossary.

The latest year's data for foreign direct investment, which is compiled from the Foreign Direct Investment survey, are provisional as these figures are subject to annual benchmarking after publication. The latest data can be found at: http://www.ons.gov.uk/ons/search/index.html?pageSize=50&newquery=foreign+direct+investment

Income (Tables 4.3 and 4.4)

Direct investment earnings include interest on loan capital, profits from branches or other unincorporated enterprises abroad and the direct investor's share of the profits of subsidiary and associate companies. It includes the direct investor's portion of reinvested earnings, which is also treated as a new investment flow out of the parent's country into the affiliate's and appears in the financial account (Table 7.3) as an offsetting entry to the earnings one. Estimates of profits are made after providing for depreciation, the companies' own estimates of depreciation being used. Although depreciation is estimated at replacement cost in the national accounts, there is little doubt that the estimates in the balance of payments are, in the main, measured at historic cost (different treatments of depreciation result in different entries in the current and financial accounts, but the sum of the two entries will always be the same).

International reporting standards recommend that direct investment enterprises report their profits on a 'current operating performance' basis and not include any realised or unrealised holding gains/losses, exceptional items, write-downs or write-offs. This is generally the case with the exception of the profits of monetary financial institutions, which report to the Bank of England on an 'all inclusive basis' and include realised and unrealised holding gains/losses, write-downs or write-offs.

Refunds of tax made retrospectively under double-taxation agreements are included in the period when they were made rather than the earlier periods in which they could be deemed to have accrued. Dividend receipts and payments include subsidiaries payments of withholding tax.

Estimates for reinvested earnings are not collected separately but are derived by deducting dividends paid from subsidiaries' profits.

Financial account (Tables 7.3 and 7.4)

The components of the direct investment financial account comprise equity capital, reinvested earnings and other capital associated with inter-company debt transactions. Inter-company transactions between affiliated monetary financial institutions and between affiliated other financial institutions (for example, securities dealers) are limited to those associated with permanent debt. The usual inter-company deposits and other claims and liabilities associated with these financial institutions are reported under other investment.

International investment position (Tables 8.3 and 8.4)

The estimate of the international investment position relates to total net asset values attributable to investing companies, that is, book values of fixed assets less accumulated depreciation provisions plus current assets less current liabilities. The book values of direct investments are likely to be less than the values at written down replacement cost and less than the market values. There are no official estimates of the market value of UK direct investment assets and liabilities. However, research by Cliff Pratten (Department of Applied Economics, University of Cambridge) indicated that, on certain assumptions, the market value of UK direct investments abroad at end-1989 might be about double their book value, while the market value of foreign direct investment in the UK might be just under double their book values at the same point of time. However there are considerable uncertainties in making such estimates.

The comparison between transactions in the balance of payments account and changes in total assets and liabilities is not affected by allowances for depreciation of fixed assets as charged to the profit and loss account; such allowances are deducted before arriving at the earnings included in the current account, and the provision for depreciation is regarded as maintaining the total book value of the existing assets. Similarly, the comparison is unaffected by the treatment of reinvested earnings from direct investments, since these appear both in the current account as earnings and in the financial account as a flow of capital adding to the stock of assets. However, the values are affected by the treatment applied in their consolidated accounts by UK companies to value newly acquired foreign companies. Under both merger and acquisition accounting the increase in the net book value can be less than the net investment to complete the acquisition. The difference represents goodwill and the other costs associated with the transaction that are written off directly against reserves.

Direct investment abroad by UK residents

Monetary financial institutions: information on the direct investment by UK registered monetary financial institutions in their foreign branches, subsidiaries and associates is collected quarterly by the Bank of England from a selection of monetary financial institutions that have a direct investment enterprise abroad. Income data are supplemented by additional information from certain monetary financial institutions that only report to the Bank of England on an annual basis. Direct investment balance sheet data are collected annually from a panel of monetary financial institutions selected by the Bank of England.

Insurance companies and other financial intermediaries: an annual inquiry forms the basis for estimates of direct investment by UK insurance companies and other financial intermediaries; these results are supplemented by a quarterly survey. Investment in foreign property by financial companies is also included here. They are estimated from the levels of such assets held by financial companies and information on their total income from abroad. In line with international standards, the investment of other financial intermediaries includes those of all holding companies.

Private non-financial and public corporations: information on direct investment by all private and public non-financial corporations is estimated from the results of ONS's annual direct investment inquiry. This inquiry covers a sample of UK companies that either have foreign affiliates or are affiliated to a foreign parent. Returns are imputed for companies that are not approached in the inquiry but which are known to have direct investment links. The estimates for the latest year are based on a quarterly inquiry with a smaller population sample. Results of the annual inquiry are available about twelve months after the end of the year and are published in a statistical bulletin and in Business Monitor MA4.

Copies of the FDI Statistical Bulletin can be found at: http://www.ons.gov.uk/ons/search/index.html?pageSize=50&newquery=fdi+statistical+bulletin

Copies of the FDI Business Monitor can be found at: http://www.ons.gov.uk/ons/search/index.html?pageSize=50&newquery=fdi+business+monitor

Households: this comprises household sector investment in property abroad. Investment in property includes the ownership of 'second homes' located outside the UK. Estimates of property ownership are based on information from the Department for Communities and Local Government (DCLG)'s Survey of English Housing (SEH). The SEH collects information from English households on the number of properties owned outside the UK. These estimates have been grossed up to estimate for all UK households. Average dwelling prices are applied as well as an estimate of property rental. For more information on the latest methodology see the *Economic Trends* article: http://www.ons.gov.uk/ons/rel/elmr/economic-trends--discontinued-/no--619--june-2005/methodological-improvements-to-uk-foreign-property-investment-statistics.pdf

Direct investment in the UK by foreign residents

Estimates for direct investment in the UK are based on the same inquiries to monetary financial institutions, financial institutions and private non-financial corporations as direct investment abroad. For direct investment in UK monetary financial institutions, the Bank of England surveys a sample of UK branches and subsidiaries of foreign-owned monetary financial institutions.

Households: limited information on property transactions was originally based on information obtained from the then Inland Revenue and on ONS estimates. From 2003, the Inland Revenue ceased to collect data, and from this point the data should be regarded as being of lower quality. ONS estimates are based on publicly reported property transactions.

Portfolio investment

Introduction

Portfolio investment comprises investment in either equity or debt securities that are not considered to have led to the acquisition of a foreign affiliate (that is, less than 10 per cent ownership) and so are classified as portfolio rather than direct investment. Portfolio investment is sub-divided into investment in equity or debt securities; debt securities are further sub-divided into investment in bonds and notes (long-term) and investment in money market instruments (short-term).

Income (Tables 4.5 and 4.6)

Earnings on equity securities consist of dividends received by investors on their holdings of shares of registered companies. Earnings on debt securities consists of interest received on investment in bonds and notes (government and municipal loan stock, and bonds and notes of private and public corporations) and money market instruments (for example commercial paper, certificates of deposit, and Treasury bills). Dividends are recorded on a paid basis and interest is recorded on an accrued basis.

Financial account (Tables 7.5 and 7.6)

Financial account transactions in equity securities comprise the acquisition or disposal in the ordinary shares of registered companies. Transactions in bonds and notes consist of the acquisition and disposal of government and municipal loan stock, and bonds and notes of registered companies. Transactions in money market instruments comprise the acquisition and disposal of government short-term paper (such as Treasury bills, certificates of deposits, and commercial paper).

International investment position (Tables 8.5 and 8.6)

As with investment income and the financial account, the international investment position is divided into investment in equity and debt securities with debt securities further subdivided into investment in bonds and notes and investment in money market instruments. Investment in both equity and debt securities are recorded at market value.

Portfolio investment abroad by UK residents

Monetary financial institutions (MFIs) (banks and building societies): estimates are derived from statutory inquiries conducted by the Bank of England. Prior to 2006, portfolio transactions by UK MFIs were based on reported transactions. From 2006 onwards, estimates of net transactions in both equity and debt securities by UK MFIs are derived from changes in reported balance sheets adjusted for both price and exchange rate effects. UK monetary financial institutions' earnings on portfolio investment abroad are collected on a quarterly basis by the Bank of England.

Insurance companies, pension funds and securities dealers: estimates are largely derived from quarterly ONS surveys. These quarterly surveys are supplemented by a more comprehensive annual survey.

Other financial intermediaries (excluding securities dealers) and private non-financial corporations: estimates are derived from survey-based asset levels to which rates of return on comparable assets shown by financial institutions are applied.

Households: estimates of investment by the household sector largely consist of investment by members of Lloyd's of London which are supplied annually by Lloyd's. They include portfolio investment income on funds which are held abroad to support business underwritten in those countries. Also included are estimates of investment in foreign equity securities acquired by UK households in exchange for their holdings of UK equities following an acquisition by a foreign direct investor. Typically, such acquisitions are funded by the issuance of shares by the investing company, rather than a cash payment. Significant levels of household ownership are most likely to exist when the UK company is a demutualised building society or privatised public utility.

Portfolio investment in the UK by foreign residents

As with portfolio investment abroad, portfolio investment in the UK is subdivided into investment in equity securities and debt securities with investment in debt securities further subdivided into investment in bonds and notes and investment in money market instruments.

Equity securities

Prior to 2007, the main sources for estimates of new investment in UK equity securities were a range of statistical surveys conducted by ONS. Data were then adjusted to take account of total levels of foreign investment in shares as indicated by the results of ONS's biennial Share Ownership Survey. The Share Ownership Survey identifies the beneficial owner of listed UK equity securities held by both UK and foreign residents. Adjustments are made to exclude holdings of a direct investment nature and to establish the beneficial ownership of nominee and third party shareholdings. From 2007, new investment in UK equity securities by non-residents is derived by residual. Non-resident investment in UK equity securities is obtained by assuming that any net transactions in UK equity securities not attributable to the domestic sectors of the UK (using all available data sources) are attributable to foreign residents.

Estimates of foreign earnings from UK equity securities consist of dividends paid to foreign holders of UK company ordinary shares. These estimates are calculated from Stock Exchange data on dividend payments, which are applied pro-rata to levels of non-resident holdings of UK shares derived from ONS's Share Ownership Surveys.

The latest Share Ownership Survey, covering end-2008, was published by ONS in January 2010. Copies of the Share Ownership Survey can be found at: http://www.ons.gov.uk/ons/rel/pnfc1/share-ownership---share-register-survey-report/2008/share-ownership---share-register-survey-report---share-ownership.pdf

No precise sector breakdown is available and an assumption is made by ONS that non-resident holdings by sector of issuer are proportional to the overall equity liabilities of each sector.

Debt securities – bonds and notes

Non-resident investment in bonds and notes are comprised of those issued by HM Government and those issued by other sectors such as monetary financial institutions and private non-financial corporations.

Monetary financial institutions: estimates for non-resident investment in bonds and notes issued by UK banks and building societies stem from statistical surveys carried out by the Bank of England and ONS estimates. Information collected by the Bank of England for identified non-resident investment is supplemented by ONS estimates. ONS estimates allocate any residual investment to non-residents (for example, any securities not identified as being held by a specific sector are assumed to be held by non-residents). Earnings on bonds and notes issued by UK monetary financial institutions are reported by those institutions to the Bank of England.

General government: investment in government bonds and notes comprises investment in British government securities (gilts) and other foreign currency bonds. Investment in British government securities by foreign central banks, international organisations and private foreign residents are measured from banking statistics and other Bank of England sources including the Central Gilts Office. Foreign earnings on British government stocks (gilts) are estimated from information on the levels outstanding and appropriate rates of interest. These earnings are calculated gross of UK income tax. Most gilts are issued by the UK Government at a discount to the redemption value. This is recorded as interest accruing over the lifetime of the gilt. Non-resident investment in UK foreign currency bonds and notes issued by central government relates to bonds issued by HM Government. Information on the total issue of these foreign currency bonds is supplied by the Bank of England. Holdings by non-residents are once again derived as the residual of total securities in issue less those held by domestic sectors. Earnings are estimated on a pro-rata basis, proportional to the levels of investment.

Other sectors (other financial institutions and private non-financial corporations): foreign investment in bonds and notes issued by other sectors is primarily estimated on the residual basis, where investment by non-residents is assumed to be the difference between total other sector bonds and notes in issues less those acquired or owned by UK residents. Information on total bonds and notes in issue and acquisition by UK residents is derived from the Bank of England and London Stock Exchange records of UK company bond issues, accumulated financial transactions, ONS surveys, and price and exchange rate movements. Earnings are estimated on a pro-rata basis, proportional to the levels of investment.

Debt securities – money market instruments

Non-resident investment in UK money market instruments consist of foreign investment in UK treasury bills, certificates of deposit and commercial paper.

Monetary financial institutions: estimates for non-resident investment in money market instruments issued by UK banks and building societies stem from statistical surveys carried out by the Bank of England and ONS. Information collected by the Bank of England for identified non-resident investment is supplemented by ONS estimates. ONS estimates allocate any residual investment to non-residents (for example, any securities not identified as being held by a specific sector are assumed to be held by non-residents). Earnings on bonds and notes issued by UK monetary financial institutions are reported by those institutions to the Bank of England.

General government: non-resident investment in government money market instruments comprises investment in UK treasury bills. Estimates for custody holdings held with UK monetary financial institutions are supplied by the Bank of England, and ONS allocates a fixed proportion of the residual (total issue less known acquisitions) to non-residents. Earnings are estimated from information on the levels outstanding and appropriate rates of interest.

Other sectors (other financial institutions and private non-financial corporations): foreign investment in money market instruments issued by other sectors is primarily estimated on the residual basis where investment by non-residents is assumed to be the difference between total other sector money market instruments in issues less those acquired or owned by UK residents. Information on total money market instruments in issue and acquisition by UK residents is derived from the Bank of England and London Stock Exchange records of UK company money market instruments issues, accumulated financial transactions, ONS surveys and price and exchange rate movements. Earnings are estimated on a pro-rata basis, proportional to the levels of investment.

Financial derivatives

Financial derivatives are defined as financial instruments that are linked to the price performance of an underlying asset and which involve the trading of financial risk. Examples of the underlying asset might include a financial instrument, commodity, bilateral foreign exchange rate, movement in stock index, or interest rate. Financial derivatives include options (on, for example, currencies, interest rates, commodities, and indices), traded financial futures, warrants, currency and interest rate swaps, forward rates agreements (FRAs), and certain credit derivatives. The rationale for separate recording of derivatives contracts in the financial account is to keep the distinction between them and other transactions (for example, securities) to which they may be linked for hedging purposes.

In Pink Book 2010, financial derivatives assets and liabilities of the banking sector were introduced from 2006 into the international investment position; these have now been included from 2004.

From Pink Book 2011, data on the derivatives business of UK securities dealers have been introduced into both the financial account and the international investment position, from 2010. An article detailing the improvements to the coverage of derivatives within the UK economic accounts can be found at: www.ons.gov.uk/ons/dcp171766_239801.pdf

Financial account (Table 7.1)

Derivatives are valued at current market prices. In Pink Book 2010, existing financial derivatives estimates for net transactions by UK banks with non-residents were revised back to 2006 as a result of methodological work to enable the introduction into the UK National Accounts of transactions with all domestic sectors. From Pink Book 2011, this revised methodology has been extended back to 2004. Prior to 2004, the banks' transactions only cover net settlement receipts/payments on interest rate swaps and forward rate agreements.

From Pink Book 2011, financial derivatives estimates for net transactions by UK securities dealers with non-residents have been included in the data from 2010.

As banks transactions are not collected, estimates are provided by the Bank of England. These are calculated by the change in the value of the derivatives portfolio, minus the net holding gains/losses. All of this information is collected by the Bank of England and explained in more detail in an article published in the *Economic and Labour Market Review* in April 2010: http://www.ons.gov.uk/ons/rel/elmr/economic-and-labour-market-review/no--4--april-2010/economic---labour-market-review.pdf

A similar method is used to derive the data for securities dealers' transactions from ONS survey data.

Balance sheets (Table FD)

Data on UK banks' gross asset and liability positions in derivatives are collected quarterly by the Bank of England through Form DQ; no data are available prior to 1998. Data on securities dealers' assets and liabilities are collected by ONS; similarly there are no data available prior to 1998.

Data published in Table FD (in chapter 8) form supplementary information, as estimates for financial derivatives have yet to be fully implemented in either the UK international investment position or in the UK's national accounts balance sheets. However, data on the financial derivatives business of UK banks are now included in the main aggregates of the international investment position from 2004, with data on the derivatives business of UK securities dealers now being included from 2010. Data for insurance companies, pension funds, unit trusts, investment trusts, open-ended investment companies, finance leasing companies, credit grantors, factoring companies and building societies are not included in the main aggregates for the UK's international investment position.

Other investment

Introduction

Other investment abroad is subdivided into trade credit, loans, currency and deposits, and other assets/liabilities.

Trade credit: consists of claims and liabilities arising from the direct extension of credit by suppliers and buyers for goods and services transactions and advance payments for work to be undertaken or currently in progress. Lending activity to facilitate trade, including those loans underwritten by the Export Credit Guarantee Department (ECGD), are treated as loans and not trade credit within the accounts. Trade credit between related firms (that is, credit received or extended between a UK business and a foreign affiliate or parent company) is treated as an investment in the affiliate or parent company, and is therefore recorded under direct investment.

Loans: comprise financial assets created by the direct lending of funds by a creditor (lender) to a debtor (borrower). This includes loans to finance trade, other loans and advances, financial leases and repurchase agreements.

Currency: consists of notes and coins that are in circulation and commonly used to make payments. UK resident holdings of foreign currency are deemed a UK asset while non-resident holdings of sterling are a UK liability. Deposits comprise both transferable (accessible on demand without penalty or restriction) and other deposits.

Other assets and liabilities: comprise any other items that are neither trade credit, loans nor deposits. The most notable other asset comprises the UK's subscriptions to international organisations while the most notable other liabilities are non-residents' prepayments of premiums and reserves against outstanding insurance claims.

Income (Tables 4.7 and 4.8)

Income predominantly comprises the interest accruing on trade credit, loans or deposits. Interest is presented net of FISIM, which is recorded within exports and imports of financial services. 'Other income payments' includes an estimate of imputed income to foreign households from UK insurance companies' technical reserves and is recorded in the balance of payments because households are regarded as owning the net equity of pension funds and life assurance reserves; that is, the funds set aside for the purpose of satisfying the claims and benefits foreseen. The estimates are derived from data collected on ONS statistical surveys.

Financial account (Tables 7.7 and 7.8)

The financial account records the drawing/repayment of loans, the addition to or withdrawals from deposits, subscriptions to international organisations, debt forgiveness, adjustments for accrued interest and prepayments of premiums and reserves against outstanding insurance claims.

International investment position (Tables 8.7 and 8.8)

The international investment position presents total trade credit, loans and deposits outstanding at end period. It also records total capital subscribed to the international organisations and levels of prepayments of premiums and reserves against outstanding insurance claims.

Other investment abroad by UK residents

Trade credit

At present only a minimal amount of data is recorded within trade credit. Some data previously recorded in this area have been reclassified as bank lending and are now within the loans data in other investment abroad. Other data are no longer suitable for inclusion and have been removed from the accounts, generally back to 1999.

Loans

These are subdivided into earnings on long-term loans and earnings on short-term loans; short-term loans are those which are repaid in full within one year.

Monetary financial institutions: MFI long-term loans comprise UK bank loans under the Export Credit Guarantee Department's guarantee. MFI short-term loans comprise sterling and foreign currency loans extended by UK banks and building societies. Information on loans extended by UK banks and from 2008, UK building societies, is collected by the Bank of England using a range of statistical inquiries. Prior to 2008, information on building society loans was supplied to the Bank of England by the Financial Services Authority. It is not possible to separate out UK monetary financial institutions earnings on lending abroad from their earnings on deposits abroad. Estimates for earnings on such loans are therefore included indistinguishably within earnings on deposits (see below).

General government: government loans are all long-term and comprise inter-government loans. Estimates are sourced from information supplied by the Department for International Development.

Public corporations: public corporation loans are all long-term and are sourced from the Export Credit Guarantee Department and the Commonwealth Development Corporation.

Currency and deposits

Currency

Estimates for transactions in foreign notes and coin by the UK private sector other than monetary financial institutions are based on tourists' expenditure.

Deposits

Estimates comprise both transferable (accessible on demand without penalty or restriction) and other deposits held abroad.

Monetary financial institutions: MFI deposits comprise UK banks' and building societies' sterling and foreign currency deposits held with deposit taking institutions abroad. Information on deposits held abroad by UK banks and from 2008, UK building societies, is collected by the Bank of England using a range of statistical inquiries. Prior to 2008, information on building society deposits was supplied to the Bank of England by the Financial Services Authority. It is not possible to separate out UK monetary financial institutions earnings on lending abroad from their earnings on deposits abroad. Estimates for earnings on such loans are therefore included indistinguishably within earnings on deposits.

Securities dealers: deposits held abroad by UK securities dealers are derived from quarterly ONS surveys. Financial transactions and interest accrued are reported directly by the institutions while end-period positions are estimated by ONS.

Other UK residents: estimates of other UK private sector deposits with banks abroad are derived from the banking statistics of countries in the Bank for International Settlements (BIS) reporting area (as defined in the Glossary). End-period positions are reported to the Bank of England, who in turn estimate net transactions. These data are then supplied to ONS. ONS then deducts deposits held abroad by UK securities dealers to avoid potential double counting. Interest on these deposits is then estimated by ONS using average quarterly levels and appropriate interest rates. Due to the limitations in the coverage of the BIS data, statistical adjustments have been applied to the financial flows data since 1994 to improve the overall coherence of the sector financial accounts. In order to maintain consistency between financial flows and balance sheet levels, corresponding coherence adjustments have been applied to the international investment position. Transactions in non-monetary gold are included here and comprise net transactions in gold which are held as financial assets by listed institutions in the London Bullion Market (LBM). These estimates are currently derived from banking statistics collected by the Bank of England. The treatment of non-monetary gold was reviewed as part of the worldwide process to revise the IMF *Balance of Payments Manual*. The main proposal is that the concept of non-monetary gold would be replaced by two categories – allocated gold (a commodity) and unallocated gold (a financial instrument). UK balance of payments will continue current practice until the treatments defined in the revised manual are implemented.

Other assets

Comprise any other items that are neither trade credit, loans nor deposits.

Central government: this includes central government subscriptions to international organisations and covers capital subscriptions to international lending bodies other than the IMF, that is, regional development banks, the International Finance Corporation and the International Fund for Agricultural Development. Some transactions are in the form of non-interest-bearing promissory notes and are included in the accounts as the subscriptions fall due, irrespective of the time of encashment of the notes. The information is obtained from official records.

Monetary financial institutions and public corporations: estimates reflect UK monetary financial institutions and the Export Credit Guarantee Department's (ECGD) debt forgiveness and offset the corresponding entry in the capital account. Information on debt forgiveness comes from the Bank of England and the ECGD.

Other sectors: these short-term assets largely relate to assets of UK insurance companies and pension funds and other financial intermediaries other than those classified under portfolio investment, estimates for which are obtained from ONS statistical surveys.

Other investment in the UK by non-residents

Trade credit

At present only a minimal amount of data are recorded within trade credit. Some data previously recorded in this area have been reclassified as bank lending (see above), and are now within the loans data in other investment abroad. Other data are no longer suitable for inclusion and have been removed from the accounts, generally back to 1999.

Loans

These are subdivided into earnings on long-term loans and earnings on short-term loans; short-term loans are those which are repaid in full within one year.

General government and public corporations: general government loans are all long-term and comprise loans received by both central government and local authorities. Central government long-term loans such as Lend-Lease and the Lines of Credit were reported by HM Treasury. The final payment on these loans was made in 2005. Also included are the loans received under the Very Short-term Financing Facility (VSTFF) taken out during 1992 and repaid in 1993. Public corporations' borrowing directly from foreign residents under the exchange cover scheme is included. Repayments under the scheme by former public corporations that have since been privatised are included under repayments from central government, to whom their foreign debt was transferred following privatisation; such debt is known as novated debt. In later years local authorities have engaged in long-term borrowing from abroad; estimates are obtained from the Department for Communities and Local Government (DCLG).

Securities dealers: estimates for securities dealers' short-term loans from abroad are estimated from information collected through ONS surveys. Since 1996 statistical adjustments have been applied to the data for securities dealers' short-term loans in order to improve the overall coherence of the sector financial accounts.

Other sectors: estimates of borrowing by other sectors are based on data reported to the Bank for International Settlements (BIS), and are generally confined to borrowing from commercial banks based within the BIS reporting area (see Glossary). End-period positions are reported to the Bank of England, who in turn estimate net transactions. These data are then supplied to ONS. ONS then deducts UK securities dealers' loans from banks abroad to avoid potential double counting. Interest on these loans is then estimated by ONS using average quarterly levels and appropriate interest rates. Due to the limitations in the coverage of the BIS data, statistical adjustments have been applied to the financial flows data since 1994 to improve the overall coherence of the sector financial accounts. In order to maintain consistency between financial flows and balance sheet levels, corresponding coherence adjustments have been applied to the international investment position. Additional information on borrowing from the European Investment Bank (EIB) is supplied directly to ONS on a quarterly basis by the EIB.

Currency and deposits

Currency

Estimates of transactions in sterling notes and coin by private foreign residents (other than monetary financial institutions) are based on ONS statistics of tourists' expenditure. While sterling bank notes are issued by the Bank of England, which is classified to monetary financial institutions, coins are issued by the Royal Mint, which is classified to the central government sector. In the absence of any separate data for notes and coin, it is assumed that notes make up 90 per cent of total notes and coin.

Deposits

Foreign deposits with UK monetary financial institutions were historically subdivided into deposits with banks and deposits with building societies. Also included are deposit liabilities of central government.

Central government: deposit liabilities of UK central government include short-term inter-government loans and transactions with non-residents under minor government accounts in the form of changes in balances not attributable elsewhere in the accounts. Since 1973 this has consisted entirely of balances held by the Paymaster General on the European Union (EU) account.

Monetary financial institutions: it is not possible to separate out foreign deposits with UK monetary financial institutions from foreign loans to UK monetary financial institutions. The estimates for foreign loans to UK monetary financial institutions are therefore included indistinguishably within deposits. Within deposits with UK monetary financial institutions, estimates for sterling deposits are derived from banking statistics and include both current and deposit accounts. Foreign currency deposits comprise all external borrowing denominated in foreign currencies by UK banks (sometimes described as euro currency transactions). They consist of changes in deposits with, and other lending to, UK monetary financial institutions from abroad. These transactions may be a reflection of (that is, the counterpart to) a variety of other foreign or domestic transactions by UK monetary financial institutions. These other transactions could be: foreign currency lending to UK residents (which are not balance of payments transactions); net purchases of foreign securities by the monetary financial institutions (which are included in direct or portfolio investment abroad as appropriate); any switching of monetary financial institutions liabilities between foreign currencies (including gold) and sterling; or any change in the amount of foreign currency capital raised by monetary financial institutions. Estimates for foreign currency deposits with UK monetary financial institutions have been calculated from the end-quarter balance sheets as reported by all UK banks and building societies to the Bank of England. Adjustments are made to the reported changes in balance sheets to exclude revaluations resulting from changes in exchange rates. UK monetary financial institutions income payments also include income payments associated with repurchase agreements and stock lending activities.

Other liabilities

These comprise any other items that are neither trade credit, loans nor deposits.

Central government: these short-term liabilities largely consist of non-interest-bearing notes, estimates for which are obtained from the Bank of England. Non-interest-bearing notes are issued by HM Government and are held by international organisations.

Other sectors: long-term liabilities consist of net equity of foreign households in life assurance reserves and pension funds, together with prepayments of premiums and reserves against outstanding claims. These are recorded in the balance of payments because households are regarded as owning the net equity of pension funds and life assurance reserves; that is, the funds set aside for the purpose of satisfying the claims and benefits foreseen. The estimates are derived from data collected on ONS statistical surveys. Short-term liabilities largely consist of additions to insurance companies' technical reserves, estimates for which are derived from ONS statistical inquiries.

Reserve assets

Introduction

Reserve assets comprise gold, convertible foreign currencies, IMF Special Drawing Rights (SDRs) and the UK's reserve position in the IMF. Currencies may be held in the form of financial instruments. From July 1979 convertible currencies also include European Currency Units acquired when 20 per cent of the gold and dollar holdings in the reserve assets were deposited on a swap basis with the European Monetary Co-operation Fund, the swap arrangement being renewed quarterly. As from January 1994 the swap was with the European Monetary Institute and as from January 1998 was with the European Central Bank. The swap arrangement was terminated in December 1998. All information on the reserve assets is recorded within the Exchange Equalisation Account by the Bank of England.

Income (Table 4.1)

Interest received on the official foreign exchange reserves and on the UK's holdings of Special Drawing Rights with the IMF and other remuneration received from the IMF (related to its holdings of sterling), is recorded within the Exchange Equalisation Account by the Bank of England.

Financial account (Table 7.9)

This item consists of the sterling equivalent, at current rates of exchange, of drawings on, and additions to the gold, convertible currencies and Special Drawing Rights (SDRs) held in the Exchange Equalisation Account; and of changes in the UK reserve position in the IMF.

International investment position (Table 8.9)

Until 1999 securities were valued at historic cost and translated to sterling. Gold was valued at the ruling official price of 35 SDRs per fine ounce until end-1977 and at end-year market rates from end-1978 to end-1999. Since 2000, all reserve assets are valued at end-period market prices and exchange rates. SDRs and convertible currencies are valued throughout at closing middle market rates of exchange.

External debt (Table 8.10)

Gross external debt is defined as the outstanding amount of those actual current, and not contingent, liabilities that require payment(s) of principal and/or interest by the debtor at some point(s) in the future and that are owed to non-residents by residents of an economy.

UK External Debt data are compiled according to the IMF's *External Debt Statistics: Guide for Compilers and Users* (www.imf.org/external/pubs/ft/eds/Eng/Guide/index.htm). The data are consistent with those contained in the UK's international investment position statement.

End-period stocks of external liabilities are classified according to institutional sector (general government, monetary authorities, monetary financial institutions and other sectors), type of instrument, and original maturity of instrument. Direct investment liabilities are separately identified.

Current transfers (Chapter 5)

Introduction

Transfers represent the provision (or receipt) of an economic value by one party without directly receiving (or providing) a counterpart item of economic value. In plain terms a transaction representing 'something for nothing' or without a quid pro quo. Transfers can be in the form of money, or of goods or services provided without the expectation of payment. Transfers are broken down into current or capital transfers. Capital transfers relate to the transfer of ownership of a fixed asset, or the forgiveness of a liability by a creditor, when no counterpart is received in return. Current transfers are all other types of transfer. Current transfers are subdivided into those made or received by general government and by other sectors. The UK's contributions to and receipts from the European Union budget are recorded on a gross basis.

General government current transfers

General government transfers include receipts, contributions and subscriptions from or to European Union (EU) institutions and other international bodies, bilateral aid and military grants. Information mainly comes from government departments (HM Treasury, Foreign & Commonwealth Office and Department for International Development).

Credits

These mainly comprise receipts of the UK general government from EU institutions, taxes on income, and social contributions paid by non-resident workers.

Current taxes on income and wealth: these are the receipts of the UK Government from taxes on the incomes of non-resident seasonal and border workers working in the UK (the incomes themselves are recorded as compensation of employees) and withholding taxes paid abroad by UK direct investment corporations. The former are estimated on the basis of the compensation of employees information derived from the International Passenger Survey and the latter from ONS surveys into foreign direct investment.

Social contributions: these represent social contributions paid to the UK National Insurance Fund by non-residents.

EU institutions: these receipts comprise the VAT Abatement and other smaller, miscellaneous EU receipts. From the 1998 edition of the Pink Book, the VAT Abatement is treated as a credit entry to the UK balance of payments, rather than netted off VAT-based contributions.

Debits

These comprise payments by the UK general government to international organisations and other non-residents.

Social security benefits: these mainly consist of National Insurance Fund retirement and war pensions paid to foreign residents.

European Union institutions: these payments are mainly the central government part of the UK contribution to the EU budget. For more detailed information, please see the methodological notes to Table 9.9.

Other international organisations: this includes contributions to the military budget of NATO, contributions to the European Regional Development Fund and agencies of the United Nations to provide economic assistance to developing countries, and subscriptions to cover the administrative expenses of various other international bodies.

Bilateral aid: this covers technical co-operation and non-project grants (project grants are included within capital transfers as they fund capital projects). Technical co-operation covers the provision of technical 'know-how' to developing and transitional countries either as qualified manpower or as facilities for the training of nationals of these countries. It is wholly funded by the UK Government and is included as a credit in 'Trade in services'.

Non-project grants are cash grants to developing countries for use in financing imports and budgetary support, together with the value of goods and services provided by the UK Government as food aid or disaster relief.

Military grants: these consist of cash grants for military purposes and the value of goods and services of a military nature provided without charge to foreign countries and international organisations by the UK Government.

Other sectors' transfers

Other sectors' transfers cover current taxes paid, receipts and payments to EU institutions, net non-life insurance premiums and claims, and other payments and receipts of households, including remittances.

Credits

Private social contributions: this consists of the actual social contributions paid by non-residents to UK private pension schemes, plus the related imputed contribution supplement, less the related service charge. Data are sourced from ONS surveys to pension funds.

Receipts from EU institutions: comprise those paid out of the EU's Agricultural Guarantee Fund and Social Fund. They are treated as non-government transfers within the national accounts and balance of payments, as the UK Government acts only as an agent for the ultimate beneficiary of the transfer.

Net non-life insurance premiums: comprise the actual premiums received by UK insurance companies from non-residents plus the related imputed premium supplement, less the related insurance service charge. The sources for these data are ONS surveys of insurance corporations, which collect premiums by type of insurance product, and Lloyd's of London.

Net non-life insurance claims: these are based on information supplied to the International Trade in Services survey on insurance claims received from non-resident insurance companies.

Other receipts of households: consists of two main components:

- Remittances, which are current transfers in cash or in kind sent by households resident in foreign economies to households resident in the UK. These estimates are statistical projections mainly based on bilateral information on partner countries' remittance flows to the UK, where these are published or have been made available to ONS, or on the basis of entries in the IMF *Balance of Payments Statistics Yearbook*, with fixed percentages of the total workers' remittances for certain countries assumed to go to the UK
- UK charities transfer receipts from abroad. These are based on information from a 1995 survey to charities

Debits

Current taxes on income: these are taxes on the incomes of UK seasonal and border workers (recorded as compensation of employees) working abroad and withholding taxes paid abroad by UK direct investment corporations.

The former are estimated on the basis of the compensation of employees information derived from the International Passenger Survey and the latter from ONS surveys into foreign direct investment.

Private social benefits: comprise private pensions paid abroad, plus the change in net equity in pension fund reserves of non-residents. The data source is ONS's survey of pension funds.

Payments to EU institutions: these comprise agricultural and sugar levies, customs duties and VAT-based contributions. The data source is HM Treasury.

Net non-life insurance premiums: this covers premiums paid by UK companies to non-resident insurance companies collected via the International Trade in Services survey.

Net non-life insurance claims: this covers settlement of claims by UK insurance companies to non-resident claimants, which are regarded as a transfer debit. The total of claims equals the total of net premiums (service charges having been deducted), as the essential function of non-life insurance is to redistribute resources. The sources for these data are ONS surveys of insurance corporations, and Lloyd's of London.

Other payments of households: these include two main components:

- Remittances, which are current transfers in cash or in kind sent by UK households to households resident in foreign economies. In many cases these are sent by long-term migrant workers in the UK to friends or relatives still resident in their country of origin. Data were obtained from exchange control records until 1979. Estimates since 1979 are statistical projections mainly based on the exchange control data and also some bilateral information on partner countries' remittance flows to the UK. The projections also take account of information on the value of gifts of money and goods sent abroad by parcel post
- UK charities' transfers abroad. These are based on information from a 1995 survey to charities

Capital account (Chapter 6)

The capital account comprises two components: capital transfers and the acquisition/disposal of non-produced, non-financial assets.

Capital transfers

Capital transfers are those involving transfers of ownership of fixed assets, transfers of funds associated with the acquisition or disposal of fixed assets, and cancellation of liabilities by creditors without any counterparts being received in return. As with current transfers, they can be subdivided into general government transfers and other sectors transfers. The main sources of information are government departments (Department for International Development and HM Treasury) and the Bank of England. Compensation payments from the EU related to the destruction of animals to combat BSE and foot and mouth disease are also included here.

General government capital transfers

These consist of debt forgiveness and project grants (there are no receipts in recent years).

Debits

Debt forgiveness is defined as the voluntary cancellation of debt between a creditor, in this case the UK Government, and a debtor in another country. Data are supplied by the Department for International Development. Project grants are cash grants to developing countries for the establishment of production and infrastructure facilities. Such transfers are distinguished from current transfers as they are conditional on the acquisition of fixed assets. Data are supplied by the Department for International Development.

Other sectors capital transfers

These include migrants' transfers, debt forgiveness and capital transfers from European Union Institutions.

Credits

Migrants' transfers: these are recorded as being equal to the net worth of the migrants, as they arrive in the UK. Estimates are based on information on number of migrants and average assets being transferred as collected on the International Passenger Survey.

Transfers from EU institutions: Regional Development Fund and Agricultural Fund for Regional Development receipts from the EU are assumed to be capital rather than current transfers as they relate to infrastructure projects. Data are supplied by HM Treasury. Other capital transfers include agricultural compensation scheme payments relating to the destruction of animals to combat BSE and foot and mouth Disease.

Debits

Migrants' transfers: these represent the net worth of emigrants as they leave the UK.

Estimates are based on information on the number of migrants and average assets being transferred as supplied to the International Passenger Survey.

Debt forgiveness: this consists of non-government debt forgiveness by monetary financial institutions and public corporations. Data on monetary financial institutions is supplied by the Bank of England and data on public corporations is supplied by the Export Credits Guarantee Department.

Sales/purchases of non-produced, non-financial assets

This heading covers intangibles such as patents, copyrights, franchises, leases and other transferable contracts, and goodwill; and transactions involving tangible assets that may be used or needed for the production of goods and services but have not themselves been produced, such as land and sub-soil assets. The use of such assets is recorded under trade in services as royalties and license fees; only the outright purchase or sale of such assets is recorded in the capital account.

The International Trade in Services (ITIS) survey has collected information on the sale and purchase of copyrights, patents and transferable contracts from 1996. Such transactions are indistinguishable from other areas of the current account for years before 1996.

Geographical breakdown on the current account and international investment position (Chapters 9 and 10)

Introduction

The geographical data is broadly consistent with level 2 of Eurostat's Vade Mecum (67 individual countries, 15 geographical regions and 5 continents). Data for the European Union (EU) relate to the membership following the enlargement of 1 January 2007. EU Institutions are included in the EU aggregate and are excluded from the International Organisations total. Separate data for Belgium and Luxembourg are not available for periods before 1999, also separate data for Serbia and Montenegro are not available for periods before 2007. Data for China exclude Hong Kong, which is shown as an individual item.

Reliability of estimates

The UK's balance of payments accounts are primarily compiled on a global basis. Not all of the data sources used in preparing the accounts attempt to distinguish transactions on a full country basis, although the majority do. Where individual country information is not reported, estimates are made by using the geographical detail for a related category; for example, the geographical breakdown of financial assets and liabilities is used to allocate some components of investment income.

In addition to the imputation of geographical detail for some categories where the data are incomplete, there remains a margin of uncertainty regarding the accuracy of reported data by country. The finer the level of geographical detail sought, the greater the likelihood of misallocation. Enterprises are encouraged to make their best estimates when asked to report geographical data but, as country allocation may not be a crucial aspect of the information from which details are extracted, a significant degree of estimation may occur.

Given these conceptual and practical limitations, these estimates should be seen as a broad indication of the economic relationships between the UK and the rest of the world economies. They will be more reliable and meaningful in terms of broad geographical areas and major partner countries than for smaller partners. Estimates for recent years are currently more reliable than those for earlier years since some data sources do not extend back over the whole published period.

Approach for country allocation

The following notes summarise the main criteria of country allocation adopted for the various categories of the current account. In general the figures are not likely to be consistent with those recorded by countries which allocate regional balance of payments estimates on a cash settlements basis. An analysis of UK asymmetries with its EU and US partners was published in the March 2005 edition of *Economic Trends*, which can be found at:
http://www.ons.gov.uk/ons/rel/elmr/economic-trends--discontinued-/no--616--march-2005/economic-trends.pdf

Trade in goods

Exports of goods are allocated to the country of destination; imports of goods are allocated according to the country of consignment. However, export figures from a country (A) to another country (B) may over-estimate the value of goods actually consumed in that country (B) if the importer forwards the goods on to another country (C). There are several reasons for this: 'the Rotterdam/Antwerp effect' (exports are properly attributed to the country where the port of discharge is located, following international convention, but are then re-exported to the country of final destination); other transit trade (goods passing straight through the country); and triangular trade (where goods are sold from member state A to B and on to C, but the goods move directly from A to C). 'The Rotterdam/Antwerp effect' is a particular issue with the UK because of exports routed through Rotterdam in the Netherlands and Antwerp in Belgium. No information is available on the value of UK exports that are subsequently shipped on to other countries, although investigations are taking place. The principal data source for trade in goods is HMRC (see the methodological notes on 'Trade in goods (Chapter 2)' for more details).

Trade in services

The geographical breakdown of exports and imports of services are largely based on the existing sources of information for the global estimates, although there is some use of proxy information for some components. The change from an industry to a product-based presentation with the introduction of the fifth edition of the IMF *Balance of Payments Manual* in 1998, and the consequent change to data collection, means that data from 1996 onwards are largely based on reported geographical breakdowns of the new products. Earlier geographical estimates are based on the industry-based geographical breakdowns in the fourth edition of the IMF *Balance of Payments Manual*, adjusted to take the changes to the trade in services classification into account.

Sea transport: estimates relating to ships owned or chartered by UK operators are taken from inquiries carried out by the Chamber of Shipping.

Geographical breakdowns of freight services on exports and cross trades are allocated using the ports at which the goods are unloaded. For non-resident operators' freight on UK imports, the nationality of the exporting country is used as a proxy to allocate the freight payments. The resulting proportions are used to calculate the shares of non-resident operators' disbursements in the UK. Disbursements abroad by UK operators are supplied annually by the Chamber of Shipping.

Passenger revenue export estimates are derived from information supplied annually by the Chamber of Shipping. Passenger revenue import estimates are based on assumptions about the likely markets for cruises and on other information relating to the movements of UK shipping.

Air transport: passenger revenue exports are based on information supplied to ONS by the Civil Aviation Authority, which gives the required country analysis of fares paid. Other transactions with foreign airlines are allocated by nationality of airline. Receipts by UK airlines from foreign passengers are allocated to the countries in which tickets are purchased. Freight services on UK imports earned by foreign airlines are allocated to the countries of consignment of the imports.

Other transport: rail passenger exports are based on assumptions of the likely nationality of channel tunnel users. Rail imports are allocated entirely to France. Estimates for road freight exports and imports are based on information supplied by the Road Haulage Association. This information includes details of vehicle load and country of destination or country of origin. Pipeline transport is based on those countries that are assumed to import / export North Sea oil and gas.

Travel: a detailed geographical split of travel expenditure, both exports and imports, are obtained from the International Passenger Survey. Allocation of expenditure of overseas visitors to the UK is by country of residence. UK residents' expenditures abroad are allocated to the country in which most time was spent or, if this cannot be determined, the furthest country visited. As a result, expenditure in countries with appreciable numbers of transit tourists may be understated.

Other services: data for communication, construction, computer and information, royalties, other business and personal services are largely based on information supplied to the

ITIS survey, supplemented with information from Royal Mail and Lloyd's registry for shipping.

Insurance services: estimates are based on detailed geographical data provided by Lloyd's of London, as well as the ITIS survey for insurance imports provided to non-insurance institutions. The geographical split of trade in goods' imports is used as a proxy for freight insurance imports. Geographical splits for other insurance services are based on fixed weights.

Financial services: regular geographical information on gross flows is obtained from the Bank of England for banking services (including FISIM), and from the ITIS survey for financial service exports and imports from non-financial institutions. The geographical breakdown of non-bank financial corporation service exports are imputed using banking geographical data as a proxy.

Government services: for the major components, detailed geographical information on the location of those receiving or making payments is available from returns provided by the Ministry of Defence, Department for Work and Pensions, and the Foreign and Commonwealth Office. The United States Air Force has also provided data on expenditure of US Forces in the UK. Expenditure by foreign embassies and consulates in the UK is based on information supplied by some overseas embassies and statistical institutions, supplemented by information on numbers of accredited diplomats by country.

Income

Compensation of employees: estimates of the geographical breakdown of seasonal and border workers' earnings are based on information supplied to the International Passenger Survey. Figures for the earnings of locally engaged staff are based on information supplied by government departments.

Investment income and international investment position

Direct investment income: figures are based on the quarterly and annual foreign investment surveys and include reinvested profits. Geographical information is based on the country of registration of the immediate foreign parent company and the location of the foreign affiliate, except for banks where the information relates to the country of residence of the ultimate owner (for inward investment) or the country of residence in which the direct investment enterprise is located.

Portfolio investment income: credits are the earnings accruing to UK residents from their investment in equities and debt securities, in the form of bonds and notes and money market instruments, issued by foreign institutions. Global estimates are derived from surveys of UK end-investors (monetary financial institutions, securities dealers, unit and investment trusts, insurance companies, pension funds and some non-financial companies).

Deriving a geographical breakdown of portfolio investment income flows has been one of the most problematic areas of balance of payments compilation. Portfolio investment income is particularly difficult to allocate correctly to the actual country owning or issuing the security, as the transactions are often made through financial intermediaries in a third country. However, with the launch and subsequent expansion of the IMF's Coordinated Portfolio Investment Survey (CPIS), an important new data source has become available. Participants in the CPIS collect a geographical breakdown of their portfolio investment assets, which are coordinated and disseminated by the IMF.

Data on the geographical breakdown of portfolio investment credits are derived from the UK's contribution to the CPIS exercise from 2001. For monetary financial institutions, Bank of England information on the geographical breakdown of levels is applied to the estimates of global earnings obtained by surveys of UK monetary financial institutions. Similarly for non-banks, a geographical breakdown of portfolio investment income is derived from the geographical breakdown of portfolio investment assets.

Information on the geographical breakdown of UK portfolio investment debits (dividends and interest payments made to overseas residents by issuers of UK securities), are based on other countries' participation in the CPIS exercise. The IMF acts as a central clearing house for the compilation of aggregate data from countries that have participated in the CPIS and disseminate the information to balance of payments compilers. These data can provide us with information on participating countries' holdings of UK-issued equity and debt securities. For earlier years, surveys of share ownership are used to allocate portfolio holdings of UK equity securities and associated dividends by country of holder. For interest on holdings of debt securities, data derived from the CPIS exercises from 2001 onwards have been used to estimate the geographical breakdown.

Other investment income: gross interest flows between UK monetary financial institutions and the rest of the world are estimated by the Bank of England by allocating global interest receipts and payments in proportion to the corresponding levels of assets and liabilities of UK monetary financial institutions. Interest flows for UK non-bank deposits with, and borrowing from, banks in the BIS reporting area are allocated in proportion to the levels supplied by the BIS. The interest on reserve assets is estimated from official records. Figures for UK monetary financial institutions are used as proxies to estimate a country breakdown for the remaining components of earnings on other investment.

Adjustments applied to the global earnings on other investment to exclude the Channel Islands and the Isle of Man have been used to estimate other investment income between the UK and the offshore islands. These data are included within 'Other Europe'.

Financial derivative balance sheets: the geographical breakdown of UK monetary financial institutions gross assets and liabilities positions in financial derivatives are collected on a quarterly basis by the Bank of England via Form DQ. A geographical breakdown was introduced into the international investment position from 2006.

Current transfers

There are very few data sources for current transfers that allocate transactions on a country basis – these are outlined below. The geographical allocation of withholding taxes is based on the geographical allocation of inward and outward direct investment as published in Business Monitor MA4. The geographical allocation of insurance premiums is based on information supplied by Lloyd's of London. Data on EU transfers are provided by HM Treasury, and the geographical allocation of social security and aid payments are supplied by the Department for Work and Pensions and the Department for International Development, respectively. Other geographical breakdowns are based on proxy data and global transfer estimates.

UK official transactions with institutions of the EU (Table 9.9)

This table presents all the official transactions between the UK Government and the Institutions of the European Union. The series are the same as those shown in Table 12.1 of the Blue Book but the presentation here reflects Balance of Payments rather than National Accounts classification of transactions.

Some of the transfers are classified to Other sectors (rather than Central government) as they are paid by or to non-government sectors; however they are still classified as official transactions because the money is collected from or paid to non-government sectors by the UK Government on behalf of the EU. The source for much of the data is HM Treasury (HMT), who are responsible for the UK's official transactions with the EU. These data represent the cash movements in and out of government bank accounts for transactions with the EU. Any divergences from this source – to accord with the reporting conventions required for Balance of Payments and National Accounts – are detailed below. The data sourced from HMT are also available in chapter 3 of the HMT White Paper on EU Finances found at the following web address:
www.hm-treasury.gov.uk/int_eu_statefraud.htm

Credits

Exports of services

This series represents the part of the import levies collected by the UK Government on behalf of the EU that the UK Government retains to cover the costs of collection. The percentage retained was 10 per cent up until 2000 and has been 25 per cent from 2001 onwards. It is treated as an export of a government service. The exports of services to EU Institutions series in Table 9.3 differs from this one in that the series includes services provided to EU Institutions by UK private companies.

Other sectors current transfers

These largely comprise receipts from the Agricultural Guarantee Fund and the European Social Fund. The receipts from the Agricultural Guarantee Fund are classified as subsidies and are recorded on an accruals basis based on the subsidies paid to farmers by the Rural Payments Agency.

Central government current transfers

These mainly comprise the Fontainebleau Abatement but also include a small number of miscellaneous payments to EU institutions and research councils. Since 1984, the UK's third own resources (VAT-based) contribution to the EU budget has been abated in recognition of the relatively low level of its receipts, compared with its contributions to the Community Budget. Broadly, the UK receives a VAT abatement of its gross contributions equal to two-thirds of the difference between its unabated contribution and its receipts. This is deducted a year in arrears. Since the 1998 edition of the Pink Book, this abatement has been treated as a credit entry to the UK balance of payments rather than simply being netted off VAT-based contributions.

Other sectors capital transfers

In most years these consist entirely of receipts from the Agricultural Fund for Regional Development and the European Regional Development Fund. Other capital transfers from EU institutions are payments to farmers under agricultural compensation schemes related to the destruction of animals during the BSE and Foot and Mouth disease outbreaks.

Debits

Other sectors current transfers

These comprise the UK's traditional own resource and third own resource contributions to the EU. The former are customs duties paid on a range of products imported from non-member states, and levies charged on the production of sugar to recover part of the costs of subsidising the export of surplus EU sugar on to the world market. EU third own resources are VAT-based contributions which represent a notional extra 1 per cent on the VAT base, but are capped at 0.5 per cent of Gross National Income (GNI), hence the adjustment to VAT contributions. Payments of both traditional and third own resource contributions are classified as taxes paid direct to the EU. Estimates are sourced from HMRC and are converted to an accruals basis using agreed methodologies.

Central government current transfers

This mainly consists of the UK Government's fourth own resource contribution. This is calculated as a fixed percentage of UK GNI, increased or rebated according to whether within the EU budget as a whole, expenditure exceeds or falls short of revenue. There are also a small number of miscellaneous payments to EU institutions under this heading.

Trade in Goods and Services additional tables (Tables 9.10, 9.11, 9.12, 9.13 and 9.14)

Tables 9.10 and 9.11 show imports of services from and exports of services to selected partner countries broken down by the 11 broad categories of services for the latest two years. The details of the methods of country allocation are outlined in the trade in services section above. To avoid disclosing data on individual companies, the tables have been arranged to remove these disclosive items. This is done wherever possible by suppressing the item so that non-disclosing headings are preserved.

Table 9.12 shows the top-50 trading partners for imports and exports of goods and services for the last two years for which data are available. Again the details of the methods of country allocation are outlined above in the goods and services sections.

Table 9.13 shows estimates of the UK's exports and imports of services with all partner countries for the latest two years. Countries not listed in the tables are assumed to have total transactions in services with the UK of less than £0.5 million. The details of the methods of country allocation are outlined in the section on trade in services above. The data sources which have full country breakdowns of transactions in services are the ITIS survey and the IPS, which between them account for around 70 per cent of the source data for total trade in services. Data from these sources have been used as proxies to estimate the very detailed country breakdowns where these are not available for other data sources.

Table 9.14 shows the UK's data for trade in services compared with world totals and those for G8 countries. The data for these are sourced from the IMF. This data is not available for the latest year as it will not have been published yet. No world balance is included as this should in theory be zero, but in practise because of asymmetries it tends to have either positive or negative values.

Further information on UK balance of payments

The following articles of interest relate to UK balance of payments statistics:

Current Account Asymmetries with the European Union, Annual Report 2004

A report on current account asymmetries for 2004.

Author: Libby Cox

Current account asymmetries occur when one country's data do not correspond to the same data for the same transaction reported by its partner countries. This report analyses asymmetries between the UK current account and the rest of the European Union. Additional data is presented regarding asymmetries between the UK and the US.

http://www.ons.gov.uk/ons/rel/elmr/economic-trends--discontinued-/no--616--march-2005/current-account-asymmetries-with-the-european-union.pdf

Analysis of past revisions to UK Trade statistics

The past revisions performance for UK Trade statistics explained.

Author: David Ruffles

This article presents an analysis of the past revisions performance for UK Trade statistics, looks at the statistically significant mean or average revisions seen in the figures for total trade, identifies the main causes of these revisions, and describes what is being done to improve the first published estimates.

www.ons.gov.uk/ons/rel/uktrade/uk-trade/analysis-of-past-revisions-to-uk-trade-statistics/analysis-of-past-revisions-to-uk-trade-statistics-.pdf

Report on impact of MTIC on UK Trade statistics

Report on further research into the impact of Missing Trader Fraud on UK Trade Statistics, Balance of Payments and National Accounts.

Authors: David Ruffles, Tricia Williams (HM Revenue & Customs)

This article was a follow-up to the article published in the August 2003 edition of *Economic Trends* which is available on the ONS website. It summarises the work carried out since July 2003 to review the estimates of the impact of Missing Trader Intra-Community (MTIC) VAT Fraud on UK Trade Statistics, Balance of Payments and National Accounts, and to investigate potential methods of estimating acquisition fraud.

http://www.ons.gov.uk/ons/rel/uktrade/uk-trade/report-on-impact-of-mtic-on-uk-trade-statistics/report-on-impact-of-mtic-on-uk-trade-statistics-.pdf

Methodological improvements to UK foreign property investment statistics

New methodology to measure ownership of foreign property by UK households and estimates the value of property owned at the end of 2003 to be £23 billion.

Author: Deborah Nicole Aspden

This article presents new methodology to measure ownership of foreign property by UK households. It is based on the Office of the Deputy Prime Minister's (ODPM) Survey of English Housing (SEH). The new methodology estimates the value of foreign property ownership in 2003/2004 to be just above £23 billion – more than double the estimate for 1999/2000. Investment is highest in Europe, with Spain and France being the preferred locations for investment.

http://www.ons.gov.uk/ons/rel/elmr/economic-trends--discontinued-/no--619--june-2005/methodological-improvements-to-uk-foreign-property-investment-statistics.pdf

Revisions Analysis to Quarterly Current Account Balance of Payments Data

An analysis of revisions made to balance of payments quarterly current account data between 1998 Q4 and 2003 Q3, an update of the previous article published in the August 2005 issue of *Economic Trends*.

Author: Mala Mistry

This article focuses on revisions to current account credits and debits and how these influence revision to the current account balance. The article also explores the chronological evolution of revisions, revisions to current account components and provides explanation for more prominent revisions occurring over the period analysed.

http://www.ons.gov.uk/ons/rel/elmr/economic-and-labour-market-review/no--5--may-2007/revisions-analysis-to-quarterly-current-account-balance-of-payments-data.pdf

Overview of UK National Accounts and Balance of Payments: Blue Book and Pink Book 2008

Accompanies publication of Blue Book and Pink Book datasets, and explains in detail the methodological changes and results.

Authors: Ross Meader and Geoff Tily

This article presents details of the Quarterly National Accounts and Balance of Payments estimates published on 30 September 2008. These are consistent with the annual Blue Book and Pink Book. The datasets reflect the introduction of a new method for measuring financial intermediation, incorporation of annual benchmark survey data and supply-use balancing of 2004-2006, and latest quarterly and monthly data for more recent periods.

http://www.ons.gov.uk/ons/rel/elmr/economic-and-labour-market-review/no--10--october-2008/overview-of-uk-national-accounts-and-balance-of-payments--blue-book-and-pink-book-2008.pdf

Methods explained: The balance of payments

Describes the main features and important trends in the UK Balance of Payments.

Author: Graeme Chamberlin

This article describes the main features of the UK Balance of Payments. The balance of payments essentially records one nation's transactions with the rest of the world - relating to conventional trade in goods and services, income flows and the transfer in ownership of financial assets across borders. The international investment position, or net asset position, is the part of the balance of payments that records net stocks of the UK's foreign assets and liabilities. The relationship between this and investment income is also analysed. Finally, the impact of the global recession and credit crunch on recent balance of payments data is presented.

www.ons.gov.uk/ons/rel/elmr/economic-and-labour-market-review/no--9--september-2009/economic---labour-market-review.pdf

Coordinated Portfolio Investment Survey, 2002 to 2007

Describes the changing patterns of UK portfolio investment holdings overseas.

Author: Kevin Madden

This article analyses the final results from the Coordinated Portfolio Investment Survey (CPIS) 2007 for the UK and compares these with the 2002 results. An article on portfolio investment holdings by country of residency was last published by the Office for National Statistics (ONS) three years ago. This article updates events since that time, focusing on proportionate movements in the estimates between 2002 and 2007 across geographical regions.

http://www.ons.gov.uk/ons/rel/elmr/economic-and-labour-market-review/no--11--november-2009/coordinated-portfolio-investment-survey--2002-to-2007.pdf

The changing nature of the UK's trade deficits, 1985–2008

Looks at the evolution of the trade deficit and the factors explaining it in the UK.

Author: Valerie Fender

This article considers changes in the nature of the balance of trade between 1985 and 2008. The first section examines the theories behind trade and the position of the UK relative to its trading partners. Periods of deficit and surplus between these dates are then analysed individually, drawing comparisons. Lastly, the composition of the balance of trade in each period and the fundamental reasons driving either the surplus or deficit are discussed. The analysis concludes that there are some fundamental similarities between the causes of each trade deficit, although there have also been large structural changes in the composition of UK exports and imports due to developments in the global economy.

http://www.ons.gov.uk/ons/rel/elmr/economic-and-labour-market-review/no--1--january-2010/the-changing-nature-of-the-uk-s-trade-deficits--1985---2008.pdf

Incorporating derivatives data in the National Accounts and Balance of Payments

Outlines how these data will be introduced into the financial accounts and balance sheets for the 2010 Blue and Pink Books.

Author: Paul Cullinane

This article outlines forthcoming changes to the National Accounts and Balance of Payments. The Office for National Statistics (ONS) aims to introduce data on derivatives business of UK banks into the financial accounts and balance sheets for the 2010 Blue Book and Balance of Payments Pink Book. Revisions will go back to the start of 2006. In the National Accounts, currently only limited transaction data is published for the bank, central government and rest of the world sectors. Data for the rest of the world sector are also presented within the Balance of Payments statistics. Additional balance sheet data are published annually in Blue Book Table 4.5 and Pink Book Table FD. Derivative transactions which take place exclusively between other sectors of the economy, such as other (non-bank) financial institutions and private non-financial corporations, will be included once reliable data sources are available.

http://www.ons.gov.uk/ons/rel/elmr/economic-and-labour-market-review/no--4--april-2010/incorporating-derivatives-data-in-the-national-accounts-and-balance-of-payments.pdf

The UK's international investment position

Describes the recent path of the UK's net asset position with the rest of the world.

Authors: Damian Whittard and Jawed Khan

This paper describes the path of the UK's net asset position with the rest of the world. Notwithstanding that the UK has run a substantial current account deficit for over a quarter of a century, at the beginning of 2009 the net asset position was not far off balance. The paper begins by detailing recent developments in both the UK's overseas balance sheet, known as the international investment position (IIP), and the current account deficit. It examines the link between the IIP and the cumulative current account deficit over the past forty years and explains that the divergence between the two is due to other changes. The paper then introduces a model which enables a decomposition of these other changes into currency, price and other volume effects. The results are reported in terms of annual and quarterly changes before conclusions are drawn.

http://www.ons.gov.uk/ons/rel/elmr/economic-and-labour-market-review/no--6--june-2010/the-uk-s-international-investment-position.pdf

United Kingdom Economic Accounts – Improving the coverage of derivatives data in the National Accounts and Balance of Payments

This article outlines changes to the National Accounts and Balance of Payments, as a result of the ONS introducing new data on derivatives business.

Author: Stephanie Duff

This article outlines changes to the National Accounts and Balance of Payments, as a result of the ONS introducing new data on derivatives business. Following the recommendation three of the article Walker G (2011) 'Developing financial statistics for policy', ONS are extending the coverage of data on derivatives in the National Accounts. From 2010 ONS has improved its coverage of derivatives business by including data from securities dealers. In the coming years ONS aims to improve further its coverage of derivative transactions which take place between other non-bank financial institutions and other sectors of the economy such as private non-financial corporations and the rest of the world once reliable data sources become available.

www.ons.gov.uk/ons/dcp171766_239801.pdf

Methods changes in the 2011 Blue Book

This article summarises the main changes being introduced in this year's annual production of the Blue Book and related publications.

Author: Glenn Everett

In the 2011 edition of the UK Blue Book (BB11), significant changes were introduced: new industrial and product classifications (SIC07 and CPA08 respectively), improved methods of deflation and some additional improvements; largely in improved methods for the financial services and planned revisions to data. This article summarises the main changes and provides information on the key changes to systems and methods, data revisions and functional modifications. It concludes with an outline of future work and improvements.

www.ons.gov.uk/ons/rel/naa1-rd/united-kingdom-national-accounts/method-changes-in-blue-book-2011/ard-method-changes-in-blue-book-2011.pdf

Other articles

Older articles which may be of interest, published in *Economic Trends*, include:

'Geographical breakdown of income in the balance of payments', November 1999

http://www.ons.gov.uk/ons/rel/elmr/economic-trends--discontinued-/no--552--november-1999/geographical-breakdown-of-income-in-the-balance-of-payments.pdf

'Geographical breakdown of income in the balance of payments: further improvements to the methodology for portfolio investment income', December 2000

http://www.ons.gov.uk/ons/rel/elmr/economic-trends--discontinued-/no--565--december-2000/geographical-breakdown-of-income-in-the-balance-of-payments--further-improvements-to-the-methodology-for-portfolio-investment-income.pdf

'IMF Co-ordinated Portfolio Investment Survey', May 2003

http://www.ons.gov.uk/ons/rel/elmr/economic-trends--discontinued-/no--594--april-2003/imf-co-ordinated-portfolio-investment-survey.pdf

'Geographical breakdown of the UK International Investment Position', June 2004

http://www.ons.gov.uk/ons/rel/elmr/economic-trends--discontinued-/no--607--june-2004/geographical-breakdown-of-the-uk-investment-position.pdf

Glossary

Acceptances

See 'Bills and acceptances'.

Accrued interest

A method of recording transactions to relate them to the period when the exchange of ownership of the goods, services or financial asset applies. For example, value added tax accrues when the expenditure to which it relates takes place, but HM Revenue and Customs (HMRC) receive the cash some time later. The difference between accruals and cash results in the creation of an asset and liability in the financial accounts, shown as amounts receivable or payable.

Advance and progress payments

Payments made for goods in advance of completion and delivery of the goods.

Affiliates

Branches, subsidiaries or associate companies.

Allocation of SDRs

See 'Special Drawing Rights'.

Arbitrage

A technique of deriving profit with little or no risk of loss by exploiting temporary misalignments in the price of financial instruments, or of one instrument in different markets.

Assets

This term commonly refers to financial assets that are claims on non-residents, from whose point of view the same item is a liability to a UK resident. Among reserve assets, however, gold and SDRs have a value which exists independently of any corresponding liabilities. Real assets such as merchandise, although they may be entered in company accounts as assets, are seldom described as assets in balance of payments analysis.

Associated companies

Companies in which the investing company has a substantial equity interest (usually this means that it holds between 10 per cent and 50 per cent of the equity share capital) and is in a position to exercise a significant influence on the company. (See 'Subsidiary').

Balancing item

See 'Net errors and omissions'.

Bank of England – Issue Department

This part of the Bank of England deals with the issue of bank notes on behalf of central government. It was formerly classified to central government though it is now part of the central bank/monetary authorities sector. Its activities include, inter alia, market purchases of commercial bills from UK banks.

Bank for International Settlements (BIS)

An international organisation which fosters international monetary and financial co-operation and serves as a bank for central banks.

The BIS fulfils this mandate by acting as:

- a forum to promote discussion and policy analysis among central banks and within the international financial community
- a centre for economic and monetary research
- a prime counterparty for central banks in their financial transactions
- agent or trustee in connection with international financial operations

Established on 17 May 1930, the BIS is the world's oldest international financial organisation, which has its head office based in Basel, Switzerland.

The most recent BIS data used within the UK balance of payments accounts covers non-bank borrowing from banks in the following countries: Algeria, Argentina, Australia, Austria, Belgium, Bosnia and Herzegovina, Brazil, Bulgaria, Canada, Chile, China, Croatia, the Czech Republic, Denmark, Estonia, Finland, France, Germany, Greece, Hong Kong SAR, Hungary, Iceland, India, Indonesia, Ireland, Israel, Italy, Japan, Korea, Latvia, Lithuania, Macedonia (FYR), Malaysia, Mexico, the Netherlands, New Zealand, Norway, the Philippines, Poland, Portugal, Romania, Russia, Saudi Arabia, Serbia, Singapore, Slovakia, Slovenia, South Africa, Spain, Sweden, Switzerland, Thailand, Turkey, the United Kingdom and the United States, plus the European Central Bank.

The data used for balance of payments purposes are locational banking statistics on a residence basis.

Banking statistics

A term used in this publication to denote an integrated set of returns, covering all UK banks, and collected by the Bank of England. The returns were first introduced in late 1974 and during 1975. Since then, various reviews of the requirements of data from banks have been conducted and forms amended, introduced or dropped as necessary. The data collected cover all listed banks up to the end of 1981 and the revised group of institutions classified as UK banks from 1982 onwards. It collects, on a regular basis, extensive information relating to the levels of, and changes in, assets and liabilities. Revised banking returns were introduced from the end of 1997 to reflect the requirements of the IMF *Balance of Payments Manual* 5th edition and to remove the Channel Islands and the Isle of Man from the definition of the economic territory of the UK.

Banks (UK)

Banks are defined as all financial institutions recognised by the Bank of England as UK banks. For statistical purposes, this includes:

- institutions which have a permission under Part 4 of the Financial Services and Markets Act 2000 (FSMA) to accept deposits, other than:
  - credit unions
  - firms which have a permission to accept deposits only in the course of carrying out contracts of insurance in accordance with that permission
  - friendly societies
  - building societies
- European Economic Area credit institutions with a permission under Schedule 3 to FSMA to accept deposits through a UK branch
- the Banking and Issue Departments of the Bank of England (the latter from April 1998)

Prior to December 2001, banks were defined as all financial institutions recognised by the Bank of England as UK banks for statistical purposes, including the UK offices of institutions authorised under the Banking Act 1987, the Banking and Issue Departments of the Bank of England (the latter from April 1998), and deposit-taking UK branches of 'European Authorised Institutions'. This includes UK branches of foreign banks, but not the offices abroad of these or of any British owned banks.

An updated list of banks appears regularly in the Bank of England's Monetary and Financial Statistics publication, available at:

www.bankofengland.co.uk/statistics/ms

Bills and acceptances

A bill is an unconditional order in writing addressed by the drawer to the drawee to pay the drawer a fixed sum on a specified date. A UK resident may draw a bill in sterling on a foreign resident representing credit extended by the UK resident to the foreign resident. If the UK resident sells the bill to a UK bank, generally at a price less than the nominal value of the bill, the bank is said to discount the bill, and the claim on the foreign resident is transferred to the UK bank.

A bill is known as an acceptance when the drawee accepts the bill. A UK bank may accept a bill on behalf of a foreign resident in which case the UK resident draws the bill on the UK bank and not on the foreign resident. The accepting bank has a claim on the foreign resident and expects to be paid by him before the bill matures.

Bond

A financial instrument that usually pays interest to the holder. Bonds are issued by governments as well as companies and other institutions, for example, local authorities. Most bonds have a fixed date on which the borrower will repay the holder. Bonds are attractive to investors since they can be bought and sold easily in a secondary market. Special forms of bonds include deep discount bonds, equity warrant bonds, Eurobonds, and zero coupon bonds.

BPM5

The *Balance of Payments Manual*, 5th Edition, published in 1993 by the IMF.

Branch

An unincorporated enterprise, wholly or jointly owned by a direct investor.

British government stocks

Securities issued or guaranteed by the UK government; also known as gilts.

Building societies

Building societies are mutual institutions specialising in accepting deposits from members of the public and in long-term lending to members of the public, mainly to finance the purchase of dwellings; such lending being secured on dwellings. Their operations are governed by special legislation which places restrictions on their recourse to other sources of funding and other avenues of investment.

Capital account

The capital account consists of capital transfers (see 'Transfers') and acquisition/disposal of non-produced, non-financial assets (see 'Non-produced, non-financial assets).

Capital transfers

See 'Transfers'.

Certificate of deposit

A short-term interest-paying instrument issued by deposit-taking institutions in return for money deposited for a fixed period. Interest is earned at a given rate. The instrument can be used as security for a loan if the depositor requires money before the repayment date.

c.i.f. (cost, insurance and freight)

The basis of valuation of imports for Customs purposes, it includes the cost of insurance premiums and freight services. These need to be deducted to obtain the **free on board** valuation consistent with the valuation of exports which is used in the economic accounts.

Collective investment institution (CII)

Incorporated (investment companies or investment trusts) and unincorporated undertakings (mutual funds or unit trusts) that invest the funds, collected from investors by means of issuing shares/units (other than equity), in financial assets (mainly marketable securities and bank deposits) and real estate. (See also 'Trusts').

Commercial paper

This is an unsecured promissory note for a specific amount and maturing on a specific date. The commercial paper market allows companies to issue short-term debt direct to financial institutions who then market this paper to investors or use it for their own investment purposes.

Commodity gold

See 'Gold'.

Commonwealth Development Corporation

A public corporation which finances development projects abroad.

Compensation of employees

Total remuneration payable to employees in cash or in kind, and includes the value of social contributions payable by the employer.

Coordinated Portfolio Investment Survey (CPIS)

A survey coordinated and disseminated by the International Monetary Fund (IMF). Participants in the CPIS collect a geographical breakdown of their portfolio investment assets.

Counterpart items

Certain items in the balance of payments exist only as counterpart items, introduced to balance the inclusion of other items that do not fall naturally into the double-entry system. The allocation of Special Drawing Rights (SDRs) is an example of an artificial counterpart item introduced into the balance of payments to offset the corresponding increase in SDR holdings within official reserves (as SDRs are no one sector's liabilities). (See also 'Special Drawing Rights').

Cross-trades

The provision of transportation services by resident operators between two foreign economies.

Currency swaps

A currency swap, also known as a cross-currency interest-rate swap contract, consists of an exchange of cash flows related to interest payments and, at the end of the contract, an exchange of principal amounts in specified currencies at a specified exchange rate.

Current account

The account of transactions in respect of trade in goods and services, income and current transfers.

Current balance

The balance of current account transactions.

Current transfers

See 'Transfers'.

Debt forgiveness

The voluntary cancellation of all or part of a debt within a contractual arrangement between a creditor in one country and a debtor in another country.

Debt securities

Debt securities cover bonds, debentures, notes etc., and money market instruments. These are split into long and short (up to one year) term, based on original maturity.

Derivatives

See 'Financial derivatives'.

Direct investment

Net investment by UK/foreign companies in their foreign/UK branches, subsidiaries or associated companies. A direct investment in a company means that the investor has a significant influence on the operations of the company, defined as having an equity interest in an enterprise resident in another country of 10 per cent or more of the ordinary shares or voting stock. (See 'Branch', 'Subsidiary' and 'Associated companies'.) Investment covers not only acquisition of fixed assets, stock building and stock appreciation, but also all other financial transactions, such as: additions to or payments of working capital; other loans and trade credit; and acquisitions of securities. Estimates of investment flows allow for depreciation in any undistributed profits. Funds raised by the subsidiary or associate company in the economy in which it operates are excluded as they are locally raised and not sourced from the parent company.

Disbursements

Operating expenses.

Dividend

A payment made to company shareholders from current or previously retained profits. Dividends are recorded when they become payable.

Equity

Equity is ownership of a residual claim on the assets of the institutional unit that issued the instrument. Equities differ from other financial instruments in that they confer ownership of something more than a financial claim. Shareholders are owners of the company whereas bond holders are outside creditors.

Equity securities

Equity securities are shares issued by companies to shareholders. Purchases of equity securities in which the purchaser does not have any significant degree of control over the company (that is, less than 10 per cent of the equity capital) fall within portfolio investment; otherwise it falls within direct investment. Equity securities include mutual fund shares.

Euro area

The euro area encompasses those member states of the European Union in which the euro has been adopted as the single currency and in which a single monetary policy is conducted under the responsibility of the decision-making bodies of the European Central Bank. As from 1 January 2011 the euro area comprises Austria, Belgium, Cyprus, Estonia, Finland, France, Germany, Greece, Ireland, Italy, Luxembourg, Malta, the Netherlands, Portugal, the Slovak Republic, Slovenia and Spain.

Eurocurrency market

All borrowing and lending by banks in currencies other than that of the country in which the banks are situated.

Euro/European Currency Unit (ECU)

The ECU was officially introduced in 1979 in connection with the start of the European Monetary System (EMS). In the EMS, the ECU served as the basis for determining exchange rate parities and as a reserve asset and means of settlement. It was a composite currency which contained specified amounts of the currencies of the member states of the European Union. The currencies making up the ECU were weighted according to their economic importance and use in short-term finance. As from September 1989 the weightings of the ECU were revised to include both the Spanish peseta and Portuguese escudo. The ECU was converted into the euro at the start of European Monetary Union on 1 January 1999, with Greece joining on 1 January 2001. From 1 January 2003, the euro became the currency of the member states of the European Monetary Union.

European Central Bank (ECB)

The Monetary Authority for the euro currency, based in Frankfurt. The ECB, together with the national central banks of the member states, manages monetary policy and the banking system across the European Monetary Union area.

European Investment Bank (EIB)

This was set up to assist economic development within the European Union. Its members are the member states of the EU.

European Monetary System (EMS)

The EMS was established in March 1979. Its most important element was the mechanism known as the ERM (Exchange Rate Mechanism) whereby the exchange rates between the currencies of the participating member states were kept within set ranges. The UK joined the ERM on 8 October 1990. On 16 September 1992 the UK's membership of the ERM and the EMS was suspended. The EMS was superseded by the single currency when 11 of the participating member states joined European Monetary Union on 1 January 1999. Since then Greece joined on 1 January 2001, Slovenia joined on 1 January 2007, Cyprus and Malta joined on 1 January 2008, Slovakia joined on 1 January 2009 and Estonia joined on 1 January 2011.

Eurosystem

The Eurosystem comprises the European Central Bank (ECB) and the national central banks of the member states which have adopted the euro in Stage Three of Economic and Monetary Union (EMU). In 2011 there are 17 national central banks in the Eurosystem. The Eurosystem is governed by the Governing Council and the Executive Board of the ECB and has assumed the task of conducting the single monetary policy for the euro area since 1 January 1999. Its primary objective is to maintain price stability.

Exchange control

A legal control imposed by governments on the ability of persons, businesses and others to hold, receive and transfer foreign currency. The extent of the *Exchange Control Act* of 1947 was considerably reduced in June and July 1979 and the Act was repealed in 1987.

Exchange cover scheme (ECS)

A scheme first introduced in 1969 whereby UK public bodies raise foreign currency from abroad, either directly or through UK banks, and generally surrender it to the EEA (see below) in exchange for sterling for use to finance expenditure in the UK. HM Treasury sells the borrower foreign currency to service and repay the loan at the exchange rate that applied when the loan was taken out. The transactions relate to net borrowing by British Nuclear Fuels plc and repayment by HM Government following the privatisation of other former public corporations (see 'Novations').

Exchange Equalisation Account (EEA)

The government account with the Bank of England in which transactions in reserve assets are recorded. These transactions are classified to the central government sector. It is the means by which the government, through the Bank of England, influences exchange rates.

Export credit

Credit extended abroad by UK institutions, primarily in connection with UK exports but also including some credit in respect of third-country trade.

Export Credit Guarantee Department (ECGD)

A non-ministerial government department, classified to the public corporations sector, the main function of which is to provide insurance cover for export credit transactions.

External debt

A measure of balance sheet liabilities owing to non-residents. Liabilities relating to trade credit, debt securities, and loans and deposits (including inter-company liabilities within direct investment) are included; equity liabilities are excluded.

Financial account

The financial account records transactions in external assets and liabilities of the UK, for example, the acquisitions and disposals of foreign shares by UK residents. The financial account consists of direct investment, portfolio investment, other investment, financial derivatives and reserve assets.

Financial auxiliaries

Auxiliary financial activities are ones closely related to financial intermediation but which are not financial intermediation themselves, such as the repackaging of funds, insurance broking and fund management. Financial auxiliaries therefore include insurance brokers and fund managers.

Financial corporations

All bodies recognised as independent legal entities whose principal activity is financial intermediation and/or the production of auxiliary financial services.

Financial derivatives

Any financial instrument that derives its value from other financial instruments (known as the underlying), events or conditions. Financial derivatives include options (on, for example, currencies, interest rates, commodities, and indices), traded financial futures, warrants, and currency and interest swaps. Under *BPM5*, transactions in derivatives are treated as separate transactions, rather than being included as integral parts of underlying transactions to which they may be linked as hedges. Estimates for foreign exchange, interest rate, equity and commodity and credit derivatives are included.

Financial gold

See 'Gold'.

Financial leasing

See 'Leasing'.

Financial surplus or deficit (FSD)

The former term for Net lending(+)/Net borrowing(–), the balance of all current and capital account transactions for an institutional sector or the economy as a whole.

FISIM

FISIM is an acronym for Financial Intermediation Services Indirectly Measured. It represents the implicit charge for the service provided by monetary financial institutions paid for by the interest differential between borrowing and lending rather than through fees and commissions.

f.o.b. (free on board)

An f.o.b. price excludes the cost of insurance and freight from the country of consignment but includes all charges up to the point of the exporting country's customs frontier. Trade in goods exports are valued on an f.o.b. basis in the balance of payments accounts.

Foreign

In this publication 'foreign' denotes residence outside the UK rather than nationality. In some contexts 'external', 'abroad' or 'non-resident' are used with the same meaning. (See 'Residency').

Forwards

In a **forward contract**, the counterparties agree to exchange, on a specified date, a specified quantity of an underlying item (real or financial) at an agreed-upon contract price (the strike price). If a future exchange of currencies is carried out in a forward contract, the counterparties exchange, in accordance with prearranged terms, cash flows based on the reference prices of the underlying items. Forward rate agreements and forward foreign exchange contracts are common types of forward contracts.

Futures

Futures are forward contracts traded on organised exchanges. They give the holder the right to purchase a commodity or a financial asset at a future date.

Gilts

Bonds issued or guaranteed by the UK Government. Also known as gilt-edged securities or British government securities.

Gold

In the accounts, a distinction is drawn between gold held as a financial asset (financial gold) and gold held like any other commodity (commodity gold). Transactions in commodity gold are recorded in the trade in goods account and include foreign trade in finished manufactures together with net domestic and foreign transactions in gold moving into or out of finished manufactured form (that is, for jewellery, dentistry, electronic goods, medals and proof – but not bullion – coins).

Banking-type assets and liabilities denominated in gold, including reserve assets) are treated as financial gold transactions and included in the financial account. The distinction between commodity and financial gold differs from that drawn by the IMF, in its *Balance of Payments Manual* (5th edition, 1993), between non-monetary and monetary gold. The UK has obtained an exemption from adopting the *BPM5* recommendations on treatment of gold in order to avoid distortion of its trade in goods account by the substantial transactions of the London Bullion Market.

The treatment of non-monetary gold was reviewed as part of the worldwide process to revise the IMF *Balance of Payments Manual* Sixth Edition. The proposal is that the concept of non-monetary gold is replaced by two categories – allocated gold (a commodity) and unallocated gold (a financial instrument). UK balance of payments will continue current practice until the treatments defined in the revised manual are implemented.

Gross

The separate identification of both credit/debit, export/import for any particular transaction.

Hedging

Hedging is accomplished by the temporary purchase or sale of futures/swaps contracts to offset movements in the position or anticipated position in the cash markets. For example, this may benefit banks, financial institutions, pension funds and corporate treasuries who hold interest rate, exchange rate or stock price sensitive assets or liabilities.

Holding companies

A holding company is a company that usually confines its activities to owning stock in and supervising management of other companies. A holding company usually owns a controlling interest in the companies whose stock it holds. Holding companies exist for legal, commercial and tax reasons. In line with international standards, holding companies are classified as other financial intermediaries.

Households

Individuals or small groups of individuals as consumers and in some cases as entrepreneurs producing goods and market services.

Import credit

Credit extended to UK institutions by non-residents, primarily in connection with UK imports.

Income

The income account forms part of the current account and consists of compensation of employees and investment income, both of which have separate entries in this glossary.

Inter-company accounts

Accounts recording transactions between parent and subsidiary or associated companies, and balances owed by one to the other.

Interest rate swaps

An obligation between two parties to exchange interest-related payments in the same currency from fixed rate into floating rate, or vice versa, or from one type of floating rate to another. A swap can be used to reshape the coupon payments of either new or existing debt. The only movement of funds is a net transfer of interest payments between the two parties. The interest payments are calculated on an agreed principal amount, which is not exchanged. The settlement receipts/payments on UK banks' interest rate swaps appear in the financial account under financial derivatives.

International investment position (IIP)

The international investment position records end of period balance sheet levels of UK external assets and liabilities. The IIP consists of direct investment, portfolio investment, other investment and reserve assets. In the 2010 and 2011 editions, for the first time, financial derivatives business of UK banks and securities dealers respectively have been incorporated into the main aggregates of the IIP. Data for insurance companies, pension funds, unit trusts, investment trusts, open-ended investment companies, finance leasing companies, credit grantors, factoring companies and building societies are not included in the main aggregates for the UK's international investment position. The financial derivatives balance sheet for all sectors is published separately in table FD of the Pink Book.

International Monetary Fund (IMF)

A Fund set up as a result of the Bretton Woods Conference of 1944 and which began operations in 1947. It includes most of the major countries of the world. The Fund was set up to supervise the fixed exchange rate system agreed at Bretton Woods and to make available to its members a pool of foreign exchange resources to assist them when they have balance of payments difficulties. (See also 'Special Drawing Rights').

Intervention Board for Agricultural Produce (IBAP)

The UK government agency which used to operate the support arrangements of the EU Common Agricultural Policy within the UK. It has now been replaced by the Rural Payments Agency (RPA).

Investment

In a balance of payments context this is categorised as either direct, portfolio or other investment. See appropriate headings for definitions.

Investment income

All investment income accruing to UK residents from non-residents or payable abroad by UK residents after allowing for depreciation. The balance on credits and debits equals 'net property income from abroad' as shown in the national accounts.

Investment trust

See 'Trusts'.

Leasing

In the balance of payments accounts all financial leases and some long-term operating leases (for example, for aircraft) are regarded as loans to finance the purchase of goods. The lessor thus makes a loan to the lessee who subsequently repays this with interest. The lessee is regarded as the purchaser of the goods.

Liabilities

In balance of payments terminology, liabilities are the financial claims of non-residents on the UK.

LIBOR

London Interbank Offered Rate. The rate of interest at which banks borrow funds from other banks, in marketable size, in the London Interbank market.

Local authorities

Elected councils responsible for the administration of certain services in particular areas within the UK.

Merchanting

Merchanting is defined as the purchase of a good by a resident from a non-resident and the subsequent resale of the good to another non-resident, without the good entering the compiling economy. The difference between the purchase and sale price is recorded as the value of merchanting services provided.

Monetary authorities

Institutions (usually central banks) which control the centralised monetary reserves and the supply of currency in accordance with government policies, and which act as their governments' bankers and agents. In the UK this is equivalent to the Bank of England and part of the Treasury (the Exchange Equalisation Account). Data is not separately available in the UK accounts for monetary authorities.

Monetary financial institutions (MFIs)

Banks and building societies.

Monetary gold

See 'Gold'.

Money market

The market in which short-term loans are made and short-term securities traded. 'Short term' usually applies to periods up to one year but can be longer in some instances.

Money market instruments

Money market instruments, within portfolio investment, generally give the holder the unconditional right to receive a stated, fixed sum of money on a specified date. These are short-term instruments usually traded at a discount; the discount being dependent upon the interest rate and the time remaining to maturity. Included are such instruments as acceptances, treasury bills, commercial paper and certificates of deposit.

MTIC

VAT missing trader intra-community fraud. A systematic, criminal attack on the VAT system, which has been detected in many EU member states. In essence, fraudsters obtain VAT registration to acquire goods VAT free from other member states. They then sell on the goods at VAT inclusive prices and disappear without paying over the VAT paid by their customers to the tax authorities.

Navy, Army and Air Force Institute (NAAFI)

A body which provides goods and services for use by the UK Armed Forces abroad.

Net

In this presentation of the balance of payments accounts, the term 'net' is generally applied only to transactions in financial assets or liabilities. Purchases of assets are recorded net of sales; similarly with liabilities. In the current and capital accounts, where the operations of UK and foreign residents are taken together in particular transactions areas, the term 'balance' is used.

Net errors and omissions

The item included to bring the sum of all balance of payments entries to zero. Also known as the balancing item.

Non-monetary gold

See 'Gold'.

Non-produced, non-financial assets

Non-produced, non-financial assets, within the capital account, include land purchased or sold by a foreign embassy, patents, copyrights, trade marks, franchises and leases and other transferable contracts, but not finance leasing. Only the purchase and sale of such assets are recorded in the capital account; earnings from them are presented under trade in services.

Novations

This term defines the reassignment of debt (for balance of payments, usually foreign debt) of public corporations to central government following the privatisation of the public corporation. This does not normally change the overall balance of payments situation as the debt is still regarded as a UK liability.

NPISH

Non-profit institutions serving households.

Official reserves

See 'Reserve assets'.

Offshores

The economic territory of a country consists of the geographic territory administered by a government; within this territory, persons, goods, and capital circulate freely. In the context of the UK, the offshore islands of the Channel Islands and the Isle of Man are subject to their own fiscal authorities and have their own tax systems, there are impediments to taking up residency, and they are not part of the EU. They are therefore not recognised as part of the economic territory of the UK for balance of payments purposes and are classified as non-resident in the UK.

Operating leasing

Operational leasing (rental) covers resident/non-resident leasing (other than financial leasing), charter of ships, aircraft and transportation equipment without crew. Leasing of ships, aircraft and transportation equipment with crew are included in the transportation account.

Ordinary share

The most common type of share in the ownership of a corporation. Holders of ordinary shares receive dividends. (See also 'Equity').

Other financial intermediaries (OFIs)

A diverse group of units constituting all financial corporations other than depository corporations, insurance corporations, pension funds, and financial auxiliaries. They generally raise funds by accepting long-term or specialised types of deposits and by issuing securities and equity. These intermediaries often specialise in lending to particular types of borrowers and in using specialised financial arrangements such as financial leasing, securitised lending, and financial derivative operations.

Other investment

Investment other than direct and portfolio investment. Includes trade credit, loans, currency and deposits and other assets and liabilities.

Parent

In a balance of payments context this means a company with direct investments in other countries.

Pension funds

The institutions that administer pension schemes. Pension schemes are significant investors in securities. Self-administered funds are classified in the financial accounts as pension funds. Those managed by insurance companies are treated as long-term business of insurance companies. They are part of S.125, the Insurance corporations and pension funds sub-sector of the financial corporations sector within the National Accounts.

Portfolio investment

Investment in equity and debt securities issued by registered companies, other than that classed as direct investment, and in equity and debt securities issued by governments. A portfolio investment, unlike a direct investment, does not entitle the investor to any significant influence over the operations of the company or institution, and represents less than 10 per cent of the equity capital.

Preference share

This type of share guarantees its holder a prior claim on dividends. The dividend paid to preference shareholders is normally more than that paid to holders of ordinary shares. Preference shares may give the holder a right to a share in the ownership of the company (participating preference shares). However in the UK they usually do not, and are therefore classified as bonds.

Private sector

Private non-financial corporations, financial corporations other than the Bank of England, households and the NPISH sector.

Promissory note

A security which entitles the bearer to receive cash. These may be issued by companies or other institutions. (See 'Commercial paper').

Public corporations

These are public trading bodies which usually have a substantial degree of financial independence from the public authority which created them. A body is normally treated as a trading body when more than half its income is financed by fees. A public corporation is publicly controlled to the extent that the public authorities appoint a majority of the board of management or when public authorities can exert significant control over general corporate policy through other means. Since the 1980s many public corporations, such as British Telecom, have been privatised and reclassified within the accounts as private non-financial corporations.

Public sector

Central government, local authorities and public corporations.

Refinanced export credit

Identified long-term credit extended for UK exports initially by banks and refinanced with the ECGD, the Trustee Savings Banks and the Central Trustee Savings Bank.

Reinvested earnings

The direct investor's share of earnings not distributed as dividends (by subsidiaries) or branch profits. As this income remains with the foreign subsidiary or branch (it is reinvested by the parent) an amount will appear in the financial account equal to (and with opposite sign) the corresponding entry within direct investment income.

Related companies

Branches, subsidiaries, associates or parents.

Remittances

Current transfers in cash or in kind sent by households resident in one economy to households resident in another economy. Closely related to *BPM5* concept workers remittances which are current transfers sent by migrants who are employed in new economies and are considered to be residents of their new economy to their home economy.

Repo/reverse repo

This is short for 'sale and repurchase agreement'. One party agrees to sell bonds or other financial instruments to other parties under a formal legal agreement to repurchase them at some point in the future – usually up to six months – at a fixed price. Reverse repos are the counterpart asset to any repo liability. Repo/reverse repo transactions are generally treated as borrowing/lending within other investment, rather than as transactions in the underlying securities. The exception being for banks, where repos are recorded as deposit liabilities. Banks' reverse repos are recorded as loans, the same as for all other sectors.

Reserve assets

Short-term assets which can be very quickly converted into cash. They comprise the UK's official holdings of gold, convertible currencies, Special Drawing Rights, and changes in the UK reserve position in the IMF. Also included between July 1979 and December 1998 are European Currency Units acquired from swaps with the European Cooperation Fund, EMI and the ECB. Reserve assets were referred to as 'official reserves' in editions of the Pink Book prior to 1998.

Reserve position in the Fund

The UK's position in the IMF's General Resources Account. This position is the sum of the UK's reserve tranche purchases, and any indebtedness to the Fund (under a loan agreement) that is readily payable to the UK.

Residency

UK residents are those with a centre of economic interest within the UK of at least one year's duration – nationality does not play a part in determining residency status. There are a number of exceptions to the standard residency classification: regardless of length of stay, UK personnel of UK embassies and military bases abroad are deemed to be residents of the UK (conversely foreign personnel of other nations' embassies and military bases in the UK are classed as non-residents), as are students studying abroad or patients being treated abroad who are normally resident in the UK. (See also 'Offshores'.)

Royalties

These form part of trade in services. They represent payments for services by, or to, UK residents in respect of the right to use processes and other information, for example, licences to use patents, trade marks, designs, or copyrights. Sales and purchases of patents are included within the capital account.

Rural Payments Agency (RPA)

The UK government agency which operates the support arrangements of the EU Common Agricultural Policy within the UK. This replaced the Intervention Board for Agricultural Produce (IBAP).

Securities dealers

Securities and futures dealers are those institutions whose main activity is dealing in securities and futures either on their own account or on behalf of customers and clients. This activity also includes stock exchange money brokers, inter-dealer brokers and dealing in commodities for investment purposes. They should not be confused with monetary financial institutions (banks and building societies) that are licensed as able to take deposits.

Security

Security against loans involves the depositing of a document or asset which is retained by the bank as a charge for an advance. This form of security may include stocks and share certificates, debentures, and insurance policies.

Smuggling

Smuggling is the importation of goods acquired duty free or duty paid in another country for re-sale in the UK without payment of UK duty and (where appropriate) VAT. (See also 'MTIC').

Special Drawing Rights (SDRs)

These are reserve assets created and distributed by decision of the members of the IMF. Participants accept an obligation to provide convertible currency, when designated by the IMF to do so, to another participant, in exchange for SDRs. Only countries with a sufficiently strong balance of payments are so designated by the IMF. SDRs may also be used in certain direct payments between participants in the scheme and for payments of various kinds to the IMF.

Spread earnings

Net spread earnings are the part of market making activities that represent payment for the provision of a service. The value of the spread earning for each transaction is calculated as the margin earned between the transaction price and the mid-market price at the time of the transaction. This represents the 'added value' gained from market making activities. Spread earnings can be made on, for example, foreign exchange, securities and derivatives transactions.

Stock lending

Lending of securities by long-term holders or custodians such as banks, pension funds or insurance companies when securities are in short supply.

Subsidiary

A registered company in which another registered company has ownership of the majority of the voting share capital, that is, greater than 50 per cent.

Subsidies

Current unrequited payments made by general government or the EU to enterprises. Those made on the basis of a quantity or value of goods or services are classified as 'subsidies on products'. Other subsidies based on levels of productive activity (for example, numbers employed) are designated 'Other subsidies on production'.

Swaps

See 'Interest rate swaps' and 'Currency swaps'.

Trade credit

See 'Export credit' and 'Import credit'.

Trade in goods

Trade in goods covers general merchandise, goods for processing, repairs on goods, goods procured in ports by carriers and commodity gold (see 'Gold'). General merchandise is defined for balance of payments purposes as covering, with a few exceptions, all movable goods for which actual or imputed changes of ownership occur between residents and non-residents.

Trade in services

Provision of services between UK residents and non-residents, and transactions in goods which are not freighted out of the country in which the transactions take place, for example purchases for local use by foreign forces in the UK and by UK forces abroad, and purchases by tourists. Transactions in goods which are freighted into/out of the UK are included under trade in goods.

Transfers

Transfers are payments or receipts where there is no corresponding exchange of an actual good or service. These transfers are split between current transfers, which form part of the current account, and capital transfers which form part of the capital account. Most transfer payments are general government transfers; that is, receipts from and payments to institutions of the EU.

Travel

The travel account gives the earnings from, and expenditure on, international tourism and business and other travel, but excludes transport between the UK and other countries (included within the transportation account). An international traveller is defined as a resident of one country who visits another country and stays there for a period of less than 12 months. This definition excludes travellers who visit another country to take up pre-arranged employment or education there, military and diplomatic personnel, merchant seamen and airline crews on duty.

Treasury bills

Short-term securities or promissory notes that are issued by government in return for funding from the money market. In the UK every week, the Bank of England invites tenders for sterling Treasury bills from the financial institutions operating in the market. ECU/euro-denominated bills were issued by tender each month but this programme has now wound down; the last bill was redeemed in September 1999. Treasury bills are an important form of short-term borrowing for the government, generally being issued for periods of three or six months.

Trusts (unit and investment)

Unit trusts are institutions through which investors pool their funds to invest in a diversified portfolio of securities. Individual investors purchase units in the fund representing an ownership interest in the large pool of underlying assets, that is, they have an equity stake. The selection of assets is made by professional fund managers. Unit trusts therefore give individual investors the opportunity to invest in a diversified and professionally-managed portfolio of securities without the need for detailed knowledge of the individual companies issuing the stocks and bonds. Unit trust units are issued and bought back on demand by the managers of the trust, the value of the unit reflecting the value of the underlying pool of securities.

Investment trusts are institutions that invest capital in a wide range of other companies' shares. Investment trusts issue shares (which are listed on the stock market) to raise this capital. The price of shares is driven by the usual market forces.

Unit trusts are 'open-ended funds' which means the fund gets bigger as more people invest and gets smaller as people withdraw their money. Investment trusts are 'close-ended funds' because there are a set number of shares and this number does not change regardless of the number of investors. (See also 'Collective investment institutions'.)

Very short-term financing facility (VSTFF)

This is a facility available within the EMS where a central bank makes short-term credit facilities in its own currency available to another central bank.

Index

Bold indicates name of chapter. **Figures** indicate table numbers. **P** indicates page number. **G** indicates the item appears in the Glossary.